Transition and Development

The MR/Censa Series on the Americas is dedicated to publishing new work on the critical issues affecting the nations of the Americas, whose destinies are becoming increasingly interlinked in the late twentieth century.

Transition
and Development

▼▲

Problems of Third World Socialism

▼▲

Edited by Richard R. Fagen, Carmen Diana Deere,
and José Luis Coraggio

Monthly Review Press · Center for the Study of the Americas

Policy Alternatives for the Caribbean and Central America (PACCA) is a national network of scholars dedicated to the formulation of an alternative vision of political, economic, and social policy toward the region.

The Regional Coordinator of Socio-Economic Research (CRIES), based in Managua, Nicaragua, is a consortium of Central American research centers committed to the same goal.

Center for the Study of the Americas (CENSA) is a nonprofit organization in Berkeley, California, engaged in research and education on Caribbean and Latin American issues.

Copyright © 1986 by Richard R. Fagen, Carmen Diana Deere, and José Luis Coraggio

Library of Congress Cataloging-in-Publication Data

Transition and development.
  (MR/CENSA series on the Americas)
  Bibliography: p.
  Includes index.
  1. Communism—Developing countries. 2. Communism—
Latin America. 3. Communism—Nicaragua. I. Fagen,
Richard R. II. Deere, Carmen Diana. III. Coraggio,
José Luis. IV. Series.
HX517.8.G73   1986   335.43'09172'4   86-12579
ISBN 0-85345-704-2
ISBN 0-85345-705-0 (pbk.)

Monthly Review Press
155 West 23rd Street
New York, N.Y. 10011

Manufactured in the United States of America

10 9 8 7 6 5 4 3 2 1

▼ Contents ▲

Acknowledgments   7

Introduction
The editors

Notes on the Analysis of the Small Underdeveloped Economy
in Transition
E.V.K. FitzGerald   28

External Finance and the Transition to Socialism
in Small Peripheral Societies
Barbara Stallings   54

The Conflict at Home and Abroad: U.S. Imperialism
vs. the New Revolutionary Societies
Roger Burbach   79

Agrarian Reform, Peasant and Rural Production,
and the Organization of Production in the Transition to Socialism
Carmen Diana Deere   97

Economics and Politics in the Transition to Socialism:
Reflections on the Nicaragua Experience
José Luis Coraggio   143

The Making of a Mixed Economy: Class Struggle
and State Policy in the Nicaragua Transition
Eduardo Baumeister and Oscar Neira Cuadra   171

State and Society in the Transition to Socialism:
The Theoretical Legacy
Carollee Bengelsdorf   192

The Role of Ideology in the Transition to Socialism
John S. Saul   212

Ideology and Revolutionary Politics in Transitional Societies
Orlando Núñez Soto   231

6 Contents

The Politics of Transition
Richard R. Fagen   *249*

Mass Organization, Party, and State:
Democracy in the Transition to Socialism
Michael Lowy   *264*

Mobilization Without Emancipation?
Women's Interests, State, and Revolution
Maxine Molyneux   *280*

War, Popular Participation, and Transition to Socialism:
The Case of Nicaragua
Peter E. Marchetti, S. J.   *303*

Bibliography   *331*

Notes on Contributors   *345*

Index   *347*

▾Acknowledgments ▴

This collection is a product of a collaborative research initiative of Policy Alternatives for the Caribbean and Central America (PACCA), a national network of scholars, and the Regional Coordinator of Socio-Economic Research (CRIES), a Managua-based consortium of Central American research centers. It is a result of two seminars, one in Washington, D.C., in October 1983, and one in Managua, Nicaragua, in September 1984, on the problems of transition to socialism in small, peripheral economies. The Washington, D.C., seminar coincided with the assasination of Maurice Bishop of Grenada; the Managua seminar with the initiation of the Nicaraguan electoral campaigns. This collection bears the stamp of both events.

The Washington, D.C., seminar was coordinated by Richard Fagen and Xabier Gorastiaga. Earlier versions of the essays by Roger Burbach, Richard Fagen, E.V.K. FitzGerald, Orlando Núñez, and Barbara Stallings included in this volume were initially presented at this seminar. The discussants included Marcia Rivera Quintero, Edelberto Torres Rivas, Carmen Diana Deere, José Luis Coraggio, Xabier Gorastiaga, and William LeoGrande.

The Managua seminar was coordinated by José Luis Coraggio and Carmen Diana Deere and hosted by the Center for the Study of Agrarian Reform (CIERA) and the National Institute of Socio-Economic Studies (INIES). We would especially like to thank their respective directors, Orlando Núñez and Xabier Gorastiaga, for their support of this endeavor, as well as the International Relations Office of INIES for logistical assistance.

The essays by Carollee Bengelsdorf, Michael Lowy, Carmen Diana Deere, Eduardo Baumeister and Oscar Neira, and José Coraggio were written for the Managua seminar. The papers benefited from the comments and criticism of the other seminar participants: Clive Thomas, Franz Hinklemmert, Edelberto Torres Rivas, John Saul, Joseph Collins, Juan Valdez Paz, Kate Young, Richard Fagen, Xabier Gorastiaga,

Rosa Maria Torres, Peter Marchetti, Orlando Núñez, Demitro Polo, and Marvin Ortega. The essays by Peter Marchetti, Maxine Molyneux, and John Saul were commissioned for this volume.

Major funding for the seminars and prepublication costs of this volume were provided by the Joint Committee on Latin American Studies of the Social Science Research Council and the American Council of Learned Societies. Finally, this volume owes much to the sharp eye and even sharper pencil of Karen Judd, our editor at Monthly Review.

Introduction

▼▲

The editors

Without exaggeration, the period following World War II can be called the third age of revolution. Now, however, it is not monarchic and feudal society that is giving way to bourgeois institutions and values as in the great eighteenth- and nineteenth-century revolutions; nor is it a replay of the overthrow of tsarist Russia and the installation in power of the Bolsheviks. Rather, an uneven and underdeveloped capitalism on the periphery of the modern world system is under assault by a very different set of social forces. The break-up of the European colonial empires, and assorted national liberation struggles against entrenched elites at home and hegemonic powers abroad, have moved the epicenter of revolutionary activity away from the core capitalist countries and into those areas frequently—if somewhat problematically—referred to as the third world. Furthermore, this revolutionary activity, with a few notable exceptions such as Iran, has been directed toward the construction of socialist alternatives.

The shift of the epicenter of revolutionary struggle for socialism away from the advanced capitalist countries and into the third world has been discussed from a wide variety of perspectives.[1] For some, this shift is the main historical proof of how wrong Marx was when he envisioned socialism springing from the rotting corpse of a fully developed capitalism—a capitalism that would eventually fall prey to its own internal contradictions, overthrown by a revolutionary movement led by a radicalized working class. For others, less interested in Marx and his theories, but deeply concerned with the East-West conflict and what they perceive to be threats to the security of the core capitalist countries, socialism in the third world is viewed as the consequence of the machinations and expansionism of the Soviet Union and its allies. For the authors represented in this volume, however, the socialist experiments in the periphery are viewed as a logical outcome of the failures of dependent capitalism, and as nationalist reactions to imperialism and underdevelopment.

But to call these experiments "a logical outcome" does not imply either inevitability or predictability. On the contrary, socialist solutions to underdevelopment do not exist as formulas that can be picked off the shelf, or magical balms that can be brewed up on the basis of the correct reading of old texts. Rather, if there is to be a new and successful social formation that can properly be called socialist, it will result from a long and complex *process of transition* that will, in turn, be deeply marked by the historical specificity of the societies undertaking the experiments.

To view the problematic of socialism in the third world through this optic, as do the contributors to this volume, thus implies a relentless questioning of both theory and practice. The fundamental nature of such questioning is suggested, but not exhausted, by the following list:

1. What in the classic Marxist tradition is relevant to today's third world realities?
2. What lessons, positive and negative, are to be learned from the experiences of the "actually existing socialisms"?
3. What are the constraints on socialist transition arising from inherited structures of underdevelopment?
4. What are the implications of relations with the first and second worlds for the construction of socialism in the third world?

Posing such questions is, however, somewhat premature. At a minimum we must first specify in more detail the phenomena we are trying to understand and the context in which contemporary experiments in transition to socialism are taking place.

Let us begin with a working definition: the experiments which are of primary interest to us are those which attempt to transform the model of accumulation and the associated social formation from what, for shorthand, we can call dependent capitalism to a socialist model. Formally, this means that the logic of capital (the profit motive) must be subordinated to and eventually replaced by a socially determined rationality of production and distribution. The basic goals of this transformation are (1) production and distribution oriented toward meeting the basic needs of the majority of the population; (2) an ending of class, gender, racial, ethnic, and other forms of privilege in access to "valued goods" such as income, culture, justice, and recreation; and (3) the reconstitution of state-society relations such that the "popular classes" have a high degree of participation in determining public policy at all levels. At a minimum, this transformation would seem to imply both the social ownership of the commanding heights of the economy and a relatively comprehensive system of planning—although these two structural changes do not in and of themselves constitute socialism.

This formulation is obviously controversial—touching economic, political, and cultural issues. It is also openended, emphasizing process and goals. It does, however, have the virtue of being elastic enough to include experiments as different as Chile under Allende, Algeria after independence, and Cuba since 1959. It also suggests, although it does not specify, the highly conflictual nature of the transition by insisting that it involves a fundamental transformation of the model of accumulation and the accompanying social formation. No matter how skillfully managed, such an attempt at transformation spells *class conflict* writ large and a prolonged and possibly bloody confrontation with imperialism. Furthermore, since the definition emphasizes the *attempt to transform,* it directs our attention to process, history, and the possibilities (very real) of failure.

What are the real-life circumstances in which such transitions are being attempted—or, it may be argued in a few cases, have actually taken place? Four features warrant special emphasis: (1) the nature of the global system; (2) the special situation of the small, peripheral economies in general; (3) the additional problems of peripheral economies attempting a transition to socialism; and (4) the lack of appropriate models for societies in transition.

The Global System

As the twentieth century draws to a close, we live in a system of production, exchange, and mass communications that is worldwide. The essential logic of this system is capitalist, and even nominally socialist countries are forced (or choose) to play by the rules of this global game in trade, finance, and investment. In short, for small countries that wish to play on the world stage in our time—or even to maintain or introduce a bit of rationality into the domestic economy— many of the key parameters are determined externally: prices, markets, technology, and tastes.

Increasingly it is thus the case that autarchical scenarios of development have become difficult to the point of impossibility. In the aggregate, this leads to the much-touted interdependence of the world economy wherein the "health" of the advanced industrial economies (overwhelmingly capitalist) deeply affects the functioning of smaller economies through trade and finance, not to mention war, immigration, and other mechanisms. The small economies, such as Cuba, that in part escape from the functioning of this system because of special relationships (with the USSR and Comecon in the Cuban case), are only the exceptions that prove the rule. So too with small economies that are so poor or geographically remote that they are still weakly integrated into the global system (e.g., Chad).

Some argue that the rise of regional and competing powers in today's world calls into question the validity of a "global system" characterization of the environment in which the small economies are attempting to develop. After all, Japan and other capitalist powers compete successfully with the United States in a variety of ways. And the Soviet Union and occasionally China successfully challenge the capitalist world politically and diplomatically. But the world is multipolar in only a limited, albeit important, sense. Certainly there are intracapitalist conflicts and even contradictions. And obviously the Soviet Union is a great power militarily, with impressive capacity to act on the world political-diplomatic stage. Furthermore, in general the actually existing socialist countries (despite all their internal schisms) stand as an ideological and political counterweight to the capitalist world—another pole of attraction and an occasional helpmate in difficult times. But the primary, critical features of the world political economy with which nations on the periphery must deal are rooted in the capitalist world system. Multipolarity provides, in some cases, a secondary structure of opportunity, some political, military, and ideological leverage on occasion, but it is not the fundamental architecture within which development on the periphery is played out.

The secondary nature of the socialist world to development on the periphery can be documented at many points: in trade, finance, transfer of technology, and even in foreign aid the world looks much more unipolar (taking the advanced capitalist nations as a bloc) than multipolar. But it is perhaps in the cultural domain, broadly defined, where the dominance of advanced capitalism is most marked. Where are the socialist alternatives to the music, dress, media productions, and consumer goods emanating from the advanced capitalist countries: Coca Cola in the backlands, "Dallas" on the TV screens of urban shacks, bluejeans on the streets of Canton and Accra?[2] At first glance this might seem to have little to do with the relentless extension of the global capitalist system. But in reality it is an integral part of the fetishism and globalization of commodities. In the political realm the rule is increasing diversity, but in the realm of consumption the rule is increasing homogenization. There is no multipolarity in the march of contemporary material culture from the urban centers of capitalism where it originated into the most distant corners of the globe. In fact, there is no more striking global monopoly in the world today.

Small Players in the Global Game

The small peripheral societies attempting to develop economically have rather tightly constrained choices in the world just described. The overwhelming majority have neither the material resources nor the productive skills and capacity to "opt out" of international trade and finance—even for relatively brief periods of time. In greater or lesser measure, in one way or another, they are subject to the rules of the only game in town. Furthermore, they are, with rare exceptions, passive players. By this we mean that they cannot as individual countries affect the rules. They are price-takers in trade, technology buyers or recipients rather than technology generators, and borrowers on terms set elsewhere. Even collectively the record is not encouraging regarding the capacity of consortia of these countries to change the rules. At the margin, through international organizations—both formal and informal—some rules have been modified and a few changed. But the overall record of the postwar period is hardly studded with successes.

Furthermore, the small, peripheral societies are particularly subject to the cultural influence of the global capitalist system. As emphasized above, the culture is transmitted in material form: as music, dress, media productions, and food habits. Given their low level of development, the capacity of small, peripheral economies to produce or sustain the production of local cultural products is not great. The onslaught from the core capitalist countries is at times overwhelming. Along with debt and traffic jams comes the internationalization of everything from consumer tastes to political practices.

None of the above would be overly worrisome from a developmental point of view if the interests of large and small players in the world system were predominantly compatible. But even relatively cautious critics of the existing international order admit that such is not the case. The small, peripheral countries want unrestricted access to core markets. Yet in many of these markets, protectionism is growing. These countries want higher and more stable prices for exports, particularly primary commodities subject to wild price fluctuations, but big buyers reject schemes that index commodity prices or take pricing "out of the market." They want inexpensive loans on the longest and softest terms. Big lenders, public and private, are more interested in getting paid back, and—quite naturally—making the most profit with the least attendant risk.

What all of this means is that economic development (defined narrowly as capital accumulation and augmenting the forces of production) is extremely difficult in today's world from a strictly systemic or structural point of view. The system and its rules were not established for the benefit of the small, peripheral countries. They were set up by the core capitalist players to ensure that their predominant position would be extended into the foreseeable future. Of course the rules have undergone changes. The core countries cannot always get exactly what they want, and there are important international and interclass disputes within and among the core countries with respect to what *is* wanted. The debate about debt restructuring and repayment suggests how heated such disputes can be. Nevertheless, the global system remains sharply skewed in favor of the interests of the core capitalist countries. The international economy viewed from the periphery is not a very congenial place.

Experiments in Transition—Additional Problems

If the small, peripheral countries face a complex and difficult international environment, it can fairly be said that those that have opted for a transition to socialism face a significantly more difficult situation. Societies in transition—like the small, peripheral economies of which they are a subgroup—cannot opt out of the global system.[3] They too must trade, borrow, and deal with the material culture of capitalism, *while at the same time attempting something even more difficult: the transformation of the basic domestic political-economic-social systems which have characterized them in the past.* In other words, societies in transition are not just trying to organize themselves more successfully to win more frequently in the global game; they are also dedicated to fundamental transformations at home in the name of social justice. Thus, the viability of the local economy in the international arena, while important, is not the primary consideration. And in fact, although not intended, the consequences of the attempt at transformation often run in exactly the opposite direction, toward making the process of transition less viable abroad both politically and economically. Put less delicately, societies in transition feel the weight of capitalist imperialism not just as the "impersonal" working-out of the rules of the game, but as economic, political, and military pressures designed to end their experiments and turn them back into well-behaved conventional societies on the periphery.

Why should this be the case? Conventional explanations usually focus on the tendency of these societies in transition to ally themselves diplomatically with one or another group within the socialist camp, thereby earning the enmity of the advanced capitalist countries (usually, but not exclusively, the United States). The enmity thus derives from geostrategic concerns, from international relations in the narrow diplomatic-military sense (horror of horrors, Grenada is going to build an airfield!). What is central to any rounded explanation of imperialist pressures on transitional societies, however, is the understanding (on the part of all concerned) that any serious experiment in transition challenges the underlying logic of capitalist relations and the global system that is the most generalized manifestation of those relations in the late twentieth century. Of course, any individual revolutionary society by itself does not threaten the global interests of capitalism—or even in some cases its most concrete local interests (e.g., Angola). But taken together, the experiments *do* challenge the legitimacy of capitalism and capitalist relations. Loudly and clearly, the societies in transition shout "Capitalism misdevelops, capitalism exploits." That they do this while still (grudgingly) attempting to survive and prosper in a world predominantly defined by capitalism is no consolation to elites in the core countries. Only when they cease to hurl defiance against the system and even begin to mumble about its virtues (China), or break with the USSR (China, Yugoslavia), does imperialism become less militant.

The challenge to capitalism is thus even more fundamental than is generally understood. The attraction of socialism to many groups and sectors in the third world often does not derive directly from either the theoretical power of Marxism or the organizational successes of revolutionary organizations and parties. *What keeps the socialist vision alive in the context of underdevelopment is the lived history of the failure of capitalism.* The failure of peripheral capitalism to deliver improved standards of living, social justice, and minimal quality of life to large sectors of the population in the small, peripheral societies gives the socialist vision a dynamic that would not be predicted from a cool analytical look at the successes and failures of actually existing socialisms in the third and second worlds. Poverty, unemployment, rampant class privilege, dictatorship and disregard for basic human rights, foreign penetration and exploitation, are the deep subsoil in which the dynamic toward socialist solutions is cultured and takes root. At a very basic level, millions understand that markets operate to their disadvantage, not to their advantage, even though they may not have the conceptual vocabulary to express this clearly. The socialist promise to replace a flawed and misallocating market rationality with a more rational and just social rationality (through planning, public ownership, etc.) has a large and potentially receptive audience (one might say a *natural* audience) in the periphery. So does the promise of democracy. When nationalist, antiforeign, and "you have nothing to lose but your chains" arguments are added to understandings of this lived reality, the appeal of socialism rooted in self-determination is potentially very powerful indeed. Socialist organizers understand these realities and the potential power of these appeals, just as their enemies fear them.

But imperialism abroad and its allies at home are not the only obstacles faced by the societies in transition. Inevitably, the transition is a *problem-generating* historical process. Quite often the old political economy worked, at least in the sense of being an integrated and functioning system of accumulation and sociopolitical control. Yet it is precisely this old system which is jettisoned or comes under frontal attack during the transition. Attempting to replace the "logic of capital" with "a logic of the majority" (to use the Sandinist language) necessarily brings to the surface class conflicts and underscores institutional shortcomings. The economy suffers, and politics loses the appearance and often the reality of "stability"—unless ironhanded dictatorial rule is invoked.

What resources can the leaders of the society in transition bring to bear as a counterweight to these inevitable problems? Although the language sounds trite—or overblown at times—the only possible answer is "the people." If the transition is a problem-generating historical experience, it is also, potentially, a person-liberating experience. Trained people flee, but new generations—initially with less training, but with a much different and higher level of consciousness—step into the breach. Production is sometimes lost in the agrarian reform, but new lands are brought into cultivation, tilled and tended by new agrarians, obeying a new calculus of motivation and using improved means of production. Class conflict perturbs the educational system, but thousands are mobilized for a literacy campaign that would have been both organizationally and politically impossible under the old regime. The transition is thus a constantly reoccuring and changing race between the problems that inhere in radical change and the resources that are generated by the liberational-transitional process itself. It is also an immense gamble: society leaps from the shore into the raging waters, buoyed by a new self-confidence and the energies released by the leap itself. In the best of cases, and with a little help from its friends, the society in transition navigates the rapids and emerges in calmer waters, strengthened and reconstituted. In other instances, the experiment either retreats into a safe reformism that fails to address basic structural issues, or—in the worst of cases—it degenerates into tyrannical and bureaucratic rule which ultimately advantages only a small military, state, or party elite.

Where are the Models?

While Marx theorized about the conditions engendered by capitalist development that would facilitate a transition to socialism, he provided neither a blueprint of what the transition would look like nor an analysis of socialism itself.[4] Furthermore, although most of the major Marxist theoreticians of the twentieth century, from Lenin to Mao and Che Guevara, have had something to say about situations in which revolutionary socialist ferment takes place on the periphery, the connecting link between these widely diverse theorists is basically the question, "How can we make the revolution?" Relatively less attention has been paid to problems of transition once control of the state has been at least nominally achieved. With only slight exaggeration, it could be said that Lenin was the last great institutional theorizer, with his tracts on party organization, his writings on the transitional state, and his debates with Trotsky and others. But with all due respect, those tracts, analyses, and debates are not sufficient to the current problematic of transition in peripheral societies, although they are often relevant.

Furthermore, it is increasingly obvious that although a great deal can be learned from the Soviets and Chinese (and other cases), no simple equation by analogy of these experiences to those of Nicaragua or

Mozambique, for example, will serve. Over the past decade, it has frequently been heard that "Nicaragua must find its own way," or "Mozambique must seek its own road"—each in accord with its distinct class structure, level of development, national history, and geopolitical insertion in the world system. Such statements, however, are basically declarations of independence rather than mappings of independently arrived-at blueprints of mechanisms and institutions appropriate to the transition. Even when carefully examined and aggregated, they do not add up to a theory of the transition geared to the realities of the global system and the third world in the waning years of the century. What we are witnessing is increasing caution in claiming that answers are definitively known or pathways clear.[5]

The essays that follow address both theoretical and empirical materials relevant to a deeper understanding of societies in transition. It should be made clear at the outset that a majority of the contributors have been heavily influenced by their involvement in, or their research on, the Nicaraguan revolution. There is thus a strong Nicaraguan cast to some of the materials that follow. Nevertheless, the collection includes work that is overtly comparative (Stallings and Deere), determinedly theoretical (FitzGerald and Bengelsdorf), and specifically non-Nicaraguan (Saul). Three broad problematics are addressed on the pages that follow: *economics*—how to combine distribution and growth in a transformed social formation; *politics*—how to create viable participatory and representative forms; and *war and imperialism*—how to accomplish the economic and political transformations in a context of aggression and emergency. These three problematics are, of course, closely interrelated. It is useful, however, as a prelude to the essays themselves, to treat them separately.

The Economics of Transition

Simply stated, the core economic problem of the transition is how to transform the inherited economic structure of underdevelopment into one that benefits the majority of the population and at the same time generates acceptable levels of growth. The constraints are formidable, since the fundamental objective is to increase popular living standards and not just to redistribute poverty more equitably. Transitional societies must thus invent and put into practice a developmental model based on both growth and equity, while at the same time replacing the logic of capital with a functioning social rationality.

As previously emphasized, all experiments in transition since 1950 have taken place in small, peripheral economies. The concept "peripheral" highlights the centrality of the export sector to the inherited model of accumulation. Specifically, it captures the external determination of the growth rate: the dynamism of the domestic economy is strongly conditioned by international commodity markets and their fluctuations, and the terms of trade. Moreover, specialization in the production of a limited number of export products makes these economies particularly vulnerable. Finally, economic growth is largely dependent on financial and technological transfers.

Smallness constrains development options in several ways. Natural resource endowments are usually thin, and human resources are equally scarce. Typically there is a small industrial base, geared to simple manufacturing and/or assembly of luxury goods. A small internal market—itself the product of poverty and the unequal distribution of income—limits the growth of manufacturing for domestic consumption. Any significant industrialization process requires the import of raw materials and semiprocessed goods in addition to capital goods.

It is thus a fundamental proposition of the essays in this volume that the economic problems posed by attempts at transition in these small, peripheral economies differ significantly from those which have shaped the debate in the Soviet, East European, and Chinese cases. This can be seen clearly in the way the transitional economy is inserted into the international division of labor, in the articulation of forms of production, and in the possibilities for planning in the transition. We will consider each in turn.

International Division of Labor

Both FitzGerald and Stallings argue that autarky is not a development option for third world economies in the periphery. The transformation of the productive structure will necessarily require external resources, with the result that the export sector will continue to be pivotal. And as FitzGerald points out, this implies that transitional economies will continue to be subject to unequal exchange in trade, while the pace of accumulation will be heavily influenced by the effects of externally determined international prices.

The main option available to a transitional economy is thus to diversify its dependence, both in export markets and in the sourcing of imports and finance. Stallings examines in detail the experiences of five of these countries in obtaining external financing in the transition. She finds that their relative success both in obtaining and diversifying their sources of funding is closely related to their ideological stance and geographic location, as well as the particular historical moment in which the transitional regime comes to power.

Articulation of Forms of Production

The classical debate assumed a one-to-one correspondence between sectors of the economy and the new organization of production:

industry, which was previously capitalist, would be nationalized and become the core of the state sector; and agriculture, previously in the hands of the peasantry, was gradually to be collectivized. In small, peripheral economies, however, the structural conditions of underdevelopment have produced myriad forms of production which continue to be reflected in the transition. Baumeister and Neira show how in the Nicaraguan case, for example, the inherited structure of production and the class relations of the revolution itself shaped both the course of agrarian policy and the maintenance of a mixed economy. Small and medium producers proliferate in both agriculture and industry. Bringing them fully into the state sector in the short run is undesirable, if not impossible. Even large capital cannot in all cases be nationalized immediately—for both economic and political reasons.

On a theoretical level, FitzGerald argues that the maintenance of a mixed economy, including an important capitalist sector, is compatible with new socialist forms of production as long as the state controls the use of the surplus and key decisions governing accumulation. This implies that state control over marketing and distribution may be more crucial than actual state ownership of the means of production. He notes that the case for not nationalizing important segments of capital rests on the superior administrative capacity of capitalists in the early stages of the transition.

Deere's review of the agrarian reforms carried out in thirteen countries that consider themselves to be embarked upon a transition to socialism shows that few have retained an important capitalist sector in agriculture. The degree of nationalization has varied directly with the degree of prior capitalist development and the penetration of foreign or settler capital. In the majority of cases, large capitalist farms were reorganized as state farms. In only a few countries have production cooperatives been the result of such nationalizations. Rather, cooperatives were expected to result from the collectivization of small producers. However, only in Vietnam in the 1960s and Cuba in the 1980s have peasant producers voluntarily pooled their land to form production cooperatives. In the majority of transitional societies, independent peasant production predominates and has often been reinforced through agrarian reform.

Baumeister and Neira emphasize that there is no one-to-one correspondence between the inherited rural structure and the transitional forms of organization of production. In Nicaragua, as elsewhere, the relative importance given to the state, cooperative, and private sectors in the transition has been a subject of continuing tension and debate. There is to date no dominant paradigm for socialist agriculture—nor, some would argue, is there likely to be in any foreseeable future.

Contributors to this volume agree that state ownership alone is insufficient to define a socialist model of production. Profound changes must also occur in the labor process—incorporating worker participation—and in popular participation in the determination of state policy.

Planning and Economic Policy

One of the main points of contention of the contributors is the relationship between central planning and economic policy—and how these in turn are related to popular participation in the transition. For FitzGerald, growing social control over the processes of production, distribution, and accumulation is central to the transition. Social control from this perspective implies centralized state planning mediated by worker participation. In contrast, for Coraggio, realistic economic policies are much more important in the initial stages of the transition than formalized central planning, which he views as feasible only in the longer run. Rather than centralized forms of control, what are desperately needed are coherent short-run policies that are also consistent with the long-run transformation of the economy.

FitzGerald starts from the proposition that the replacement of the law of value by planning based on social and economic priorities is at the heart of the transitional process. This in turn requires centralized social control to subordinate the operation of capitalist relations and allow and encourage the creation of other economic forms. Central planning increasingly should establish prices, distribute labor to different sectors, and regulate the pace and course of accumulation. Price stability is needed to articulate different forms of production, allow the decentralization of management in state enterprises, and allocate the internal surplus. He argues that there is a single (optimal) set of prices compatible with reproduction of the economy and planned investment, and that this set is derived fundamentally from the insertion of the economy into the international division of labor—as conditioned by the domestic articulation with petty producers at a given level of supply. Any other set of prices leads to inflation, black markets, and other problems. A central task of planning, from this point of view, is forecasting this "correct" set of prices and putting them into practice.

Coraggio reminds us that state intervention in the economy is not a neutral process. It affects different groups in different ways and is inherently political. He sees the conjunctural control of the economy as a fundamental component of the revolutionary order, a basic test of the legitimacy of that order. Working from this perspective, he analyzes a series of problems in the design and implementation of economic policy in Nicaragua that support his claim that central planning in transitional societies is a long-run proposition. Lack of theory relevant to economic transformation in small peripheral economies, lack of knowledge about the concrete reality to be transformed, and the fragmentation of the transitional state, all contribute to making central planning difficult if not impossible. To this Fagen adds what he calls a basic paradox: private capital is proportionally more important in the economic sphere than it can be allowed to be in the political sphere. This suggests that no matter how carefully economic policies are crafted, political conflict will be endemic to the transition.

The Politics of Transition

No problem has so vexed and discredited socialism in our day as the absence of an associated democratic political practice. Exclusionary and authoritarian institutions, the bureaucratization of governance, and—in the worst of cases—high levels of repression, have been the rule rather than the exception.[6] Yet nothing could be further from the spirit of the classics and the dreams of millions of advocates of socialism. As Bengelsdorf points out in her review of the Marxist theoretical legacy, notions such as the rule "of the immense majority in the interest of the majority," and "the withering away of the state in the future communist society," are profoundly democratic in spirit and intent. But as she also emphasizes, the classics are thin to the point of silence on the need for political mediation, on the design of agencies and institutions required to turn the abstractions into realities.

Saul is somewhat less sanguine, suggesting that the Marxist tradition embodies a double legacy: Marxism as a frozen "scientific" dogmatism vs. Marxism as a form of critical inquiry; ideology used to conceal realities rather than to expose contradictions; the vanguard party as an infallible source of wisdom vs. the party as the instrument of the masses. Although lamentable, it is not surprising that the dogmatic and elitist interpretation of the tradition should frequently dominate in practice. Thus it is essential for the future of democracy in transitional societies, he argues, that this duality be confronted directly.

In this context, of theoretical and normative emphasis on the importance of democracy and a concrete practice to date which is still overwhelmingly nondemocratic, a major theme of the essays in this volume can thus be summarized as follows: What might democracy in the transition look like, and what are the obstacles that impede its realization? Marchetti speaks for many when he elevates meaningful mass participation to an absolutely central place in the transition to socialism. Lowy shares this point of view, and emphasizes that transitional societies face huge obstacles, both material and human, to the institutionalization of meaningful participation. The common legacy of underdevelopment—lack of resources, trained personnel, and democratic and participatory traditions—coupled with the heritage of authoritarian models in actually existing socialisms—militate against such participation. So too do imperialist intervention and the centralizing and bureaucratizing tendencies evident when attempts at comprehensive planning are made in fragile and impoverished economies.

In this context, Lowy speaks boldly in favor of representative and direct democracy in the political realm and self-management in the productive realm. At all levels, persons must be involved in choosing between alternative economic and political policies. This in turn requires political pluralism, with contested elections and different groups contending for leadership within the revolutionary vanguard. Political pluralism implies freedom of expression: the only way the popular classes can educate themselves ideologically is through an open confrontation of revolutionary ideas with bourgeois ideas. Along with Marchetti, Lowy argues that democratic practice of this sort is not a luxury, but rather an essential condition of survival in revolutionary states engaged in a struggle with underdevelopment at home and imperialism abroad. Fagen suggests, however, that the dilemma is more delicate: silencing dissent is counterproductive to the legitimacy of the revolutionary state, but allowing the full range of classical liberal freedoms may run the risk of tipping the balance in favor of those who do not want any changes at all. A central "constitutional" issue thus becomes developing a doctrine of dissent which, while still democratic in spirit, is compatible with the construction of a working consensus supportive of the new political and economic order.

Although much of the discussion of democracy in the transition involves concepts and issues applicable to a wide range of other circumstances, there are three problematics which are rooted in tensions specific to the construction of democracy in a context of revolutionary socialism: vanguard and mass, the state and class struggle, and planning and popular participation.

Vanguard and Mass

As Saul emphasizes, there is a continuing tension between vanguard and mass action, between party-directed change and popular participation that initiates and shapes change. On the one hand, there is a need for the leadership to transcend the limitations of spontaneous class action and to guide the development of revolutionary consciousness and the revolutionary process. On the other hand, there is a strong temptation for the leadership to view itself as the (sole) agency of the popular classes, and consequently to downplay or repress autonomous mass action.

Marchetti and Núñez both see this problem as related to the class base of the revolution as well as the class composition of the vanguard. In most small peripheral countries there is no significant proletariat to act as the leading social force in the revolution. Revolutionary transitions have been initiated by broad and heterogeneous social move-ments. There is thus no single dominant center of class power. Often, as a result, the vanguard party is staffed by state functionaries with little experience or trust in popular participation. When this distrust of popular participation is widespread, it leads naturally to the dogmatic claim that "the vanguard can do no wrong." In such circumstances, internal democracy—criticism and contestation with the party—are absolutely essential to avoid a degeneration into party dictatorship.

The State and Class Struggle

Nuñez presents the most comprehensive analysis of class forces and their complex relationship to the state. He draws attention to the importance of what he calls the "third force" (petty bourgeoisie, youth) in the overthrow of the old order. After the victory, these social forces, along with the peasantry, remain critically important to the legitimacy of the new order. Furthermore, given the relatively small size and economic weight of the proletariat, there is no clear class hegemony in the transitional period. Thus at the heart of the transitional political process is the dilemma of developing a "proletarian project" in the absence of proletarian hegemony. Stated most bluntly, the key ques-tion for Nuñez is how to proletarianize a process that cannot be directed—in any organized way—by the proletariat. The transitional state must represent or at a minimum reflect the interests of a diversity of popular classes, while at the same time ensuring that the main dynamic of transition moves toward the construction of socialism, not the restoration of capitalism. Inevitably, state-society tensions will be continuing and complex.

Coraggio argues that a revolutionary project based on national unity puts a brake on class struggle in its traditional forms. There is thus a very real danger that mass organizations, and other institutions of popular participation, will be transformed into mere implementors of state and party policy instead of evolving as autonomous articulators of agendas for social change. As Saul notes, if the inevitability of fundamental contradictions between state interests and class interests in the transition is not recognized, then the basic rationale for the progressive empowerment of the popular classes disappears. There is then no need for an upward flow of information and pressure, since the state is seen as automatically representing mass interests.

Lowy takes the argument one step further, suggesting that it is central to socialist democracy that individuals and groups be allowed to organize around their own immediate interests as they perceive them, and that they be encouraged to press for the realization of those interests. Molyneux makes this argument concrete in the context of gender issues, which by definition cannot be subsumed under class issues. An organized women's movement cannot simply be a transmission belt for party or state policy. Rather, it must be a relatively autonomous mass organization which can influence official policy. Inevitably, gender issues as conceptualized and articulated by such an organization will not always be in one-to-one correspondence with formulations and policies generated in the state or party apparatuses.

Planning and Popular Participation

Several authors warn that centralized economic planning, in one degree or another indispensable in socialist transitions, also creates the conditions for the bureaucratization of decision-making. Lowy, Fitz-Gerald, and Marchetti all explore ways in which planning can be democratized and controlled through popular and workplace organizations, as well as community-based groups.

Deere examines the tensions between planning and participation in her review of the relationship between forms of productive organization in agriculture and peasant-worker control. She finds very little evidence of worker participation in the management of the state farms created in socialist third world agrarian reforms. In contrast, in the production cooperatives established by these reforms, much higher levels of participation are found. The successful development of cooperatives in turn is linked to autonomous peasant and rural worker organizations.

Finally, Coraggio provides another argument in favor of high levels of popular participation in the planning process. When the planning apparatus is weak, understaffed, and data-poor (as is inevitable), popular participation is a resource that initiates and facilitates projects that would otherwise be impossible. This perspective is seconded by Fagen's observation that in the politics of transition, popular mobilization must often substitute for economic and organizational resources that are in short supply. To underutilize "the people" is to hobble the transitional effort by tying it too mechanically to what—from the point of view of technical cadres—appear to be the objective limitations imposed by shortages of material and financial resources.

War and Imperialism

Several essays point out that most transitional societies today (and earlier both the Soviet Union and China) have had to face armed imperialist aggression or, at a minimum, carefully organized and well-funded destabilization campaigns. War and destabilization must thus be considered an organic rather than an exceptional feature of the transition. As such, theories of the transition must incorporate imperialist aggression as integrally into the basic paradigm as ideas about the incomplete economy or dependence on the external sector.

Different authors approach this challenge from different perspectives. For FitzGerald, a primary consequence of aggression is to accelerate the process of disentanglement from the capitalist world system. A frequent corollary, of course, is a relatively rapid integration of the transitional society into the socialist bloc. Internally, military mobilization reduces the size of the productive labor force, eventually affecting the production of export goods (and thus accumulation) and consumption goods (and thus basic needs). Higher labor productivity can counter this trend, but it is difficult to achieve in the short run. Furthermore, the allocation of centrally controlled resources for defense creates inflationary pressures and makes rationing the only logical distributive response. Overall, a reduction in popular living standards is almost inevitable.

Marchetti argues that the primary resource which a revolutionary society possesses in the face of armed aggression is subjective: ideological mobilization. This mobilization, in turn, can only be maintained on the basis of sustained popular participation—for him, a precondition of socialist democracy. On the other hand, he recognizes that conditions of war also tend to lower the capacity of the vanguard for self-criticism and restrict the scope of mass participation. It becomes logical and easy to blame the enemy for problems, rather than addressing failures of economic policy and political blunders directly. Moreover, aggression and associated states of emergency lead to a curtailment of the flow of information—necessary for meaningful participation—and a heightened sense that criticism automatically plays into the hands of the enemy, or—in the extreme case—is treasonous.

War may also change the relationship between the state, the party, and the mass organizations. In addition to the need to enhance state power—including coercive power—in the face of armed aggression, as Marchetti points out, there are also strong pulls toward the fusion of party and state. Concomitantly, as Coraggio adds, war weakens the mass organizations, draining them of key cadres and encouraging the state and party functionaries to view them as simple transmission belts for directives from above. Implicit in Molyneux's essay is a related theme: the defense effort severely restricts the state's capacity to provide the material and political resources necessary to address gender-related issues. Concrete goes to bunkers, not to daycare centers. Health care professionals go to the front, not to clinics serving civilians. The attention of leaders is focused on war-related questions, and gender issues—which even in the best of times do not easily make it onto the national agenda—are pushed even further into the shadows.

In a more positive vein, Marchetti notes that aggression may contribute to new styles of leadership and new strategies centered on building consensus for the war effort. Defense requires the revolution to construct the broadest possible alliance—with peasants, workers, the private sector, and ethnic, religious, and regional interests. Imperialism thus has the potential for consolidating the revolution. But here too there is a potential cost. Coraggio emphasizes that a renewed alliance with the private sector is reflected in a decline in the participation and power of mass organizations. Class struggle in the form of takeovers of land and factories is subordinated to the war effort. As FitzGerald notes, an acceleration of the transformation of the economic structure may still take place. But if so, it will certainly threaten the broad alliance seen by many as essential to a successful defense effort.

On balance, it is thus clear that the overall impact of war and defense on any transitional society is overwhelmingly negative. The few benefits of a mobilizational and integrative sort are more than offset by the human, material, and political costs incurred in fighting the aggression. In most cases, transitional societies eventually "win" in the sense of surviving. But the scars of battle remain to remind all citizens that the right to determine their own future is neither easily nor cheaply won.

There is, of course, another road by which the topic of war and imperialism can be approached. Burbach's essay focuses on the sources of U.S. behavior in an age of declining hegemony, rather than on the consequences of that behavior for societies in transition. In particular, he points out that policy elites have come to perceive a multiplicity of threats to U.S. interests in the postwar world: economic, geopolitical, ideological, and strategic. Thus, in Latin America and the Caribbean, for example, experiments as diverse as Arbenz in Guatemala, Castro in Cuba, Allende in Chile, Bishop in Grenada, and the Sandinistas in Nicaragua have all been viewed as inimical to officially defined U.S. interests. Experience of imperialist aggression in the third world is by now sufficient to allow revolutionary regimes to make some assessments of future behavior—what are the constants and where, by contrast, they can hope to find some cracks or divisions in the foreign policy establishment that can be exploited to create some room for maneuver. Moreover, the United States is home to a diverse set of groups and social forces. Increasingly, Burbach suggests, many of these groups and social forces are not objectively advantaged by imperial practice. To the contrary, they have much to lose—including their lives in some cases—under a foreign policy regime that is interventionist and determinedly counterrevolutionary. Thus as domestic consciousness and political organization catch up with changing realities, there is hope that the most destructive actions of the United States toward societies in transition may be reined in. Such changes cannot happen too rapidly for those who live in the small peripheral societies that have embarked on a transition. They live the consequences of imperialism, and with each passing day they continue to suffer for their audacity in having rejected models of development stamped "made in USA."

Notes

1. See, for example, the edited collections by Desfosses and Levesque (1975), Rosberg and Callaghy (1979), Szajkowski (1981), Wiles (1982), and White, Murray, and White (1983).
2. This statement is not meant to denegrate either the folk culture or the "high" culture of the Soviet Union, China, or other socialist countries. The generation and diffusion of commodity culture is an issue apart, and quite clearly the provenance of the advanced capitalist countries.
3. With the exception of China, and to a limited extent North Korea and Vietnam, all the postwar third world experiments in transition to socialism have taken place in relatively small economies. This smallness, and the key related role of the external sector in accumulation, are crucial to setting limits on the political economy of transition.
4. Toward the end of his life, Marx began to consider how noncapitalist forms of production might also provide the preconditions for socialism, suggesting a possible multiplicity of transitional paths (Shanin 1983).
5. See Saul (1985) and Harris and Vilas (1985), for example. An early attempt to theorize the problems of transition specific to small peripheral economies is Thomas (1974). Also see the special issue on "Socialism and Development," in *World Development* (1981) edited by Charles Wilber and Ken Jameson.
6. These of course are characteristics of many of the small, peripheral societies as well.

Notes on the Analysis
of the Small Underdeveloped Economy
in Transition

▼▲

E.V.K. FitzGerald

In the second half of the twentieth century, national liberation struggles led to a series of attempts to construct socialism in the "third world." Beginning in China and continuing in Vietnam, North Korea, Cuba, Algeria, Angola, Ethiopia, and Mozambique, this group includes the tragic cases of Chile and Grenada, and has its most recent expression in Nicaragua. These experiences, as the result of their "dependent" or colonial past, are very different from those of Europe. In addition to their incipient industrialization and heterogeneous production forms, these economies are "peripheral" to the dynamic of world trade. The three Asian examples had the advantage of a certain geostrategic rearguard in the form of the existing socialist bloc, and relatively large populations. The others are much smaller economies, dependent upon foreign trade and technology transfer for both simple and expanded reproduction. Their subordinate position in the international division of labor, and their exposure to metropolitan pressure because of this, is a defining feature of the group; it is also a characteristic of their internal economic organization.

However, with the notable exception of China, the rich historical experience of these transitions has yet to be incorporated into the body of socialist economic theory. Particular debates, such as those on production incentives in Cuba or the peasantry in Vietnam, have been significant; but they have not led to systematic theorization. In particular, the central problem of how insertion into the international division of labor affects the process of reproduction, and thus the limits of social transformation, has yet to be addressed.

The aim here is to attempt to establish, on the basis of the common experiences of "socialist transition on the periphery," some elements of the necessary modification of existing transition theory. This article will examine a series of generalizations rather than resort to an endless

Translated by Scott Otteman

28

bibliography. Similarly, it will not attempt a precise definition of the transition, beyond observing that the social formation involved "combines relations of distinct modes of production in such a way that the transformation of the dominant relations of production is a possible outcome of the class struggle" (Hindess 1976:3).

A Formal Model for the Transition

The Marxian reproduction scheme proposed by Kalecki (1972, 1976) provides a useful frame of analysis. As an empirical model it is not only simple, but also particularly suited to the inflexible production structure typically encountered during the first stages of the transition. In the classical reproduction scheme, production is divided between two Departments: the means of production (Department I) and the means of reproduction of the labor force (Department II). The former refers to the capital goods and joint inputs that are used by both Departments, while the latter refers to wage goods and wage services for the workers employed in them. With fixed technical coefficients, a given balance of production will generate both the growth rate and income distribution.

However, in the case of the peripheral economy, Department I is incomplete; foreign trade becomes the essential source of producer goods (cf. Braun 1975). Although some of its components, such as construction materials, energy, and higher education, do exist, imports are the principal source of the means of production, exchanged for semiprocessed raw materials. Strictly speaking, the Department I of this economy is located abroad, in the industrialized countries with which it trades at prices that they determine. However, for the purposes of analysis we shall define the export sector as Department I because it performs this function. Moreover, historical experience indicates that this will hold true long into the initial stages of the transition, during which the economy is developing its own producer goods capacity and technological base.[1]

Kalecki expands his Marxian scheme for a developing economy along the lines indicated in the *Grundrisse,* by dividing Department II in two: Department IIa, which producers "necessities" for the consumption of workers; and Department IIb, which producers "non-necessities" for consumption by the capitalists. We must modify these definitions for the case in hand. First, Department IIa should include not only wage goods as such but also services such as health, education, and transport (even culture and sport) to the extent that they are socially necessary for the reproduction of the labor force; in other words, what is now known as "basic needs."[2] Department IIb should be considered as not just the luxury goods that still reflect continued social differentiation during the transition, but rather as "incentive goods" to raise the productivity of both workers and small producers.

For instance, a typical such economy might have mining or agroexports as Department I, peasant food production as the basis of Department IIa, and national light industry as Department IIb. Department I exports provide inputs to Department IIb; Department IIa provides food for the workers in Departments I and IIb in exchange for Department IIb goods, which also make up part of the wage goods basket. The dynamics of such an economy are not difficult to work out: it is not difficult to see how the assignment of labor force and imported inputs between the Departments will determine their respective production levels, trade balances, and the standard of living. The assignment of (imported) investment goods to each Department generates a clear accumulation model (cf. FitzGerald 1985c).

The classical problem of the optimum rate of accumulation is then expressed as the balance between export production and basic needs production (both closely linked to agriculture), which determine, respectively, the rate of growth and the standard of living, with the complication that both worker and peasant productivity will depend upon the availability of incentive goods. The whole model will also rest upon a given set of technical coefficients and external (world) prices, which condition the reproduction of the economy as a result of the level of development of its productive forces and its insertion into the international division of labor.

When we attempt to apply existing theoretical interpretations of transition to this sort of economy, however, we encounter several problems, each of which will be analyzed separately.

Problem 1: The Articulation of Different Forms of Production

Diverse forms of production necessarily exist within the developing economy in transition. State enterprise on the "commanding heights" and extensive cooperativization are added to the remnants of the existing capitalist and the petty mercantile sectors. It is to be expected that during the transition, the former two are strengthened at the expense of the latter.

The theory of this articulation has been worked out in the context of the early history of capitalism and, more recently, applied to underdeveloped countries.[3] Analysis focuses on the dynamic relationship between the reproduction of the capitalist sector on the one hand and that of those productive (or reproductive) units based on "noncapitalist" social relations on the other. Although capitalism is the dominant production form within the social formation, the articulation with the other forms is a struggle for their survival, because the relations of exchange are essentially a way of appropriating surplus labor and controlling the social distribution of the means of production. Specifically, it is necessary to develop a diversity of (a) types of ownership of the means of production; (b) forms of expropriation of the surplus; (c) degrees of division of labor; and (d) levels of development of productive forces (Laclau 1977).

Applying this logic to the case in hand, it is clear that the rupture implicit in the revolution itself produces disarticulation, so that one of the major tasks of the transition is to rearticulate the economy so as to assure the required material production levels while at the same time transforming social relations of production and exchange. During the transition, the state is clearly the hegemonic force in the economy, although not necessarily the dominant property owner, while the degree of the division of labor and the level of development can only be advanced in the long run. Articulation must be planned (that is, it cannot be simply the result of various conflictive dynamics) while the socialization of the principal means of production and exchange initiates the construction of a new economy, no longer based on the private appropriation of surplus labor. However, the different production forms must also be assured the conditions for their reproduction to sustain the economy while this construction takes place; so the mode of appropriation of the surplus becomes the central economic question. Moreover, the conditions of scarcity and atomisation of production processes imply that value forms must be used to express much of this economic articulation.

The "classical" debate on the transition initiated by Lenin (1978) supposes a complete coincidence between departments, production sectors, and forms of production. Industry and agriculture are Departments I and II, and organized as state firms and peasant farms, respectively. Central planning of industry is assumed, foreign trade is not significant, and the problem is reduced to the determination of the correct level of the terms of trade between town and country to assure both the reproduction of the peasantry (and thus an adequate future food supply for the towns) and the transfer of surplus labor (as food or migrant workers) to industry. The former factor also conditions the transformation of production relations in the countryside, leading to cooperativization, which allows a degree of family control over the surplus and the labor process itself.[4] Unfortunately, this line of analysis of the multiform socialist economy has not been systematically applied to two similar problems: the articulation of the state with other groups of petty producers and with nonstate enterprises, although both phenomena are widespread in practice.[5]

The diversity of forms of production is not just a matter of strategic choice, because it depends on the combination of the level of development and location within the international division of labor inherited from the previous capitalist order. The revolution inherits these conditions and proceeds to transform them, but they have their own dynamic, which must be understood as Bukharin (1979) pointed out in 1919.

The insertion of the economy into the international division of labor results in the development of an export sector (our Department I) organized according to the needs of the main export markets. This often results in large production units, with relatively high technology, a proletarian labor force (albeit seasonal), and even foreign ownership when the capital requirements are high. However, in other cases direct production is carried out by small or medium producers, while supplies, credit, storage, processing, marketing, and so forth are controlled by monopoly interests, which can thereby also control technology and appropriate the surplus. These systems may also be combined. Typically, the state will obtain ownership of the large production units or of these control points early on in the transition, the usual economic objective being to gain control over the surplus, that is, foreign exchange.

It is logically possible to maintain individual juridical ownership even of quite large production units, at least in the initial stages of the transition. This would imply social control of the appropriation of the surplus, and thus of the reproduction of the enterprise, but leave the organization of direct production in the hands of capitalists. The labor process itself would also be conditioned by legislation, wage controls, and trade union organization. Essentially then, the capitalists would cease to be such, becoming in effect subcontractors to the state, paid for their administrative capacity with a proportion of the surplus (Mandel 1962; Wheelock 1984).

Political conditions may not permit this solution, but in essence it is the same sort of arrangement that is usually proposed for the petty producers, except that rather than the underdevelopment of production being the problem, it is the relatively advanced nature of the larger firms and their administrative requirements which limit the efficacy of state control. This argument is important in Department I because of its key role in the inherited economic structure, but much the same argument can be made for other sectors, such as manufacturing. It should be noted that in any case multinational corporations have this sort of relationship with the state in many socialist countries. Clearly, once the state sector has acquired the technical and managerial capacity to take these firms over, this can be done, subject to political considerations. Moreover, it is reasonable to suppose that the inevitable concentration of accumulation in the state sector will lead to its predominance over time.

There is another facet to this argument. The mere fact of juridical ownership of large firms by the state does not automatically imply their socialization, so long as the appropriation of the surplus, investment decisions, organization of the labor process, commercial relationships, and so on are still decided by the management (Bettleheim 1975b). Social control over the articulation of these state firms with the economy (that is, planning) is required in order to define a form of noncapitalist or even socialist production and exchange.

Department IIa ("basic needs") in underdeveloped economies tends to have a large component of peasant and artisan production, simply because it is through this form of social organization that capitalism initially found the cheapest method of reproducing its labor force: through unequal mercantile exchange with this form of production, by employing temporary labor which returns to this sector when it is not needed, and also by using the family as the cheapest social security system. In the long run, these small producers must enter a more complex division of labor and superior social organization if the productivity of Department IIa is to rise and elevate overall living standards.

Yet petty producers, particularly peasants, historically resist collectivization, which has not only political but also economic consequences. Experience has shown, therefore, that it is possible to leave juridical ownership of the basic means of production (land or workshop) in the hands of the family, and also the organization of the labor process itself, albeit in the form of simple cooperatives. The state can, through the control of inputs, marketing, and technical assistance, maintain social control over the appropriation of the surplus and the production of use-value.

The social transformations brought about by revolution themselves create a new form of production: popular mobilization for such activities as literacy campaigns, preventive health programs, housing construction, and civil defense. The success of these programs, especially if they are to be sustained over a long period of time, depends upon their raising the standard of living of the immediate community, so they are naturally concentrated in Department IIa. Although it involves an increase in labor intensity, no further surplus is thereby created because the product is an immediate use-value. The case of voluntary labor for such activities as harvesting is an exception, but this is notoriously difficult to sustain except as an ideological exercise. It should also be noted that this sort of "popular production" requires considerable state support in the form of inputs, technical assistance, publicity, and so on.

The articulation of these forms of production assumes that their reproduction under state hegemony is in fact compatible; in practice there is always conflict between them, and specifically between the old (capitalist and petty producer) forms and the new (state and cooperative) ones. The process of social transformation implies that at the very least expanded reproduction (accumulation) is concentrated in the new forms, and that the old forms sustain simple reproduction at the most. The socially feasible rate of change will depend both upon the factors considered above, and the availability of surplus for accumulation.

Problem 2: A New Insertion into the International Division of Labor

Many of the characteristics of the underdeveloped economy in transition are inherited from its previous subordinate position in the capitalist world economy, affecting the products traded, markets, prices, technology transfer, and credits. Because this subordination is a determining factor in revolutions of "national liberation," overcoming it logically becomes a central objective of transition strategy.

The composition of trade inherited from the past cannot be altered rapidly, because this would mean transforming the domestic technological structure through a sustained process of accumulation: experience indicates that this process is a long one.[6] In consequence, primary commodities (albeit semi-processed) and perhaps some simple manufactures are the basis of exports, forming the equivalent of Department I to the extent that they can be transformed through trade into capital equipment and production inputs.

The prices at which this exchange takes place (and thus the use-value which can be obtained) between the industrialized capitalist countries of the metropole and the small underdeveloped economies of the periphery are defined largely by the former, generating a process of surplus transfer known as "unequal exchange." The terms of trade result from a determinate relationship between import prices for raw materials and export prices in the metropolitan economy, based on real wage and profit levels resulting from the rate of accumulation and the strength of organized labor. The internationalization of the metropolitan profit rate through capital flows, and the depression of wages on the periphery due to the low costs of reproduction of labor, then determine income levels on the periphery.

The internal transformation of the economy during the transition will clearly affect the volume, nature, and disposition of the surplus available internally, but continued trade with the capitalist metropole implies continued exploitation through the terms of trade and thus an unequal valuation of labor. The return on foreign investments will presumably be reduced by renegotiations, taxation, control of transfer pricing, and even limitations on profit remittance, while the local bourgeoisie would no longer be able to export capital. Simultaneously, the standard of living of workers would rise as Department II expands, possibly at the expense of foreign trade. In other words, the process of income distribution is changed, although not the terms of trade. A single small third world country is in no position to affect these prices substantially.

Just as before the revolution, the economy may benefit from a certain differential rent at an international level due to having a better natural resource base or more favorable geographic position than its competitors. Nonetheless, the excess profits earned in the prerevolutionary export sector as a result of low labor costs logically disappear in the transition, placing our economy at a disadvantage compared to its capitalist competitors. The solution to this dilemma is sought in the establishment of a New International Economic Order to redress the terms of trade via collective negotiation of supply.

So long as capitalist countries are willing to extend loans, the import costs can be displaced in time, even though the existing terms of trade are not affected. Similarly, the existence of secondary centers of capitalism and even the industrial maturation of some of the large third world economies permits a certain autonomy in foreign trade; this may alter the geopolitics of the situation, but not the economics of unequal exchange.

The construction of socialism on the periphery opens up the perspective of a new insertion into the socialist division of labor. While this reinsertion may be a strategic objective—a means of assuring an "economic rearguard" and long-term technical cooperation—the speed at which it takes place may well be a tactical reaction to economic aggression from the former hegemonic power. The immediate cost of the shift can be high: the increased transport costs implied by new trading partners; the need to replace inherited production technologies that can no longer be reproduced; and the organizational effort required to adapt to a new system. In addition to military aid, the transition itself requires financial assistance (i.e., transfer of surplus) in its initial stages because of the low productivity resulting from the transformation of social relations and the need for rapid accumulation to overcome underdevelopment.

Economic analysis of socialist trade, both among developed socialist economies and between them and underdeveloped countries, lacks a sound basis in trade theory. The view of orthodox socialist economists is that such trade is determined by "internationalist principles" and "mutual advantage" but the principles of the resulting price formation are not explained in analytical terms. What is more, the practice of socialist planners is to set most trade prices (except explicitly subsidized ones) with reference to world markets; that is, those determined by the law of value in capitalist unequal exchange (Rumantsiev 1983; Szentes

1971; Bogomolov 1983). Even if this were not so, a rigorous theoretical construct would presumably show that the relative prices of raw materials and producer goods (i.e., terms of trade) in a "socialist trade area" would logically reflect costs of production, wage rates, and the margins of surplus required to finance accumulation in the developed socialist economies according to their own planned economic calculus (Steedman 1979). These prices cannot be arbitrarily adjusted to reflect the logic of peripheral production.

In strictly technical terms, therefore, the exchange of raw materials for producer goods between industrialized socialist economies and the periphery is still "unequal," not only because of the transmission of capitalist market prices, but also because of the inevitable differences in wages for similar kinds of work and national control over the rate of accumulation, quite independent of the different levels of development or the form of social organization. Joint negotiation of production and trade does allow for long-term price stabilization, which permits better planning; but the subordinate position in terms of exogenous prices and continual foreign exchange shortages will persist even if both center and periphery are socialist, unless wage levels are explicitly equalized.

In sum, during transition and until a further stage of economic development is reached, our economy will face a given and unequal structure of foreign trade prices; this will affect both the internal articulation of the economy and the disposition of the surplus.

Problem 3: Labor and Distribution

Typically, the labor process and workers' standard of living before the revolution will have had the following characteristics specific to underdeveloped capitalism. First, intensive work schedules were enforced by means of institutionalized violence and economic pressures such as unemployment, seasonal labor, differential access to social services, and lack of individual means of production, particularly land. In other words, a process of absolute exploitation and primitive accumulation ensured an ample and cheap labor supply and made low technology, extensive production forms profitable, especially in the primary export sector (Department I) which is the center of accumulation. Second, low wages and unequal internal terms of trade in Department II permitted a minimization of the real wage, while social services were provided only to salaried workers at the level required to maintain urban stability. Third, the expansion of production for the domestic market (particularly Department IIb) was limited by the lack of domestic demand, even though the process of urbanization and the expansion of the wage labor force permitted a certain degree of industrialization of wage goods, such as textiles and beverages.

The revolution necessarily upsets this framework. First, in the absence of the former methods of coercion, work intensity naturally declines, leading to falling production or to intense labor shortages. Wage pressure rises with new labor legislation and free trade unions. Labor discipline as a whole will also be reduced, until new methods of social organization are introduced. When social services such as health, education, housing, and food rationing are extended to the whole population, including those in the non-wage sector, the economic incentive for proletarianization is reduced (all the more so if the land reform distributes land to rural laborers and artisan cooperatives are supported). Second, the effective demand for wage goods, and generally for the output of Department IIa, is increased by the social pressure that the poor (and also the party organizations) place upon the state to improve living standards rapidly. Moreover, the socially acceptable quality and contents of the wage goods basket itself are extended by political change and the spread of urban standards to the countryside, effectively transferring goods and services from Department IIb to IIa.

Thus, in the initial stages of the transition at least, the socially necessary labor time for production increases, while at the same time the social cost of labor reproduction rises, against a background of stagnant or declining production. This necessarily puts a severe strain on the economy and creates inflationary pressure which may affect the social base of the revolution itself.

The recovery of labor productivity begins with the restoration of previous levels of labor intensity, because higher levels of technology require a longer period of accumulation. How to achieve this recovery has led to debates about the relative value of moral and material incentives to the labor force.[7] Moral incentives (i.e., more effort for a given wage) are sometimes regarded as a precursor of communism, as a demonstration of an ability to overcome production relations based on the sale of labor power. This is logically connected with the ability to distribute wage goods according to need. However, except at certain moments of national cohesion (emergencies, aggression, etc.) when voluntary labor may also be forthcoming, the experience in socialist economies has been that the more elementary socialist principle of "to each according to the amount of work" is more effective for sustained productivity, where wages are essentially based on piecework. This does not have to lead to individualistic attitudes among workers: union negotiation of work norms and piecerates imply collective control of the labor process, while the increasing technical division of labor in turn requires the definition of productivity in terms of teams or even sections of the enterprise. Material incentives can take the form of wage increases or specific items (televisions, vacations, etc.), but in any case these incentives must be supported at the macroplanning level by an increased supply of goods and services which are not part of the basic needs (Department IIa) package.

In consequence, Department IIb plays a key role in stimulating productivity in every sector of the economy, not just enterprise workers, but also professionals and petty producers. It is not by nature a "non-necessary" sector in the Kaleckian sense, nor is its expansion merely a desirable improvement in the standard of living; rather, it is an essential component of the reproduction of the new economic system. In this sense, increased consumption is needed for growth, although not necessarily as a proportion of the total social product because the incentive payments may not represent the entire value of the increased output. Curiously, although material incentives are an integral part of what might be termed "socialist microeconomics" consumption is not reflected in the corresponding theory of aggregate economic balances.[8]

In the longer run productivity will increase with the increased use of technology (machines, inputs, and labor skills), although the real wage bill as a whole can only increase if the output of Department II increases as well. However, in the medium term considerable increases can be achieved by the reorganization of the labor process itself, better care of machinery, reduction of wastage, and so on. To be able to mobilize this creative force effectively, widespread worker education is necessary, as is effective participation in the management of the enterprise. Participation does not become merely a matter of access to the surplus (that is, wage incentives based upon the profitability of the firm), therefore, but rather one of social control over the labor process itself as part of the transition to socialism.

The aspirations of workers for increased real wages early on as a result of the revolution itself are usually confronted with limited wage goods production capacity, declining productivity, and pressure for improved terms of trade by the peasantry. Improvements in community living standards, particularly if based on voluntary labor which receives its social reward directly, may be regarded as a right rather than an incentive. At the same time, the consumption claims of technicians, administrators, and professionals (many inherited from the past) must also be met; as must those remaining claims of capitalists in the initial stage of the transition if they are to achieve simple reproduction—that is, stay in the country. Finally, if an increased supply of wage goods is to be obtained from peasants and artisans (i.e., if they are to increase their work intensity under prevailing low levels of technology), then they too must receive increased amounts of incentive goods in return.

In sum, there are two contradictory characteristics of labor and distribution for the underdeveloped country in transition. The first is the tension between the political requirement to overcome the grinding poverty of the majority of the population through expanded supply of basic goods and services (Department IIa) on the basis of need, on the one hand, and the economic necessity of real wage differentiation (Department IIb) in order to recover labor productivity and secure sufficient labor supply, on the other. This may require the dedication of an increased proportion of the social product to consumption (Department II rather than Department I) and thus reduce the rate of accumulation or bring about a foreign trade crisis.

The second characteristic is the competition between the different forms of production for the available labor supply, where the widespread existence of petty mercantile production may become an increasingly attractive alternative for wage laborers, particularly when extensive land distribution has taken place or proletarianization has been a relatively recent historical phenomenon. This in turn may lead the state to constrain or even supress these petty forms of production in order to secure the labor force, as both an economic and a political strategy.

Problem 4: Price Formation and the Appropriation of the Surplus

In order to integrate an economic structure by the articulation of the forms of production, insertion in the international division of labor, and the conditions of reproduction of the labor force, a price structure is necessary that is also consistent with the desired pattern of appropriation of the surplus.

The advance toward collective relations of production is often understood to mean that social labor would be realized in a form other than that of value. The measure of value in capitalism is socially necessary labor time, but the "necessity" is that of appropriation of the surplus. Fulfillment of the needs of the population as a whole is thus a matter of assuring the reproduction of the labor force at a minimum cost, or of permitting the valuation of domestic production, or at most a response to pressure from organized workers. Under socialism, the concept of socially necessary labor time changes radically, because the objective of production is no longer the appropriation of surplus value but the satisfaction of social needs. However, in a small underdeveloped economy, the need to organize accumulation centrally, and maintain large groups of unproductive workers (army, teachers, etc., as well as bureaucrats), means that a surplus must still be appropriated. The form that this takes should be a major determinant of social relations in the transition.

Unfortunately, we do not possess an appropriate theoretical framework to analyze this process.[9] But as we have seen, early on in the transition progress is typically made toward fulfilling basic consumption requirements (distribution of Department IIa output) on the basis of need. Similarly, decisions on accumulation and foreign trade (distribution of Department I output) are made on the basis of a plan rather than on criteria of profitability. Even the "incentive" consumer goods (Department IIb) are distributed according to the contribution of the recipient to production, and not merely according to ability to pay. Thus distribution becomes largely socialized, despite the fact that prices (value forms) must be used as a detailed rationing device because of the shortage of goods relative to social requirements.

On the other hand, it has always been clear that the existence of multiple forms of production in an underdeveloped economy requires that there be mercantile exchange between them (Preobrazhensky 1965). To maintain control over the economy, this exchange will have to be organized by the state to prevent the reemergence of the law of value as the determinant of economic activity. In our case, this is obviously true in relation to peasant and artisan production, which may represent a significant part of output. Insertion of a large part of the primary sector into the international division of labor also implies mercantile exchange for industrial inputs and capital equipment.

In foreign trade, the small economy confronts a virtually elastic demand schedule and a price vector which is essentially exogenous, while supply is endogenous to the plan. These prices represent the valuation of the labor time incorporated in the export products used to pay for the imports in question. In turn, the price offered to petty producers by the state will depend upon the volume demanded from them in order to fulfill the plan, because supply is price elastic. The price represents the labor value of the industrial goods that the state offers these small producers in exchange for their products (or labor time). These two exchanges are essentially "unequal" because of the different ways in which prices are formed and imposed. As we have seen, foreign trade involves a transfer abroad of the surplus centralized by the state, even through this may be compensated by foreign aid. Similarly, the internal terms of trade imply a transfer of value from small producers to the state, even though this too may be compensated by specific transfers in the form of social services or infrastructure. Even when the institutional exploitation of the peasantry characteristic of the prerevolutionary past is overcome, there will still exist unequal exchange because prices in the state enterprise sector include margins to cover accumulation requirements, while petty producer prices are based on the cost of reproducing the family unit. Small producers, in other words, value their labor power at the margin or below the existing wage level in the enterprise sector, and thus well below the latter's prices (Caballero 1984).

In the planned (state enterprise) sector, prices should reflect an "economic calculus" based on the costs of production and the required surplus margin to be distributed between social expenditure in the firm or its locality, direct investments, and contributions to the central accumulation fund. This is clearly necessary in order to impose criteria of economic efficiency on the enterprises and to allow them some degree of administrative flexibility. However, in view of the importance of the petty production sector in determining the relative prices of domestic output in relations to wage goods supply (and thus real wages) on the one hand, and the external sector in setting input and output prices on the other, a planned rate of accumulation and certain provisions for surplus distribution will more or less fix producer prices in the planned sector as well.

These three factors would tend to support the argument that the law of value is maintained during the transition, even though it reflects not the logic of the accumulation of private capital, but rather that of the (conflictive) reproduction of international economy, the petty producers, and the state sector.[10] However, this does not mean that the plan will automatically reproduce existing social relations or base foreign trade on a crude principle of comparative advantage.

The importance of internationally traded goods in the economy means that, for their efficient use, they must be priced according to their foreign exchange value within the production system. This correspondence need not include short-term fluctuations (especially in the case of primary products) but to set prices at any other level would lead to wasteful use of foreign exchange under the rules of the economic calculus. Nonetheless, this does not represent a return to neoclassical comparative advantage, because the volumes of exports and imports in the medium term can be based on more strategic considerations as part of the plan, including specific trading agreements with other planned economies. Moreover, production decisions can be based on criteria other than comparative cost; for example, on national food security. It is still necessary, however, to know how much this will cost in foreign exchange losses, precisely because this represents the social surplus. In other words, the problem is one of consciously modifying the international operation of the law of value rather than ignoring it.

Once the production and distribution plan is determined, prices (including indirect taxes as a form of price) will serve to distribute the monetary surplus among production units and between them and the central fund. For any given investment program, there then exists a corresponding price structure that guarantees both the reproduction of individual enterprises and a centralized financial surplus equivalent to the planned level of investment or other state activities. Alternatively, the state banks can be used as the mechanism for redistributing the surplus. These requirements for price setting, along with the considerations mentioned above, close the system of price formation.

This relatively complex interlocking system of prices implies that any set of administered prices that does not correspond to this structure will lead to such distortions as inflation, black markets, shortages, and unrealizable money balances. Even so, the existence of non-state production forms will make it very difficult to control the monetary incomes of firms and individuals. It is thus necessary to have some sort of "sink" in the system with flexible prices to clear excess demand in the economy; this is a particular function of Department IIb markets, where high clearing prices in state stores may be seen as a form of taxation.

In empirical terms, the economic surplus is usually defined as the difference between the total material product (net of replacement of the means of production used up therein) and the consumption socially necessary to reproduce the labor force. Within our stylized framework, this surplus manifests itself in two forms peculiar to the economic structure. First, the workers and producers from Department II produce more than enough to maintain themselves (and their families), and to sustain those in other Departments that produce the inputs they need or the goods they receive in exchange. This surplus maintains the army, public administration, and the Department I workers who produce for accumulation. Any attempt to increase this surplus by pressuring the internal terms of trade (providing fewer industrial products to the peasantry, for example) tends to result in a reduction in petty commodity production, and thus a fall in real wages. Moreover, this form of the surplus cannot be simply materialized as in the classical closed-economy case, where it allows more labor to be sustained in the capital-goods sector. Nor, for that matter, will the centralization of monetary balances in the central accumulation fund automatically provide the investment goods required, although it may serve to reduce inflation by helping to adjust domestic consumption demand down toward the output of Department II.

The surplus that can be accumulated is essentially that acquired through foreign trade: the excess of exports from Department I (or credits, of course) over the imports (M') needed for the simple reproduction of all the sectors is available to import capital goods and the inputs to the limited domestic production of, for instance, cement. This is equivalent, of course, to the previous definition of the accumulable surplus in macroeconomic terms—the difference between total net product $(I + II - M')$ and socially necessary consumption (II)—except that one form is not translatable into the other because consumption goods and services are not generally traded. To the extent that Department II output requires imported inputs, the reduction of this output will release foreign exchange to import consumer goods, but the effect will be disproportionate (depending on the import coefficient) and lead to severe distortions in the economy. Thus the only way to increase accumulation is to increase exports, which means investment in Department I.

As the foreign trade sector is centralized by the state and the other forms of production are paid in local currency, these cannot accumulate at will and the accumulable surplus is in fact in the hands of the state—a particular form of "primitive socialist accumulation." The extent of this surplus is a complex matter. On the one hand, it will depend upon the structure of Department I itself: its previous capitalization, the extent of the natural resources, the intensity of the labor process, and the import content of real wages (which depends on productivity in Department II), and the import content (direct and indirect) of the inputs it requires. On the other, it depends upon the international terms of trade for the commodity basket exported and imported, and the extent of the differential rent for the country in question. However, the two key strategic variables will be (1) the allocation of labor and inputs to exports; and (2) the level of international prices.

Prior to the revolution, nonessential consumption (that is, Department IIb) is often identified as a potential source of surplus, in the sense that capitalist consumption can be drastically reduced without affecting the workers' standard of living (Mandel 1962). This may be true at an early stage in the transition, but to the extent that the nature of Department IIb is transformed into one of incentive to the productivity previously obtained by coercion, the saving may not be as large as expected. Moreover, much of the luxury consumption was in the form of housing, personal services, and so on, which cannot be converted directly into the foreign exchange needed.

In sum, for our underdeveloped economy in transition, the accumulable surplus is represented by the balance of payments position, while the "internal" surplus available to support unproductive state labor is limited by the articulation of the forms of production and the need to maintain labor productivity. The appropriation and distribution of the accumulable surplus by the state takes the form of decisions about foreign exchange allocation. For any particular allocation decision and production pattern, there will exist a matrix of consistent prices which must, in turn, be consistent with the wage vector, the reproduction of the non-state sectors, and external prices. This limitation on the scope for surplus appropriation on the part of the state ultimately represents the prevailing social relations.

Problem 5: Macroeconomic Management and Planning

Growing social control over the economy, in terms of central planning as well as worker participation in enterprise management, is essential to the concept of transition. As we have seen, this does not necessarily imply state ownership of all the means of production and distribution, but the state must control enough of them to eliminate the driving forces of capitalism and ensure the reproduction of another social formation which behaves according to other economic laws, those of socialism (Mandel 1962). Neither is this state property merely a legal concept; it must represent effective social control over production, a control expressed through subordination to the plan, which is itself the expression of a collective social decision materialized through the state.

It is usually assumed that the law of value in the capitalist economy is replaced by planning in the socialist economy: production, distribution, and accumulation decisions are no longer based on the search for the expansion of capital, but rather on the increasing satisfaction of social needs (Bettelheim 1975b).[11] In socialist planning theory, this presents apparently technical problems of determining what these needs are, and of maintaining sufficient enterprise autonomy for efficient management, both of which require decentralization and the use of value forms (Ellman 1973). Nonetheless, it is usually assumed that all economic activities are potentially subject to the administrative authority of the plan, which is based in turn on the extensive use of material balances (Rumantsiev 1978).

Our small economy in transition requires modification of this standard scheme, which in turn helps to overcome some of its more obvious shortcomings. First, reduced size means that it is simpler to obtain centralized information on the main production units and investment projects and to construct the main material balances. This can also compensate to some extent for the relative lack of technically qualified management that decentralization requires. Second, the relatively low standard of living implies that it is easier to identify the more pressing social needs and to standardize them for planning targets. Third, the existence of a unique and constrained set of "correct" prices closely linked to international prices permits the establishment of economic calculus based on central decisions without recourse to domestic market forces. Fourth, a centralized banking and fiscal system can permit worker participation in management without the danger of creating independent centers of surplus appropriation.

The advance toward the effective socialization of the enterprise sector of the economy through subordination to the plan may therefore be more rapid than in a larger, more developed economy. What is more, the definition of planning criteria for each sector is simplified by the particular role of each Department. The objectives for Department IIa are defined in terms of the gradual achievement of defined levels of nutrition, health, education, clothing, housing, and other services; the enterprise criteria will be based on cost-minimization so as to use the available resources most efficiently. The export targets for Department I, in contrast, are defined in terms of the maximization of the available foreign exchange surplus, which are easily turned into profitability and efficiency criteria for enterprises. Finally, required Department IIb output in the plan depends upon negotiated productivity and wage agreements, so once more, the enterprise criteria must be based upon cost-minimization in the fulfillment of plan targets.

In the initial stage of the transition, before the economy is organized into state enterprises and production cooperatives, the traditional instruments of economic policy continue to play an important role. In a capitalist economy on the periphery, economic policy can guarantee a certain degree of domestic demand stability so as to allow the convertibility of the currency without undue strain on the balance of payments; in other words, to allow the law of value to operate. This, in turn, means that government expenditure is limited to a low level of tax receipts, while monetary policy is designed to provide capitalist enterprise with the required credit, backed up by private savings. In the transition economy, demand stability is also required, but for quite different reasons: to restrain total expenditure in the face of foreign exchange controls, and to guarantee the required centralization of financial surpluses in the hands of the state. In both cases, inflation is to be avoided, but while in the capitalist economy this is for balance of payments reasons, in the transition economy it is to stabilize the price set and permit the correct articulation of the different forms of production without distorting the planned income distribution.

Maintaining the required macroeconomic equilibrium, and thus financial balances, is extremely difficult. The coexistence of different property sectors makes the task of economic administration delicate in any case, while the socioeconomic equilibrium is highly unstable. Moreover, the objective of economic policy is not to preserve this equilibrium but rather to control the dynamic of change (Nove 1983). Trade union pressure for increased wages and the expansion of social services typically creates a budget deficit due to the lack of taxation capacity when income is being redistributed downward. The increase in state investment requires the inorganic expansion of credit until state enterprises generate the necessary financial surpluses. In a closed economy, the consequent expansion of the money supply, unless it is supported by equivalent foreign credits, will inevitably lead to a rising rate of inflation unless there is absolute administrative control of commerce, which is hardly possible in an underdeveloped economy.

This inflation effectively represents the imposition of "forced saving" on the population as a means of financing the state, and in this sense is another means of primitive socialist accumulation. However, even if workers' real wages can be protected by rationing, the inflation will inevitably distort the relative price set and thus lead to disarticulation of the different forms of production (turning the terms of trade against the peasantry, for instance) and undermine attempts to implement the economic calculus as a means of ensuring enterprise efficiency. An essentially "conservative" monetary policy (with its implications for fiscal and financial restraint) becomes therefore a key element in the maintenance of state hegemony in the transition economy.

However, the problem of stabilization has not even been overcome in the centrally planned economies. A major difficulty in the past has been the gradual accumulation of liquidity in the hands of the population as the result of increasing wages, fixed prices, and the scarcity of consumer goods. This eventually led to parallel markets and falling real wages, with attendant social consequences. Enterprise surpluses were centralized and thus did not create a demand problem, while foreign trade fluctuations were dealt with via reductions in imports and rationing. In the past decade, nonetheless, the administration of exports and explicit flexibility of real wages have been used as more efficient policy variables (Portes 1979), while the practice of enterprise decentralization through the market has produced demand disequilibria in the producer goods market, requiring the use of more traditional monetary instruments of control.[12]

The structural rigidities on the supply side for both exports and real wages in a peripheral economy make these difficult if not impossible to use as policy variables, while the use of import restrictions in the short term would have to be confined to Department IIb in order to avoid reducing exports or basic needs standards. This in turn means that not only must overall monetary stability be maintained, but certain key prices must be continually adjusted to balance the supply pattern generated by fluctuating foreign exchange allocations. Moreover, faced with uncertainty even in the annual plan, the economy should carry sufficient foreign exchange reserves (with consequent implications for extra emphasis on Department I production) to compensate for external fluctuations.

In sum, the substitution of planning for the law of value in the transition can advance relatively rapidly, but the plan must be supported by the administration of a consistent price set and the maintenance of a considerable degree of monetary stability.

Problem 6: Accumulation and Economic Development

I have attempted to make some generalizations about the economic logic of the simple reproduction of the small underdeveloped economy in transition in order to have a series of definitions and logical deductions to compare with established economic transition theory. It is now necessary to analyze the logic of expanded reproduction and the corresponding economic transformation, even though the literature is even more scarce on this topic.

We can distinguish tentatively among three different stages in the transition: contracted, simple, and expanded reproduction. Immediately after the revolution, a period of reduced production, and thus diminished available surplus, is usually experienced. This is the phase of "contracted reproduction," in which falling production in one branch (such as agriculture) reduces that of others (such as food manufacturing), capital flight occurs, the maintenance of plant and equipment is neglected, and the labor force is mobilized for military purposes. This is sometimes thought of as a "frictional period" that logically follows the destruction and disorganization of the revolution (Bukharin 1979) but from which there should be a rapid return to simple reproduction, defined minimally as on the one hand, an equilibrium between total exports and imports of productions inputs, and on the other, the recuperation of previous real wage standards.

However, the recovery of prerevolutionary production levels has proven a longer task in practice, not only because of external aggression but because the effect of the dissolution of previous social relations of production upon labor productivity and administrative efficiency is usually underestimated. The political mobilization of the population for the tasks of reconstruction and extensive foreign aid are characteristics of this phase, as "extra-economic" means of overcoming the decline in productivity. The optimism on this topic, despite historical experience, is surprising in view of the recognition of the historically specific nature of capitalist production relations which are firmly grounded in the social and ideological structure.

The second stage could be defined in terms of the level of simple reproduction mentioned above. The sources of surplus are diverse, but typical of this phase is "primitive socialist accumulation" in the sense we have described in the previous problem. As we have seen, the extraction of greater surpluses from the petty production sector is counterproductive, as it eventually leads to a decline in the availability of wage goods, forcing the proletariat to work more strenuously for less sustenance. The transfer of surplus from remaining capitalist enterprise (which is only required to maintain simple reproduction) through price and tax mechanisms thus becomes an important mechanism for internal state finance and the repair and replacement of productive assets destroyed earlier on. The maintenance of this property form, although in the constrained sense we have discussed, has thus an economic as well as a political importance. An essential source of investable surplus must be long-term foreign credits, because of the impossibility of generating the necessary trade surpluses to finance the import of capital goods. Popular mobilization as a means of resolving pressing problems in the social services continues in this stage.

The third stage could be properly considered as that of expanded reproduction, even though the standard of living of the population may have improved and some investment have taken place in the previous stage. The fundamental source of internal surplus in this stage is the rising productivity of labor, especially in the expanding state sector, due as much to improved organization and skills as to capitalization. Foreign credits may continue, but they can now be serviced regularly as a commercial transaction, because the trade balance is more than enough for simple reproduction. This situation is then sustained while the production structure is transformed.

The concept of the "development of the forces of production" as used in socialist economic theory tends to refer to the acquisition of plant, machinery, and equipment; "industrialization" in its narrowest sense (Rumantsiev 1978). In our case, it will not be so much the means of production that are given sole priority; in the peripheral developing economy the development of the objects of production (natural resources, infrastructure, etc.) and the training of the labor force itself are even more important. This means that agriculture, energy, and education comprise the logical "center of accumulation." With the changing nature of Department I, the external surplus is transformed from a combination of Type I rent and superprofits (from low wages) to normal profits and international differential rent of Type II based on the application of technology to the exploitation of natural resources. Likewise, labor productivity increases pass from reliance on the intensity of the labor process to the application of technology.

The "choice of technique," or the relative degree of capital intensity in different branches, is a key determinant of any development model, affecting as it does the distribution of income and the growth rate in the long run (Dobb 1970). The logic of our analysis so far would indicate several things. As high a degree of economic autonomy (i.e., minimum imports) as possible would be sought in basic needs production (Department IIa) so as to guarantee minimum standards of living for the population independently of external fluctuations. The maintenance of petty production (albeit in cooperative form) in this sector would seem to imply, in combination with the autonomy criterion, a relatively low level of mechanization and thus high absorption of the labor force. In contrast, the need to raise real wages and maintain international competitiveness in Department I would involve a relatively high level of technology (and thus import-dependence), and a correspondingly lower rate of labor absorption.

The transition process itself, however, creates new accumulation possibilities. First, the expansion and standardization of consumption, as a result of redistribution of income, permits the expansion of basic industries in Department IIa to mass produce consumer goods (textiles, footwear, etc.), inputs for the social services (books, medicines, etc.), and basic production as part of Department I (cement, fertilizers, etc.). This planned expansion of the internal wage goods and input supply (which the previous model was unable to create because of narrow markets and enterprise competition) allows the necessary standardization and economies of scale to be reached more easily and costs to be kept down to international levels. Second, our economy can benefit from a certain advantage of its reduced size in the sense that it can import the latest technologies embodied in capital goods without setting up a heavy industry of its own, making a virtue out of a necessity. Third, it is possible to specialize in the technology pertaining to a selected few of its own activities, such as agricultural inputs or natural resource processing—initially to develop the economy itself, but later as export activities in their own right.[13] Fourth, it should be repeated that the massive training of the labor force is the best possible form of investment, allowing the best possible use of existing resources as well as the effective absorption of imported technologies. This, above all, is a fundamental option for a socialist economy, which the peripheral capitalist economy finds very difficult to achieve because of its social nature.

In this broad sense, industrialization is the essence of economic development in the transition. This does not mean priority for "industry" over "agriculture," as if the former led necessarily to faster productivity growth or more rapid proletarianization of the workforce than the latter.[14] Industrialization should be understood as technological advance in any branch, but particularly the process of overcoming the subordinated export model, the exploitation of the workforce, and the persistence of petty commodity production. In this sense, the effective transfer of technology to the primary sector should be the heart of technical cooperation with the more advanced socialist economies.

Once the development model is defined, the optimal rate of accumulation itself can be set in the plan. In essence, this should be derived from a long-term objective in terms of the living standards of the population, which in turn requires a certain rate of investment in a previous stage. We have noted how higher rates of accumulation require a greater assignment of the investable surplus to Department I (exports), and logically investment must be larger in Department I than in Department II to allow expanded reproduction at all. Orthodox socialist planning theory (e.g., Rumantsiev 1976) suggests that a maximum rate of investment consistent with stable per capita consumption (i.e., Department II output growing at the same rate as the population) should be kept up for an extended period to bring forward a further stage of higher consumption on the basis of previous investment. However, as we have argued, this bias against consumption may well lead to lower labor productivity and thus inefficient use of installed capacity. This "accumulation bias" appears to be a common feature of socialist economies, and is probably connected to the interests of the state managers themselves (Nuti 1979).

The process of economic development leads to a greater division of labor, a more skilled workforce, and a progressive socialization of production; it will also permit the transformation of the relations of production and exchange. In this sense, the dominance of state enterprise and cooperative forms of production as the basis for both the social structure and the new articulation of the economy will depend upon the advance of industrialization as defined here.

Problem 7: The Defense of the Transition Economy

Military and economic aggression against nations attempting the construction of socialism is a central element in the reality of the transition. In the cases that concern us here, the taking of power itself assumes the form of a "war of national liberation" against a colonial power or its domestic proxy. Despite this general experience, the topic of defense is not included in the body of theoretical literature on the transition, even though it profoundly affects the development of both productive forces and social relations.[15] I can only offer some initial observations on the "defense economy" insofar as it affects the conclusions drawn so far. It is assumed that the defense in question takes the form of a "popular war" based on the mass mobilization of workers and peasants, armed by other socialist countries.

The war has an immediate effect on the level of production, by way of the destruction it causes. Indeed, this may be a strategic objective of the aggressor in order to reduce the support capacity for defense or even the social base of the revolution. The loss of export income, moreover, has the further effect of reducing import capacity and thus production in branches otherwise unaffected by the war. Investment activity, logically, will be severely reduced as well.

In relation to the international division of labor, the effect of military aggression, and such measures as trade or credit embargos, is to accelerate the shift away from subordination to the capitalist metropole and the corresponding integration into the socialist trading area. This abrupt reorientation involves high costs in terms of new technologies and separation from regional trading partners. This is only partly compensated for by the natural tendency in these circumstances to make greater efforts toward self-sufficiency and therefore reduce the external trade coefficient of the economy.

Because defense is based on mass mobilization, particularly of labor-intensive militias, it has a double impact on the economy. On the one hand, mobilization removes a significant part of the workforce from production. On the other, the troops need a disproportionate share of consumer goods (food, clothing, etc.) and support services (health, transport, etc.) which thereby reduces per capita availability to the civilian population. However, the consequent rationing implies the equalization of real incomes between social classes and the forced socialization of distribution, which may become ideologically acceptable in wartime. Similarly, productivity may be maintained without the requisite economic incentives on the basis of ideological commitment.

Even though the need to divert both internal and external surpluses toward defense may reduce accumulation possibilities severely, it should tend to reinforce the mechanisms for the centralization of the surplus in the hands of the state. Failure to achieve this, particularly when the economy is not yet fully planned, leaves excess effective demand in the hands of the population with a reduced availability of consumer goods. This imbalance is expressed through a budgetary deficit unmatched by tax increases or expenditure reductions; once monetized it creates inflation and becomes in effect a "war tax." This crude way of centralizing surplus, however, has the undesirable effect of further disarticulating the economy (declining real wages, speculation, etc.) and leads, under the circumstances, to the application of complex administrative controls which may require a high degree of coercion to be even partially effective. Financial discipline therefore may be even more necessary in wartime (Lê Châu 1967).

The residual role of private capital may be eliminated rapidly, particularly if it is associated with the aggressor, while the first experience of socialization for many (above all the peasantry) may well be the army as a prelude to proletarian life. Central control of strategic material balances required by the war economy can be the prelude to full central planning. The centralized and vertical nature of the military command structure may well be reflected in the civilian administration and affect subsequent social organization.

In sum, apart from the destructive effect of the war itself and the inevitable delay in economic development implied by a subsistence economy, the logic of defense may well lead to the implementation of "war communism." This, as in the case of the USSR, implies a form of social organization inconsistent with the level of development of the economy itself, requiring the reconstruction of an integrated set of production forms at a later stage as the basis for the transition. This experience of external aggression, nonetheless, is the birthmark of socialism in the real world.

Notes

The author would like to thank the editors of this volume and many Nicaraguan colleagues for their valuable comments on what is still a very preliminary analysis. The views expressed here should not be interpreted as being those of the Nicaraguan government, for whom the author acts as economic adviser.

1. Logically, products from the secondary sector (textiles, for instance), or even from the tertiary sector (tourism, for example), can be exported too. The point is that there exists a sector specifically geared to exports, as an inheritance from the capitalist past.
2. As Rowthorn (1980) indicates, it is logically necessary to extend Marx's concept of "productive labor" (i.e., labor which generates surplus value) to activities such as education and health care, which make the direct labor force productive in the first place.
3. For Wolpe "the notion of articulation . . . refers to the relationship between the reproduction of the capitalist economy on the one hand and the reproduction of productive forces organized according to pre-capitalist relations and forms of production on the other" (1980:41). In other words, it is the antithesis of both the dualism of orthodox development economics and the monism of orthodox Marxism. In this more empirical analysis I am referring to the complex economic relationship between various forms of production; a relationship expressed through both market forces (prices, markets, credits, labor supplies, etc.) and social structures of power, custom, ownership, and so on.
4. See White and Kroll (1985), for example. Unfortunately, critical analysis of socialist agriculture tends to concentrate on the peasantry in itself, without facing the problems of proletarianization or national accumulation.
5. Nove (1983) discusses the undoubted advantages of small business (repair shops, restaurants, etc.) in terms of consumer service in developed socialist economies; while Horvat (1982) constructs an entire theory of the labor-managed economy as an idealization of Yugoslavia. But neither explains how the self-managed forms are supposed to articulate with the centrally organized state enterprise apparatus.
6. Cuba, for example, continues to export mainly sugar and nickel, while importing oil and machinery twenty-five years after its liberation; see McEwan (1981). For an explanation of this socialist comparative advantage see Rodriguez (1983); a similar argument is made in a general context by Bogomolov (1983). For a survey of peripheral socialist economies which clearly demonstrates this feature, see Jameson and Wilber (1981).
7. Guevara (1968). In his introduction to this collection de Santis suggests a dialectical relationship between Guevara's "idealist" position on moral incentives and the more "materialist" positions held by Mandel and Bettelheim,

as well as Castro himself. Rodriguez (1983) points out, however, that Guevara never argued for the complete elimination of material incentives.

8. Rumantsiev (1978), for example, contains this inconsistency in his exposition of the "General Law of the Socialist Economy": he emphasizes the importance of material incentives for workers, but then ignores the logically consequent positive relation between consumption and growth at the aggregate level.

9. Bettelheim argues for this, but only at the micro level.

10. This is, in the last instance, what concerns Guevara (1968); the attempt to constuct an independent manufacturing economy in Cuba probably sprang from this intuition (see O'Connor 1970).

11. Unfortunately, Bettelheim does not define the political structure needed to guarantee this expression.

12. However, it should not be forgotten that, as Kalecki points out, "the problem of avoiding inflationary pressures in economic development is not 'monetary.' It is solved by assuring, by a variety of methods, a correct structure of national expenditure" (1976:154).

13. The obvious parallel is with small developed economies such as Denmark and New Zealand, which have achieved a high level of "industrialization" based on agriculture and a skilled labor force. Bulgaria is another example.

14. Although even in the Cuban case, as Rodriguez (1983) points out, this was a theoretical distinction given that the adopted strategy was rather more of the type discussed here.

15. An exception, of course, is Bukharin (1979). It should not be forgotten that Lenin was an admirer of his colleague's work, although he noted its defects.

External Finance and the Transition to Socialism in Small Peripheral Societies
▼▲

Barbara Stallings

A crucial question in any discussion of transition to socialism is whether the transition can occur without external resources.[1] As E.V.K. Fitz-Gerald points out elsewhere in this volume (see also FitzGerald 1985c), the classical literature assumes a sufficiently "large" country that even foreign trade is not required. In practice, however, most attempts at transition have occurred in small peripheral economies, so that large country assumptions do not hold. In fact, a brief review of the inherited characteristics of small peripheral economies and their articulation with the world economy makes clear that external finance is essential in such a transition process. The problem then becomes one of identifying potential financiers and the circumstances under which they might finance economies in transition to socialism.[2]

The External Finance Debate

The relative merits of open vs. closed economies have long been debated in both capitalist and socialist contexts. In the last decade the argument has become especially heated under the rubric of "delinking" or "self-reliance" (Amin et al. 1982). The exact meaning of these terms varies considerably—from near autarky to the selective use of tariffs and exchange controls—a fact that tends to confuse the discussion.

Samir Amin (1974, 1976, 1977), perhaps the best-known proponent of a "self-reliant" development strategy for countries attempting a transition to socialism, defines a self-reliant economy as one which can complete the entire circuit of capital internally since it produces its own capital goods. The other main production component of such an economy is mass consumption goods; thus relatively high wages are essential to maintain a domestic market for these goods. This is the model of a mature capitalist economy. Peripheral economies, by contrast, produce mainly exports and luxury consumption goods, with the result that the market is either outside the country or centered on a very small portion of the local population. Thus the living standard of the large majority can be ignored.

If peripheral countries are to attain self-reliant economies, Amin says, two conditions are essential. First, there must be genuine political concern for the mass of the population, as evidenced in political leadership and its support movement. Second, a radical break with the capitalist world economy is necessary because the economic mechanisms of dependency (e.g., unequal exchange and profit repatriation), together with its political components (local classes which benefit from the status quo and their foreign allies), will prevent an economic and social transformation. Whether such a break can be accomplished, and how, is left very vague. Also unclear is the role to be played by existing socialist countries, but there is at least the implication that self-reliance requires distance from the second world as well as the first.[3]

My own view, while sympathetic to the concerns Amin expresses, is that a radical break with the world economy is virtually impossible for a small peripheral society today. It is not feasible for a country of several million people to eschew international trade. Furthermore, the demands that such a country has for foreign exchange will most likely far exceed that available from export revenues, thus necessitating international finance as well as trade. The political and economic consequences of *not* having foreign exchange are extremely negative. The resulting inability to carry out a project to better the lives of the population puts the government itself in jeopardy. While in principle we could talk of a break only with the capitalist countries, to be substituted by aid and trade with the socialist world, there is little evidence that the Soviet Union and other nations are willing or able to step in to the necessary extent. "Another Cuba" seems as undesirable to them as to the Reagan administration.

What seems more useful for a small transitional society than Amin's vague prescription for total self-reliance are the late Carlos Diaz-Alejandro's (1978) proposals for "selective delinking." Agreeing with the need for a strong state as a starting place—"the fundamental precondition of a policy of selectivity is, of course, the power to be selective" (ibid.:110)—Diaz-Alejandro outlines several specific suggestions: (1) diversification of markets for goods and capital; (2) promotion of commercial and financial links among third world countries and with smaller advanced capitalist nations; (3) emphasis on competitive markets (e.g., the Eurocurrency market and commodity markets); (4) attempts to break up components of import packages (e.g., finance, technology, equipment, and management); (5) search for ways to limit spillover effects in domestic economies (e.g., geographical isolation of foreigners); and (6) attempts to enter world markets in phases favorable to buyers.

In order to substantiate the claim that external finance is necessary, I will review the demands for foreign exchange together with the possible sources of supply. Following FitzGerald's (1985a) general approach, I begin with the Kaleckian version of Marx's economic departments whereby total product is divided into Department I (means of production), Department IIa (basic consumer goods), and Department IIb (luxury consumer goods). As stated above, Department I is generally nonexistent in small peripheral economies and thus the full circuit of capital cannot take place within the countries themselves. Almost all capital goods and substantial quantities of raw materials must be imported. Spare parts also become crucial if the plant is to be kept functioning. The absolute and relative importance of these imports will depend on the role assigned to industry and the mechanization of agriculture, but under any circumstances Department I imports will be considerable. An important question that arises is whether the lack of Department I capacity should be considered a permanent aspect of the transition period or whether the construction of a capital goods industry is a viable goal for the future. Insofar as it makes sense to single out transition in small peripheral economies in contrast to the classical literature, the distinguishing characteristic would seem to be that their "small" size places severe limits on the development of Department I. Thus, while some capital goods may eventually be produced locally, the majority will continue to be imported, unless economic integration with similar countries becomes possible in the future.

Department II items are more mixed in terms of local vs. international production. At least in theory, all Department IIa goods could be produced locally, assuming that the necessary capital goods can be obtained and kept in working order. It may be useful, however, to divide the transition period into at least two stages—the years immediately after a revolutionary government takes power and those that follow. Special problems will arise in the former period if the economy has been partially destroyed in the process of takeover. Even food imports may be required if planting has not taken place and animals have been slaughtered. Clothing, shoes, and other basic consumer items may also be impossible to produce in the short run if industrial capacity has been badly damaged. In addition, even if extensive damage has not occurred, less food may be marketed as superexploitation is eliminated, and productivity may temporarily fall as new relations of production are introduced. In the medium term, however, all basic consumer goods should be able to be locally produced.

Department IIb goods present different kinds of problems. One alternative is drastically to curtail the supply of such goods in line with their supposed "luxury" nature, but if we adopt FitzGerald's characterization of the small transitional economy, such action is not possible as so-called luxury goods are necessary as incentives. A full discussion of this issue would involve consideration of the debate on moral vs. material incentives, which is far afield from the topic of this essay. Based on historical trends, however, it seems realistic to assume that the outcome of such a debate will lead to the decision that these goods must be made available in fairly substantial quantities. The question then becomes whether they should be produced at home or imported. Local production is clearly preferable in terms of employment and foreign exchange savings, but the need for technology and imported inputs may offset such advantages. This is likely to be especially true in the early period of transition when priorities are on the export sector and basic consumer goods. Thus, a significant, although probably declining, portion of these goods will come from abroad.

Another class of goods that does not fit conveniently into the Marxian-Kaleckian schema—because it is almost never considered in such discussions—is defense items. Even the Soviet Union was faced with an outside military challenge after the 1917 revolution, and small peripheral countries trying to move toward socialism are obviously far more vulnerable. The typical situation has involved not large-scale military confrontations but guerrilla warfare, where the specific aims are economic sabotage and political disruption with the general goal of alienating citizens from the government. Such guerrilla forces, while in the main staffed by disaffected citizens, receive the vast bulk of their economic and logistical support from foreign governments and other groups that want to overthrow the revolutionary governments. Under these circumstances, a large share of resources must be devoted to defense. The key point for this discussion is that a substantial portion of these resources involves either gifts or foreign exchange since weapons and support equipment are not produced locally.

Finally, in addition to merchandise imports that will require foreign exchange, a revolutionary government will also have to deal with outflow of foreign exchange in both legal and illegal forms. The latter will be most important in the period immediately after taking power as citizens and foreign corporations alike try to get resources out of the country. But legal outflow—through profits, interest payments, and amortization—will continue on both old and new debt and foreign investments. The only way to prevent such outflows would be to repudiate the previous debt and seek no new international financing. If the basic premise of this discussion is correct, however, such policies are not viable. Exactly how large the outflows will be, and what form they will take, will depend on the type of external finance that is obtained.

Given capital goods, luxury consumption goods, defense equipment, and capital outflow as the primary demands for foreign exchange, what are the sources of supply? Leaving aside external finance for the moment, there are only two other sources: export revenues and currency reserves. The latter does not require much discussion. However large a supply of reserves a revolutionary government may have inherited, it is a finite amount which is likely to be quickly consumed. Furthermore, a certain quantity of reserves is essential, especially for a government of the type being considered here. In fact, building and maintaining reserves may better be seen as a source of demand for, rather than supply of, foreign exchange.

Exports, then, are the principal means of obtaining foreign exchange. Again, it may be helpful to think of two stages in terms of export capacity since it too may be negatively affected by destruction during the taking of power. Similarly, as an extension of the external military aggression a boycott against exports may be instituted which will prove especially disruptive in the short run until other customers can be arranged. In the medium and long run, other problems are likely to occur in terms of both volume of exports and price fluctuations.

The source of these problems goes back to the traditional insertion of small peripheral countries into the world economy. The vast majority rely on one or a few primary products, whether agricultural or mineral, to provide export revenue. The small size of such economies may mean that they can increase the volume of their exports without affecting the price, but not all of them are price takers, and volume increase itself may be difficult without extensive investment, including a large foreign exchange component. In addition, agricultural products are subject to the vagaries of the weather, and both agricultural and mineral products can be displaced by synthetic substitutes. Beyond questions of volume, the much-discussed problem of price fluctuations is especially severe for primary goods exporters. In the extreme case, prices may vary by a factor of two or three from year to year, and the structure of the international economy is such that primary producers have little control over prices. These kinds of fluctuations in prices, and thus revenues, are the very antithesis of the economic planning that a society in transition to socialism is trying to institute. A large quantity of reserves is the most obvious way to deal with the situation, although commodity agreements or favorable trade contracts may be alternatives. Foreign exchange problems will be vastly exacerbated if the government does not control the entire export sector.

In summary, I am arguing the following points: (1) The need for foreign exchange is crucial since the size and inherited economic structure of a transitional economy makes autarky an impossible alternative. Another way to express the situation is that some part of the surplus produced in the economy, defined as total product minus basic consumer goods, must take the form of foreign exchange. (2) The volume of export revenue is unlikely to be sufficient, even in the medium run, to cover all of the requirements for imports. In fact, part of the very definition of a developing country, whether capitalist or socialist, is that it consumes more resources than it produces. The more ambitious a revolutionary government's goals, the larger the shortfall. (3) Even in the unlikely event that average volume of export revenues were sufficient to cover import requirements, the problem of price fluctuations nevertheless remains as a major impediment to a planned economy. (4) The lack of foreign exchange can become a *political* as well as an *economic* problem. Projects essential to the government's attempt to provide better lives for its citizens cannot be undertaken. The resulting discontent provides fertile ground for domestic opposition to gain support and unite with hostile forces on the outside. (5) Thus, for both political and economic reasons, it is hard to imagine the possibility of a transition to socialism in a small peripheral economy without external finance even in the medium run. This does not mean that there are no dangers from seeking and receiving such finance. It merely means that the objective conditions are such that external finance is indispensable, and therefore strategies must be established for dealing with it. I will return to this issue in the concluding section of this essay.

How Can External Finance Be Obtained?

If the above conclusion is true, attention must be turned to possible sources of external finance and their respective characteristics. These can be grouped under five categories: governments, international organizations, private banks, suppliers, and direct investment. In addition, restructuring of existing debts from the first four can increase the net inflow through lowering amortization payments; alternatively, refinancing can provide new loans to be used to cancel payments due. The first issue is whether or not any finance would be available to the revolutionary government. Beyond that, the important topics to be considered for each category of finance include amount available, the economic terms on which it would be provided, and the political terms likely to be attached. Table 1 summarizes some estimates for the net amounts available for *all* developing countries from the five sources during the 1980–83 period.

Bilateral government loans. Bilateral loans must be subdivided into at least two categories: capitalist and socialist governments. In the Latin American context, a further subdivision of the former into the United

Table 1
Net External Long-term Financial Flows for All Developing
Countries, annual averages, 1980–83 ($ millions)

Source	Amount	Percent
Bilateral	$32,086	36.2
Capitalist	(22,737)	(25.7)
Socialist	(3,046)	(3.4)
OPEC	(6,306)	(7.1)
Multilateral	13,807	15.6
Private Banks	21,493	24.3
Private Suppliers	9,175	10.4
Direct Investment	1,967	13.5
Total	88,531	100.0
GNP	$2,433,703	
Total/GNP	3.6%	

Source: OECD (1985). Countries include 111 nations in Africa, Asia, Latin America, the Middle East, and Mediterranean Europe.

States and others is also important. For all peripheral countries, bilateral loans accounted for 36 percent of foreign capital available in the early 1980s; this was 6.4 percent from the United States, 19.2 percent from other capitalist donors, 7.1 percent from the Organization of Petroleum Exporting Countries (OPEC), and 3.4 percent from Comecon countries (OECD 1985). Bilateral "aid" loans are usually on very favorable economic terms with long maturities and low interest rates. The main purpose is economic and social infrastructure, although general purpose program loans have been given. The favorable economic terms, however, may be offset by the political character of the loans. Bilateral "aid" tends to be the most political of all forms of external finance; donor governments provide money to recipients with whose politics they agree. For transitional economies this has meant that the United States has provided little aid, while the Soviet Union has provided substantial amounts to Cuba but little to others. Thus, most bilateral funds have come from Europe, especially from the Scandinavian countries, which have concentrated their aid on a small group of countries of the transitional type. In addition to bilateral "aid" funds, there are also export credits or guarantees that are tied to purchases in the respective countries. Although partially subsidized, these loans are provided at near market terms so that the so-called grant element is small. These export credits constitute a substantial portion of the bilateral funds available to transitional economies.

Multilateral loans. The principal multilateral donor is the World Bank, representing 46 percent of total multilateral loans in 1980–83 (OECD 1985). Like the regional development banks, the World Bank has both "hard" and "soft" loans. The former, provided by the International Bank for Reconstruction and Development (IBRD), are extended at close to market interest rates although with maturities up to fifteen years. The latter, under the International Development Association (IDA), carry fifty-year maturities with only a processing fee charged. These loans are also generally intended for infrastructure projects and require the submission of elaborate feasibility proposals. Although World Bank loans are less directly political than bilateral funds, several qualifications must be kept in mind. First, to obtain loans, a country must be a member of the Bank and the International Monetary Fund (IMF). Second, the United States has been known to organize boycotts against loans to revolutionary governments or even some less radical (e.g., Peru under Velasco). Third, the Bank itself refuses to lend to countries that have expropriated foreign property without compensation. Fourth, the Bank emphasizes development projects that favor private enterprise. In addition to the World Bank, other important multilateral lenders are the European Economic Community, the regional development banks, and the various U.N. agencies.[4] Of these, only the U.N. groups lend with minimal political/economic strings attached, but their funds are relatively scarce.

Private banks. The international commercial banks have been lending large amounts of medium- and long-term money to peripheral countries only in the last ten or twelve years; previously their clients were multinational corporations and European governments.[5] Their loans are the most expensive of all those considered here. For example, between 1970 and 1978, their average interest rate was 9.2 percent compared to 6.2 percent for the World Bank; maturities were 7.1 years and 26.4 years respectively (Stallings 1982). In addition, interest rates on private loans "float," thus passing the risk of rising rates onto the borrowers. Nevertheless, despite their shortcomings, private loans have major advantages. During the 1970s they were the largest and fastest growing source of money. Few strings were attached as long as a government did not run into a liquidity crisis. The banks have also been less political then public agencies, willing to lend to a number of transitional economies in the third world and East Europe. Since the onset of the debt crisis in 1982, however, the banks have provided few new loans other than those connected with rescheduling packages.

Suppliers' credits. Suppliers' credits, by definition, are tied to the purchase of particular goods from particular companies. Here we are talking only about private suppliers' credits since those provided or guaranteed by governments are included in bilateral loans above. Maturities will vary, depending on the type of good involved. Interest rates are likely to be similar to those for private bank loans and in fact the credits may even be made by the banks but arranged by the suppliers. Their advantage is that while they are economically tied they are unlikely to be politically tied. In addition, because they are the counterpart to company sales, they may be more available to transitional economies than some other kinds of loans.

Direct investment. Moving from loans to equity, we arrive at direct investment by foreign corporations. These investments could be completely owned by the foreign corporations, or they could be joint ventures with the government or private citizens of the "host" country. During the 1970s, third world governments generally thought that bank loans were preferable to direct investment because the former provide the borrowing government with greater control over the funds. In the case of direct investment, especially when not a joint venture, it is the company that decides what and how much to produce, when and how much to invest, and the technology to be used. In the current situation of debt crises, the question is being reconsidered, since profit outflows are likely to be lower in times of economic difficulties, while debt service payments continue at the same level or may even rise. In addition, the advantages of technology and export markets, which direct investment by multinationals may provide, are again seen as attractive possibilities. If joint ventures can be arranged, third world governments are apparently thinking that direct investment can bring significant benefits without allowing control to escape their hands.

What, then, would appear to be the best possibilities for governments in their search for external finance? Public money is cheaper than private, but it also tends to have more political strings attached. Suppliers' credits and especially direct investment entail powerful economic strings. Bank loans are currently in very scarce supply. If one recommendation seems obvious, it is diversification, so that no one source becomes dominant. This holds for individual lenders within categories as well as across categories themselves. Nevertheless, these sources are not really separate alternatives that can be selected at random; often they are tied together. Three types of interrelationships are especially important. First, project loans tend to involve various kinds of finance, e.g., government export credits, World Bank loans, private bank loans, and suppliers' credits. No one source is willing to undertake the entire project, and there is a tendency to wait until all have been lined up. Second, cross-default clauses are typically included in loan contracts such that a default on any loan, public or private, is considered to be a default on all. Likewise, any individual bank in a loan syndicate can declare a default which will then bind all other lenders as well. Third, the International Monetary Fund is still seen as the linchpin of the international lending system. Its role is most important when a crisis occurs, but a country's failure to join the Fund, and accept its annual fact-finding missions, is taken by some lenders as a yellow if not red light in terms of a country's creditworthiness.

Access to External Finance: Five Case Studies

Moving beyond the previous discussion of possible sources of external finance, I now want to look at the actual success that five revolutionary governments have had in obtaining it and (insofar as it is possible to ascertain) the political and economic price they have had to pay. In order to interpret these results, I will also summarize some basic political and economic features of each case, together with a notion of what "socialism" means in each. The cases were selected to illustrate different approaches to international finance; obviously others could be added, e.g., Grenada in the Caribbean; Angola, Algeria, Zimbabwe, and Ethiopia in Africa; and Vietnam and North Korea in Asia.

Cuba. In chronological order, the first to take power of the five governments examined here was the Castro government in Cuba in 1959.[6] Backed by the 26th of July Movement and, to a lesser extent, the Popular Socialist (Communist) Party, Castro won a military victory over the Batista dictatorship. The rebel army became one of the pillars of the new regime; the other was the single political party (now called the Communist Party). Together with the departure of most of his enemies, the new institutions gave Castro a wide latitude for economic experiments to overcome Cuba's backward productive structure and highly uneven distribution of income and wealth.

In ideological terms, the Cuban revolution was initially social democratic, but by April 1961 it was declared "socialist," and by December 1961 this was further clarified as socialism of a "Marxist-Leninist" character. The ideological radicalization was accompanied by a breaking of ties with the United States and the establishment of close economic and political relations with the USSR. With respect to the former, foreign investments were expropriated without compensation and foreign debt was repudiated. The chronology of events (Boorstein 1968; Blasier 1971) provides convincing evidence that the particularly close economic and political relations that Cuba had with the United States—especially but not only in trade—together with the U.S. control of the world economy at the time left little choice to the Cuban government. If it wanted to make certain domestic changes, such as the agrarian reform and the control of basic industries, it had to loosen its ties with the United States. Given U.S. power over Europe and Latin America, the only available option seemed to be the socialist countries. With the value of hindsight, Castro might have chosen a different strategy, although it is not clear that this was possible in the particular international context of the late 1950s and early 1960s. Subsequent revolutions trying to achieve similar goals might have more options and an example to learn from. Cuba suffered from the liabilities, and perhaps the advantages, of being among the first.

The economic strategy eventually came to include state ownership of virtually the entire economy, with the exception of one-third of the agricultural sector, and a national system of planning. Economic policy emphasis nevertheless has varied substantially over time, from the initial push toward rapid industrialization and the downgrading of the role of sugar, to a returned focus on agriculture, to a more moderate attempt to diversify the economy. Even the agricultural strategy was fairly capital intensive, however, thus requiring large quantities of resources. Defense also took substantial amounts of money as an attack from the United States was seen as a real possibility. A third type of major expenditure has been on social services (e.g., health, education, housing). Indeed, insofar as Cuba has a clear record of success, it has been in the social service field rather than in macroeconomic management and growth (Brundenius 1983).

The financing of the economic project has depended very heavily on external sources. Following the break with the United States, the Soviet Union became the major source of external financial support. One expert on this topic, Carmelo Mesa-Lago (1982:150), calculates that Cuba received $16.7 billion in Soviet economic aid between 1960 and 1979; of that total, one-third was in the form of loans and the rest was grants. Loans included credits to finance the Soviet-Cuban trade deficit and for economic development projects. Grants involved subsidies on the price of Cuban sugar and nickel exports and on oil imports and military equipment.[7] Terms on the Soviet loans have been very favorable—ten to twenty-five years with interest rates of 2.5 percent (Mesa-Lago 1981:103–4). In 1972 Cuba's debt with the Soviet Union was deferred for thirteen years, with both interest and principal put off. A further rescheduling for at least five years was arranged in 1984.

Cuba's economic relations with the Soviet Union have thus been extraordinarily favorable, at least in quantitative terms. Financing has been available in large amounts, reportedly up to one quarter of GNP per year (U.S. Congress 1982), and on very soft terms. Export subsidies have smoothed out the usual boom/bust cycles of primary exporters, and many economic and social projects have been facilitated. There have also been costs, of course. Even leaving aside the supposed influence on Cuban foreign policy, the aid flow has undoubtedly led to major inefficiencies in the Cuban economy. Soviet and East European goods have been late and of poor quality, and the ability to rely on such large amounts of money means that costs were not always seriously considered. External finance apparently went not only for social and economic investment, but also to keep the economy running on a day-to-day basis. Finally, the sugar subsidy has contributed to the continuing dominance of exports by a single product.

Contrary to popular opinion, however, Cuba has also been heavily involved with capitalist countries (Eckstein 1980). This relationship includes not only trade but also its financial counterpart. By 1984 Cuba had a debt with Western countries of $3.0 billion. According to the 1985 Economic Report of the Cuban Central Bank, this was divided into 50 percent from governments (mostly export credits), 42 percent from banks (short-term deposits and medium-term Euroloans), and the rest from other lenders including suppliers and multilateral agencies. The multilateral total is low because Cuba is not a member of either the World Bank or the Interamerican Development Bank. Since debt service on Western loans began to take a heavy toll on dwindling hard currency exports, a rescheduling of $550 million was carried out, covering payments due between September 1982 and December 1983 (*Latin America Weekly Report,* May 13, 1983). A further rescheduling for 1984 maturities was also negotiated (*Quarterly Economic Review,* no. 3, 1984). Of the Western creditors, the most important have been Italy, Japan, France, Spain, and some Latin American countries (OECD 1983:68; Mesa-Lago 1981:104); the United States still maintains its boycott. West German refinancing, as well as trade credits, are being held up by Cuba's refusal to sign the "Berlin clause" which supports the claim that West Berlin is a state of West Germany (*Latin America Weekly Report,* April 19, 1985).

Finally, Cuba is actively seeking direct foreign investment. In February 1982 new legislation authorized joint ventures with public or private companies from any country. The main interest is in industrial investment for both exports and the domestic market. Incentives include 49 percent ownership (more in special cases); full repatriation of profits; tax breaks; autonomy in hiring; overseas sources of supply if Cuban products are not competitive; and a "stable and disciplined" workforce with a relatively high educational level (Schmidt 1983). Whether such investment will be forthcoming remains to be seen; so do its political and economic costs if it materializes in substantial amounts.

Tanzania. Tanzania gained its independence from Britain in 1961, with "socialism" as a stated goal, but it was not until six years later that President Julius Nyerere clarified the meaning of the term in the Arusha Declaration.[8] As dominating a figure in Tanzania as Castro is in Cuba, Nyerere has a quite different vision of socialism than does his

Cuban counterpart. His is an avowedly non-Marxist socialism, referred to as *ujamaa* (roughly translated as "familyhood"), which is based on the supposed socialism of traditional African society. Its central focus in the early 1970s was the resettlement of the rural population into communal villages where they were encouraged to engage in communal production. In actuality, villagization has entailed provision of social services rather than changes in organization of production, which remains household based. At the national level, Tanzanian socialism involves state control of the "commanding heights" of the economy. Initially, this translated into nationalization with full compensation of banks and insurance, the milling industry, export-import firms, seven major multinational companies, and 60 percent of the sisal industry. Later the list was extended to include at least 60 percent state ownership of most commercial and industrial firms in the country, resulting in some 500 state firms—the so-called parastatals (Clark 1978).

Of the cases studied here, Tanzania is the poorest, with per capita GNP around $265. Over 90 percent of the population consists of peasant farmers so that Nyerere's problems have not been so much overcoming a capitalist past as preventing a capitalist future. The main tool for this purpose is the single party (now called CCM or Party of the Revolution). Unlike the other cases, no foreign government has attempted to overthrow the Tanzanian regime, but a large amount of the country's resources in 1979–80 were taken up by the campaign to depose Idi Amin in neighboring Uganda. Expected international assistance was not forthcoming (Coulson 1982:309–11).

Although "self-reliance" is supposed to be a major aspect of Tanzanian socialism, the country is one of the highest aid recipients in the world—although it probably receives less than Cuba. The importance of aid increased from 2 percent of GNP in 1964–68, to 7 percent in 1969–73, to 16 percent in 1975–79 (Clark 1978; *Quarterly Economic Review,* 1979). The vast majority of Western finance has come from bilateral loans. Of this category, the Scandinavian countries have dominated, providing some 40 percent. West Germany is the next highest donor, with former colonial power Britain trailing behind. During the late 1960s and early 1970s, West Germany cut off aid over Tanzania's relations with East Germany, and relations were broken with Britain over policy with respect to Rhodesia. The consequences were not the same kind of blow that a U.S. aid cutoff has been in Latin America, however, because of the availability of alternate sources of aid. The United States has played a minor role in Tanzania except during the immediate postindependence period before the Arusha Declaration (Coulson 1982).

Other than the Scandinavian countries, the single most important source of Tanzanian external finance has been the World Bank. Bank loans, of which about 75 percent have come from the IDA's "soft" window, have mostly gone for agricultural projects with infrastructure and industry as secondary areas. Some funds have come from the socialist countries, especially China in connection with its construction of the Tanzanian-Zambian Railway (TAZARA) in the early 1970s; the Comecon total has been minuscule. In terms of the private sector, most funds are from suppliers. Direct investment has been sought, but little has materialized although some joint ventures with parastatals do exist (OECD 1983, 1985).

The large amounts of external finance in Tanzania have obviously had their costs. On the economic side, these have not been overly burdensome. According to the *World Debt Tables,* the country's low per capita GNP has made it a prime candidate for "soft" loans, so that debt service has taken up less than 10 percent of export earnings because of very low interest rates and long maturities. A less visible economic cost derives from the fact that most aid has been for large-scale projects for which equipment must be purchased in donors' countries and for which counterpart requirements absorb funds that the government might prefer to spend in other ways (Harris 1983:17–18). Nevertheless, the main costs must be measured in political terms, although as usual it is hard to determine the exact situation.

The two most controversial lenders are the World Bank and the International Monetary Fund. Several observers (Payer 1982a; Mittelman 1981; Von Freyhold 1979) state that the Bank refused to lend to Tanzania for communal production and actively discouraged moves to implement such policies. On the other hand, some of the same critics agree that the Bank has lent for industrial projects that it disapproved of, and apparently it has made no effort to bring about a shrinkage of the state's role in the economy. Currently the main conflict with international financiers centers on the IMF. In 1980, Tanzania broke off negotiations with the Fund, but deteriorating economic conditions eventually led to their renewal. Major items of contention include a large devaluation, wage ceilings, massive price increases to farmers, and a cut in government spending, including social services. The last item has been the most resisted because Nyerere considers social services the main achievement of Tanzanian socialism (Singh 1983). Although the June 1984 budget introduced some policies—especially increases in producer prices, cuts in subsidies, and a devaluation—that the IMF had sought, agreement still has not been reached. It seems only a matter of time, however, since all of the major donors are urging it. Ironically, the alternative to IMF policies—focusing on food self-sufficiency, import controls, and the development of heavy industry—appears to be precluded by lack of foreign exchange (*Quarterly Economic Review,* no. 1, 1985).

Chile. In October 1970 Salvador Allende was confirmed by the Chilean Congress as president of the republic after receiving a 36 percent plurality in the general elections.[9] For the first time in the Western hemisphere, a declared Marxist had been elected as head of government. Allende was head of a multiparty coalition (the Popular Unity) composed of Communists, Socialists, and various smaller leftist parties pledged to prepare the way for a transition to socialism. The definition of socialism was left rather murky, but the Chilean version appeared to include government control of the most important sectors of the economy, central planning, and some form of worker participation. More specific policy goals were increased production, greater equality, expanded political participation, and increased international independence.

Unlike the other cases under discussion, the Popular Unity did not have control over the entire state apparatus. The coalition had won the presidency, but lacked a majority in congress and control over the judiciary and the comptroller (an agency that could rule on the constitutionality of laws and decrees). In addition, although the military was formally under the presidency, in reality it functioned quite independently. At the same time, the Chilean case was also different in that Chile was more economically—and thus more socially—developed than the other four. Specifically, there was a substantial industrial sector, and thus an industrial bourgeoisie and proletariat, together with a large "middle sector" defined primarily in terms of aspiration toward a lifestyle similar to its counterpart in the United States and Western Europe.

In early 1971 the structural transformation program got underway with an agrarian reform, the expansion of the state-controlled area of the economy, and the nationalization of the copper mines. The third item provided the excuse for the United States to move ahead with an economic blockade of Chile although the decision to oppose the Allende government had been made immediately after the election. Despite the fact that the United States had not been as dominant in the Chilean as in the Cuban economy, it had nevertheless been the major financial power in Chile. Most of the bilateral loans came from U.S. AID or the Eximbank; most private investment was of U.S. origin; and trade finance was handled almost exclusively by U.S. banks (Petras and Morley 1975). The blockade hit all of these areas, plus the U.S. government pressured multilateral agencies to cease loans to Chile. Only the IMF committed new money through its automatic facilities, but loans "already in the pipeline" from other sources were disbursed (NACLA 1973; U.S. Congress 1974).

Allende's chief economic advisor states that the resulting external financial crisis could have been dealt with by finding alternative sources

that "had no direct or indirect economic involvement with the nationalization process" (Guardia 1979:81). The two obvious sources were
Western Europe and the socialist countries; another was Latin America
itself. Indeed large amounts of loan commitments were obtained from
all three. Most of the loans from the socialist countries, however, were
long-term credits for import of capital goods from those countries.
While they might have been helpful in the long run—had there been a
long run—they did not help to resolve the immediate need to finance
spare parts and raw materials from U.S. firms that had constructed
existing Chilean plant. Thus by August 1973 only 20 percent of the
more than $400 million of socialist credits had been drawn (ibid.:99–
100).

Of more immediate relevance were short-term lines of credit in
convertible currency. Another $400 million was obtained in this form,
of which 43 percent came from Western Europe, 40 percent from Latin
America, 5 percent from the socialist countries, and 12 percent from
other areas (ibid.:101). The problem with these credits was that most
were tied; that is, they too could only be spent to finance goods in the
countries of origin. Nevertheless, they did help resolve the liquidity
crisis and gave some indication that perhaps the external financial
problems could be overcome with time. New arrangements for direct
investment were also underway in 1973 with deals pending with
Peugeot, Citroen, Pegaso, and various Japanese, Finnish, Dutch, Belgian, and West German firms. Additional help was obtained by a partial
refinancing of foreign debt payments, since repudiation was not considered; here too the United States tried to block progress.

In the Chilean case, the question was not the costs of accepting
external finance but the costs of not having it. The opposition to the
Popular Unity—the local bourgeoisie, the "middle sectors," the military and their foreign allies—decided to make the economy the center
of their political battle. Thus the shortages that came about, in part
because of the lack of foreign exchange, increased opposition to the
government. The situation was exacerbated because the government
sought to increase its chances of winning the municipal elections in
1971 by increasing consumption. Real wage increases of 30 percent
stimulated demand for imports as well as for domestic goods (Griffith-
Jones 1981). Whether the foreign exchange crisis could have been
resolved eventually is now a moot point; time was not available as the
government was overthrown three years after its inception. The problem of external finance was not the dominant cause, but it was a
contributing one.

Mozambique. The second African country considered here gained
its independence in a different way than did Tanzania.[10] Mozambique
fought an armed struggle for independence from Portugal although it

actually achieved it in 1975 as a result of the revolution in Portugal itself. The military campaign was led by the Front for the Liberation of Mozambique (FRELIMO), which then became the official party with its leader, Samora Machel, becoming president. Even as a guerrilla group, FRELIMO had advocated socialism, and at the 1977 party congress Marxism-Leninism was formally adopted. Unlike the Party of the Revolution in Tanzania, FRELIMO is a vanguard party with the goal of creating a dictatorship of the proletariat. Although the proletariat is currently a minuscule part of the society, it is seen as the leading revolutionary force.

FRELIMO inherited a chaotic economy. Within a year after independence, 90 percent of the 250,000 Portuguese settlers had left, taking their skills and everything else they could carry with them. The nature of Portuguese colonialism was such that there were virtually no trained Mozambicans in any field. Thus the first year and a half were little more than crisis management; the first long-range policy statements were those of the 1977 FRELIMO party congress. The policy pursued from then until the beginning of 1980 was one of increased centralization and state control. Banks, retail trade, and some industries were nationalized, and much of state resources in the countryside went into state farms. In 1980 a shift was made toward decentralization and even denationalization although the commitment to socialism remained strong.

Economic problems were compounded by political ones. From 1976 to April 1980, Mozambique closed its border with Rhodesia in compliance with international law and thereby lost an estimated $500 million in trade revenue (Isaacman and Isaacman 1984:173). It also housed many Rhodesian refugees and ZANU guerrillas and so became the target of frequent Rhodesian air raids. Since 1980 the Mozambique National Resistance (MNR), an anti-FRELIMO group with major South African backing, has carried out a campaign of economic sabotage that has destroyed transportation and communication links, schools, health centers, farms, and villages. Defense activities thus account for some 30 percent of government expenditures (Legum 1984:B680). The MNR's activities, together with the drought that has affected much of East Africa, produced hardship and even starvation in some areas. Finally, in March 1984 the Mozambique government signed a nonaggression pact with South Africa, aimed at eliminating the latter's support for the MNR in exchange for an end to Mozambique's military support for the African National Congress (Isaacman 1985).

Mozambique has tried to maintain an autonomous, nonaligned international posture despite considering the socialist countries as its closest allies. Even the former U.S. ambassador, Willard DePree, stated, "Sure, FRELIMO's Marxist, but they keep their distance from

Moscow. They're very independent, pro-Third World" (Isaacman and Isaacman 1984:183). This independence, which has included the refusal to provide Moscow with port facilities, has perhaps been partly responsible for the lack of large amounts of economic aid from the socialist countries. Although substantial military aid has been provided, and some economic assistance for the state farms and industries, the amount actually disbursed is said to have been only about $25 million (Somerville 1984). Mozambique's application to join Comecon was also turned down, although recent trips by government leaders to socialist countries have provided consumer goods needed to stimulate peasant agricultural marketing. Since FRELIMO did not want to become completely reliant on the Soviet Union, it has sought aid from the West since the late 1970s. Some results have been forthcoming. Various Scandinavian countries have supported social services and rural development efforts. The Italians signed a comprehensive economic pact in 1981 to carry out various projects in return for access to Mozambique's natural resources (*Quarterly Economic Review,* no. 1, 1984).

The major change, however, came after the signing of the nonaggression treaty and the promulgation of the new foreign investment law. The latter—which is similar to Cuba's new law—provides protection against nationalization (except under "exceptional circumstances") and guarantees profit remittance at a rate to be agreed between investor and the government. It encourages joint ventures but also permits totally foreign-owned companies. Priorities for investment are sectors that increase exports, substitute imports, and create jobs for Mozambican workers. The most enthusiastic new investors have been the South Africans, but the Italians remain the largest investors, and even U.S. firms have been awarded contracts (*African Business,* December 1984).

Relations with the public sector in the West have also improved substantially, apparently based on Mozambican initiative. In August 1982 Mozambique acquiesced to West Germany's demand that it sign the "Berlin clause" (which Cuba has refused to do as mentioned above), thus opening the way for substantial aid from the EEC as well as West Germany itself. Portugal and the United Kingdom have also provided military and economic aid. Perhaps most surprising is a thaw in relations with the United States which helped negotiate the nonaggression pact. The U.S. Congress lifted the ban on bilateral aid in August 1984 which led to increased food aid (already exempted under the ban) and a $500,000 donation for repairs on Maputo's water treatment plant. AID sent a team of experts to look into the funding of projects, and $1 million of nonlethal military aid has been offered (*African Business,* August 1984; *Africa News,* January 28, 1985). Other recent changes have derived from the need to renegotiate Mozambique's $1.4 billion foreign debt, which gives that country the highest debt service ratio— 45 percent of export revenue—in Africa. The *quid pro quo* was that Mozambique drop its long-standing objections and join the World Bank and the International Monetary Fund; this occurred in September 1984. Mozambique has also signed the Third Lome Convention. Exactly what benefits will accrue to the country from its political and economic concessions remains to be seen. Thus far, despite the nonaggression pact, the guerrilla war still overshadows development planning.

Nicaragua. The most recent of the five cases began with the Sandinista overthrow of the Somoza dictatorship in Nicaragua in mid-1979.[11] Once again, as in Cuba and Mozambique, the rebel army defeated the old military force, and military victory was transformed into Sandinista control of the political apparatus of the state. For a variety of reasons, however, including the financial ones discussed below, an attempt has been made to maintain a broad coalition in support of the government. U.S. government statements to the contrary, the Nicaraguan regime has not defined itself as Marxist-Leninist but as nationalist and anti-imperialist, preparing the way for an eventual Nicaraguan version of socialism.

The initial postrevolutionary period was defined as one of national reconstruction, since a vast amount of the country's productive capacity and infrastructure had been destroyed during the fighting. In addition, of course, the Sandinistas inherited a dependent, backward, unequal economy typical of the other cases already discussed—especially similar to Cuba in its intimate links with the United States. A set of structural reforms was begun almost immediately, including an agrarian reform and the establishment of a state sector of the economy, mostly based on the old Somoza holdings. The major part of the economy, however, remained in private hands, with private control of some export crops of particular importance. Thus, the opposition forces had a powerful economic base which could be used to promote political opposition. The military opposition, primarily consisting of the Honduran-based Nicaraguan Democratic Force, has been heavily supported by the United States. The CIA has not only provided weapons and training but has also directly participated in covert operations, including the mining of Nicaragua's harbors.

The Sandinistas came to power in 1979 with a desperate financial situation. They faced a $1.6 billion debt and only $3 million in reserves. The latter was largely attributable to Somoza's taking the resources of the national treasury when he fled the country (Sholk and Maxfield, 1985). Fortunately, international support was overwhelming, with both bilateral and multilateral pledges of aid. Agencies from Mexico, Venezuela, Cuba, East and West Germany, Holland, Sweden, the United States, the World Bank, the Interamerican Development Bank, and the

Central American Bank for Economic Integration provided Nicaragua with enough foreign exchange to finance its total 1980 import bill (Weinert 1981). The $75 million loan from the United States was especially important in symbolic terms with its implication that a Chilean-type blockade would not occur.

The strong international support meanwhile provided the backdrop for negotiations with the private banks over Nicaragua's debt. In order to maintain good relations with Western financial sources, the Sandinistas agreed to pay all of Somoza's debts except those used for some arms purchases in the final days of the revolution. For their part, the private banks agreed to much more lenient terms than had been arranged for other countries. Thus $582 million was rescheduled over twelve years with a five-year grace period. No up-front fee was charged, and no conditionality was imposed. Most surprising, interest arrears were capitalized as were interest payments exceeding 7 percent over the five-year grace period (Dizard 1980; Weinert 1981; Maxfield 1982).

The completion of the rescheduling in late 1980 marked the high point in Nicaragua's relations with the Western financial community. The Reagan election quickly led to a change from cooperation to confrontation, and the elements of the Chilean blockade were reproduced. Bilateral aid was cut off and pressure was exerted on the multilateral agencies and other donor governments. As a consequence, commitments from the World Bank and the Interamerican Development Bank fell substantially after 1979–80. Likewise, both long- and short-term loans from private banks have almost disappeared, despite the agreement to continue lending that was part of the renegotiation (Conroy 1985). The Nicaraguan government calculates that it had lost some $350 million by 1983 as a result of U.S. "economic aggression"; another analysis indicates that the figure may be over $600 million (Sholk and Maxfield 1985). In mid-1985 that aggression was further stepped up as the Reagan administration instituted a formal trade embargo against Nicaragua and the U.S. Congress reinstated aid to the military opposition (*New York Times,* May 2, 1985 and June 13, 1985).

As for alternatives, a situation similar to that in Chile has occurred. The socialist countries offered Nicaragua some $600 million through 1983 (Conroy 1985), but most consisted of long-term credits for capital goods imports, so less than $200 million has been used (OECD 1985:177). Western Europe and Latin American credits are also tied to their own exports, but these are nevertheless more useful, especially the oil credits from Mexico and Venezuela. In general, reliance has had to be placed on bilateral trade credits so that choice of technology is based on the availability of finance (*Latin America Weekly Report,* July 29, 1983).

Although lack of data for the period after 1983 prevents detailed analysis, it seems clear that Nicaragua's international financial situation remains precarious. Government officials indicate that some 40 percent of domestic resources are going to the war effort (*New York Times,* March 19, 1985). Exports continue to stagnate, and the lack of foreign exchange was a main cause of the unpopular austerity measures introduced in February 1985. The government has recently settled its arrears with the IMF, and an agreement has been signed with the private banks covering principal and interest through June 1986, but Nicaragua's loans from the World Bank have been declared nonperforming (*New York Times,* June 17, 1985). New commitments of some $400 million have been obtained from West and East Europe, which should cover most of the current account deficit, although they leave little room for new projects. Given their firm political control, the Sandinistas do not face the same immediate pressures for building political support as did the Popular Unity in Chile, but neither can they count on the amount of aid that Cuba has received. The resulting lack of financial resources will be an important cause of increasing political discontent, especially with the military struggle continuing.

Conclusions

In order to facilitate a comparison of the five transitional economies discussed here, and between them and other developing countries, Table 2 summarizes some rough estimates on external finance in the same categories shown in Table 1. Some similarities can be noted among these five in contrast to other developing countries. First, all transitional economies have a much higher reliance on bilateral flows. Second, private banks and direct investment are relatively unimportant for all of these economies. Third, all of them (with the exception of Chile) have had a much higher financial inflow than have other developing countries.

Among the transitional economies, however, there are also important differences. Most obvious is the role of the Soviet Union. In one case (Cuba), it represents the vast majority of all financial flows. For the other countries capitalist support is more important, although in all cases some Soviet aid has been received; in Tanzania, China was also a key source of aid. Another important difference among the five concerns multilateral aid. For Tanzania and Nicaragua, multilateral development banks have been an important source of funds. Cuba, which does not belong to the World Bank/IMF, and Mozambique, which joined only recently, have not received much multilateral money. Chile was a member but its loans were blocked by the United States; this is now happening with Nicaragua as well. Another type of differ-

Table 2
Net External Long-term Financial Flows for Five Countries, annual averages, 1980–83 ($ millions)

Source	Cuba	Tanzania	Chile*	Mozambique	Nicaragua
Bilateral	$2993	$519	$166**	$165	$160
Capitalist	(-7)	(498)	(136)	(142)	(87)
Socialist	(3000)***	(3)	(30)	(16)	(47)
OPEC	(—)	(18)	(—)	(6)	(25)
Multilateral	6	176	25	45	88
Private Banks	-167	4	78**	7	5
Private Suppliers	23	59	50	173	12
Direct Investment	0	14	-24	2	0
Total	2855	771	295	391	264
GNP (GNP per capita)	12400 (1240)	4928 (265)	9187 (950)	4722 (357)	2460 (877)
Total/GNP (percent)	23.0	15.6	3.2	8.3	10.7

Sources: OECD (1985) for Tanzania, Mozambique, and Nicaragua; OECD (1985), Banco Nacional de Cuba, 1985, and U.S. Congress (1982) for Cuba; OECD (1978), IMF Balance of Payments Yearbook (1977), and World Debt Tables (1978) for Chile.

*1971–73.
**Includes refinancing
***Includes sugar subsidy

ence focuses not on the composition of financial flows but on the total amounts. Looking at the latter as a percentage of GNP indicates that Cuba has had access to a substantially higher amount of aid (23 percent) and on much better terms. Tanzania was next highest (16 percent), with Nicaragua and Mozambique at a similar level (11 and 8 percent, respectively), while Chile trailed far behind (3 percent).

How can these differences be explained? One hypothesis would focus on the degree of "radicalization" of the five governments. A categorization along these lines would put Cuba and Mozambique on the left as avowedly Marxist-Leninist regimes, Chile and Nicaragua in the middle representing moves toward a *sui generis* socialism, and Tanzania on the right as a non-Marxist, humanist version of socialism. This hypothesis can account for some of the differences observed, namely, the high Soviet aid to Cuba, the large amount of Western aid to Tanzania, and the medium level of aid from various sources to Nicaragua. It cannot deal with the small amounts of Soviet aid to Mozambique nor the minuscule amount of aid of any kind to Chile.

Some light can perhaps be shed on the Mozambique and Chile cases, as well as additional comprehension of the others, by considering two other factors: timing and the extent to which a specific blockade is imposed. With respect to the former, those governments that came to power later in time may have learned some lessons from earlier ones. Nicaragua and perhaps Mozambique would fall into this category, in the sense of trying to diversify sources of external finance. Similarly, the very existence of one outcome may prevent a repeat: for example, Soviet support for Cuba seems to have prevented similar support for another country even if it were desired.

The question of blockades has been mostly related to U.S. activities in Latin America, although the British ceased their aid to Tanzania at one point, and West Germany has blocked three of the countries' access to funds over the issue of recognizing West Berlin as a West German state. U.S. blockades have been especially harsh because of Latin American countries' strong historical dependence on the United States; furthermore, the United States has not hesitated to pressure other funding sources to join its blockades. This was true for Cuba in the early 1960s and for Chile in the early 1970s. Now in the 1980s, a repeat is being seen in Nicaragua although support for the U.S. line is weaker than before. The United States has not provided much financial aid to the two African countries, but its lack of traditional involvement puts the current lack of finance in a different light.

To summarize, then, a transitional regime's ideological stance appears to have some effect on the amount and type of external finance it receives. Likewise, its geographical location is important, as is the time at which it comes to power with respect both to other transitional economies and the political-economic situation of the world. Since the last two factors are not under the control of the government itself, careful planning with respect to foreign exchange needs and sources becomes absolutely essential. A balance of payments crisis is the easiest way in which a transitional regime can be undermined.

Although I have argued that the political and economic needs for foreign exchange make international finance essential, I want to close by stressing the problems involved and the need to seek ways to deal with them. History provides ample evidence that those who oppose revolutionary governments will try to use financial leverage to undermine them. Thus policies must be developed to accompany the use of international finance. A number of specific recommendations could be made, but three fairly general ones are of particular importance. First, development of expertise with respect to sources of international finance and techniques of negotiation is an essential prerequisite to adequate management. Such expertise can be acquired abroad initially, but local experts should be trained as soon as possible. Second, in choosing sources, diversification is the most urgent priority. This includes diversification among lending countries as well as general types of finance. Third, the amounts of money to be sought should be as small as possible, and ways of servicing the loans should be considered in advance. The balance of payments cannot be left to take care of itself. Furthermore—the justification for an essay such as this one—governments in transitional economies should pay attention to the experiences of similar countries and try to learn from them, both about what to look for and what to avoid. If proper precautions are taken, I still believe that the advantages of external resources outweigh the costs. The "care and feeding of gift horses" (Over 1983), however, demands great skill.[12] The possibility of them turning into Trojan horses is a very real danger.

Notes

The author would like to thank Steve Orvis for research assistance and Carmen Diana Deere, Richard Fagen, and Crawford Young for comments on earlier drafts of this article.

1. For a book that deals with the *internal* aspects of finance in the transition to socialism, see Griffith-Jones (1981).
2. Contributors to this debate include Samir Amin, Giovanni Arrighi, Andre Gunder Frank, and Immanuel Wallerstein. For several positions see Amin et al. (1982).
3. Cheryl Payer takes a position close to Amin's, focusing particularly on international finance. In her earlier book on the IMF, Payer (1974:210–

11) argued that nations have failed to develop "not because they had too little international money, but because they had too much." In her more recent discussion of the World Bank (1982b:363), she reluctantly agrees that aid from "good" (as opposed to "imperialist") international agencies might be acceptable "in limited quantities for specific, well-thought-out needs, on a case-by-case basis."

4. The IMF is traditionally excluded from data on international agency loans because countries do not formally obtain loans but purchase currency from the Fund.

5. Excluded here is discussion of short-term trade and other credits of under one-year duration. These are extremely important but information is difficult to obtain.

6. Major sources on Cuban socialism, and especially Cuba's experience with international finance, include Banco Nacional de Cuba (1985), Blasier (1971), Boorstein (1968), Brundenius (1984), Eckstein (1980), Mesa-Lago (1981, 1982), Schmidt (1983), and U.S. Congress (1982).

7. In an unpublished paper (Yale University, 1985) Richard Turits calculates that the Soviet sugar subsidy was not important until 1976. Before that time the U.S. preferential price was generally *above* the Soviet price. Afterward, the sugar subsidy alone averaged about $2 billion per year.

8. For sources on Tanzania, see Clark (1978), Coulson (1982), Mittelman (1981), Payer (1982a), Singh (1983), and Von Freyhold (1979).

9. On Chile, see especially Griffith-Jones (1981), Guardia (1979), NACLA (1973), Petras and Morley (1975), and U.S. Congress (1974).

10. Mozambique is discussed in Hanlon (1984), Isaacman (1985), Isaacman and Isaacman (1984), Mittelman (1981), and Somerville (1984).

11. On Nicaragua, sources include Conroy (1985), Irvin (1983) , Maxfield (1982), Sholk and Maxfield (1985), Walker (1985), and Weinert (1981).

12. This is not the sense in which Over used the phrase.

The Conflict at Home and Abroad: U.S. Imperialism vs. the New Revolutionary Societies

▼▲

Roger Burbach

From 1974 to 1980 fourteen new revolutionary states emerged in the third world. Seizing state power in countries that ranged in size from the tiny island state of Grenada to the sprawling expanse of Angola, these revolutions represented diverse political movements, from a fundamentalist Moslem regime in Iran to a self-proclaimed Marxist-Leninist state in unified Vietnam. In spite of their diversity, however, the new revolutionary governments had two things in common: they took power in third world societies struggling with the immense problems of underdevelopment, and with only one exception—Zimbabwe—they encountered the hostility of the United States. Four of the revolutionary governments—Angola, Cambodia, Iran, and Vietnam—are not even recognized by the United States today. Two of them, Grenada and Nicaragua, have been or are the victims of large-scale U.S. aggression, while counterrevolutionary forces in two more, Angola and Afghanistan, are supported and funded by the CIA.[1]

What are the dynamics of the U.S. system that account for the opposition of the United States to revolutionary governments? Is such opposition inevitable? And if so, what does it portend for the future development of third world countries? These are central questions that must be answered if we are to understand the options available to new revolutionary societies as the twentieth century draws to a close.

In order to understand the fundamental forces that drive the United States to maintain a generally belligerent position toward revolutionary governments, we need to review the history of U.S. opposition to revolutionary governments, focusing on the evolution of U.S. policy in the 1970s; we can then examine more closely U.S. policy toward three revolutionary movements: Iran, Angola, and Nicaragua.

The Historical Context

U.S. hostility toward revolutionary governments is not of course a new phenomenon. The counterrevolutionary policies of the United States can be traced back to the beginning of this century, when the United States joined the ranks of the great powers and developed international economic interests that could be adversely affected by revolutionary movements. The two great social and political upheavals of the early twentieth century, the Mexican revolution and the Bolshevik revolution in the Soviet Union, encountered the open hostility of the United States. U.S. expeditionary forces were sent into both countries to engage the revolutionary armies and to weaken or overthrow the governments. In the immediate aftermath of World War I, the United States conspired with the major European powers to block the revolutionary movements in Europe, particularly in Hungary, where the communist government of Béla Kun was overthrown (Meyer 1967:827–52).

Since then, the United States, in a century beset by world wars, major regional conflicts, and enormous material and technological transformations, has remained largely steadfast in its opposition to radical revolutionary movements. In the 1920s and 1930s, when revolution and social unrest threatened in Latin America and the Caribbean, the United States dispatched the marines to several countries and fought the first counterinsurgency war in the Western Hemisphere, against Augusto César Sandino in Nicaragua.

In the aftermath of World War II, U.S. counterrevolutionary policies toward the third world were institutionalized, becoming a cornerstone of U.S. foreign policy. According to NSC-68, the National Security doctrine proclaimed in 1950, the entire world, developed and underdeveloped, was to be regarded as an arena of competition between the United States and the Soviet Union. In this context radical revolutionary movements in the third world were viewed as abetting the Soviet challenge, and "any means, covert or overt, violent or nonviolent" could be employed against the Soviet Union or any other state or movement that might be viewed as its ally (National Security Council 1975:51–108).

Thus the major revolutionary governments that came to power in the postwar period—in North Korea, Cuba, and North Vietnam—were viewed as threats to the United States, and a succession of U.S. administrations moved to contain or overthrow them. Even elected left-of-center leaders that were not Marxist-Leninists—such as Mohammed Mossadeq in Iran, Jacobo Arbenz in Guatemala, and Salvador Allende in Chile—met with the determined and effective opposition of the United States. Among the newly independent governments in Africa and Asia, only those that adopted neocolonial relationships with the major imperial powers enjoyed the support of the United States. When a radical nationalist, Patrice Lumumba, took power in the Belgian Congo (now Zaire) in the late 1950s, the United States launched a destabilization program which ultimately led to his overthrow and death (see Weissman 1974).

The fourteen different instances in which revolutionary movements successfully seized power from 1974 to 1980 presented an historic challenge to U.S. counterrevolutionary policies. The disastrous defeat of U.S. policy in Vietnam, the successful replacement of the Portuguese colonial regimes in Africa by Marxist-Leninist governments, the anti-Western Iranian upheaval in the strategic Persian Gulf area, and the Grenadan and Nicaraguan revolutionary governments in the U.S. "backyard"—all these developed in a relatively short period of time and compelled U.S. leaders to reevaluate their counterrevolutionary strategies and to make some adjustments in their policies.

The Realignment in U.S. Foreign Policy

The sharp policy debates that occurred in the United States over these revolutionary upheavals did not result in the emergence of consistent policies. U.S. leaders were in fact deeply divided over what the movements meant for the United States and how they should be dealt with. From 1975 to 1979 U.S. policies toward third world revolutionary governments can be characterized as erratic and somewhat contradictory; there were even a few halting steps to find a *modus vivendi* with some of the new governments. By 1979 however, the United States began to move back to its policy of across-the-board hostility toward revolutionary governments, a policy that was consolidated with the election of Ronald Reagan.

What accounts for these swings in U.S. policy? The decade of the 1970s was a period of realignment within the dominant U.S. foreign policy circles, precipitated in large part by the Vietnam war (Burbach and Flynn 1985:70–75). Even before the war ended two major cleavages had developed within the eastern establishment that had guided U.S. policy since World War II. One pole was determined not to allow the erosion of U.S. global power as a result of Vietnam. Epitomized by Henry Kissinger, this camp had no intention of accommodating the United States to radical or revolutionary regimes in the third world. But it did realize that popular sentiment in the United States against involvement in another land war made it virtually impossible to use direct military force in the third world. As an alternative defense of empire, the Kissinger foreign policy team developed a strategy of using regional military bulwarks (Iran, Brazil, etc.) to protect U.S. interests and squelch any new revolutionary movements. Simultaneously, this camp attempted to use covert operations (as in Angola) to deal with revolutionary challenges (Morris 1977:293).

The other pole that emerged within the eastern establishment regrouped mainly within the liberal wing of the Democratic Party. Cyrus Vance, Robert McNamara, Paul Warnke, and Clark Clifford, all of whom had served in the administration of Lyndon Johnson, came to view the Vietnam war as a "mistake" that required a reassessment of U.S. involvement in third world conflicts. *Foreign Policy,* a quarterly publication founded in 1970 by liberal intellectuals and junior foreign service officers, became a major organ for articulating this new perspective. In its premier issue the quarterly proclaimed that "in the light of Vietnam, the basic purposes of American foreign policy demand reexamination and redefinition."

Many members of this second school believed that a major mistake of the United States in Vietnam was to see the war as an extension of the global competition with the Soviet Union and China. They argued that henceforth the United States should treat third world conflicts as separate from the challenges posed by the dominant communist power, the Soviet Union. There would be changes in the third world, and even possibly new radical revolutionary governments, but the United States should view these developments as distinct from the competition with the Soviet Union.

There was one more small but significant splinter in the eastern establishment, significantly to the right of the other positions. As articulated by presidential security adviser Paul Nitze, this position argued that the United States could have won the Vietnam war if only it had used its full military might early in the conflict, instead of engaging in a gradual build-up which sapped domestic support for the war and gave the North Vietnamese time to build up their forces (Sanders 1983:142–45; Josephs 1981:143). The members of this group, many of whom later became known as neoconservatives, soon broke completely with the eastern establishment and began to forge alliances with right-wing organizations in the southern and western United States. They provided the foreign policy basis of the New Right coalition that brought Ronald Reagan to power in 1981.

The formation of these three camps provides the backdrop for understanding the twists and turns in U.S. policy toward third world revolutionary governments in the 1970s. When the revolution in Portugal in 1974 made it inevitable that four centuries of Portuguese colonial rule in Africa would come to an end, Kissinger began to search for ways to ensure that the new governments would not be dominated by Marxists. In Angola he ordered an intensive CIA effort to support the pro-Western National Front for the Liberation of Angola (FNLA) forces against the more radical Popular Movement for the Liberation of Angola (MPLA) led by Agostinho Neto (Danaher 1985:112).

But this policy did not enjoy bipartisan support in the United States. Congressional leaders, fearing another Vietnam-like conflict in which the United States would become more and more entangled, reversed U.S. policy by cutting off funds for CIA operations in Angola.

The lessons of this setback were not lost on the new foreign policy leadership that came in under President Jimmy Carter. In its early days this group embarked on a systematic, if somewhat tepid, effort to see if a *modus vivendi* could be worked out with some of the third world revolutionary governments. In Africa, the Carter administration moderated U.S. hostility toward the Angolan and Mozambican governments, and even pressured the South African apartheid regime to soften its policies toward the revolutionary forces fighting for independence in Namibia. In Asia, some contacts were made with the Vietnamese government, although these foundered over the question of U.S. soldiers missing in action and the dispatch of Vietnamese troops into Cambodia. In Latin America, U.S. relations with Cuba were upgraded to the subambassadorial level and some initial discussions were held in an effort to normalize relations between the two countries.

The two boldest moves by the Carter administration to establish normal relations with revolutionary governments occurred in Nicaragua and Zimbabwe. In Nicaragua, Carter recognized the Sandinista government when it took power in July 1979, and pressured Congress into passing a special $75 million aid package for the government. In the case of Zimbabwe, the United States supported agreements worked out in Great Britain, known as the Lancaster agreements, that provided for free elections and a constitution that would lead to black rule. When Robert Mugabe, an avowed Marxist, won, the United States along with Great Britain and other West European governments stood by their original commitment to recognize the new government and provide extensive economic assistance.

A common view of U.S. policy is that these accommodationist efforts were dramatically reversed in 1981, when the Reagan administration came to power, ushering in a new era of confrontation. But this is a misreading of history. In 1979–80, at the very time that the agreements with Nicaragua and Zimbabwe were being worked out, the Carter administration was backing away from its policy of seeking an accommodation with third world revolutionary governments. The efforts to normalize U.S. relations with Cuba ended with the alleged "discovery" of a brigade of Soviet troops in Cuba, and as U.S. opposition to the Iranian mullahs and Ayatollah Khomeini demonstrated, even before the taking of the embassy hostages, the United States was not about to cozy up to a new revolutionary government that had tossed a trusted U.S. ally out of power. Even in the case of Nicaragua, the Carter administration in its waning months in power became disillusioned with the Sandinistas and laid the legal groundwork for ending U.S. aid to

Nicaragua. What accounts for this reconsolidation of U.S. opposition
to revolutionary movements?

U.S. Interests and Revolutionary Movements

Marxist scholars traditionally focus on economic factors in analyzing
the roots of U.S. intervention abroad. While economic considerations
are clearly central to an understanding of U.S. policy, the twists and
turns of foreign policy cannot be explained entirely by an analysis of
economic interests and motives. An imperial power such as the United
States has a complex network of interests that evolve and expand over a
period of time. In the early stages of the U.S. empire, for example, U.S.
interests abroad were viewed as predominantly economic, thus explaining why the term "Dollar Diplomacy" came to characterize U.S. policy
in the Caribbean Basin at the beginning of this century (Feis 1965:v).

But as the United States became the ascendant world power, it was
no longer sufficient to focus simply on protecting U.S. business
interests abroad. The dictates of empire required that the United States
consider geopolitical and military factors along with purely economic
interests. As the century advanced, an integrated imperialist system
emerged, and when the foundations of this system were challenged,
first by Germany and Japan in the 1930s and 1940s, and later by the
Soviet Union in the late 1940s and 1950s, the United States reacted by
building a series of alliances with other advanced industrial nations and
by encouraging or coercing third world countries into accepting U.S.
leadership.

Moreover, in order to mobilize popular support at home and to
appeal to sentiments in other countries, particularly in Latin America,
U.S. leaders in the post-World War II era forged a "free world"
ideology based on the principles of democracy, free trade, and
anticommunism. Although the principles themselves are sometimes
contradictory (anticommunism for example often leads U.S. leaders to
support undemocratic, authoritarian regimes), this ideological package
has acquired a certain life of its own and interacts with U.S. economic,
military, and geopolitical interests.

The complexity of these interests means that it is often difficult to
determine what particular interests are at stake in a given country or
region. U.S. leaders themselves often obfuscate these interests by
declaring that "U.S. national security" is at stake whenever they
conclude that a certain combination of U.S. interests is being threatened by the activities of other governments or revolutionary movements. In some instances U.S. military, corporate, and political leaders
may even be deeply divided over what particular interests are at stake
and over just how the United States should respond, thereby making it
even more difficult to decipher what precise interests are driving the
United States to intervene abroad.

The interaction of these interests in the shaping of U.S. foreign policy can best be understood by looking at three key upheavals in the 1978–79 period—Iran, Angola, and Nicaragua. Each of these (very different) revolutionary movements affected a particular set of U.S. interests. By examining these specific cases we can better understand what drives the United States to intervene against third world revolutions.

Iran: The Non-Marxist Challenge

The Iranian revolution is particularly illustrative of how concrete U.S. interests not related to cold war concerns are adversely affected by third world revolutions. Since its inception, the Iranian revolution has been dominated by deeply conservative Islamic fundamentalists; thus, unlike other revolutions, U.S. opposition cannot be attributed to anticommunism. Specific U.S. economic, military, and geopolitical interests were at stake in Iran, and they were threatened by ultranationalist forces determined to eliminate the influence of the decadent West, rather then any danger of an emerging "Marxist-Leninist regime."

On the eve of the Iranian revolution, U.S. economic interests in the country were quite extensive. In 1978, the last stable year of Iranian oil production before the revolution, Iran provided over 13.5 percent of U.S. petroleum imports (IMF 1982:380). Perhaps even more important than the actual amount of oil that came from Iran is the fact that the Shah of Iran was responsive to U.S. efforts to hold down oil prices in the Organization of Petroleum Exporting Countries (OPEC) cartel. While the Shah went along with the price rises in 1973–74, in subsequent years the Iranian government consistently worked with the more conservative Arab governments to limit future rises in oil prices.

Moreover, the Shah helped ensure that a major portion of the increased Iranian oil revenues flowed into U.S. corporate coffers. In the 1970s the U.S. stake in Iran mushroomed as U.S. multinationals rushed to the country to build factories, to set up new oil refineries, and to market luxury commodities for the burgeoning upper and middle classes. Billion-dollar construction projects were drawn up by such firms as the Bechtel Corporation. U.S. banks also benefited by serving as the depositories and the investors for Iranian petrodollars.

The largest single beneficiary of Iranian petrodollars in the 1970s was the U.S. armaments industry. Iran became the biggest U.S. arms purchaser in the third world, averaging $3.2 billion annually in purchases between 1973 and 1978. At the time of the revolution the Shah had outstanding arms contracts for approximately $15 billion (Klare 1984:127).

The U.S. geopolitical stake in Iran was also quite significant. The Nixon Doctrine proclaimed in the early 1970s that the United States would look for regional third world allies to front for U.S. interests. In accordance with this doctrine Henry Kissinger, first as head of the National Security Council and then as secretary of state, moved to strengthen the Shah and make him the U.S. regional gendarme in the volatile and strategic Persian Gulf region (ibid:40).

Iran also played an important role for the United States in its global competition with the Soviet Union. In 1953, when the CIA managed the ouster of the neutralist, left of center president, Mohammed Mossadeq, and installed Shah Reza Pahlevi as the effective ruler of Iran, the United States and its Western allies won a significant victory in the unfolding cold war. Iran's oil and its proximity to the Soviet Union made it a critical third world outpost. The establishment of a major CIA listening post on Iran's northern border to monitor Soviet military testing and engage in electronic eavesdropping on a wide range of Soviet activities underscored the geopolitical and military importance of Iran to the United States.

With this array of interests, it is small wonder that the United States tried to prop up the Shah in his final days. When in December 1978 the Carter administration realized that this was no longer possible, it sent the head of NATO to try to preserve the regime while the Shah went into what was thought to be temporary exile. But this scheme fell apart in a month and a half, and in February 1979 the Islamic fundamentalist forces of Ayatollah Khomeini took power.

The revolution in Iran had immediate repercussions within the United States. According to the *U.S. News & World Report* (February 19, 1979), shock waves were felt throughout the U.S. arms industry as the new government canceled future orders. The nation's business community as a whole became extremely disgruntled with the Carter administration, believing that it was in large part responsible for the Iranian turmoil. A special issue of *Business Week,* titled "The Decline of U.S. Power" (March 12, 1979), asserted that the fall of the Shah signaled "an accelerated erosion of power and influence," and called upon the Carter administration to employ U.S. covert and military forces to protect U.S. interests around the world. Well before the taking of the Iranian hostages, which enabled U.S. leaders to whip up broad-based anti-Iranian hysteria in the United States, the predominant U.S. ruling circles had already decided that the United States should adopt a tough policy toward the new Iran government.

Angola: An Ideological Thorn

While Iran demonstrated that the United States will act to protect concrete material interests that are adversely affected by third world revolutionary movements, the Angolan experience has shown that the

United States has a fundamental hostility toward third world Marxist revolutionary movements, even when those movements do not directly threaten U.S. economic or geopolitical interests.

In 1974 the Portuguese empire was on the verge of collapse after the revolution in Lisbon that brought reformist military officers to power. In Angola, the largest and most important of the Portuguese colonies, the United States had only limited interests. In geopolitical terms, Angola and central Africa were of secondary importance compared to such regions as Western Europe, Latin America, and the Middle East. Economically, U.S. investments were marginal except for the petroleum fields owned by Gulf Oil.

Nonetheless, when three political movements in Angola vied to take over the reins of political power—the National Union for a Totally Independent Angola (UNITA), the National Front for the Liberation of Angola (FNLA), and the Popular Movement for the Liberation of Angola (MPLA)—the United States stepped into the foray to oppose the latter movement, which was avowedly Marxist. In January 1975 the three movements agreed to establish a tripartite transitional government and a unified national army, but the administration of President Gerald Ford moved to sabotage the agreement. The CIA began providing covert funding to the FNLA, and the United States' most reliable ally in central Africa, Mobutu Sese Seko of Zaire, became a conduit for shipping U.S. arms to the FNLA. With this newly acquired arsenal, the FNLA launched an attack on MPLA forces and began to move on the capital city, Luanda, the MPLA stronghold (Danaher 1985:112–13).

From then on, the conflict escalated rapidly. The MPLA appealed for and received Soviet military aid along with 200 Cuban military advisers. When this began to turn the tide of the conflict, the South African government, with tacit American approval and CIA support, launched an invasion from the south. This offensive threatened to topple the now independent MPLA government in Luanda, and the new president, Agostinho Neto, appealed for more Cuban and Soviet military aid. Cuba sent 20,000 troops, whose support proved decisive in turning back the South Africans.

The conflict in Angola provoked deep divisions within U.S. ruling circles. The U.S. government, under the leadership of Henry Kissinger, maintained that the United States had to stop the MPLA from consolidating its control because of its ties to the Soviet Union and Cuba. Kissinger clearly viewed the Angolan war as part of the East-West conflict. As the CIA officer in charge of the Angolan operation later noted: "Kissinger saw the Angolan conflict solely in terms of global politics and was determined the Soviets should not be permitted to make a move in any remote part of the world without being confronted militarily by the United States" (Stockwell 1978:43).

However, sectors of the U.S. corporate community took a different stance. Gulf Oil, the largest single foreign investor, received assurances from the MPLA government that Gulf could maintain its operations. As a result, the company established cordial commercial relations and announced it would make royalty payments to the government. The Ford administration initially blocked these payments, but Gulf Oil later prevailed in its efforts to pay the new government (Danaher 1985:116–17).

The inability of the Ford administration to forge a consensus for its Angolan policies extended to Congress. Fearing another Vietnam-type involvement, Congress in early 1976 first refused to authorize more funds for covert operations in Angola, then passed the Clark amendment, which made it illegal for the CIA to support the armed opposition movements. But the issue was not resolved. Even the Carter administration refused to recognize the Angolan government. And in 1985 a different Congress repealed the Clark amendment.

The Angolan intervention demonstrated that there is a deep-seated political commitment among U.S. political leaders to oppose Marxist-Leninist revolutionary movements everywhere because of their potential alignment with the Soviet Union. This commitment does not arise from immediate economic interests, at least not in the short term, but out of the belief that U.S. interests on a global scale are furthered by stopping any revolutionary movement that threatens to align itself with the socialist bloc countries. The counterrevolutionary policy which it fuels began with the Bolshevik revolution, was reenforced by U.S. national security doctrine after World War II, and remains a cornerstone of U.S. foreign policy today.

But owing to disagreement over immediate and long-term U.S. interests, support for counterrevolution on a world scale is not automatic; it must constantly be remobilized. In the case of Angola, in 1976 U.S. corporations, as well as some members of Congress and sectors of the foreign policy establishment, did not support CIA operations because they worked at cross-purposes with U.S. economic interests and threatened to embroil the United States in another regional war coming on the heels of the Vietnam debacle. A decade later, with the liberal foreign policy establishment routed, and a popular anticommunist president, a campaign to support covert operations in Angola began afresh—this time to UNITA, the only remaining Angolan opposition.

Nicaragua: Threat of a Good Example

The Nicaraguan revolution presented a very different threat to U.S. interests compared to the Iranian and Angolan situations. The ouster of dictator Anastasio Somoza in July 1979 initially had a minimal effect on U.S. interests. U.S. investments in Nicaragua were a small fraction of what were at stake in Iran, and while Somoza had served as a regional gendarme of sorts for the United States in Central America, by the late 1970s his repressive policies and the isolation of his regime rendered him increasingly ineffective in the regional defense of U.S. interests. Moreover, the presence of Nicaraguan business representatives in the Sandinista government, the non-Marxist orientation of some leaders, and the moderation of the new government's policies (no U.S. holdings were expropriated and unlike Iran there were no summary executions of former government personnel) led the Carter administration to push a special $75 million aid package through Congress to help rebuild Nicaragua's wartorn economy.

However, the new Sandinista government soon came into conflict with the United States for one simple reason—the Nicaraguan revolution served as a catalyst and inspiration for revolutionary movements in Central America, thereby provoking concern that a broad range of U.S. economic, military, and geopolitical interests in the Caribbean Basin would be adversely affected. In its waning days, the Carter administration began to abandon the policy of supporting the Sandinista government precisely when it realized that its effort to prop up the government in El Salvador were in part undermined by the Nicaraguan revolution. While the administration focused on alleged Nicaraguan arms shipments to the Salvadoran revolutionaries as the reason for cooling relations with the Sandinistas, this type of direct support was only the most visible manifestation of how the revolution adversely affected U.S. interests.

Placed in historical context, it is easy to understand why U.S. leaders view developments in any given Central American country as having far-reaching consequences. Political movements in the Caribbean Basin have in fact often had effects that extend far beyond national boundaries. The Mexican revolution, for example, was a factor in precipitating the upheaval that gripped Central America in the second quarter of this century. Both Augusto Sandino in Nicaragua and Farabundo Martí in El Salvador were deeply affected by the Mexican revolution, and Sandino's war against the U.S. marines in the 1920s and 1930s was aided by arms and supplies arriving from Mexico. Secretary of State Kellogg declared in 1927 that Mexico was manipulated by "Bolshevik leaders" intent on overthrowing governments in Central America.

This historical backdrop explains why the Nicaraguan revolution had a profound impact in Central America, affecting in particular the Salvadoran and Guatemalan insurgencies. Nicaragua served not only as an inspiration and a model for other movements, but also as a place where revolutionary leaders from other countries could find refuge, regroup, and discuss political strategies for challenging their respective governments.

Thus the Nicaraguan revolution, like the Cuban revolution twenty years earlier, quickly became a threat to U.S. hegemony throughout Central America and the Caribbean, thereby stirring up deep concern in U.S. ruling circles that the extensive U.S. interests throughout the Caribbean Basin would be adversely affected. The United States has a total of $23 billion invested in Central America and the Caribbean, and another $5 billion tied up in Mexico (excluding over $90 billion in international debt), making this the most important third world region for the United States (Burbach and Flynn 1984:91–92). And as U.S. military leaders point out, the existence of "a string of hostile or nonaligned governments" to the south would complicate U.S. efforts to allocate military forces or wage war in other parts of the world.

The threat to these interests explains why the Reagan administration made Nicaragua, El Salvador, and the Caribbean Basin in general a top priority on its foreign policy agenda as soon as it took office. During its early years the Reagan administration fought a running battle with many of its domestic adversaries over how best to contain the Nicaraguan revolution and prop up the Salvadoran government. But by early 1984, congressional hearings and the report of a special Kissinger Commission on Central America revealed that a broad range of U.S. leaders, including Democratic and Republican party leaders as well as U.S. corporate and military officials, believed that a major commitment of U.S. resources had to be made to preserve Central America and the Caribbean for U.S. interests.

Domestic Polarization and the Crisis of Empire

The debate and maneuvering that has occurred within the established policy circles over U.S. foreign policy is part of a broader political process at work within the United States. Over the past two decades U.S. conflicts with third world revolutionary movements have produced two contradictory tendencies at home. On the one hand U.S. intervention has stimulated the growth of domestic movements that oppose U.S. counterrevolutionary policies. First the Vietnam conflict, then subsequent interventions—ranging from the CIA-backed coup in Chile in 1973 to the current U.S. military build-up in Central America—sparked major opposition movements. However, the very growth of the anti-intervention movements combined with the erosion of U.S. power abroad have fomented the development of an opposing tendency—a right-wing movement that demands an ardent defense of U.S.

imperial interests and that seeks to impose its will on third world radical movements.

This polarization over foreign policy issues reflects the fundamental crisis of the U.S. empire. Because the informal empire that was forged in the early twentieth century is an integral part of the U.S. system today, it is logical that its demise would inevitably have profound reverberations within the United States. As the conflicts in El Salvador and Nicaragua (not to mention Vietnam) demonstrate, the loss or threatened loss of small countries that have historically been in the U.S. "sphere of influence" can spark major foreign policy debates that drag on for years. This is a new stage in American politics in which foreign policy issues are internalized, that is, they are increasingly at the cutting edge of domestic debates and they divide the United States into distinct political camps.

The development of two conflicting poles is rooted in the impact the crisis of the U.S. empire has on different social sectors. The dominant strata of U.S. society are driven to defend the empire because they have a material interest in doing so. The corporate elites, the beneficiaries of the military-industrial complex, and the state managers who run the foreign policy apparatus—these groups all have a definite stake in preserving the present imperial system and in utilizing U.S. resources to prevent third world societies from breaking out of that system.

U.S. corporate interests, which have spearheaded the integration of the United States into the global economy, are particularly dependent on the maintenance and expansion of the U.S. empire abroad. In a survey of the top 100 U.S. corporations active in industry, banking, and commerce, *Forbes* magazine found that sixty-two of them have 25 percent or more of their assets abroad while twenty-two earn over 50 percent of their profits from international operations. The importance of this for the U.S. corporate world was underscored by the *Forbes* declaration that "in economics, if not in politics, it's one world now" (July 2, 1984, p. 129).

Those who control the U.S. military complex (armaments manufacturers, military officers, and the civilian officials in the Pentagon) also have a major stake in perpetuating the imperialist system. They gain prestige and power from managing the swollen military budgets and from running the string of bases and military alliances that the United States possesses around the globe. As the fall of the Shah of Iran demonstrates, the U.S. military and the armaments industries are fundamentally opposed to the victory of revolutionary movements and the loss of staunch U.S. allies in the third world.

Aligned with the defense interests are the foreign policy managers who jockey for positions of power and reap promotions and material benefits by "protecting U.S. interests" abroad. And grouped around

these state managers are an array of think-tanks, foreign policy associations, and lobbies that are funded by private business groups or by
lucrative government contracts. These elites all have a personal and
material stake in maintaining the U.S. empire, and they use their
positions to propagate the belief that U.S. society as a whole will be
undermined if "Communists" or, more recently, "Marxist-Leninists" in
the third world are not contained or defeated.

The Domestic Adversaries of Empire

There are broad sectors of U.S. society—the unemployed, much of
the working class and even middle class, as well as certain business
sectors—that do not have a direct stake in the U.S. empire. Some of
these groups have benefited from U.S. expansion, particularly in the
1940s, 1950s, and early 1960s when the U.S. empire reached its
apogee. The growth of export markets in the developed and underdeveloped worlds, the inflow of profits from U.S. corporate activities
abroad, and the creation of a military-industrial complex "to protect the
free world" abroad—these and other expansive endeavors created jobs,
generated income, and in general contributed to the growing prosperi-
ty of U.S. society.

However, the Vietnam war combined with the erosion of the U.S.
economic position abroad in the late 1960s and early 1970s reduced the
rewards of empire that accrued to the lower strata of U.S. society. No
real cost-benefit sheet can be drawn up on who gains or loses from the
U.S. imperial system at any given moment, but one can perceive that as
challenges arose to U.S. prerogatives abroad—challenges from third
world revolutionary movements, from West European and Japanese
economic competitors, and even from the newly industrializing third
world countries—the U.S. empire generated less revenue that re-
dounded to the general benefit of the U.S. populace. And as the
challenges to the U.S. system mounted, the costs of defending the
empire were borne disproportionately by the lower social sectors. The
most dramatic intervention on behalf of the informal empire, the
Southeast Asian war, demonstrated that U.S. blacks and Latinos along
with white working class youth paid inordinately in blood and wasted
lives for U.S. interventionary policies.

Today it is still minorities, along with most women, the poor, the
elderly, and even sectors of the middle and business classes that bear
the (increasing) burden of U.S. imperialist policies. The "Reaganomics"
program is the clearest declaration of who is to pay the price necessary
to prop up the U.S. empire in its waning years. From 1981 to 1985 this
program enabled the military-industrial complex to consume an ever-
expanding percentage of the U.S. national wealth while fundamental

social programs (medical care, educational programs, unemployment benefits, housing facilities, etc.) were curtailed or eliminated in order to sate the appetite of the Pentagon. Simultaneously, the tax rates of the wealthy and the corporations dropped while an increasing proportion of the U.S. tax dollar needed to finance this military machine came from the middle and lower sectors of U.S. society (Navarro 1985:46–48).

The Emerging Alternative

Within the electoral arena, Jesse Jackson's campaign for the Democratic nomination in 1984 made anti-intervention a principal theme—and rallied many progressive forces around the Rainbow Coalition and the Democratic Party. Yet only a small minority in the party is committed to fundamentally changing U.S. foreign policy; the party leadership clearly repudiated the Jackson position. Moreover, while Democrats do often differ with the Reagan administration over foreign policy issues, they provide support for Reagan's policies at critical moments. This occurred around El Salvador, when after the election of President Napoleon Duarte in 1984, the Democrats granted Reagan everything he requested in military and economic aid, and was painfully demonstrated again in June 1985, when Congress voted to provide aid to the contra forces trying to overthrow the Sandinista government in Nicaragua.

The Democrats cannot be counted on to consistently oppose Reagan's policies in part because many Democratic leaders are themselves an integral part of the system's hierarchy and reap benefits from the exercise and maintenance of U.S. power abroad. The Democrats, even more than the Republicans, helped create the military-industrial complex in the aftermath of World War II and today they are a central part of the political coalition that sustains it. Some Democrats, such as Senator Lloyd Benson of Texas and Senator Sam Nunn of Georgia, use their positions in Congress and the party to actively further the interests of the military-industrial complex.

The most liberal perspective put forth in Washington foreign policy circles, the so-called neorealist position, advocates a certain modus vivendi with third world revolutionary movements. Heir to the Cyrus Vance wing of the Carter administration, this position asserts that new revolutionary governments are both more stable and ultimately more reliable than third world dictatorships with which the United States has traditionally been allied; the new regimes must inevitably turn to the United States for assistance, since they need trade and financial relations with the world's largest economic power in order to prosper and retain the support of their people (see Feinberg 1980).

This argument has a certain appeal in some foreign policy circles, particularly those that are concerned about U.S. involvement in another Vietnam-like conflict. But ultimately it ignores the real processes that occur when an imperialist power sees its position threatened abroad. It is one thing for foreign policy analysts out of office to argue that a revolution should be able to run its course, that eventually it will come around to realizing that it needs the United States. It is quite another for anyone in government to argue such a view when trusted allies are falling and revolutionary governments articulate new interests and adopt development strategies that curtail or eliminate military and economic prerogatives. As a consequence, the neorealists have had little real impact, in either the Democratic Party or the government.

A number of domestic groups, however, are increasingly convinced that the maintenance of the U.S. empire is not in their best interests. Over the past decade many local and regional organizations along with single-issue movements have begun to put forth fundamentally new perspectives on U.S. military and foreign policies. The antinuclear movement; the increasingly militant protests against U.S. support for the apartheid regime in South Africa; the solidarity organizations that mobilize public support in the United States for revolutionary movements in such countries as the Philippines, El Salvador, Nicaragua, and Chile; local trade union committees across the country that provide material support for third world movements and that challenge the cold war positions of their national trade union leadership; the many Catholics and mainline Protestant churches that take stands against U.S. policies that violate basic human rights and the principle of self-determination—these are some of the social and political forces in the United States that are working on a day-to-day basis to check the more aggressive tendencies of the U.S. imperialist system and to build piece by piece a new vision of a noninterventionist foreign policy.[2]

Polarization in the 1980s

Despite the efforts of liberal as well as progressive forces to articulate alternative visions of U.S. policy, it is clear that the New Right has been much more successful in building a popular base for its views. In the 1970s the New Right mounted a concerted campaign that played upon public feelings of insecurity and doubt about the U.S. role in the world and that stoked the chauvinistic and anticommunist strains deeply ingrained in the American consciousness. This political effort led to the election of Ronald Reagan in 1980 and explains why large sectors of U.S. society that have no objective stake in interventionary policies are in fact supportive of actions such as the overthrow of the Grenadan government in 1983.

In the early 1980s, moreover, ruling-class differences over Central American policies compelled the Reagan administration to move to consolidate U.S. corporate support. The Caribbean Central American Action (C/CAA) organization, a little known but influential group of business leaders from many of the country's leading corporations, began to work closely with the Reagan administration in 1981 to encourage the broader business community to invest in the Caribbean Basin and to publicly support counterrevolutionary policies (Burbach and Flynn 1984:204–7).

The C/CAA played a key role in the passage of the Caribbean Basin Initiative, in 1983, which provided $350 million for pro-U.S. governments and gave special incentives and tariff concessions to U.S. businesses that invested in the Basin. The C/CAA itself has directly benefited from government support, receiving millions of dollars from the Agency for International Development (AID) for its "private-sector" activities in the Caribbean Basin and for publishing pro-corporate and anticommunist views in the United States.

Subsequently, right-wing business groups were mobilized to support the Reagan administration's efforts to topple the Sandinista government. When Congress temporarily restricted the CIA's ability to fund and direct the contra forces in Nicaragua, a number of private groups stepped in to provide assistance. Such business leaders as J. Peter Grace and Adolph Coors raised millions of dollars from business and corporate donors to provide material aid for the contra forces. Right-wing evangelical churches also raised millions, which supported, in addition to the contras, like-minded religious groups in Guatemala and El Salvador. At the same time, U.S. mercenaries were recruited by groups linked to *Soldier of Fortune* magazine to advise the contras and even to fight with them in Nicaragua.

However, as the administration has escalated the conflict in Central America, accelerated the arms race, and adopted a supportive approach toward right-wing regimes ranging from General Pinochet in Chile to the apartheid government in South Africa, a broad-based movement of opposition to U.S. policies has also begun to build. Indeed, the social composition of the antiwar movement is much broader today than it was during the Vietnam war. The student community is perhaps less prominent, but its lack of numbers has been more than compensated for by the involvement of the religious community. Mainline Protestant churches, Catholic bishops, liberation theologists, religious orders, and local church congregations have all concluded that fundamental moral principles are being violated by U.S.-sponsored wars in the third world. Moreover, through the Sanctuary movement, Church leaders are taking a stand in support of Salvadoran and Central American refugees in the United States. The religious community also plays a key role in the Emergency Response Network that has signed up close to 100,000 people who have committed themselves to engage in civil disobedience if the United States intervenes more directly in Central America.

Today, the anti-intervention movement is a major force that is able to challenge the influence of the well-heeled and well-financed right wing. This is why President Reagan and other New Right figures are constantly complaining about their inability to get their interventionist message across to the American people and decrying the "disinformation campaign" of opposition forces. Public opinion polls indicate the vast majority of the American people do not believe that U.S. troops should go into Central America, nor do they think that we should prop up right-wing authoritarian regimes, even if they are "guardians against communism" (LeoGrande 1984:16–39).

This does not mean, however, that the task of the anti-intervention forces will be easy. The dominant sectors in the United States, including the Democratic Party, will strive to maintain the counterrevolutionary policies of almost a century and they will be able to mobilize the vast resources of the state against third world revolutionary governments and movements. But these interventionist activities no longer serve U.S. society as a whole, and this basic contradiction means that revolutionary struggles in countries as disparate as El Salvador, Chile, the Philippines, and Nicaragua will be at the center of internal political debate and conflict within the United States in the coming years.

Notes

1. The seven other countries where revolutionary movements seized power from 1974 to 1980 are Cape Verde, Ethiopia, Guinea-Bisau, Laos, Mozambique, and Sao Tome.
2. In addition, an array of small research and lobbying organizations are putting forth new policy perspectives based on nonintervention, an end to U.S. militarism, and respect for the principle of self-determination. Although virtually all operate on shoestring budgets and are understaffed, they, together with critical analytical journals, are putting forth some of the most effective critiques of the interventionist policies of the Reagan administration and the New Right.

Agrarian Reform, Peasant and Rural Production, and the Organization of Production in the Transition to Socialism

▼▲

Carmen Diana Deere

The process of agrarian transformation in small peripheral societies in the transition to socialism raises the theoretical question of *what is* socialist agriculture. The empirical inquiry examines how new social relations of production in the countryside have been fostered, focusing on the organization of production and the role of peasant and rural worker participation in shaping the process of agrarian reform.

The thirteen countries here reviewed, all of which have declared themselves to be "socialist" or in a transition to socialism, differ markedly in terms of how socialism is conceptualized; not all are inspired by Marxism. Nonetheless, all of them have attempted to bring about revolutionary changes in agriculture in the name of "socialism," although they differ with respect to the political and economic means of such a transformation.

These thirteen countries, spanning Africa, Asia, the Middle East, and Latin America, differ not only as to where they are going, but also as to their initial conditions for a socialist transformation. The one structural characteristic they share is that at the moment of their revolutionary rupture, the majority of their population was rural, engaged in agricultural production. They differ, however, as to the importance of agriculture within the national economy. Seven of the countries—Cuba, Ethiopia, Guinea Bissau, Mozambique, Nicaragua, Somalia, and Tanzania—are still agroexport economies, with the agricultural sector generating over half of export earnings; the other six—Algeria, Angola, Syria, Vietnam, The People's Democratic Republic of Yemen, and Zimbabwe—are not agroexport economies today, but at the initiation of their respective transitions, the agricultural sector generated over half of Gross Domestic Product (GDP).

Since the work of Marx, Engels, and Lenin has informed the goals of agrarian socialist transformation in crucial ways, we will briefly review their work on socialist agriculture before taking up the changes in land tenure and property relations introduced in small peripheral societies.

We can then examine the organization of agricultural production, the priority given to state farms, and the history of peasant collectivization in each country.

Theoretical Conceptions of Socialist Agriculture

While Marx and Engels provided the theoretical basis for an understanding of socialism quite different from that of their utopian predecessors, they did not provide a blueprint of the process of transition to socialism, especially in agriculture. Characteristically, they viewed the process of socialist construction within the political and economic conditions peculiar to each historical moment and social formation.

Four basic elements of their theoretical vision of socialist agriculture can be deduced from their writings: (1) the nationalization of land; (2) a high level of development of the productive forces; (3) the socialization of production based on collective control over the labor process and of appropriation and distribution of surplus labor; and (4) the worker-peasant alliance.

While the theoretical basis for the first three emerges out of their analysis of capitalism, the fourth principle, the worker-peasant alliance, has a different status. It reflects the fact that capitalism may not be predominant in a social formation, or at least, that capitalism co-exists with other forms of production and class relations. An alliance between the working class and the peasantry may be necessary to bring about a revolutionary transformation.

For Marx, the nationalization of the land was a precondition for the collective ownership of the means of production in socialist agriculture as well as for successful capitalist development. Marx first developed his critique of private property through the lens of humanism; in the *1844 Manuscripts* he presented private property as the basis of alienation. But in concert, Marx sketched out his theory of rent, in which private property in land resulted in "absolute rent," a payment by capital to landlords due to their monopoly ownership of a crucial means of production, which in turn lowered the rate of accumulation of capital in agriculture.[1] Thus private property in land was both a condition of existence and a fetter on capitalist development.

This analysis found its political expression in the *Communist Manifesto* of 1850. The demand for the nationalization of land was one of ten measures to be advocated by the working class as reforms which could be achieved within the formal limits of bourgeois democracy (Carr 1972:9). As such it was a capitalist reform, but one that would provide an important precondition for the transition to socialism. But Marx and Engels later recognized this demand to be at odds with an alliance between the peasantry and working class in either the bourgeois or proletarian revolutions, primarily due to its incompatibility with peasant aspirations.[2]

Socialism would also require a strong material base. Marx's admiration for capitalism in developing the productive forces is well known: capitalist competition unleashed not only an unending chain of technological innovation, but also the concentration and centralization of capital. Marx and Engels assumed that the process of capitalist development in agriculture would be similar to that of industry, leading to the predominance of large-scale scientific farming, and the ruin of the peasantry and its subsequent proletarianization. The process of primitive accumulation and capital concentration would lead to another important precondition for socialist development: a fully proletarianized and socialized workforce. And the contradiction between private ownership of the means of production, private appropriation of the surplus, and a socialized labor process would engender the *objective* basis for the transition from one mode of production to another.

Thus three of the elements of socialist agriculture—the nationalization of land, large-scale scientific agriculture, and a rural proletariat collectively working the means of production—were to be engendered by the process of capitalist development. They would provide the foundation for socialist agriculture and, by the replacement of planning for market forces, allow the efficient allocation of resources and a rapid growth of the marketable output and of accumulation (Ellman 1979). The worker-peasant alliance, by contrast, was a result of Marx and Engels' recognition that the process of capitalist development was uneven and incomplete. Moreover, it reflected their recognition that the transition to socialism depended on subjective factors, the degree of organization of the working class, class alliances, and class struggle.

Marx first focused on the potential for a revolutionary alliance between the proletariat and peasantry in "Class Struggles in France 1848 to 1850," in which the question was viewed as a conjunctural one. The alliance depended on the weight of the peasantry, their degree of organization, and their particular grievances and demands. Out of his analysis of the experience of revolutionary struggle in France in this period, Marx concluded that the proletariat could ally with the peasantry in the bourgeois-democratic revolution; in the socialist or proletarian revolution, it must ally with the rural proletariat.

Engels, in his major historical work of this period, *The Peasant War in Germany* (1850), identified the primary class interest of the peasantry in the anti-feudal struggle. The peasantry was thus a natural ally of the proletariat in the bourgeois-democratic revolution. This insight subsequently led Marx to concede that the proletariat might have to back a program of peasant proprietorship in the democratic revolution when such was an anti-feudal demand (Carr 1972:387).

Later on, Engels recognized that the support of the peasantry would be crucial to the success not only of the bourgeois-democratic revolution but also of the proletarian revolution. Moreover, a socialist program might require the protection of peasant private property. In *The Peasant Question in France and Germany* he struggled with the recognition that "we can win the mass of the small peasants forthwith only if we make them a promise which we ourselves know we shall not be able to keep. That is, we must promise them not only to protect their property in any event against all economic forces sweeping upon them but also to relieve them of the burdens which already now oppress them" (1955:27).

He concluded with what we may call the substantive principle of the worker-peasant alliance:

> when we are in possession of state power we shall not even think of forcibly expropriating the small peasants . . . as we shall have to do in the case of the big landowners. Our task relative to the small peasant consists, in the first place, in effecting a transition of his private enterprise and private possession to co-operative ones, not forcibly, but by dint of example and the proffer of social assistance for this purpose. (Ibid:28)

It is perhaps because of the thorniness of building a worker-peasant alliance on a program based on the abolition of private property that Marx began to favor the possibility of constructing socialism on the basis of the precapitalist peasant commune. As Teodor Shanin (1983) and others argue convincingly, Marx devoted a good deal of attention in the latter part of his life to conditions in rural Russia and the debate among Russian populists and Marxists concerning the possibility of skipping a stage of capitalist development and building socialism directly on the basis of the Russian peasant commune, the *mir.*

While Marx and Engels' views on the nature of the *mir* fluctuate over the 1875 to 1894 period, their writings present a fairly conclusive answer to the theoretical question: a noncapitalist path of socialist development was indeed possible. This is stated most unequivocally in the Preface to the Second Russian edition of the *Manifesto of the Communist Party* (1882): "If the Russian revolution becomes the signal for proletarian revolution in the West, so that the two complement each other, then Russia's peasant communal land-ownership may serve as the point of departure for a communist development" (Shanin 1983: 139).

One of the important implications of this view, although not developed by Marx or Engels, is in terms of the nature of the alliance between the proletariat and peasantry. For if Russia was "to skip a stage" and proceed as a result of the revolution to build socialism, capitalist development would not yet have created a proletariat of significant size or strength, and the task of socialist construction, by default, would have passed to the peasantry.[3]

The Dictatorship of the Proletariat and Peasantry

It is now a fact of history that most socialist revolutions have taken place in countries where the peasantry form the majority of the population. In this regard, the small, peripheral economies of the third world differ little from the Russian case. In the first decade of the century, 90 percent of Russia's population was rural, and agricultural activities contributed approximately 50 percent of national income (Carr 1972:24). In Russia, as in the third world, the socialist revolution depended critically on the support of the peasantry.

This makes Lenin's work on the "agrarian question" particularly significant. For Lenin elevated the concept of the worker-peasant alliance from a tactical consideration to a theoretical innovation within Marxism.[4] He first elucidated the concept in 1905, in "Two Tactics of Social Democracy in the Democratic Revolution," where he called for the establishment of a "revolutionary-democratic dictatorship of the proletariat and peasantry" in the context of the bourgeois-democratic revolution. Lenin did not simply discover the peasantry in the course of the first (1905) Russian revolution (Levine 1982). But in the 1895– 1905 period he viewed the worker-peasant alliance primarily as an anti-feudal alliance. Thus in "The Worker's Party and the Proletariat" (1901) he argued that the Social Democratic program must include such anti-feudal demands as the abolition of redemption payments and the restitution of the lands of which the peasantry had been deprived in the tsar's 1861 agrarian reform (the so-called cut-off lands). He also noted that the party's work in the countryside must include the establishment of peasant committees so that its work would be focused on the concrete and most pressing needs of the peasantry (Lenin 1971:14).

In "To the Rural Poor" (1903) Lenin gave his first full explanation of the role these committees could play in developing the class struggle in the countryside as well as in the worker-peasant alliance. The peasant committees were to be elected at the village or district level and represent each class segment in the countryside (including the middle and rich peasantry). They were to be at least relatively autonomous from the party and formulate their own demands based on local conditions:

> No one knows better than the peasants themselves what bondage oppresses them. No one will be able to expose the landlords, who to this day live by keeping the peasants in thrall, better then the peasants themselves. The peasant committees will decide what cut-off lands, what meadows, what pastures, and so forth, were taken from the peasants unfairly; they will decide whether those lands shall be expropriated without compensation, or whether those who bought such lands should be paid compensation at the expense of the high nobility. . . . The peasant

committees will rid the peasants of interference by officials; they will show that the peasants themselves want to and can manage their own affairs; they will help the peasants to reach agreement among themselves about their needs and to recognise those who are really able to stand up for the rural poor and for an alliance with the urban workers. The peasant committees will be the first step towards enabling the peasants even in remote villages to get on to their feet and to take their fate into their own hands. (Ibid.:70)

Lenin never wavered in his view of the proletariat as the *vanguard* of the worker-peasant alliance. But what is striking about this work is the degree of autonomy that he gives to the peasantry in formulating its own demands. Moreover, in this piece, he commits the party to what we previously termed the substantive principle of the worker-peasant alliance: "the Social-Democrats will never take away the property of the small and middle farmers who do not hire labourers" (ibid.:50). He points out that the interest of the Social Democrats is only in expropriating the property of landowners, "those who live on the labour of others."

In the pre-1905 period, debate raged within the party not only over the revolutionary potential of the peasantry, but over the political feasibility of land expropriation, thought by most Social Democrats to be too divisive (Haimon 1967:145; Baron 1963:229). Events during 1905 proved beyond a doubt that the Russian peasantry was a revolutionary force, and settled the debate over the character of the peasantry in Lenin's favor. From the beginning of that year, in concert with the urban industrial strikes, the peasantry was seizing land, including landlord's land. The Social Democratic party quickly had to adjust its program to catch up with the revolutionary peasantry.[5]

By 1906 debate within the party concerned forms of land tenancy in the bourgeois-democratic revolution. While Lenin argued forcefully for the nationalization of all land as an important precondition for socialist agriculture, he insisted that the inclusion of this demand in the party platform must be contingent on its coming from the peasantry. In a most important footnote to his draft agrarian program Lenin noted that he had attached a variant to the nationalization clause in order "to remove any idea that the workers' party wants to impose upon the peasantry any scheme of reforms against their will and independently of any movement among the peasantry. . ." (ibid.:132).[6]

The Peasantry's Agrarian Reform, 1917–18

After almost a ten-year lull, peasant mobilization began again several months after the fall of the tsar in February of 1917. As in 1905, the peasant land takeovers were synchronized with, but autonomous from, the development of industrial strikes all over Russia, and the growing desertion of soldiers from the front (Wolf 1969:85). The Provisional Government installed in February included the Social Revolutionaries who were placed in charge of the agrarian program. But as the peasant land takeovers escalated over the summer months, the Socialist Revolutionaries refused to declare an agrarian reform due to their support for the war effort. Only the Bolsheviks fully backed the peasant land takeovers as well as an end to the unpopular war.

In April, Lenin announced the strategy that would move the revolution from its first stage, the bourgeois-democratic revolution, to the second stage, the proletarian revolution based on an alliance with the poorest strata of the peasantry (Carr 1972:26). Thesis 6 of the "April Theses" provided for the confiscation of all landlord estates which were to be put in the hands of the soviets of poor peasants and the peasant deputies. But how land was then to be apportioned was left ambiguous, except for a clause that noted that large estates were to be turned into model farms worked under the control of poor peasants.

Meanwhile, the peasantry was already developing its own guidelines for the agrarian reform. The May-June Peasant Congress produced a draft composed of 242 instructions compiled by local peasant deputies. Lenin, commenting on the instructions in an article in August 1917, noted that the majority of the demands followed the Social Revolutionary principles and that the peasants really did want to retain "small-scale" farming (Owen 1963:239–41).

By August the peasantry had begun implementing its own agrarian reform, confiscating and redistributing landed estates; by the end of the year the poor peasantry had moved on to the holdings of the rich peasantry. In October Lenin made good on his promise and simply confirmed the course of events:

> As a democratic government, we cannot ignore the decision of the masses of people, even though we may disagree with it. . . . We trust the peasants themselves will be able to solve the problem correctly, properly, better than we could do it. . . . The point is that the peasants should be firmly assured that there are no more landlords in the countryside and that they decide all questions, and they arrange their own lives. (1971:205)[7]

The Organization of Production in the First Transition

The final Soviet land reform decree, promulgated in February 1918, made clear the purpose of a socialist agrarian program: collectivization. Article 11 stipulated the objective: "To develop the collective system of agriculture, as being more economic in respect both of labour and of products, at the expense of individual holdings, in order to bring about the transition to a socialist economy" (see Carr 1972:44).

The specific form that collective agriculture would take, however, and how it was to be achieved, could only be determined by actual practice. Lenin was well aware that the path of collectivization would be difficult in underdeveloped Russia. He often stressed that the transition to socialist agriculture would in fact be different in countries where large-scale agriculture predominated vis-à-vis countries characterized by small-scale peasant production (1971:211, 243, 260). In the former, where land was already concentrated and worked by a rural proletariat, collectivization required only the expropriation of the capitalists; the farms could be worked by either the state or a cooperative organization of the workers. In the latter, by contrast, the process of collectivization had to be gradual and go through a series of stages (ibid.:244). Peasants had to be shown the superiority of large-scale farming by proof of example. Only then would they *voluntarily* pool their individual plots and move gradually toward more advanced forms of cooperation.

Lenin viewed collectivized agriculture as composed of both state farms and production cooperatives. Nowhere in his writings are state farms considered to be a "higher form" of collective enterprise than cooperatives. In fact, in the prerevolutionary period his writings include only production cooperatives in the description of the future form of collective agriculture. For example, in "To the Rural Poor" (1903) Lenin notes that "when the working class has defeated the entire bourgeoisie, it will take the land away from the big proprietors and introduce *co-operative farming* on the big estates, so that the workers will farm the land together, in common, and freely elect delegates to manage the farms" (ibid.:66).

However, the draft agrarian programs of the Social Democratic party in this period usually contained a plank providing for the most advanced scientific farms to become model state farms. And this was maintained in the 1917 decree on land.

In one of Lenin's major writings in the postrevolutionary period, "Economics and Politics in the Era of the Dictatorship of the Proletariat," he notes the place of both state farms and production cooperatives in the transition:

> The state organisation of large-scale production in industry and the transition from "workers' control" to "workers' administration" of factories and railways—this has, by and large, already been accomplished; but in relation to agriculture it has only just begun ('state farms', i.e., large farms organised by the workers' state on state-owned land). Similarly, we have only just begun the organisation of various forms of co-operative societies of small farmers as a transition from petty commodity agriculture to communist agriculture. (Ibid.:297)

Lenin's most forceful statement on the importance and role of production cooperatives is to be found in the article "On Co-operation" written in 1923. It is apparent from his comments that he was concerned with the negative attitude of many of his comrades toward the cooperative movement, believing that insufficient resources had been directed toward this sector. The New Economic Policy had been underway for more than a year, and Lenin stressed that cooperatives were now more important to the transition than ever. In order to be sure that cooperatives not be written off as a form of capitalist cooperation, Lenin goes to great pains to locate them theoretically in the transition to socialism:

> Under our present system, co-operative enterprises differ from private capitalist enterprises because they are collective enterprises, but do not differ from socialist enterprises if the land on which they are situated and the means of production belong to the state, i.e., the working class. This circumstance is not considered sufficiently when co-operatives are discussed. It is forgotten that owing to the special features of our political system, our co-operatives acquire an altogether exceptional significance . . . co-operation under our conditions nearly always coincides fully with socialism. (Ibid.:372–73)

Lenin continually returned to the importance of organizing the cooperatives on a *voluntary* basis. In his report on work in the countryside at the Eighth Party Congress in 1919, he warned about the dangers of using coercion to organize the peasantry: the task is to persuade the peasantry to form associations, to "gain the peasants' voluntary consent," and this is done by practical deeds (ibid.:267). Lenin later commented that the party congress confirmed that "there can be no question of forcibly imposing socialism on anyone" (ibid.:309).

What followed in the Soviet Union is well known. Stalin's forced collectivization of the peasantry, and its costs, are now history (Lewin 1968). In a period of seven years, between 1928 and 1935, 94 percent of Soviet farmland was collectivized (Nove 1982:150, 174). Subsequent socialist agrarian reforms, in China and Eastern Europe, would conform more closely to the gradual vision of collectivization of the Marxist classics.

In all of the early socialist agrarian reforms land initially was redistributed to the peasantry, conforming to what perhaps may be called the "classical" path of socialist agrarian transformation. But in contrast to the Soviet Union, in China and Eastern Europe land was not nationalized; it was redistributed to the peasantry as private property, and collectivization proceeded by stages. In Poland and Yugoslavia, private peasant property to this day predominates. In none of the socialist countries, with the exception of the Soviet Union, do state farms predominate over production cooperatives in terms of the distribution of farmland.

What is perhaps not well understood, and important to our subsequent analysis, is the fact that the Soviet industrialization drive was based on production cooperatives (the *kolkhoz*) (Dunman 1975). Not until the late 1950s was emphasis placed on building the state farm sector. The view of state farms as the "highest form of socialist agriculture" is part of the Stalinist legacy. As I have tried to demonstrate, however, it is not part of the legacy of Marx, Engels, and Lenin on the agrarian question.

The Transformation of Land Tenure and Property Relations

Apart from the African countries, few of the small peripheral countries have found it possible, or necessary, to nationalize all land as part of a socialist transformation.[8] More common has been for the state to intervene in the regulation of property relations through an agrarian reform that limits the amount of land any individual may own as private property. Most often, the expropriated land is "nationalized"; it constitutes a new form of social property, what we will term "agrarian reform property." What distinguishes such property from bourgeois private property is that the land cannot be sold; it is no longer a commodity. Usually, the land can be inherited, but not subdivided.

As Table 1 shows, seven countries, six of them African, have nationalized all land, in each case, due to the legacy of precolonial and precapitalist tenure patterns. In all except southern Ethiopia and Yemen, where feudal tenancy predominated, precolonial land tenancy had been based on some form of communal land ownership. Colonial rule had resulted in the gradual alienation of the African majorities from the lands to which they held hereditary tenure.

For example, in Mozambique and Angola, land nationalization was both a vindication of precolonial norms of land tenure and a direct response to the particular form of agrarian capitalist development. Under Portuguese colonial rule, Africans in both Mozambique and Angola were restricted to "native reserves"; these lands were part of the state domain and ceded in usufruct to tribal chiefs for redistribution. The best lands, of course, became the private property of Portuguese settlers who developed them as capitalist farms (Guerra 1979:96). In Mozambique, upon independence in 1975, all land was "socialized" but private property was to be respected (Wuyts n.d.:6). The massive exodus of Portuguese settlers (90 percent fled) resulted in the nationalization of their properties. In Angola, private property was to be protected, but here as well, the exodus of the settler colony resulted in their land being nationalized by default (Kaplan 1979:119). In both countries land, in effect, became the domain of the state.

In Cuba, Nicaragua, and Algeria, the nationalization of some land has been carried out in quite a different context. Partial land nationalization

Table 1
Agrarian Reforms in the Socialist Third World

Country	Land Nationali- zation	Land Expropriations	Land Redistribution*
Vietnam (1954)	None	1954: landlord class	peasant property
Cuba (1959)	Substantial	1959: 402 ha. ceiling 1963: 67 ha. ceiling	state & peasant prop. state & peasant prop.
Algeria (1962)	Some	1963: settler farms 1971: public lands, absentee landlords	state farms prod. coops
Syria (1963)	None	1963: 55/300 ha. ceiling, public land	peasant prop. & agrarian reform lands
Yemen (1967)	All	1970: anti-feudal; 20/40 ha. ceiling	peasant holdings
Tanzania (1967)	All	1967: settler farms ujamaa	state farms peasant holdings
Somalia (1969)	All	1975: ceilings	state farms
Ethiopia (1974)	All	1975: anti-feudal; 10 ha. ceiling commercial farms	peasant holdings state farms & coops
Guinea Bissau (1974)	All	1975: no one to expropriate	
Mozambique (1975)	All	1975: settler farms	state farms
Angola (1975)	All	1975: settler farms	state farms
Nicaragua (1979)	Some	1979: Somoza farms 1981: 35/350 ha. ceilings	state farms prod. coops & peasant holdings
Zimbabwe (1980)	None	1980: unused, abandoned land, absentee ownership	peasant property

*Refers to predominant beneficiary; the term "peasant holding" is used to distinguish agrarian reform titles from peasant private property.
ha. = hectare.

occurred in response to particular processes of capitalist development: the concentration of land in the hands of foreign (Cuba) or settler (Algeria) capital or, in the Nicaraguan case, by a dictator.

While significant amounts of prime agricultural land were nationalized in Cuba, Nicaragua, and Algeria, all three countries also protected private property, within the limits on landholdings provided for in the agrarian reform legislation. In the Cuban case, however, capitalist private property was effectively eliminated by the 1963 agrarian reform law, which provided for the expropriation of all landholdings above sixty-seven hectares in size. Individual peasant farmers, however, were assured of their right of land ownership. Indeed, the Cuban agrarian reform created an important sector of smallholding property owners.[9]

In both Nicaragua and Algeria, not only peasant property, but also capitalist property was protected by the agrarian reform. The 1979 Statute of Rights and Duties of Nicaraguans guaranteed the right to private property as long as it functioned in the social interest. This was further amplified in the 1981 agrarian reform, which not only guaranteed the right of private property, but did not set a size limitation on holdings that were efficiently managed as capitalist enterprises.

In the case of Algeria, private property was never viewed as problematic (Leca 1975:134). But under the 1971 agrarian reform law, lands owned by absentee landlords could be expropriated, as could "excess" lands, loosely defined as holdings capable of generating an income three times that of a permanent worker on a state farm (Sutton 1978:54). Capitalist enterprises (other than the French estates nationalized in 1962) have not been affected by the agrarian reform law.

Syria's agrarian reform has also been compatible with private capitalist property. The agrarian reform of 1963 expropriated land above certain ceilings, which was redistributed as private and agrarian reform property (Havens 1980). Zimbabwe has also sought to protect private property (that of the white settler community) while generating a new sector of African property holders through the agrarian reform. According to 1980 decrees, the state was first to redistribute unused or abandoned land and absentee landlord holdings; subsequently underutilized land would be affected and redistributed (Cleary 1980:30).

Interestingly, North Vietnam, which has achieved the highest degree of collectivization of agriculture among the third world countries here examined, neither nationalized land nor prohibited the existence of private property in land. The 1954 agrarian reform primarily expropriated the lands of the landlord class which was then redistributed as individual private property to some 8 million peasants (Moise 1976). A number of countries have created what we termed "agrarian reform property," property distributed through an agrarian reform which guarantees inheritable usufruct rights but which cannot be freely sold.

In Algeria, Nicaragua, Syria, Ethiopia, and Yemen, this form of property has been distributed both to individuals and to collectives of various sorts.

This brief review illustrates the great diversity of agrarian reform experiences, given such different initial conditions. Land nationalization has come about in quite a different circumstance than originally envisioned by Marx, however. Rather than removing a fetter on capitalist production, land nationalization has often been a vindication of precapitalist landholding systems. Here, Marx's insights concerning the Russian *mir* seem particularly relevant; precapitalist collective ownership can provide a precondition for socialist agrarian development.

Where agrarian capitalism was well developed, nationalization of *all* land was impossible. The significance of capitalist private property in these transitions has been quite heterogenous. While on the one hand, the existence of capitalist agriculture has facilitated the partial nationalization of land (and subsequent creation of state farms), under specific circumstances (settler, foreign, and dictator owned lands), the strength of the agrarian bourgeoisie has often been sufficient to prevent a more fundamental restructuring of property relations.

The Organization of Production: State Farms in the Third World

In few of the small, peripheral countries in transition is the majority of land cultivated collectively. As Table 2 shows, only in Cuba and Vietnam do collective forms (state farms and production cooperatives) predominate over private, individual production. These are followed by Algeria and Nicaragua, where approximately one-third of the cultivable land is farmed in collective forms; interestingly, both these countries also feature an important agrarian capitalist sector. In the socialist countries of Africa, individual peasant production predominates.

Within the socialized sector of production, the relatively more important place of state farms vis-à-vis production cooperatives is apparent, accounting for a significantly larger share of the cultivated area in Cuba, Algeria, Nicaragua, Angola, Mozambique, Somalia, and Ethiopia. Production cooperatives constitute the bulk of collective production in only Vietnam and Tanzania. In order to examine the conditions that have given rise to this emphasis on state farms and its implications for the transformation of social relations, we first consider the Cuban case, where state farms dominate the agricultural sector.[10]

Cuba: Why State Farms?

Of the countries here reviewed, only in Cuba are state farms explicitly viewed as the goal of socialist agriculture. At the First Party

Table 2
Distribution of Cultivable Land
According to Organization of Production (in percent)

Country	State Farms	Prod. Coops	Service Coops	Peasant Holdings	Peasant and Capitalist Farms	Total
Vietnam	5	90		5		100 (1975)
Cuba	80	11		9		100 (1983)
Algeria	27	14			59	100 (1980)
Syria	1		23		76	100 (1977)
Yemen	10		70		20	100 (1980)
Tanzania		8		92		100 (1979)
Somalia	4		9		87	100 (1980)
Ethiopia	4	3		93		100 (1981)
Mozambique	4	1		93	2	100 (1982)
Angola	12	2		86		100 (1980)
Nicaragua	24	6	16		54	100 (1983)

Sources:

Vietnam: Bhaduri (1982); the bulk of peasant holdings are cooperative lands distributed for family farming.

Cuba: Benjamin et al. (1984); majority of peasant holdings belong to credit and service cooperatives.

Algeria: Kifle (1983); only 72 percent of the land noted above in production cooperatives was farmed collectively in 1977 (Pfeiffer 1981b).

Syria: Havens (1980).

Yemen: derived from Halliday (1983); production cooperatives reported to be growing in number out of the service cooperatives.

Tanzania: Ellis (1982) estimate of use of village lands only; there are some state farms encompassing approximately 1 percent of cultivable lands (Kaplan 1978).

Somalia: Kifle (1983); some production cooperatives are included among the service cooperatives.

Ethiopia: Kifle (1983); majority of peasant holdings belong to peasant associations and service cooperatives.

Mozambique: Kifle (1983).

Angola: Government of Angola (n.d.); there are still a few capitalist settler farms.

Nicaragua: CIERA (1984).

Congress in 1975, Fidel noted that there were two roads toward "superior forms of production": state plans and production cooperatives. While thereafter production cooperatives were to be promoted, he made clear that state farms were the far superior path. State farms were considered a more advanced form of socialist agriculture because they represented ownership by all of the people; the wealth they generated would benefit the society as a whole.[11]

At the time of the 1959 revolution, Cuba was the classic agro-export economy. The agricultural sector was characterized by extreme land concentration (farms greater than 500 hectares held approximately 50 percent of the cultivable land), and dominated by sugarcane plantations and cattle estates producing for export (Pollitt 1982:Fig. 1). The preponderate place of the agricultural proletariat within the economically active population (EAP) in agriculture distinguishes Cuba from other third world socialist countries at the eve of revolution. According to the 1953 census, agricultural workers comprised 61 percent of the agricultural EAP (ibid.:Table 1). While this may be an overestimation, as Pollitt has argued, it is clear that the majority of agricultural semi-proletarians and proletarians were dependent upon the sugar sector for their livelihood.

The 1959 agrarian reform law set a ceiling of 400 hectares on agricultural properties, but this could be doubled for highly productive farms, partially exempting the sugar estates, many of which were U.S.-owned, from total expropriation. The hostile U.S. reaction to the Cuban revolution, summarized briefly by the cutting off of Cuba's sugar quota in the U.S. market and then the aborted Bay of Pigs invasion, led to the total expropriation of U.S.-owned agricultural enterprises. As a result, almost three-fourths of the land expropriated under the 1959 reform had not been foreseen in the law itself (Benjamin et al. 1984:ch. 12).

The 1959 law provided for the expropriated estates to remain intact and to be worked as cooperatives. There was little question of dividing up these estates, due both to the perceived economies of scale of large-sized production units and the fact that it was not a demand of the rural proletariat (MacEwan 1981:48; Rodriguez 1965:64). What initially emerged on the expropriated estates were cooperatives based on wage labor, with managers appointed by the Agrarian Reform Institute (INRA). While in theory the members were to elect their own councils to play a role in the administration of the enterprises, participatory forms of management never were consolidated.

Among the reasons cited for the subsequent decision to operate the large estates as state farms rather than as production cooperatives was the fear that the heterogeneous production conditions and productivity of the estates would lead to severe inequality among rich and poor cooperatives. Moreover, it was felt that cooperatives run by permanent workers would do nothing to ameliorate the seasonal unemployment problem of temporary workers, exacerbating income inequalities among the rural workforce. Further, the lack of experienced administrators and technicians at the local level favored the centralization of production decisions within INRA. This, combined with the state's concern to assure sufficient exports and food supplies, led to the conversion of the cooperatives into state farms by late 1961 (MacEwan 1981:49–51).

With the nationalization of banking, external commerce, and the major share of transportation, construction, and industry, the bulk of the Cuban economy was in state hands by 1962 (ibid.:70). The 1963 agrarian reform law responded to the growing tension between state control of the economy and the continuing importance of capitalist producers in agriculture. On the one hand, the state did not want to build up the economic strength of this sector, and was thus not providing the incentives or even agricultural supplies to stimulate it. On the other hand, medium-sized farmers controlled some 20 percent of the farmland and should have been producing an important share of foodstuffs and export crops. Another issue was that this sector relied on wage labor, which was increasingly viewed as incompatible with the now explicitly socialist character of the Cuban revolution. Ideologically, these farmers inhibited the organization of small farmers by their vocal denunciations of the threat they perceived to private property. These tensions were finally solved by their expropriation in 1963 (ibid.:71; Rodriguez 1965:65–66). As a result of the implementation of the 1963 agrarian reform law, the state sector mushroomed to occupy 63 percent of the cultivable land. But the private peasant sector gained as well, and the government reiterated its commitment to the maintenance of a smallholder sector in agriculture.

In the late 1960s, in the face of the renewed emphasis on increasing sugar exports, the state began pressuring independent farmers to sell or lease their land to the state (Eckstein 1981:192). Social and demographic factors (old age, lack of heirs, labor shortage) also encouraged private farmers to sell their land to the state (Valdes Paz 1980:94), and between 1967 and 1970 the state purchased 24,000 farms; by 1982 the state sector had expanded to 80 percent of the cultivated land area (Pollit 1982:12). As a result of the policy decision to support production cooperatives, the state sector has stabilized in size in the 1980s.

Workers within the state farm sector are organized into the Confederation of Cuban workers (CTC). While formal mechanisms for worker participation in decisionmaking on the state farms are limited, some important changes have been noted in labor union activity in the 1970s as compared to the 1960s. In the late 1960s unions, to the degree that they existed at all, were institutions of the state, rather than organizations of workers; their main activity was to maintain labor discipline and encourage workers to work harder (MacEwan 1981:152). As part of the general reemphasis on mass organizations in the 1970s, the CTC began to play a greater role, at least in national level decisionmaking (Carciofi 1983). The first trade union congress in 1973, for example, provided an occasion for workers at all levels to discuss such policy issues as work incentives and wage structures. However, it is unclear from the availble literature how much this reorientation has resulted in greater participatory structures within the state farms themselves.

Nicaragua: Somoza Property and People's Property

The constitution of Nicaragua's state farm sector was facilitated by Somoza's concentrated landholdings. Not only was there national unity behind the confiscation of the properties owned by Somoza, his family, and close associates, but there was near unanimity that these farms should be run by the state in the interests of the "whole people."

The confiscation of the Somocista properties began during the last months of the war, largely as a result of land takeovers organized by the Rural Workers' Association (ATC). The farms were initially farmed collectively by landless peasants under FSLN direction in order to assure the provision of foodstuffs for the armed struggle. Upon the Sandinista victory on July 19, 1979, the farms were officially confiscated and reorganized as state farms under the direction of the newly created Nicaraguan Institute for Agrarian Reform (INRA).

Dividing these properties up into individual holdings was never an issue. First, there was no pressure from the landless peasants and rural workers on the estates to do so. Accustomed to working as wage workers in the agroexport economy, they viewed security of employment as a much more important issue than access to land as direct producers. Second, the majority of the ex-Somocista properties were modern large-scale operations; as in Cuba, it was generally assumed that for reasons of efficiency they would continue to be worked under centralized management.

A potential issue was whether these farms should be organized as production cooperatives or as state farms. The factors that favored their organization as state farms, as in the Cuban case, had to do with their importance in the productive structure of the Nicaraguan economy, and concerns over ameliorating inequalities in the countryside. Nicaragua is an agroexport economy, with the agricultural sector in the prerevolutionary period generating close to 70 percent of the country's foreign exchange, and the ex-Somoza farms, which represented approximately half of the estates over 355 hectares in size and some 20 percent of the nation's farmland, generating an important share of sugar and tobacco exports in particular. And in addition to not generating new differences between permanent and seasonal workers, it was argued that creating a socialized sector would allow the surplus produced on these farms to be directed toward a broader segment of the rural population. As a result, the thrust of agrarian reform efforts in the 1979–81 period focused on the consolidation of the state farm sector, known as the APP (Area of People's Property).

It was initially planned for INRA and the Rural Workers' Association to have joint responsibility for managing the state farms. The ATC quickly organized the permanent state farm workers into unions; the next task was to train rural workers for their future responsibility in participatory decisionmaking within the state enterprises. Worker participation was to be assured through representation in the administration of the enterprises as well as through periodic general meetings of workers and management.

A truly participatory decisionmaking structure was difficult to implement (Ortega 1985). Only in 1983 was a major effort launched to experiment with greater worker participation on a selected number of state enterprises, only to be abandoned in 1984 due to the war effort. Nonetheless, the ATC has been a rather effective representative of rural workers' concerns, demanding social services and access to plots for basic grain production by worker collectives at the state farm level, and participating vigorously in national debates over wage levels, prices, and the pace of the agrarian reform.

Discussion surrounding the formulation of the 1981 agrarian reform law rekindled debates as to whether the agrarian reform should favor state farms or production cooperatives. Those favoring state farms argued that the agroexport sector should be the motor force of accumulation in the transition period. This required heavy investment in modern infrastructure and machinery which would be better managed directly under state control. Others questioned the performance of the state sector in the first two years; while production had largely been reactivated on these farms, organizational and production difficulties remained. The majority felt that the agrarian reform should give priority to production cooperatives over state farms since the former were more participatory structures and were favored by landless and poor peasants (Deere, Marchetti, and Reinhardt 1985).

The agrarian reform legislation (which provided for the expropriation of another 20-40 percent of the nation's farmland) left the issue unresolved. This gave the Sandinista leadership considerable flexibility in responding to rural worker and peasant demands and changing economic, political, and military conditions. By 1982 arguments favoring the expansion of the state sector were heard less frequently as the Sandinistas adopted a more decentralized state structure and allowed the mass organizations considerable autonomy in the shaping of the agrarian reform. Beginning in 1983 state farms that could not be managed efficiently as part of a given productive unit were turned into cooperatives and state farmlands were increasingly given to individual producers. These developments responded to the growing organizational capacity of the mass organizations, the demands of workers and peasants, and also to the military and economic pressures of the counterrevolution.

Algeria: The Rise and Fall of Worker Management

At the time of independence in 1962 French settlers held approximately one-third of the cultivable land, producing cereals, wine, and fruit for the export market (Blair 1969:62); agriculture contributed 81 percent of exports (World Bank 1982:127). These were generally capitalist farms, employing some 10 percent of the EAP (Pfeiffer 1981b:44). In the final year of the liberation struggle the French settlers began to leave *en masse,* creating chaos in the agricultural sector. Rural workers, organized in the Union Générale des Travailleurs Algeriens (UGTA), began seizing the settler farms and estates. These were then organized as cooperatives, largely at the initiative of the workers.

In 1962 the newly independent state attempted to bring these excolonial estates under state control. Apparently, the workers on the cooperative estates resisted, since it was rumored that these would later be resold to Algerian landlords. Finally, workers were granted the right to use the estate land in perpetuity, although property rights passed to the state. *Autogestion,* or worker-management of the estates, was accepted, with production on them to be integrated into a national plan (Leca 1975:131).

The initial structure of these farms suggests that they were highly participatory enterprises. Workers were paid a fixed salary as well as a share of the profits which they themselves determined. The general assembly of the enterprise (made up of all the permanent workers) elected a workers' council which in turn elected a management committee and a president to make the day-to-day farm decisions. The president of the management committee shared ultimate management responsibility with a director appointed by the National Office of Agrarian Reform (Foster and Steiner 1964:24, 62).

According to most accounts, over the years these *autogestion* farms have gradually lost their participatory character as they have become increasingly managed by state-appointed managers and integrated into a centralized planning apparatus. There now appears to be little worker participation in decisionmaking (Pfeiffer 1981a:6; Smith 1975:267; Blair 1969:108).

The end of *autogestion* appears to parallel the general demobilization of the mass organizations and unions after the 1965 coup by President Boumediene (Pfeiffer 1981b:58). The 1965 Chartre d'Alger decreed that the period of combative syndicalism was over; the role of unions in Algeria would be to cooperate with the state. And since 1969 UGTA has been under direct state control (Blair 1969:116). The state farm sector has remained relatively stable in size since the 1960s, and continues to play an important role in the Algerian economy.

State Farms in Angola and Mozambique

In both Angola and Mozambique, the development of the state farm sector responded to the pressing need to organize production on the farms abandoned by the departing Portuguese settlers in 1975. In Angola, Portuguese settlers had held approximately 35 percent of the cultivated land in farms largely devoted to export agriculture (coffee and cotton) (Kaplan 1979:207). In Mozambique, Portuguese settlers, along with other foreign capital, occupied approximately half of the cultivable land. Their property included both large-scale plantations producing for export and modern, capitalist farms oriented toward domestic foodstuff production.

The massive flight of the Portuguese required that the newly independent states move quickly to expropriate the farms and reactivate production. But due to the loss of management and technical skills as well as severe damage to the productive infrastructure in both countries, the cultivable area in state farms is now less than that previously farmed by the Portuguese, occupying 12 percent of the cultivable land in Angola and 4 percent in Mozambique.

Both countries concentrated human and financial resources almost exclusively on the state farm sector in an attempt to reactivate production. In Mozambique, communal villages and production cooperatives had been given initial priority (Roesch 1984:5); but by the 1977 Third Party Congress state farms were established as the focus of the socialist transformation of agriculture (Isaacman 1983:148). It was hoped that by concentrating resources on the state farms, the severe food shortages in the cities could be overcome and the balance-of-payments crises ameliorated.

The 1980s produced a reevaluation of priorities in both countries. In Mozambique, the almost exclusive focus on the state farms produced a crisis in production, due to the lack of attention to the peasantry (Roesch 1984:1). Food imports in 1980 constituted almost 50 percent of total imports. Moreover, while state farms were producing some 56 percent of the marketed output in 1981 this was far below target, and the state farms, characterized by low productivity, were financially insolvent (Isaacman 1983:150). At the 1983 Fourth Party Congress it was decided both to support independent farming and decentralize the state sector (in order to increase efficiency) and to diversify production (in order to generate more year-round employment). Moreover, unproductive state lands were to be redistributed to the peasantry.

A similar trend is evident in Angola, where state farms control a much larger share of the cultivable land than in Mozambique (Wolfers and Bergerol 1983:139). Since 1982 investment on the state farms has been scaled back in favor of individual peasant producers, and planning is being decentralized to take place at the level of the productive unit rather than at the national level (Zafiris 1982:73). Here too, some state land is being redistributed to the peasantry and some state farms converted into production cooperatives (Kaplan 1979).

Neither Angola nor Mozambique advanced very far with respect to worker participation in management of the state farms. In Angola, state farm workers are organized into the National Union of Angolan Workers (UNTA); they comprise 80 percent of all unionized labor in the country (Wolfers and Bergerol 1983:120). The 1976 Law of State Intervention illustrates the initial commitment to worker participation. It provided detailed guidelines for state/worker management on the state farms. Management teams were to be composed of only one state delegate and two worker delegates, who would have collective responsibility for the enterprise. Apparently, this structure was ineffective, because by the next year the law was amended so that a state-appointed director had responsibility for running the firm, charged with following guidelines established by the central planning authority. The management committees were expanded to include more representatives of management, but these had no decisionmaking power; neither did the workers' assemblies which, while still to be convened monthly, were limited to an advisory role.

State farm workers in Mozambique are not unionized. The production councils which are organized in the state enterprises are considered the primary mechanism to engender worker participation and new socialist relations of production. However, the production councils (which have been fairly successful in urban industry) were not organized on the state farms until 1980 (Isaacman 1983:152), before which there was a low level of political mobilization among state farm workers. It was hoped that by extending the production council structure to the rural enterprises both the skill and education level and consciousness of rural workers would be raised, a continuing problem in rural Mozambique.

State Farms or Cooperatives?

This review of the organization of state farms shows that in all except Nicaragua and Algeria, the size of the state farm sector loosely corresponded to the degree of capitalist development on the eve of revolution. What Nicaragua and Algeria share with the other experiences is that what facilitated the constitution of a state farm sector was foreign, settler, or dictator control of a sizable portion of the nation's farmland. While subdivision was never an issue, the question we must ask is why these estates have generally been converted into state farms rather than production cooperatives.

The main argument for state farms has been their importance in the national economy. In the majority of countries, these former capitalist enterprises were central to the agroexport sector. Whether or not they were the base of an agroexport *economy,* their contribution to export earnings was sufficiently significant to support the argument for state control. In Mozambique, Algeria, and Ethiopia, these capitalist farms also produced a disproportionate share of marketable foodstuffs. And, in Nicaragua, Mozambique, and Angola, the devastation of the economy through war and sabotage was another compelling reason for the state to directly assume economic reactivation. Thus, not just balance-of-payments considerations, but assuring a food supply for the cities, have been among the reasons justifying the creation of a state farm sector.

The other major reason for the conversion of these capitalist estates into state farms was that in the majority of cases their conversion into cooperatives was not demanded by the workers. Only in Algeria did a well-organized and mobilized rural proletariat put forth the demand for the conversion of the estates into self-managed farms on a cooperative model. What is important to take into account is that this happened only after the estates had been taken over by their workers and managed by them, apparently successfully, for a period of time.

Thus it is not just rural worker and peasant participation in the revolutionary struggle that produces the demand for economic democracy at the point of production (for in Nicaragua, Angola, Mozambique, and Guinea Bissau, they participated actively as well), but rather, the experience of "learning by doing." This is important because it is precisely the lack of training and preparation of rural workers for self-management which is often cited as the main reason why expropriated capitalist estates cannot be turned into production cooperatives. The role of these excapitalist farms in the economy is usually seen to be too important to leave their productive performance to "chance."

Equity considerations are also important. It is often felt that the adjudication of highly capitalized enterprises to the workers within them would exacerbate income inequalities in the countryside between less and more well endowed enterprises, permanent and temporary workers, and between cooperative members and independent peasant producers. If one assumes a neutral state policy with respect to taxation, pricing, investment, and so on, this certainly could be true; but an interventionist state policy could ameliorate such a result.

Another reason given for conversion to state farms is the lack of sufficient technicians to service a cooperative sector; this is often the justification for the centralization of management and decisionmaking of the state farms under a national planning apparatus as well. But centralization of management and decisionmaking, of course, can only lead to a deemphasis of worker participation in management and decisionmaking.

What is quite disheartening in this review is that it seems that no country in the transition to socialism in the third world has had a successful experience in participatory management. And even more alarming, while most consider worker participation as an integral aspect of the transformation of social relations, few have even experimented with worker participation at the point of production. While the reasons for this lack of attention to worker participation are varied, it raises some fundamental questions about the nature of the state in the transition.

Collectivization and the Peasantry

All of the countries here reviewed view the collectivization of the peasantry as a goal of socialist agriculture. They differ as to the time frame—whether collectivization is to be achieved immediately or evolve gradually—and the means. They also differ tremendously with respect to the initial conditions for such a transformation. My objective here is to analyze the factors that have facilitated or encumbered collectivization as well as peasant participation in the general cooperative movement.

Massive Collectivization Attempts: Vietnam and Tanzania

Only two countries have attempted massive collectivization drives, Vietnam and Tanzania, with widely different results. In Vietnam, within nine years 95 percent of peasant households belonged to production cooperatives, while in Tanzania, a decade after *ujamaa,* collective production was being carried out on perhaps only 8 percent of village land (see Table 2).

The Vietnamese collectivization process represents the most successful in the socialist third world. It was carried out on a voluntary basis, with reasonable peasant enthusiasm, implemented fairly quickly, and resulted in short-term production gains. Nonetheless, the consolidation of production cooperatives as the basis of socialist agriculture in Vietnam has been marked by ups and downs. Twenty-five years later, private, household-based production within the cooperatives is now being officially encouraged.

Collectivization was designed to pass through three gradual stages, similar to the Chinese process. First, mutual aid teams based on labor exchanges between households were to be encouraged to demonstrate the advantages of pooling labor. Second, low-level cooperatives were to be promoted, in which land, tools, and work animals would be pooled, though remaining the private property of the household. The cooperative would remunerate the households for their use. The labor process was to be collective with each member remunerated according to his or her contribution. Third, high-level cooperatives would be established based on the collective ownership of the means of production as well as collective labor; households would no longer derive income from private property.

The land reform carried out between 1954 and 1956 redistributed land according to the principle of equalization of the size of holdings. Given Vietnam's high population density, this resulted in extremely small holdings: the average middle peasant owned .161 hectares, poor peasants, .144 hectares, and laborers .14 hectares (Moise 1976:Table 3). While the lot of poor peasants and laborers had been much improved through the reform, their living standards were still quite low. There was no question of trying to squeeze a surplus from the peasantry; the challenge was how to raise production.

In this land-poor country of intensive rice cultivation, the development of production cooperatives offered a number of advantages. Pooling land would result in less land being wasted on boundaries and small dykes; there could be better use of existing irrigation; and an improved division of labor would allow the mobilization of labor for capital investment—new irrigation and drainage works. It was hoped that greater specialization and more rapid technological development could be achieved.

The peasantry apparently agreed, for by all accounts, the initial process took place relatively smoothly, without physical coercion (White 1983:248). But as Bhaduri (1982:36) stresses, the cooperative movement was essentially a political movement, guided by the party, rather than a spontaneous reaction among the peasantry to perceived benefits. It was conducted according to "the triple principle" of voluntariness, mutual benefit, and democracy, and based on the poor and lower middle peasants who had the most to gain from collectivization.

Voluntary cooperative development may also have been facilitated by the provision in the regulations allowing members to leave the cooperative with their own means of production (if a low-level cooperative) or the right to an average-sized share of land (if a higher level cooperative). In addition, family security was provided for by the equal distribution of 5 percent of the cooperative land to households for garden and animal production.

In 1958 only 4.8 percent of all peasant families belonged to cooperatives. By 1960, 73.4 percent belonged to low-level cooperatives and another 12.4 percent to high-level cooperatives (Vickerman 1982:Table 2). Over 20,000 small hydraulics works were built and as the irrigated crop area increased, so did per capita rice production, providing concrete evidence to other peasants of the benefit of collective work. By 1968 the process of collectivization was virtually complete: 88.1 percent of peasant families were in high-level cooperatives, 6.7 percent still in low-level cooperatives, and only 5.2 percent, independent farmers (ibid.).

The high-level cooperatives are important not just as a productive unit, but also as a political unit. In the absence of a peasant mass association they serve as the primary vehicle for peasant political participation for nonparty members. There have been recurrent drives to assure democratic decisionmaking in the cooperatives. The cooperative general assembly elects by secret ballot all important administrative committees and boards as well as the chief accountant and the manager. The managing committee is the key administrative link to the relevant organs of the state, entering into contracts regarding production targets, the provision of inputs, and state procurement levels. However, the genuine participation of the membership at the cooperative level has not necessarily resulted in influence in agricultural planning within the apparatus or party (Bhaduri 1982:54).

The war both increased the local autonomy of the cooperatives and stimulated family-based farming. The loss of cadres to the war front required an intensified labor effort; many cooperatives resolved this by subcontracting tasks and land to families. White (1983:251) reports that after considerable debate about the significance of family-based farming within the cooperatives, the party finally responded with a new policy that made the alienation of cooperative land illegal and ended its use by individual families. Private trade was also curtailed.

But in 1980, as part of the general economic liberalization, cooperatives were once again encouraged to subcontract their land to individual households or groups of households for cultivation. Despite significant productivity increases since collectivization, per capital food production has decreased substantially from the early 1960s to the late 1970s, primarily due to rapid population growth (Hiebert 1984:6). White (1983:251–58) suggests that during the late 1970s the leadership became increasingly aware of the limits of the cooperative system as the basis for further growth in productivity. Moreover, the new policy also emerged out of a critique of the bureaucratic style of agricultural management which was seen to place "administrative fetters" on economic decisionmaking.

Under the new system, cooperative members negotiate with the cooperative management to produce a specified output on a given amount of land, with the inputs (seed, fertilizers) supplied by the state. Peasants may sell any surplus above this, as well as what they produce on their individual allotment, on the private market. Households are also encouraged to raise their own buffalo and cattle, and to rent them to the cooperative (Wiegersma 1983:102).[12] Over 90 percent of the cooperatives now use the contract system and agricultural production reportedly increased by 20 percent in the first three years of the new policy.

Tanzania's path of socialist development was based on the concept of *ujamaa,* which means "familyhood" in Swahili and implied the creation of communal village production units (Hyden 1980:96).[13] The goal was to transform independent peasant production to communal farming in ten years (McHenry 1979:210). The policy did result in the largest resettlement effort in African history, with perhaps 5 million or more rural Tanzanians moved into villages within ten years (Hyden 1980:130). But this was based on compulsion, and compulsory villagization did not produce collective agriculture.

It is important to note that 94 percent of the Tanzanian population in 1967 lived in rural areas, and 91 percent of the rural population lived in scattered homesteads (McHenry 1979:2, 44). The creation of villages was seen as a prerequisite for rural development, not only to facilitate the provision of social services, but to engender the spatial conditions for cooperation among peasant producers.

In the first two years, the development of ujamaa villages was limited; only 5 percent of the rural population responded favorably to the new policies (McHenry 1979:150). Although the principle of ujamaa stressed self-reliance and popular participation, the lack of trained party cadres for political education and mobilization convinced the government in 1969 to begin offering material incentives including land access (where this was scarce), agricultural supplies and equipment, credit, schools, medical dispensaries, and potable water. Only another 10 percent of the rural population responded, however. Barker (1974:100) explains that the material benefits of villagization were not widely demonstrated and the peasantry remained skeptical of rural socialist policy. Finally, in 1972, it was made compulsory for rural Tanzanians to live in villages. The goal for full implementation was set for 1976, and force was needed to accomplish it. By 1976, 90 percent of the rural population lived in villages.

Each household in the new village was guaranteed a usufruct plot and then expected to provide labor for a communal plot or other community enterprise such as small industries or shops. It was up to each village to determine how land would be distributed between individual and collective production. On average, each household received between two and five acres, sufficient to guarantee their subsistence food requirements. In the villages constituted in the 1974–75 drive, "block" farming was instituted; households received their individual plots side by side in the hopes that this would lead to future collectivization.

Collective farming appears to have been most successful in those villages formed in the 1967–69 period, since these had been formed voluntarily, apparently by people who wanted to experiment with collective forms of production. In the majority of villages, diverse sanctions (usually fines) had to be imposed to force people to carry out communal work. By 1974 some 5,008 villages were in existence but only 7.8 percent were registered as cooperatives. McHenry (1979) reports that registration as a cooperative did not necessarily mean the village constituted a production and marketing cooperative. In a 1974 survey of four regions he found that only one-third of the adults in the villages participated in communal farming or fishing; they averaged only twenty-three days of communal labor per year. Some 40 percent responded that they participated in collective work only because they felt compelled or obligated to do so.

The policy of required communal farming was reversed in 1975, following two bad harvests. The 1975 Villages and Ujamaa Villages Act established communal farming as voluntary, but reaffirmed the aim of encouraging cooperative village industries and shops. It also declared that only those villages with extensive communal farming would be known as ujamaa villages. Ellis (1982:68) estimated that approximately 8 percent of the land under village cultivation was farmed collectively in 1979. But while production cooperatives have not advanced very far in rural Tanzania, it appears that most villages do have some kind of cooperative activity, such as a shop, a grinding mill, or a small communal farm (Holmquist 1983:27).

The effort to explain what went wrong with ujamaa has generated a voluminous literature.[14] Two factors of particular importance are the nature of peasant-state relations and the issue of the relationship between technology and collectivization. Most observers agree that ujamaa was implanted upon the countryside by the state and party with little peasant participation; the net result was a peasantry unconvinced of the benefits of complying with the state's development strategy.

Moreover, what participatory structures had existed in rural areas before ujamaa (district councils and marketing cooperatives) were dismantled as threats to the implementation of central government policy. These were replaced by a new set of village-level political and self-help structures which generated little popular enthusiasm. As Holmquist put it, "bureaucratic initiative inevitably pre-empted peasant initiative" (ibid.). Other observers are more optimistic (Maecha 1982). But in any event the Tanzanian government has been reevaluating the ujamaa experience recently, attempting to revive some of the local structures that had been dismantled in previous years, such as the marketing cooperatives.

The technological issue turns on whether there are economies of scale in rainfed agriculture based on hoe technology that would result in benefits to villagers. Despite such assertions, villagers remained unconvinced. This was compounded by the policy of allowing peasants to farm a private plot for their own subsistence, designating the communal farm as the mode to generate a marketable surplus. Hyden argues that many peasants did try to comply with collective farming but that it conflicted with their need to guarantee subsistence. Few peasants viewed the generation of a surplus as an end in itself; moreover, poorer households could not afford "to gamble with their food supply" (Hyden 1980:115). And since communal farming was given such limited attention, it was unprofitable, discouraging peasants even further.

In comparing the collectivization experiences of Vietnam and Tanzania, the differences in technology and the type of farming system certainly stand out. While in the Vietnamese case, the benefits of economies of scale and division of labor could be readily demonstrated in hydraulic agriculture, in the case of hoe agriculture this is not self-evident. Indeed, mechanization appears here to be a precondition for economies of scale.

Another important difference relates to the pattern of settlement. For not only are villages the primary form of settlement in Asia as compared to much of Africa, but in Vietnam these have traditionally been important socioeconomic units. They often had precisely the kind of collective responsibility for communal activities (such as irrigation works) further developed by collectivization.

But just as important in distinguishing these two experiences was the form and content of peasant mobilization. The Vietnamese certainly had more experienced cadres, trained by the trial and error of the land reform experience. Moreover, they had a clearer class line in a situation where perhaps class differences were more acute and the poorer peasantry had substantial amounts to gain. The process was also sufficiently gradual to prepare the peasantry for each step toward further cooperation and full collectivization.

Looked at comparatively, the Tanzanians attempted to skip a stage—to pass from individual peasant production to full collectivization without the learning process of cooperation among households (Bhaduri and Rahman 1982:4). Moreover, doing so in the context of forced villagization was clearly a factor of alienation rather than of preparation for further cooperation.

Production Cooperatives as a Product of Land Reform: Algeria and Nicaragua

Nicaragua and Algeria are among the countries that have successfully spurred the development of production cooperatives through an agrarian reform. Both have relied upon material incentives to promote collective rather than individual production on agrarian reform lands. But the experience of these two countries differs markedly with respect to the role of autonomous peasant organizations within the cooperative movement.

In Algeria, while plans for an agrarian reform based on "land to the tiller plus cooperativization" was laid out in 1962, it was almost ten years before the program was implemented, by which time, agrarian reform was seen by most analysts to serve the requirements of capitalist, rather than socialist development (Leca 1975:142; Pfeiffer 1981a:6).

In 1971, when the "agrarian revolution" was announced, close to 900,000 peasants were landless or lacked adequate land to reproduce their families (Sutton 1978:10).[15] These were to be the beneficiaries of the reform. By 1974 less than 10 percent of the potential beneficiaries had received land (Pfeiffer 1981a:7).

A wide assortment of cooperatives was created, with the most advanced form being the production cooperative and the lowest, mutual aid societies (Pfeiffer 1981b:167–69). These cooperatives (along with the *autogestion* state farms and private farms) were to be linked by a district-level service and marketing cooperative to facilitate the provision of inputs and sales.

Beneficiaries were required to join a cooperative in order to receive land, but were not allowed to choose which form to join; this was decided by the *Associacion Popular Communal* (Pfeiffer 1981b:131).[16] Production cooperatives were apparently favored, for these constituted 72 percent of the 5,841 cooperatives organized by 1977. While some beneficiaries apparently managed to avoid joining a cooperative, Pfeiffer reports that a significant number of potential beneficiaries did not acquire land precisely because of the requirement that they would be forced to do so. Moreover, the cooperatives also have had quite a high withdrawal rate.

The degree of peasant participation in these cooperatives appears to be minimal. The director of the cooperative is appointed by the state and is charged with assuring that the cooperative's production fits into the national plan. Cooperative members also belong to the National Union of Algerian Peasants which was created in 1971 to mobilize peasants for the "agrarian revolution." But this association appears to be dominated by the larger private farmers. Until 1973, when it was expanded to include agrarian reform beneficiaries and landless peasants, its membership had been restricted to property owners. In that year, 44 percent of the membership owned more than twenty-five hectares of land; this group controlled most leadership positions.

As Pfeiffer argues, it appears that the major effect of this agrarian reform has been to create a large pool of seasonally employed wage workers or urban migrants. Sharecropping, renting, and other precapitalist relations were abolished, yet 90 percent of the potential beneficiaries did not receive access to land. This fact certainly supports the argument that the reform simply bolstered capitalist development in rural Algeria.

Nicaragua's approach to cooperative development differs markedly from that of Algeria in that cooperative development has been carried out at the behest of the rural mass organizations. Not only have they had primary responsibility for organizing both production cooperatives and service and credit cooperatives, but they have effectively represented peasant demands before the state, significantly shaping the course of the agrarian reform.[17]

In the first six months of the revolution, state attention focused almost exclusively on the reactivation of production on state farms, as already described. By early 1980 it was evident that in order to attack the problems of rural unemployment and poverty, as well as of foodstuff production, the agrarian reform had to be broadened. But the Sandinistas' options were constrained by the policy of national unity with the patriotic bourgeoisie, which depended upon government commitment to a mixed economy and private property. A fundamental restructuring of property relations was considered to be impossible at that time.

The Sandinistas, however, had to respond to popular demands for access to land and employment opportunities. And the Rural Workers' Association (ATC) had been leading land takeovers of non-Somocista land. The government tried to respond to these pressures while at the same time reassuring landlords about the commitment to private property. The properties under ATC membership control were expropriated, but it was made clear to the ATC that more land takeovers would not be tolerated. At the same time landlords were required to abide by a new set of land rental regulations which lowered rents by 85 percent and prohibited the eviction of tenants. The government also began to cede, rent-free, unused and underutilized state farm land to groups of workers willing to work the land collectively. The other thrust of Sandinista policy in this period was the diffusion of massive amounts of credit to peasant producers and the new collectives, in an effort to stimulate basic grain production as well as cooperative development.

The task of organizing rural workers and peasants into cooperatives fell upon the ATC with some support from the ministry. The response in rural areas was tremendous: by June 1980 2,512 cooperatives had been organized with 73,854 members, encompassing approximately 60 percent of rural households. Over half of the cooperatives were some form of production cooperative on either state or rented private land. The greatest number of cooperative members, however, were individual peasant producers, members of the 1,184 credit and service cooperatives.

ATC membership also expanded in the process; by June of 1980 it claimed approximately 120,000 members. But this membership was increasingly heterogeneous, ranging from landless proletarians on the state and capitalist farms to medium-sized farmers who employed wage labor, making it difficult for the ATC to attend to the sometimes conflicting demands of this constituency. Finally, in the spring of 1981, the ATC gave birth to a new mass organization, the National Union of Farmers and Cattlemen (UNAG), which later took responsibility for organizing small and medium producers as well as all cooperative members.

UNAG quickly took up the demand for a thorough agrarian reform, protesting a lack of landlord compliance with the land rental decrees, the existence of substantial amounts of idle land, and of decapitalization by landlords. Added to this pressure was the government's concern over basic grain production. The credit program had been relatively successful the previous year in raising peasant consumption levels but marketable output was less than sufficient. It was also becoming apparent that if the production cooperatives were to become consolidated, security of tenure was a precondition.

Discussion of a comprehensive agrarian reform was thus reinitiated, with UNAG and the ATC actively participating, leading to the enactment of the July 1981 agrarian reform law. The law provided for expropriated lands to be distributed to individuals, collectives, and state farms. But it did not prioritize one form of agrarian reform property over another, reflecting the diversity of opinion on this matter.

UNAG had argued forcefully that any form of cooperative association must be voluntary, and that peasants and rural workers should be given the opportunity to choose the form of productive organization they wished. While they viewed production cooperatives as the long-term goal of the transition, they favored a gradual policy, one that meant giving land to peasants as independent producers if they so demanded it. As they saw it, these peasants could be encouraged to join credit and service cooperatives as a first step toward more collective practices.

Other policymakers feared that the distribution of land to individual producers, by emphasizing individual rather than collective interests, might spur the development of capitalist class relations. They argued for a reform in which land would be collective property only, but with peasants allowed to work individual parcels if they so chose. These were termed "cooperatives with dead furrows" and were seen as a middle road between production cooperatives and credit and service cooperatives. Nonetheless, most agreed that priority attention should be given to the development and consolidation of production cooperatives.

The implementation of the agrarian reform law was initially quite slow, reflecting ongoing debate over the organization of production in the reform sector and the consensus that cooperatives should be on a strong organizational footing before receiving land. Moreover, great care was taken to identify and expropriate only those landholdings that fell strictly within the scope of the agrarian reform law in order not to alienate those of the private sector cooperating with the revolution.

Of the agrarian reform land distributed as of October 1982, some 68 percent had gone to production cooperatives, the majority formed on expropriated estates and composed of landless workers and poor peasants. Some of the latter had voluntarily pooled their private parcels into the production cooperative, but production cooperatives formed totally in this way are few.

The internal organization of the cooperatives is quite democratic. The membership elects the cooperative officers and, in some cases, the members of the various commissions (e.g., production, finances, services, etc.). In smaller cooperatives (thirty members or less), every member will sit on one commission, leading to a highly participatory structure. The cooperatives are totally independent of the Ministry of Agriculture. While they receive technical assistance from the ministry, and credit from the National Development Bank, cooperative members themselves draw up their production plans, organize the work process, and decide upon the allocation of the surplus produced.

At the time of the 1982 cooperative census, production cooperatives (CASs) made up 20 percent of the total, while "dead furrow" cooperatives made up 13 percent. The vast majority of cooperative members (63 percent) were independent producers organized in credit and service cooperatives, which made up 45 percent of the total 2,849 cooperatives in existence. Women represented 6 percent of the total cooperative membership of 68,434 (CIERA 1984c).

By the fall of 1982, the agrarian reform process was being increasingly decentralized and at the same time speeded up. Both factors were a response to the defection of much of the agrarian bourgeoisie to the counterrevolution as well as to the military situation. As the intensity of the U.S.-backed contra attacks escalated, the military urged a quicker implementation of the reform to increase the defense capabilities of the war zone. Combined with the pressure for redistribution from the rural organizations, this led to a sharp increase in the pace of expropriation and titling.

While in the first eighteen months only 93,000 hectares had been redistributed, over twice that amount was titled in 1983. By the time of the fifth anniversary of the revolution, in July 1984, the rapid pace of titling had raised the total amount of distributed land to close to 1 million hectares, nearly 20 percent of the cultivable land. At that point 42 percent of the land had gone to production cooperatives, 4 percent to indigenous communities on the Atlantic coast, and 54 percent to individual producers. The total number of households receiving land through the agrarian reform amounted to 45,000, 32 percent of Nicaraguan rural households (CAHI 1984b).

The increased pace of the reform is a clear response to the counter-revolution; but it also reflects Sandinista commitment to popular participation and the role of the mass organizations in shaping the agrarian reform. It is this that differentiates the Nicaraguan agrarian reform from the Algerian: the Sandinistas have created important preconditions for both economic and political democracy, while it is fairly clear that Algeria has not.

Other Collectivization Experiences: Angola, Mozambique, and Ethiopia

Peasant production cooperatives in Angola are currently viewed as equal in status to state farms with respect to socialist collective production. They are to develop on a voluntary basis alongside state farms and smallholdings (which have received state protection). The process of collectivization was initiated in 1978 with the formation of peasant "associations." These could be considered precooperatives, focusing primarily on marketing arrangements. With the amount to be based on individual private landholdings, members were to contribute to a fund to purchase farm equipment collectively.

The formation of the peasant associations got off to a good start. Some 92,000 peasants joined in 1976–77 and by the late 1970s 417,800 peasants were organized in 3,521 associations (Angola n.d.). Initially, the associations had been promoted by Ministry of Agriculture technicians with limited success. Subsequently it was decided that peasants should organize themselves; "rural dynamizers" were chosen from the villages and given a short training course. Going by the response of the peasantry, this approach seems to have been quite successful (Wolfers and Bergerol 1983:141).

The problem soon became that the government was unable to deliver on its promised support. Not only land (which was plentiful) but seed, fertilizer, equipment, and the provision of country stores had been promised; but the means and organization to deliver on these promises were not in place. Consequently, collectives that had been organized began to fall apart and the process of constituting production cooperatives has moved slowly. In 1977, 150 production cooperatives, farming 9,000 hectares, were in existence (Kaplan 1979:207). Subsequently, it was reported that some 60,000 hectares (the bulk coffee plantations) were being farmed collectively, corresponding, perhaps, to some 304 production cooperatives in 1980. The peasant members continued to farm their usufruct parcels outside the cooperatives.

Available reports suggest that the Angolan peasantry has been receptive to the development of cooperative organizations, perhaps as a result of their long experience in collaborative forms of organization during the lengthy independence struggle. More than by peasant resistance, cooperative development has been plagued by the lack of trained cadres as well as the minimal capacity of the state to deliver on technical assistance, means of production, and transportation. And marketing problems at times have been severe (private traders predominate in rural areas). The overwhelming problem that plagues any development effort in Angola is the war being waged against it by South Africa; but these difficulties were compounded by the allocation of scarce human and material resources to the state farm sector, rather than to peasant producers, in the initial years.

Mozambique's approach to the peasantry in many ways parallels the Tanzanian experience. Collectivization of peasant production was to follow from "villagization" which was seen as necessary not only to develop collective forms of work, given the sparsely settled and scattered rural population, but to allow the delivery of basic services to the rural population. But villagization in Mozambique has not proceeded as rapidly as in Tanzania, perhaps because it has been strictly voluntary. In 1982 only 19 percent of the population were in communal villages (Isaacman 1983:Table 4).

Communal villages were initially seen to be the "backbone" of the country's rural development strategy, conceptualized as "integrated economic, social, political and cultural totalities" (Roesch 1984:5). The economic base of the communal village was to be a production cooperative based on collective access to land and collective labor; social services (schools, health centers, etc.) would be built by the villagers around this productive kernel (ibid.:155).

Production cooperatives were to be formed by first promoting the use of collective labor on groups of family plots, leading quickly to production cooperatives and the communal villages. In fact, case studies show that both peasant integration into cooperatives and their movement into communal villages was slow. Peasants appeared to show little enthusiasm for either (Roesch 1984:17; Harris 1980).

Part of the problem was that while the state formally favored cooperative development, few resources were put at its disposal. Neither were trained cadres available to foster cooperativization. Recognizing the limitations of its resources, and the need to quickly solve the impending food crisis, in 1977 FRELIMO decided to concentrate on state farms. Over the next five years, only 2 percent of total state agricultural investment went to the development of production cooperatives. State farms were favored not only with credit, but inputs, machinery, and trained personnel.

This only aggravated the crisis in rural areas, and cooperative development came to practically a standstill. In 1982 only 37,000 farmers (a large proportion of them women) belonged to production cooperatives (Kifle 1983:72; Urdang 1984:12). This represents less than 2 percent of the agricultural EAP. In total, only 229 out of 1,352 communal villages had production cooperatives (Isaacman 1983:Table 7.4).

Many of the cooperatives studied in detail have been found to be quite weak, with a low level of participation of the membership in either collective work or in decisionmaking, leading to general apathy (Harris 1980). Since cooperative members are usually allowed to farm usufruct plots for subsistence purposes, the time dedicated to collective production is oftentimes minimal.

By 1983 peasant production—without inputs, marketing channels, or consumer goods—was in crisis. This crisis of "reproduction of the peasantry," as it is called, was especially severe in the south due to a major flood in 1979 and the drying up of seasonal labor migration possibilities to South Africa (ibid.:28; Wuyts 1981).

FRELIMO recognized that given the present difficulties, collective forms of production would not solve the crisis and that if the peasantry is to deliver adequate levels of agricultural output, it must be supplied with the means to do so (Roesch 1984:36). In 1983 the party thus reoriented its agricultural development strategy to favor the peasantry. The development of production cooperatives, however, was not abandoned; these were to receive increased state support (Isaacman 1983:198).

Perhaps one of the problems in rural Mozambique is that peasants have not been organized into their own mass organization, capable of expressing their needs before the state. It may have been assumed that peasant participation would be assured through the new institutions of self-government—*poder popular*—whereby local assemblies throughout the country would in turn elect district, provincial, and national assemblies. But this form of broader political participation is quite different from being organized on a class basis. Moreover, peasants were to be integrated into the party cells, but their extension into the countryside has been limited and concentrated in a few areas (Isaacman 1978:35). It was also assumed that peasant membership in cooperatives and communal villages would expand rapidly, assuring another form of participation. But given that these did not expand at a rapid rate, one is left with the impression that the period of socialist transition has been characterized by the demobilization of the peasantry.

Ethiopia: Who Will Collectivize?

While peasant collectivization is still incipient in Ethiopia (3 percent of cultivable lands are in cooperatives), the government has set a goal of one-half of the country's cultivated land to be in production cooperatives by 1990 (Cohen 1984:23). The issue at present is whether this will be carried out at the behest of the peasantry or the military.

In order to implement the agrarian reform, the Ethiopian government formed "peasant associations" on a territorial basis (to encompass 800 hectares). Besides land expropriation and its redistribution (based on the principle of equity), the peasant associations were given broad political powers and development duties. They were to establish judicial tribunals to hear land cases (thus substituting for previous state structures and traditional local leaders), build schools, clinics, and other social services (with state support), carry out villagization programs, and establish marketing and credit cooperatives. Initiated with the help of high school and university students (the Zemecha), by 1981 there were 23,497 of these associations with a membership of 5.1 million households (ibid.:9, 16).

Initially, a number of experimental communal farms were set up. These were to be complementary to the individual peasant holdings distributed through the agrarian reform, but by 1978 the number of peasant associations with communal farms, as well as their size, was dwindling (Abate and Teklu 1982:75–80). Only at this point did the state turn its attention to cooperative development. Service cooperatives, grouping a number of peasant associations, were organized, charged with distributing agricultural inputs, machinery rental, grain storage, the operation of consumer stores, and the development of small rural industries. These were seen as an interim step to the development of full production cooperatives.

According to government guidelines, the development of production cooperatives was to pass through three stages, corresponding roughly to the low-level (shared means of production) and high-level (collective ownership of the means) cooperatives of the Vietnamese and Chinese experience, with the highest level resembling the Chinese commune. The government offered fairly strong incentives for collectivization. Production cooperatives receive credit subsidies, tax advantages, and priority access to farm inputs and extension services. Yet as of 1982 only some 1,006 low-level cooperatives had been formed with some 60,000 members (representing only 1 percent of peasant association members). The majority of these had been formed on the excapitalist farms and their membership consists of formerly landless peasants or poor peasants without oxen (ibid.:22–23).

The available literature differs markedly in its interpretation of why production cooperatives have been slow to form on a voluntary basis as well as on the nature of the peasant associations. Cohen, for example, claims that in the south, former tenants want to control their own land, farming it individually, while in the north, peasants "have strong traditional ties to their holdings that are incompatible with group farming approaches" (1984:23). Left-wing critics of the Ethiopian military government, on the other hand, argue that the peasant associations have been taken over by the rich peasantry and that they are simply an organ of state control (Bekele 1982:62–63; Halliday and Molyneux 1982:108).

Yemen: Slow but Steady

In contrast to Ethiopia, in the People's Democratic Republic of Yemen peasant mobilization in the antifeudal reform seems to have maintained its momentum in the period of cooperative development. Here, too, peasants acquired the usufruct of land they formerly farmed as tenants and were urged to join a service cooperative as a first step. The 1972 land law established three kinds of producer cooperatives: mutual aid teams and low-level and high-level production cooperatives. The strategy was similar to that of the Vietnamese, in that peasants were to be urged to gradually but continually move to a higher form of cooperation (Nyrop 1972:121; Halliday 1979:15). Apparently the strategy was successful, for in 1972 there were only twenty-one cooperatives in existence, yet by 1980 there were forty-four, with 40,000 members farming 70 percent of the cultivable land (Ismael 1982:765).

While there is little information on the Yemen experience, comparing it to the other African countries here analyzed suggests the importance of a gradual collectivization process, based on stages leading to growing cooperation. This, plus the importance of a supportive state policy, is also demonstrated by the Cuban experience.

Voluntary Collectivization in Cuba

In contrast to many of the above experiences, Cuba offers a model of successful, voluntary collectivization of the peasantry. As we noted earlier, the 1959 and 1963 agrarian reforms *created* an important small farm sector, holding some 37 percent of the cultivable land (MacEwan 1981:175). Over the next fifteen years, the holdings of this sector would be diminished both through attrition and state policies aimed at containment (Huberman and Sweezy 1969:120–29). However, not until the late 1970s did it become official state policy to encourage these private producers to pool their land into production cooperatives. The peasantry responded quite positively to the new incentives; within five years, over half of all peasant households belonged to production cooperatives.

The National Association of Small Producers (ANAP) was formed in 1961, as an interest group of the beneficiaries of the agrarian reform and other smallholders. According to its bylaws, however, it was integrated into INRA and charged with carrying out many of the functions usually carried out by a ministry of agriculture (Amaro and Mesa-Lago 1971:359). While the general administrator of ANAP was appointed by INRA, the peasant membership did elect its local, regional, and provincial representatives (MacEwan 1981:57). Membership in ANAP was voluntary, but access to services in effect required membership.

In the early 1960s ANAP was charged with credit provision, the supply of inputs, the purchase of peasant production, as well as with organizing various forms of cooperative organizations. While cooperation was viewed as the first step toward an eventual transition to collective forms, little stress was placed on organizing either credit and service or production cooperatives in this early period.

By the mid-1960s the majority of peasant households (60 percent) belonged only to loosely organized peasant associations that facilitated their coordination with ANAP's annual production plans. Credit and service cooperatives claimed 28 percent of peasant households, primarily tobacco and sugarcane producers. Only 3,200 households (3 percent) belonged to some 270 Agricultural-Livestock Societies, where land was worked collectively and profits distributed according to the amount of labor contributed (Amaro and Mesa-Lago 1971:360). The production cooperatives represented a semi-spontaneous peasant movement; yet they were given only erratic official support in this period apparently due to the determination of the government to deny its hostile U.S. neighbor any chance to accuse Cuba of "imposing" collectivization on the peasants (Pollitt 1982:21; Gomez 1983:64; Rodriguez 1965:69).

Various authors suggest that the lack of official support for production cooperatives in the 1960s also had to do with the preference Cuban planners had for state farms as the superior form of organization. Fidel noted as much in his 1977 speech to the fifth ANAP congress: "The truth is that we, and I myself, six years ago still believed in the idea of only one path [to socialist agriculture]. We had not understood reality clearly and the advantages of not using only one path" (quoted in Gomez 1983:157).

In the 1960s it had been assumed that the peasant sector would eventually disappear once the benefits of state farms were apparent in terms of higher productivity and the higher standard of living of the workforce. Only for a brief period in the late 1960s was strong pressure exerted upon peasant producers to encourage them to sell or lease their lands to the state farms. In this period, farmers were increasingly required to plan their production in collaboration with a state farm plan, to work part time on state land, and were prohibited from hiring labor. Private sales of agricultural products were also prohibited. This regulation of peasant sector activities appears primarily to have been designed to increase the supply of labor for the sugarcane export drive and to make available increased acreage for the planned production of foodstuffs (Eckstein 1981:192). It did succeed in reducing the number of peasant producers and expanding the state sector.

In the early 1970s the state once again relaxed its controls over the peasant sector, allowing it to hire labor and carry out private sales. Moreover, there was less pressure exerted on peasants to work on state farms or join plans. As a result, the number of peasant associations integrated to state plans dropped by half between 1973 and 1977 (Eckstein 1981:192–93). Eckstein suggests that the relaxation of controls was a response to strong peasant dissatisfaction and a recognition that the private farms were more productive than state farms in the production of labor and quality-intensive crops.

A new strategy to deal with the peasantry was clearly needed. At the First Party Congress in 1975 Fidel offered two roads toward superior forms of production: peasant integration into state farms or the development of production cooperatives. As noted previously, state farms were still considered the superior road for theoretical reasons, but the development of production cooperatives was from now on to receive full support (Gomez 1983:69).

The theses emanating from the Party Congress were discussed by the ANAP membership over the subsequent year, and production cooperatives (CPAs) were officially adopted as a priority for the organization in 1977. Great emphasis was placed on the need for this pooling of private holdings to be voluntary in nature (Pollitt 1982:21; Gomez 1983:165). Regulations were adopted governing the independent valuation of land and means of production, for these cooperatives would be immediately what the Vietnamese would call "high-level cooperatives." Guidelines for self-management and democratic participation were also approved.

The state provided a very strong package of incentives for peasants to join the production cooperatives, including preferential access to equipment, inputs, and lower interest credit as well as tax advantages. For the first time, the social security system (which guarantees a fixed income in old age, death insurance, and maternity leave) was extended to these farmers. Another important incentive was priority access to construction materials for the members to build what are termed "agricultural communities," previously built for workers on state farms. These are full service communities, with a school, daycare facility, laundry, store, recreational facilities, besides good quality housing with electricity, indoor sanitary facilities, and so on.

Peasant women were often among the most interested in pooling their private plots to join the production cooperatives because of the benefits offered them and their families. The agricultural communities potentially ameliorated the burden of housework and childcare. Moreover, women were guaranteed their place as full members of the cooperatives with the right to employment and their own incomes (Deere 1984; Gomez 1983:105–8).

It is impressive how quickly the number of production cooperatives has grown. In 1977 there were only 44 of these; two years later there were 725. By 1983 there were 1,480 with 78,000 members, 26 percent of whom were women. The production cooperatives in 1983 covered 53 percent of the land in the private sector; the goal is that by 1990, 90 percent of the private farmland will be so organized.

Benjamin et al. (1984) report that the production cooperatives have thus far been a success, most showing profit whereas the state farms continue to run at a loss. They suggest that this is due to two factors: motivation and democratic participation in decisionmaking.

The Lessons of Collectivization

What can be learned from this broad range of experience? The most salient feature of *voluntary* collectivization is that it must make economic sense to the peasantry. As Engels warned almost a century ago, the peasant smallholder will pool his or her plot when, by show of example, it makes sense to do so. In the particular conditions of Vietnam, the peasantry stood to gain through economies of scale at a low level of technological development, due to the specific features of the farming system. These advantages have not been repeated elsewhere in the absence of mechanization. In the Cuban case, the possibility of mechanization, along with other strong economic incentives, is what appears to have made collectivization attractive to the peasantry after twenty-five years of revolution.

Another strong incentive for production cooperatives is access to land that already constitutes a modern productive unit, particularly excapitalist farms. Where these have been adjudicated to landless workers and poor peasants, such as in Nicaragua, and on a more modest scale in Ethiopia, Angola, and Mozambique, there has been little pressure for subdivision.

Economic incentives provided by the state and potential economic benefits from economies of scale may be necessary conditions for the formation of production cooperatives, but neither is sufficient. The political aspects of the process have certainly been central to successful collectivization efforts, whether due to the role of the party (and its numerous peasant cadres) in Vietnam or autonomous rural organizations in Nicaragua. What seems to fail is collectivization directed by the state alone, without sufficient party or peasant organization.

The Vietnamese "stages" model allowed the peasantry to gain confidence in cooperative forms and democratic processes, while the party provided leadership toward the goal. Many of these experiences seem to get "stuck" at the stage of service cooperatives, particularly when these are structurally an agency of a ministry of agriculture. What has to be kept clearly in mind is that receiving credit or inputs *from* the state is not necessarily a cooperative practice, one that fosters participatory democracy or builds a new social relation. Receiving a specified sowing plan from the state is also not the equivalent of collective decisionmaking or praxis. The first stage, mutual assistance, does seem to play a very important role in fostering cooperative practices where this has been tried.

Nor has it worked very well to attempt to skip stages, as in Tanzania, where the peasantry was expected to go from independent production to a fully collective form without experiencing successive collective practices. On the other hand, if a process is too slow, or given insufficient state attention, the danger of demobilization of the peasantry arises, as occurred in Mozambique. What emerges from these comparative experiences is the thin line that must be traversed between a continuous, yet gradual, process of collectivization and state support, but not control, of cooperative development.

Organization of Socialist Agriculture and Worker-Peasant Participation

This review has, above all, illustrated the tremendous diversity of experience in attempts to build a socialist agriculture. It has also made clear the difficulty shared by each: building socialist agriculture on a noncapitalist base.

In retrospect, Marx and Engels' theorization of capitalist development providing certain preconditions for socialist development is most insightful. At the micro level, the socialization of the agrarian capitalist enterprise is certainly an easier task than the socialization of individual peasant producers. Nonetheless, collective ownership of the means of production does not necessarily ensure economic and political democracy at the point of production or in the society at large.

One of the most difficult theoretical and policy issues is in fact what constitutes socialist relations of production and how these are expressed in the relationship between the micro (productive enterprise) and macro (societal) level. The basic issue has usually been defined in terms of whether state farms or production cooperatives better serve the purpose of social accumulation. But just as important is which organizational form better fosters new social relations of production, particularly if one considers participatory democratic norms integral to this goal.

As we have seen, the majority of postrevolutionary countries in the third world have favored state farms, due to the importance within the economy of the expropriated capitalist farms. The argument for state farms is that they are more easily integrated into a national planning apparatus, assuring state control over the generation of a marketable surplus.

It is useful to contrast here the formal differences between state farms and production cooperatives. In a state farm, wages are a cost of production and the state directly appropriates whatever surplus is produced. The risks of production fall directly on the state; but the state is also assured of whatever output is produced, whether to guarantee food supplies and/or the generation of foreign exchange. The state enterprises need not be financially viable to guarantee certain minimum levels of output.

In a production cooperative, the level of worker remuneration (irrespective of whether an "advance" is paid) is determined by the surplus produced. Here the risk of production falls primarily on the membership. It may be shared by the state, depending on whether taxation is proportional to output or fixed (in the latter case it would be equivalent to a cost of production for the cooperative) and on credit policy. The usual argument favoring production cooperatives centers on motivation, since the size of the surplus directly determines the level of worker remuneration.

Various writers have suggested that production cooperatives are a much better vehicle for socialist accumulation than are state farms. Kifle (1983) for example, argues that this is what the Soviet experience shows, and in fact explains why the *kolkhoz* predominated over state farms up until the 1950s. He also suggests that this is why production cooperatives have been favored over state farms in East Europe. The argument is that the state, through fixed taxation policies, can assure itself of a target level of deliveries, and leave the level of remuneration of the membership to their collective motivation. In the Soviet Union, until very recently, the level of remuneration on the *kolkhoz* was significantly less than that of the average state farm worker (Dunman 1975). The state can also indirectly influence the level of output and of membership remuneration through price policy and the terms of trade.[18]

Whether collectivization based on production cooperatives in the Soviet Union actually provided the basis for socialist accumulation and the industrialization drive is the object of a major debate, beyond our immediate concerns (see Millar 1974; Ellman 1975). What is interesting is that the majority of the socialist third world countries (the major exception being Vietnam) initially have chosen a different route, prioritizing state farms.

The most disconcerting aspect of this review of state farms in the third world is what appears to be the minimal degree of worker participation in management and decisionmaking within them. There appears to be very little progress in instituting changes in the relations of production as capitalist enterprises are converted to state enterprises.

The view that state farms are a superior form of production to cooperatives rests on the state representing the interests of the whole society; that only the state can ensure the collective control over production and the appropriation and distribution of the surplus. The problem here, of course, is the relationship between the state and the meaning of socialist democracy. And can one have socialist democracy without participatory mechanisms, not just in a formal political sense, but at the point of production?

I think not, and this is the case for the importance of production cooperatives in societies in the transition. What production cooperatives offer is worker control over the labor process and over the appropriation and allocation of the surplus produced. The state has a considerable number of mechanisms at its disposal to ensure that these collective, but still "private," enterprises function in the interest of the whole society. The problem, as we have seen, is that the state may intervene to such an extent that worker control over the labor process is lost.

The question for countries in the transition to socialism is: At whose behest is collectivization to take place? The Nicaraguan experience thus far offers a new model, one based on the autonomous organization of rural workers and peasants. This has already shaped the course of the agrarian reform in a more participatory and democratic way than any other transitional experience. As such it comes closest to the reading of the classics offered here.

Notes

This essay is an abridged version of "The Peasantry and Agrarian Reform in the Transition to Socialism in the Third World," Kellogg Institute Working Paper #31, December 1984. The author is indebted to Lynn Duggan, Mieke Meurs, Hannah Roditi, and Antonella Stirati for research assistance, and to the Graduate School of the University of Massachusetts for a Faculty Research Grant. Thoughtful commentary and advice on earlier versions by Carollee Bengelsdorf, Frank Holmquist, Nancy Wiegersma, Jeanne Henn, Teodor Shanin, Peter Marchetti, Joe Collins, José Luis Coraggio, and David Ruccio is gratefully acknowledged.

1. See "Private Property and Communism" and "Rent of Land" in *Economic and Philosophical Manuscripts* and Volume Three of *Capital.*
2. See Levine (1982) for a convincing rebuttal to those who consider Marx and the Marxist legacy to be "anti-peasant." He also provides an interesting analysis of the continuity in the thinking of Marx, Engels, Lenin, and Mao on the agrarian question.
3. Nonetheless, it is quite clear in Marx and Engels' writings that they considered it feasible for Russia to "skip a stage" to socialism *only* in concert with a proletarian revolution in West Europe. First, Russia would have to rely on the advanced socialist countries to develop its productive forces. Also, in their internationalist vision, they assumed that the borders of nation-states would melt away. Thus, perhaps, it was the proletariat of West Europe that was to provide the leadership for the Russian peasantry.
4. While Western analysts of the Russian revolution have often chosen to interpret Lenin as opportunistic and anti-peasant, his contribution was certainly not lost on Lenin's Social Democratic colleagues. Owen (1963:89) quotes Zinovyev in 1924 as writing: "The first new idea that Lenin introduced [into Marxism] was his outlook upon the peasantry . . . the union of a working class revolution with a peasant war."
5. It was in this context that Lenin developed the slogan of "the revolutionary-democratic dictatorship of the proletariat and the peasantry." But Lenin's theoretical innovation to Marxism was not received lightly. Plekhanov and others objected that the proletariat and the peasantry could not act with a "single will." Plekhanov was even to accuse Lenin of leaning toward populism for his pro-peasant ·deviations (Shanin 1983: 19, 37).
6. The 1906 party congress (the so-called Unity Congress of Bolsheviks and Mensheviks) failed to approve land nationalization among its demands, agreeing to call only for the confiscation of church, state, and landlord land. Lenin continued to argue the importance of nationalizing all land, but directed his attacks primarily at the other Marxist party, the Social Revolutionaries (the heir of Narodism), and at the liberal parties participating in the various parliaments convoked under the Stolypin government. The Social Revolutionaries' agrarian program of 1906 called for the "socialization" of land and the distribution of land to the peasantry based on the principle of equalization (this takes into account the number of workers and consumers in each household). The various liberal parties, in turn, were attempting to promote agrarian reforms which would leave the landlord's land intact. Meanwhile, the Stolypin agrarian reform of the 1906–11 period proceeded on a frontal attack on the peasant commune.

   In response to these developments, Lenin in 1907 wrote one of his most important treatises on the agrarian question, "The Agrarian Programme of Social Democracy in the First Russian Revolution 1905–1907." His objective was to propose a revision of the Social Democratic agrarian program, based on an overall assessment of events in the 1905–07 period. It was here that he developed the conceptualization of the now famous "two paths" of capitalist development: the junker path, based on the internal transformation of the feudal estate, and the American path, based on individual family farming. He analyzed the junker path as primarily favoring the landlord class and concluded that this was the main intent of the Stolypin reforms. In contrast, the American path favored the peasantry and since the whole rural population would be involved, it should result in a more rapid development of agrarian capitalism. The outcome, of course, would be a rapid process of social differentiation, leading to the creation of a rural proletariat and the concentration of land in the hands of a peasant bourgeoisie. The American farmer path was thus the "revolutionary" path of capitalist development (1971:157).

7. The main features of the October 26th "Decree on Land" were (1) the abolition of landlord ownership without compensation; (2) the placement of landlord, crown, and church lands at the disposal of the land committees and the Soviets of Peasant Deputies pending the convocation of a Constituent Assembly; (3) the adoption of the "Peasant Mandate on Land" as the main guide to implementation of the reform until legislated otherwise by the Constituent Assembly (1971:202).

Lenin highly supported the main provision of the Peasant Mandate, the abolition of private ownership of land. All land was to become the property of "the whole people" and form part of a national land fund. Local and central self-government bodies were to be in charge of its distribution and all citizens "without distinction of sex" were to be given the right to use it as long as they worked the land with their own labor. Land was to be distributed according to the equalization standard of the Social Revolutionaries. A provision was also made for farms with a high level of "scientific farming" to be turned into model farms either under state or commune control. Most interestingly, the Peasant Mandate emphasized that there were to be no restrictions on the form of land tenure that might arise; included as possibilities were the "household, farm, communal, cooperative" or whatever was decided at the individual village or settlement level (ibid.:202–4).

8. Space precludes a detailed comparative analysis of the prerevolution agrarian structure of the thirteen countries under consideration. But obviously, such factors as the inherited distribution of landed property and the existing relations of production, as well as the level of development of the productive forces and person-land ratios, condition the feasible paths of socialist agrarian development.

9. In 1959 there had been only some 40,000 to 45,000 smallholders in Cuba (owning farms under 67 has. in size). By granting every tenant, sharecropper, and squatter the right to claim the land upon which they worked up to this limit, some 110,000 households received land under the first reform (MacEwan 1981:56–57). By the time that the 1963 agrarian reform law was implemented, the smallholder sector had mushroomed fourfold, to approximately 200,000 households (Rodriguez 1965:65).

10. I cannot analyze in any detail the performance of the state farm sector since insufficient data is available for such an evaluation. However, changes in state policy often speak to the problems of this sector. We will see that a number of countries have reevaluated the priority initially placed on state farms, and have increasingly focused state resources on previously neglected peasant producers and on cooperative development.

11. See Departamento de Orientación Revolucionaria del Comité Central

del PCC, *Sobre la Cuestion Agraria y Las Relaciones con el Campesinado: Tesis y Resolucion* (1976), summarized in MacEwan (1981:207) and discussed subsequently.

12. See White (1982) for an analysis of the implications of this renewed focus on the family economy for women's workload and status.

13. Hyden (1980:98–100) points out this conceptualization went far beyond anything in Tanzanian precolonial history. Mutual aid and reciprocity among neighbors (*ujima*) was a traditional practice, but ujamaa applied only to the household, not the community. A similar point is discussed in Barker (1979:102–3).

14. Barker (1979) provides an excellent summary of the debate up to the mid-1970s.

15. Since in Algeria the settler estates had been expropriated previously, land in the private sector was not so much highly concentrated as unequally distributed and under indirect forms of tenancy; approximately half of all farm units were sharecropped or rented (Pfeiffer 1981b:138, 69).

16. The APCs are elected local assemblies (reportedly from an FLN prepared list). They appear to be dominated by the rural petty bourgeoisie (middle level proprietors, shopkeepers, civil servants). Also charged with expropriating land during the agrarian reform, they were slow to do so and facilitated evasion (Pfeiffer 1981b:153–56).

17. This section on Nicaragua draws heavily on Deere, Marchetti and Reinhardt (1985) and will not be referenced in detail.

18. Dunman (1975) has argued that recent Soviet experience points to the convergence of state farms and production cooperatives. Over time, the differences between the two forms of organization of production are fading as more worker participation in decisionmaking is introduced on state farms and the level of remuneration is more closely tied to an incentive structure. On the production cooperatives, the form of remuneration has increasingly shifted to a guaranteed monthly payment and production is tightly coordinated with an overall plan. He argues these changes have made the two forms more like each other, and that only minor differences remain in their respective levels of mechanization and capitalization. In contrast, in the socialist third world, "conversion" seems to be far off. To the extent that production cooperatives are to be formed primarily through the collectivization of peasant plots, the differences between the capitalized state sector and the socialized peasant sector will remain large for some time to come, particularly if resources are not channeled specifically toward the peasantry.

Economics and Politics in the Transition to Socialism: Reflections on the Nicaragua Experience

▼▲

José Luis Coraggio

In a capitalist society, a separation appears to exist between economy and politics. This appearance, however, is a manifestation of capitalist domination itself, and it has been the task of revolutionaries to demystify the phenomenon by demonstrating the effective relations between the economic interests of the dominant classes and the structures which sustain its political power (Evers 1979).

In processes of social revolution, where the government plays a guiding role in defining the project of the majorities, the overlap between economy and politics tends to become even more evident. Certain ambiguities, of course, persist with respect to whether the political determines the economic process, or vice versa. The post-revolutionary correlation of political forces endeavors to build its corresponding economic bases: the development of a state productive sphere, state control of the sphere of circulation, a reinsertion into the world market, the development of new social forms of production, and so on. This process requires an economic policy which combines the long-run transformation of the economy with short-run measures consistent with the strategic program. The conjunctural control of the economy becomes a fundamental component of the revolutionary order.

The macrosocial transformations required by the popular project take place through the intervention of those wielding political power (and not only state power) in property relations, those of exchange, accumulation, and consumption, which in one way or another affect specific interests. The relationship between these specific interests and the "general interest"—as well as the timing over which of these interests are addressed or are negatively affected—is a central question on the political stage, where different social sectors play out their expectations of what the revolutionary project will mean for their own

Translated by Molly Molloy and Consuelo Soto

material existence. The political actors include not only certain sectors of the previously dominant classes, but also broad segments of the popular classes, who may perceive their everyday lives in sharp contrast to expectations as well as to the official state discourse, which is at times utopian, at times realistic.[1]

In addition to the problems caused by the contradictions of implementing a revolutionary project in an underdeveloped economy are the complications brought on by the efforts of the counterrevolution to destabilize the economy by exacerbating these contradictions (if not by sabotage or directly destroying the productive apparatus). The political alliances entailed in a project of national unity may also condition economic policy, in that particular interests must be addressed that limit the transformations in favor of the popular sectors. The need to materially sustain the revolutionary process is another factor that conditions the timing and forms of the political revolution. Thus, attaining the active cooperation of the productive sectors of the bourgeoisie implies, at a minimum, guaranteeing the economic reproduction of these classes (Coraggio 1985). The class bases of the revolution—workers, the subproletariat, peasants, artisans, small businesspeople, professionals, and technicians—in turn expect a response to their economic demands. Their political support is not indifferent to their perception of the attempts made and the results obtained by the revolutionary government's economic measures. To the extent that the political vanguard directly assumes government positions, its legitimacy is vulnerable if it does not favorably resolve the diverse particular interests of its social bases.

This essay starts from the proposition that in the current period, and in the historical context of a revolution such as that of Nicaragua, economic policy plays a fundamental role, undoubtedly more important than in models of centralized planning designed for other situations.[2] It is evident that processes such as that which Nicaragua has experienced since July 19, 1979, are affected by certain economic and political determinants which cannot be dealt with solely through the exercise of economic policy, nor be confronted only from this perspective. But economic policy remains a fundamental instrument for building revolutionary hegemony.[3]

It is possible that, in practice, not only the formal and institutional separation of economy and politics will be preserved, but also that a tendency may persist to regard the exercise of economic policy and of political power as if they responded to separate logics, causing contradictions in overall revolutionary practice. This situation could be seen as a smokescreen to allow for the domination of the popular classes over the minorities (thus inverting the prerevolutionary situation). However, I believe it actually creates the conditions that deter a revolutionary transformation by blocking an understanding of the relationship between the "general interest" and the particular interests of the popular sectors. This phenomenon is also related to the nature of the state in the process of social transition, as in the Nicaraguan case, a point I will return to in the conclusion.

It is from this perspective that I hope to contribute to the analysis of economic policy in the Nicaraguan revolutionary process. It is difficult to write about the Sandinista revolution today without focusing on the phenomenon whose dynamic impregnates the overall movement of the society at this moment: the war of aggression. But I will try to draw out more general relationships between economy and politics, which I contend are valid for the entire six-year period since the overthrow of Somoza, as well as for the years to come. If the economy and the internal political scene are thought of as the rearguard of a war against imperialism at the present historical moment, the question of the political system, democracy, and popular power (the state/civil society relation) on the one hand, and the handling of market relations on the other, are central in the construction of popular hegemony—the political basis of a successful resistance against the aggressor.[4] I will draw some lessons from the Nicaraguan revolutionary process, referring to partial, but central, aspects of the process that should illuminate the relationship between economics and politics in the process of transition.

The Influence of Politics on Economic Policy

Economic policy—that ensemble of government interventions on economic conditions and relationships of private and public agents—is effectively shaped by political factors. This is in part because the possibility of carrying out socioeconomic transformation requires the consolidation of revolutionary power, but also because the revolutionary project itself requires a conception of the political system which it wants to establish, of the nature of the state and its relations with the civil society whose development is codetermined by the exercise of economic policy. If a social revolution implies a transformation not only of civil society, but also of the state, and of the relations between them, then economic policy, which affects the material base of the society as a whole—but especially as it differentially affects various groups and sectors, public and private—becomes a privileged arena for the exercise of revolutionary power. Economic policy is also the terrain of confrontation of the revolutionary government with private corporate forces, of the consolidation or weakening of class alliances, all within the overall struggle to sustain or modify given socioeconomic conditions. In addition, within a political project such as that promoted by the Sandinista revolution—to deepen the social revolution on the basis of popular consensus, to advance simultaneously in the processes of democratization and social transformation, to create new patterns of socialization while maintaining a mixed economy—the efficacy of economic policy must pass another test: that of persuading the social agents. This persuasion obviously should be manifested in the acceptance by the majority of the political-ideological hegemony of the revolution, but also in the modification of economic behavior in relation to the revolutionary project at each conjuncture.

The immediate (and long-run) economic interests of the members of society are not a marginal "factor," to be compensated for by developing revolutionary consciousness. Rather, economic interests must be given a revolutionary response, whether in immediate practice, or in the expectations generated by the project itself. Thus economic policy, which in Nicaragua today forcefully affects these interests, is an essential condition for popular consensus. A fundamental political challenge for the revolution is to transcend the contradictions which continually arise due to the narrow material base upon which the revolution seeks to build a new society, organizing, in the process, the popular forces around revolutionary economic tasks. Part of this challenge demands that popular creativity be empowered, gradually breaking the alienation generated by the market system and developing people's ability to conscientiously control their own lives at all levels of society. In this process, it is crucial to incorporate popular wisdom, with its behaviors and expectations, in the formulation of official discourse and in the proposals for change. The ideology of the people is also being shaped through economic practices, particularly in its relation to the state and the political vanguard.

A popular revolution must bring out into the open what occurs, although partially hidden, in all societies: economic policy is not designed and implemented by a neutral state apparatus, but rather, organized sectors and groups who are subject to and beneficiaries of policy participate in its formulation. The exercise of economic policy implies intervention into the complex, interlocking conflicts among the specific interests that constitute society. Even while appearing to be a neutral mediator, the state exerts force, imposes decisions, and sets limits on private activity. This may require the more or less open deployment into the political arena of the social forces who benefit most from the state's policies. The popular forces, who in this case make up the fundamental social base of the revolutionary project, must be organized to participate in the development and implementation of the state's economic policies. Moreover, the political viability of a popular economic policy may require the particular social forces which sustain it to be clearly on the social stage, within the framework of the alliances and counterbalances necessary for the consolidation of revolutionary power.

The exercise of politics in the economic arena has a special dimension in the case of revolutions in small countries of the capitalist periphery. In these situations, imperialism has an enormous capacity to directly attack the revolution militarily, thus calling into question the stability of the new correlation of forces. Indirectly, through ideology or an economic boycott, it attacks the social bases that sustain the revolution's power. Thus when an economic boycott is imposed, for example, the causality of the subsequent economic scarcity is not obvious to all of the population. (Some may even attribute it in the final instance to the fact that the political leadership has "gone too far" in its defiance of the U.S. colossus.) In any case, the revolutionary state appears as the political mediator of the socioeconomic impact of the external action. Here, as well, economic policy is fundamental in the managing of the impact. It must respond not only to the foreign aggression, but also to the exacerbated conflict of competing interests within the national society. If policy is designed to focus exclusively on the macroeconomic effects, the political consequences can be startling and of extraordinary magnitude. This is what the foreign aggressor is ultimately counting upon.

Economic Logic and Political Logic

Having emphasized the political component of economic policy, we must emphasize equally an aspect that the "overpolitization" of these processes may conceal: economic policy must also respond to specific economic laws, conditions, and mechanisms, whose logic cannot be ignored for long without seriously affecting the revolutionary order itself.[5] A fundamental feature of the revolutionary order is that the economic system—even when undergoing a process of transformation—must function at minimally acceptable levels of reproduction (even within the difficult conditions imposed by external forces). The economic system provides the context which gives meaning to the practices of its agents, articulating or counterposing private interests with the new social interests. Optimally, it would systematically stimulate those tendencies compatible with the project for a new society and discourage retrograde ones. The question of economic logic may be dealt with on the macrosocial level, analyzing the major balances of the economy and the contradictions they imply. However, in order to tie in the political aspects, an analysis must be made of political forces and their relationship to the social forces at their base. Thus it is essential that this analysis conceptually integrate the reality and behavior of the concrete agents of the society.

Within revolutionary theory there is a tendency to resort to generalities, to all-embracing concepts that do not have a clear and direct operational referent. Thus agents are conceptualized as mere sustainers of economic and social structures. However, in reality, the "structures" one is attempting to change or develop do not have an independent life above and beyond the systems of relations between concrete agents of the society. To alter the structures is to alter social relations, and this entails changes in the individual and collective behavior and consciousness of the social agents. But in reality these agents are multivalent and not reducible, even within the economic sphere, to a single social category, or to a pure, exclusive relation, that would completely define its identity.[6] To speak of the "bourgeoisie" and the "proletariat," or more specifically, of the "cotton-producing bourgeoisie" and the "industrial proletariat" in Nicaragua, is to speak of a subset of productive agents that cannot be separately attributed to the position designated by their name. Neither the economic behavior of the private cotton producer nor that of a Managua factory worker will be exclusively determined by their productive function. What defines the boundaries between the producer of cotton or sorghum, the industrialist or the merchant? What distinguishes the salaried industrial worker from the active participant in the informal sector? Although economic policies are designed around abstract economic players, these policies concretely affect multivalent subjects and units of reproduction with complex strategies. Failure to take this reality into consideration provokes unexpected effects.[7]

This phenomenon, which applies to any country with an advanced division of labor, is a crucial factor in a society such as Nicaragua, where classes and agents do not have the consistency, or the level of crystallization, presupposed by structuralist theories. Nicaraguan society is enormously malleable. Its class structures are in many ways like gelatin, highly unstable and vulnerable to changes in the conditions of their reproduction and, in addition, disposed to dizzying mobility that defies prediction (see Arico 1980). If in Nicaragua it was possible to speak about the minimal quantitative importance of the proletariat as a class, now we must also speak about its loose consistency, its inorganic character, and the still unstable ascription by its members to their class identity (Núñez 1983). The same must be said for the poor peasantry. Peasants may not only cease to be peasants in their productive function, but may also cease to be rural dwellers, becoming urbanized and altering their way of life drastically and irreversibly. These social reversals cannot fail to have an effect upon consciousness and organizations and, consequently, upon the play of political forces. In effect, just as the classes are "gelatinous," so are their corporate organizations, including those with the longest traditions of struggle (however limited), which are the urban proletarian organizations. The recent tendency on the part of the Nicaraguan proletariat and wage earners in general to join the urban informal sector clearly demonstrates that there is nothing inherent in the wage-earning class that makes its members less inclined to abandon their positions within the social division of labor, just as in the case of peasants who migrate to the cities. Under conditions of difficult reproduction, immediate economic interests take priority.

Moreover, the imperatives of defense against external aggression as well as the project of national unity prevent the class from organizing itself autonomously and carrying on the internal class struggle in a traditional manner or even with new variants.[8] Thus, during extremely critical situations, the class may tend toward disintegration, instead of retrenching and consolidating itself as the working class. In addition, this decomposition may take place by illegal methods, which are nevertheless legitimized by their magnitude (the "logic of the majority" operates here in a regressive manner, or at best, as a signal to the state of the objective contradictions it must take up) and by the vast network of "accomplices" required by the new modes of survival. It would be paradoxical for the revolution to unleash a process that would contribute to the disintegration of its essential class base—the only classes that will continue to the end. And even if this process had fundamentally objective determinants, inadequate policies or faulty methods of ideological and political work by the state and the revolutionary vanguard also have contributed to it.

A possible consequence of economic crisis may thus be that the mass organizations—prevented from growing and consolidating themselves through the struggle for their specific demands—become "emptied" of their rank and file. Economic policy plays a crucial role in this phenomenon, not only because of its objective effects on the conditions of reproduction of the diverse social sectors, but also because of the pedagogic nature of its implementation, which, if not taken into account, may produce alienating effects on the rank and file and their political will.

Thus, economics and politics permeate one another; they are mutually dependent. Economic policy—state policies that affect the material base of society—is a fundamental element of politics and of the construction of revolutionary power, of popular power. To separate, tactically and strategically, economics from politics is to precipitate the dynamics of a disintegrating dialectic.

If in addition the reorganization of the economy is to be built with *the consensus* of those affected by the changes, the tactical use of economic policy is imperative. Economic policy must regulate the development and/or transformation of the class identities advocated by the revolution as well as those it wishes to discourage. But this process must be governed by an overall strategy of transformation or else face the risk of counterproductive results.

The social, political, and ideological transformation of a society implies not only organization and construction, but also disorganization and destruction, and this process must be conscientiously directed, based on scientific knowledge regarding these processes. Otherwise, economic policy in the context of crisis may not only weaken the classes that are considered to be fundamental pillars of the revolution, but may also simultaneously reinstate forms of production that were considered to have been abolished by decree. For example, the resurgence of sharecropping may be a response to the reproductive strategies of the poor peasantry, and small and medium agrarian producers and the agrarian bourgeoisie. These relations of production have been associated historically with local-level interpersonal relations that lend themselves to manipulation by nonrevolutionary forces.

In the case of landless workers in an inflationary economy (when wage restraints are imposed and where basic goods are acquired by paying high prices on the parallel market), the best and most secure use of labor power may be that which permits direct access to use values for self-consumption or sale. A phenomenon similar to that of payment in kind arises which for workers is not equivalent to a money wage if they anticipate inflation and foresee that wages will trail behind prices.

Another problem—in the absence of a global strategy that puts forth alternatives to the relations being destroyed—may arise when the state attempts to accelerate its control of the economy, and gives incentives to specialized and "formal" modes of production and circulation, in order to facilitate its control. This may conflict with the survival strategies of the popular and middle sectors of society, without simultaneously providing them with a "formal" effective alternative. In fact, the political and ideological characterization of "speculators" as unproductive and antisocial may encompass broad popular sectors that span the class spectrum. If these sectors are not offered adequate productive alternatives, on acceptable terms, they may easily become disaffected.

If these contradictions are objective and cannot be resolved at will, the political imperative of the central struggles taken up by the revolution, and/or overall economic imperatives, may require decisions that negatively affect the sectors which make up the social base of the revolution, or who make up part of its fundamental alliances. Nevertheless, the absence of a strategic framework and an integrating analytical system of diverse state policies may favor ineffective decisions, precipitating unexpected phenomena that aggravate the situation, thus exacting an unnecessary "political cost" for the revolution.

Problems in the Design and Implementation of Economic Policy

In his exposition on the rectification of economic policy undertaken in 1984, Cmdte. Jaime Wheelock added a "fourth determining cause" to the three previously recognized causes of economic problems (the Somocista legacy, the international economic crisis, and foreign aggression): namely, errors in economic management committed since the revolutionary triumph.[9] Following are some hypotheses concerning the factors which may have contributed to these errors, and an analysis of their costs in economic and political terms.

The Fragmentation of the State

Part of the Somocista legacy was the need for the new government to build the revolutionary state upon the remains of a backward and corrupt system. The institutions and instruments of economic policy were very poorly developed. The changes made in the organization of the state were unable to overcome a crucial problem: the divisions among spheres of decisionmaking did not necessarily correspond to the concrete relations and subsystems that constituted the economy. The ministerial units corresponded to state practices inspired by a Latin American tradition based on theories of economic policy ill-suited to a revolutionary process such as the separation between production and circulation, between the real and the monetary, between distinct spheres of production according to branches or sectors, between state finance and all others, and so on.

Thus any subsystem that includes both production and circulation, such as cotton production, which extends from the importation of agrochemicals to the export of cotton and the production of textiles, falls under the domain of numerous ministries and state agencies, each of which tends to have its own institutional logic for meeting certain specific objectives. The Ministry of Domestic Commerce (MICOIN) fixes consumer prices, attending to problems of consumption and distribution; the Ministry of Agricultural Development and Agrarian Reform (MIDINRA) or the Ministry of Industry (MININD) fixes the prices that the producer receives, according to production objectives; the Central Bank fixes interest and exchange rates, following credit and monetary policy; the Finance Ministry (MIFIN) sets tax structures, attends to budgetary policy, and so on. If each concrete situation is confronted by a group of isolated decisions made on the basis of sectoral or distinct institutional objectives and criteria, there is no guarantee of consistency in the resulting group of government interventions. The need for coordination, for unified direction is necessary in order to create a planning framework, and should have been provided by the Ministry of Planning (MIPLAN).[10] In addition, some of the special programs, such as the National Basic Foods Program

(PAN), should have coordinated the activities of the various agencies addressing a similar problem, in this case the production and distribution of basic grains.

The proliferation of interministerial coordinating committees did not resolve the problem of the need for unified direction of the economy.[11] To give one example, prices, which should have responded to the logic of an integrated subsystem, were fixed at different points in time and according to diverse criteria, unsettling production decisions. At the same time, this process generated the conditions for speculative behavior,[12] an uncontrollable increase in the cost of subsidies, and subsequently, an expansion of the money supply.[13] All of this, in turn, led to excess demand for national and imported products with respect to the supply of goods available. The pressure on the balance of payments was thus accentuated above and beyond objective pressures arising from the inherited productive model, deteriorating terms of trade, and the costs of foreign aggression.

By 1984 it was evident that the goal of deterring inflation was impossible to achieve, even if money wages were frozen. In 1983 there had been a lengthy discussion of the wage issue in the context of the military emergency. It was concluded that wage demands must be controlled in order to avoid economic problems which might affect national defense.[14] But prices, which were established in order to respond to cost increases or the pressures exercised by various productive groups, both private and state, were reviewed case by case.[15] This provoked not only the aforementioned distortions along the chain of production and circulation, but also distortions due to relative prices that did not respond to production priorities or to the country's real resource availability.

Profit margins, which were fixed for each productive sector separately on the basis of a negotiated margin over variable costs, did not take into account the decisionmaking strategies of the heterogeneous producers within each sector. Some producers opted for less risky products that have a faster rate of turnover of capital (sorghum rather than cotton, for example) and that require a lower investment per cordoba earned. The calculation of prices thus led to enormous differentials in intrinsic profit rates, which are those that tend to guide most private decisions.[16] Moreover, the price of imported products, resulting from an exchange rate that did not reflect the real foreign exchange cost to the country, promoted conspicuous consumption and overinvestment for a period of time.

As a result, and since the partial fixing of prices was upsetting the logic of the resource allocation system, prices were being quoted in terms of the "official" and the "parallel" price, neither of which corresponded to the real conditions of the economy. But this duality, which became permanent, generated opportunities for easy income. A worker had only to acquire small quantities of products at the official price and resell them to merchants in the parallel market in order to double or triple his or her wages. The migration of peasants to Managua (and of workers and artisans away from their productive activity) was in part a result of these price structures. Smuggling was also stimulated for the same reasons. As a result, incentives for productive work were diminished and a strata of newly wealthy speculators emerged. They in turn interacted with a vast network of small-scale speculators. Corruption proliferated among state officials and even within the mass organizations involved in the distribution of basic goods.

In general, economic calculus was dismissed as a criterion of decisionmaking and those who advocated it were judged "economistic." Concrete analyses of costs and profits, of the structure of capital, and so on, which should inform decisionmaking, were nonexistent, and furthermore, they were considered unnecessary by many state officials, who preferred to base decisions on their "own experience." Empiricism predominated, and the absence of elemental economic theory was the norm in many spheres of government decisionmaking. Phenomena such as differential rents—basic for understanding the configuration of interests in the agricultural sector—were ignored and prices were fixed on the basis of averages, always loosely estimated. The state attempted to abolish the rents by fixing uniform, very low rental rates for land. In reality, this procedure transferred revenues from certain agents to others, and abolished one of the mechanisms for the rational allocation of resources, without replacing it with a new efficient and effective rationality. Ironically, at the same time, attempts were made to make headway on a system of central planning.

Why was this lack of coordination in the design and implementation of state economic policies maintained? One relevant factor was the lack of accepted channels of coordination. Every decisionmaking sphere allocated resources or implemented measures without considering macroeconomic implications or the needs of other state spheres. The overall result was excess demand, a kind of "collective voluntarism." This was one of the fundamental reasons for the changes in economic policy introduced in February 1985. The magnitude of the changes dramatized the seriousness of the situation.[17]

The Lack of an Operating Strategy

Each decisionmaking sphere nonetheless attempted to respond to the political directives of the revolutionary project, interpreting these according to their sectoral or institutional vision. Here, another hypothesis may be put forth: a vacuum in direction was created which could not be filled by coordinating meetings aimed at resolving specific problems, due to the lack of an economic strategy based on the overall framework of a political strategy. Such an economic strategy needed to have met two fundamental conditions: (a) to integrate, visibly and logically, the basic principles orienting revolutionary action, with the objectives and modes of action corresponding to each sphere of state action; and (b) to be known and assumed by those in charge at the different levels of the diverse spheres of decisionmaking.

There are various reasons for this vacuum, which allowed for the fragmented and discretionary actions of different state agencies. In the first place, in order to recognize the very need for a strategy of this type, it is necessary to have a theoretical conception of society and of the transformation process which goes beyond a macrohistorical vision. This conception must integrate the scientific knowledge that has been accumulated in Latin America about phenomena which also occur in Nicaragua (i.e., theories on the peasant economy, on the so-called informal sector, on market functioning, etc.). Without this it is impossible to mediate the great tasks of the historic class project and the specific conjectural tasks of the revolution in its present stage. Another factor is the distribution of power among the diverse state spheres. This has allowed the execution of projects and the presentation of programs according to sector-generated logic, as *faits-accomplis* sweeping along the rest of the state administration. Another fundamental factor has been the empirical ignorance of social reality at the time of the triumph. The difficulties of exercising social science under Somoza meant that there was little research generating rigorous empirical knowledge.[18] But undoubtedly a more fundamental factor hindering the development of an economic strategy such as the one proposed has been the counterrevolutionary aggression. The war has created a situation whereby all data relating to the functioning of the economy is considered as being of strategic importance to the enemy. As a consequence, the imperative of defense impedes the socialization of information, programs and plans, projections and results of economic activity. This dilemma, whether to socialize information in order to achieve greater integration in public and private decisionmaking, or to confine information to restricted circles, thus handing down only general guidelines or very specific tasks, is in some ways analogous to the dilemma which confronts revolutionary organizations when fighting against a dominant power.[19]

A strategy that is not analytical and that is unknown in its detail does not permit the incorporation of criteria such as the opportunity cost of decisions (i.e., what one will no longer be able to do or the interests affected if certain decisions are made), nor does it permit the incorporation of part of the knowledge generated by revolutionary practice itself (since this has not been systematized and written down). It also hinders the participation of society as a whole in decisionmaking, which is in some cases an essential condition for the society to assume a strategy as its own and abide by its dictates and consequences. The alienation provoked by the circumstances of being subjected to (often abrupt) shifts in the economy may have a discouraging effect on productive efforts and their rationalization in accordance with the general interests. A strategic economic framework that was publicly known would help to make sense of these reversals, or even to anticipate them. Moreover, it is not sufficient to have a clear vision only of the broad picture and to visualize what would be a correct policy. Policy implementation requires other subjective conditions that if not met can impede the rectification of economic policy. It may be necessary to first overcome certain problems, such as the aforementioned fragmentation of the state, or to carry out a process of collective discussion whose logic and timing are determined by political rather than economic factors, until the new policy is assumed in its entirety by the state.[20]

The Central Role of the State in the Transformation Process

At the time of the 1979 triumph, Nicaraguan society was characterized by a weak civil society. Given this, it was not difficult to conclude that the fundamental transformations in society, especially economic ones, would have to be directed and implemented by the state. As practical experience demonstrated, the state that was inherited was also backward, and its endemic inertia would exert a powerful influence. So-called institutional feudalism, bureaucracy, and the corrupt tendencies of the state's agents did not disappear with the triumph. Instead, a permanent tendency arose to reproduce and even extend this behavior, against which the revolutionary political leadership fought, and continues to fight. The problem is to determine to what extent, and for how long, the revolutionary transformation of the state can be carried out exclusively by the top leadership. To revolutionize the state implies revolutionizing power structures, and this requires the action of organized political and social forces whose objective is to democratize society, becoming protagonists of the revolution. These forces are rooted in civil society itself; thus, in this process, the relation between the revolutionary party, the state, and the mass organizations is fundamental.[21]

On the other hand, the state's limited capacity to assume all of the tasks of the revolution means that many of these tasks will necessarily be postponed, unless the people's creative energy is utilized. But drawing on this energy requires changes in the typical attitude that assumes that the initiative and direction of the transformation will be in hands of the state. In fact, the problem is related to the very concept of power. If power is seen as a given, as something which has already been "taken" and which can be distributed or centralized, in such a way that power granted to one social group is "extracted" from another, then there is no recognition of the fact that social power regenerates and expands with the development of society. The revolution, in fact, creates new sources and possibilities for the exercise of power. In a revolutionary project such as the Sandinista revolution, in which popular power and hegemony are constituent components, endless possibilities are opened up for the exercise of people's power, which not only competes with but strengthens state power within the joint project of revolutionary consolidation. Moreover, in a process of social transformation oriented toward achieving effective socialization of power and the economy, the state cannot move ahead of civil society in all areas; the relation between the state and civil society must be defined in each specific area. An economic policy favorable to the popular project should, in its design and implementation, count not only on the state but also on the mass organizations, from the diagnosis of the situation to implementation and follow-up of policy. But this is not an easy matter; it demands communication and a special relation between the state and the leadership of the mass organizations, and, in turn, between that leadership and the masses themselves.

The Limits of Class Struggle

In order to sustain itself in the face of imperialist aggression, the Nicaraguan revolution must place the economy at the service of defense and the basic reproduction of the population, while taking into account the material interests that sustain national unity. This entails objective political contradictions that are extremely difficult to resolve.

From the start, the revolutionary leadership set out to create a revolutionary order that would provide the context within which the project of national unity would be realized. While this was a necessary condition to sustain the ongoing struggle against imperialist aggression, it also entailed curbing the class struggle in its traditional forms, including those that enabled the revolution to defeat the National Guard. Seizures of land and workplaces were stopped, as well as strikes for economic demands that were impossible for the economy to meet. Moreover, the mass organizations led by the FSLN were transformed from forces enunciating their own specific demands to supportive forces, which often merely implemented the guidelines handed down to them by the revolutionary leadership and the state. This directly contradicts the materialist conception of social change assumed in revolutionary discourse.[22]

The organization of the masses has come to depend on their leadership's capacity for mobilization and access to state resources, rather than on the development of the class struggle itself. If the accumulation and sustenance of forces is achieved in opposition to "visible" class adversaries, against which one can advance, winning demands through struggle and organization, then the Nicaraguan mass organizations were to develop with a congenital weakness. To the extent that the countless advances attained by the popular classes were going to be mediated by the state, the conception would almost inevitably arise that, as the representative of the revolution, it is the state that struggles and that delivers or postpones the fulfillment of demands. As objective conditions make it increasingly difficult to respond favorably to these demands, it is the state itself that appears to be denying them. In any case, for objective reasons, the class struggle, even with an internal correlation of forces very favorable to the popular majority, cannot be actualized in continual or notable gains in the living conditions of the masses. But in the absence of direct experience with struggle and its obstacles, this fact requires an explanation, a very special pedagogy to justify just why the class struggle would take the form of defense, of the fight against the counterrevolution, of increases in productivity and efficiency, or, at a more abstract level, why the class struggle should center on the battle against backwardness. The level of consciousness and global vision needed to assume these lines of action is difficult to attain if not located within the framework of growing class organization. This, in turn, is hindered if struggles of a specifically class nature are held back by the needs of the revolutionary order.

Another consideration is that the nature of popular demands and needs has not been adequately or systematically investigated and defined. This is important, because in the absence of the free play of forces and tensions that result from particular economic interests, only scientific study will make it possible to discern those underlying tensions and their predictable consequences. For example, during the first years of the revolution, it was often asserted that access to land was not a basic demand of the Nicaraguan peasantry. This assumption, partly based on the limited peasant struggles during the Somoza period, turned out to be incorrect. After 1983 the Agrarian Reform Ministry changed its policy, distributing land to individual families. Three fundamental factors influenced this change in policy: (1) the changed socioeconomic context resulting from the revolutionary triumph, which opened up new expectations or permitted the manifestation of demands that had remained hidden by the Somocista repression; (2) the economic crisis itself, combined with the direct and indirect economic costs of the aggression, which affected the conditions of reproduction of the peasantry; and (3) the realization that even where it was not an "active" demand of the peasantry, the redistribution of lands promised to spur production.[23]

A factor which must be considered is the time lapse between the moment in which subjective conditions demand a response and the moment in which that response is finally given. During the interim, the receptivity to state measures may be modified by the delay itself. What would have been regarded as a revolutionary conquest is then reticently received from a state that is distrusted. The possibility should be taken into account that the Nicaraguan peasantry, on the basis of its social nature and historical experience, has "antistate" tendencies, preferring not to depend on the state, and desiring to minimize state interference in household economic reproduction. These tendencies may have been accentuated by the inadequate execution of policies by functionaries unprepared to deal with this new "clientele." As a result, certain groups of the peasantry may reject policies intended to favor them from the state's point of view—such as credit, the substitution of state channels of commercialization for private ones, or even the distribution of free land. This is so because they anticipate that all these measures imply coming under the domination of the state, whose logic and objectives are alien to their immediate economic reproductive practices, which are based on different types of relations, the possibilities and limitations of which they at least believe they know.

The Absence of a "Social Pedagogy"

A mercantile economy functions as an ensemble of microeconomic decisions made by numerous and diverse agents on the basis of their particular objectives. Their behavior is conditioned not only by their history, and by the material resources at their command, but also by their expectations, which are in turn reinforced or revised on the basis of practice. As a consequence, economic policy, which seeks to orient the overall course of the economy fundamentally through the manipulation of the variables that condition individual behavior (prices, legal restrictions, compulsory marketing relations, etc.), should be grounded in theoretically based empirical knowledge of the various agents and their integration into the economic system. In the absence of such knowledge, the design of economic policy must be based on (1) the theories that are most suitable to the situation and/or (2) the direct participation of the agents themselves, organized toward that goal.

Economic policy proposals must be designed within a theoretical framework that incorporates the basic concepts of the class struggle, and an understanding of mercantile logic that in many ways continues to rule the country's economy. It is also necessary to incorporate the direct protagonists of production and trade in the discussion and elaboration of economic programs so that they can contribute their experience and vision of the economic situation, and so that they assume formal commitments and agreements with the state. In this way, policy initiatives will result in something more than wishful thinking, and lead to the attainment of goals that reflect the general interest.

The Sandinista government has always maintained a posture of open negotiation and dialogue with the productive sectors, particularly with the bourgeoisie.[24] However, it was not easy to implement private sector/state agreements, and only in 1985 were these agreements pursued more vigorously. Similarly, incentives began to be linked to the level of managerial efficiency or to workers' productivity. In fact, in practice, the revolution has learned the limits that the market in a mixed economy imposes on political will. Thus, the rectification of economic policy is geared toward acknowledging these limits in order to operate within the laws of the marketplace while continuing to be under the direction of the revolutionary state.

In any cases, the new measures and the successive waves of readjustment since February 1985 have constituted a strong check on production and circulation as well as on consumption (the predicated inflation rate for 1985 is close to 200 percent). It is crucial to thoroughly explain the new measures and devise a system for continually gathering feedback from the diverse sectors, in order to avoid the accumulation of contradictions which would again necessitate drastic changes in economic policy. These changes generate great instability and increase alienation when there is inadequate comprehension of the reasons for them. A pedagogy to accompany the design and implementation of economic policies must be a fundamental element in the building and strengthening of consensus in a pluralist political system based on popular hegemony.[25]

Political competition, incorporated by the revolution as a component of the new society, opens the door to opposition attacks designed to capitalize on the discontent generated by the difficult economic situation. In this respect, it is essential to keep in mind that although the popular sectors may not have a scientific vision of the functioning of the economy, nor readily understand the language code usually employed in government communications, they do have popular wisdom concerning the conditions necessary for their own reproduction. Their survival experience shapes their ideological consciousness and vision of the state, the economy, and their own immediate interests. It is from this ideological configuration that they interpret the phenomena to which they are submitted. Understanding these origins of popular consciousness is crucial for effective communication between the revolutionary leadership and its social bases. Even the best pedagogic efforts to explain the new policies thus far appeal to a communications code that does not come from the masses, but rather from the middle sectors of society.[26] In political terms, this is a critical aspect of economic policy, as it affects the ability to develop and sustain consensus and to confront tensions in the popular arena. But in addition, its absence prevents the enrichment of revolutionary practice through the creativity and wisdom of the people.

The Political Costs of the Economic Policy

The current stage of the Nicaraguan revolution is characterized by the need to consolidate revolutionary power in accordance with the principles of popular power and political pluralism. It also implies confronting the economic and human costs of imperialist aggression within the context of an inherited economic structure incapable of flexibly responding to the international crisis, and a level of development which places Nicaragua among the three poorest nations of Latin America. If during this stage political conditions determine economic change, how can we reconcile this with the materialist principle that gives primacy to economic processes?

To begin with, "economic change" must be interpreted more broadly, in the sense of "material change," that which relates to the reproduction of human life. This is important in a country confronting a war of attrition, where limits on life itself come not only from the difficulties of economic reproduction for the popular classes, but also from the ever-present possibility of death in the anti-imperialist war. In this sense, the assurance of military protection against counterrevolutionary attacks and the assurance of economic reproduction (access to productive resources and basic goods) cannot be disassociated, as both are necessary to the cohesion of civil society during this critical period.

The society as a whole confronts the challenge of maintaining the program of national unity in order to consolidate the anti-imperialist front and to strengthen international alliances with strategic allies of the United States, who question the legitimacy of U.S. intervention in this country. This requires the reproduction of the privileged classes (productive sectors of the bourgeoisie, professionals, and technicians, the formal commercial sector), while simultaneously attaining the reproduction of the classes constituting the historical subjects of the revolution: the workers and peasants, and the impoverished sectors, not formally integrated into the social division of labor, but who played a determining role in the insurrection (see Vilas 1985; 1986).

The claim that the political struggle has relative autonomy is valid in certain cases, and is particularly applicable in the case of the Sandinista revolution. As a political revolt against a dictatorship, the revolution emerged triumphant before the economic crisis in the agroexport economic model ruptured. Nevertheless, political will cannot endlessly substitute for the material conditions of human existence, and at a certain point, the crisis of economic reproduction can begin to have ideological and eventually political effects contrary to the consolidation of the revolution. The limits above and beyond which economic scarcity—or the unsatisfied private interests of privileged sectors—can begin to bring about a reversal of support for the revolution are difficult to determine. The Nicaraguan people have shown that they have a historical dignity which the revolution has turned into a national force, capable of confronting the foremost world power. This phenomenon makes it difficult to establish limits (even biological ones) to the material sacrifice the Nicaraguan people are willing to endure to defend their right to self-determination. Nevertheless, the new society, the "new human being" is still a project, and values and norms of behavior forged in the Somocista past continue to operate.

With respect to the masses, the fact that the laws of history indicate that the revolution is their historical project does not guarantee that they will always be willing to follow all dictates concerning their economic behavior, however functional it may be to the revolutionary project. Below a certain minimum standard of living, the search for a survival strategy that will at least guarantee the reproduction of the family is primary. And in this respect, Nicaraguans have shown the great ability to rapidly adapt to changing situations, constantly searching for ways to reinsert themselves into a system of economic relations in order to improve their position, or at least prevent its deterioration. This stems from a long history of survival in conditions of poverty, but also from the experience of six years of revolutionary government. In this sense, the revolution has already helped to consolidate certain models of economic behavior through its handling of economic policy. Speculation, for example, is a product not only of scarcity, but also of the possibilities systematically opened up during these six years by state management of the marketplace.

It is particularly important to point out that the fragmentary treatment of different sectors of the market produced a crisis of economic direction. This crisis broke out in the two market sectors which integrate the entire economy: the money market and the labor market. But it was the latter that evidently made it politically impossible to postpone the decision to rectify economic policy, as its distortions had not only economic implications, but also direct sociopolitical ones (i.e., tendencies toward the disintegration of the class bases of the revolution).

When the masses perceive the effects (although not the ultimate logic, nor the objectives) of economic policy, personified in the faces and behaviors of the state (public officials), it is natural that as a mass, given the incomplete process of organization and formation of class identity, they will tend to resist the restrictive directives concerning what they must do "to be revolutionary." This is especially so when conditions for their own economic reproduction differ from the content of revolutionary discourse.

Of course, it is essential to differentiate the factors attributable to inevitable objective decisions (the economic crisis, the costs of the aggression, the Somocista legacy) from the margin of action which the state had and has for economic management within this framework. The February 1985 rectification actually confirmed that this margin was important, and established as a principle that political vigilance of economic policy would be a built-in part of the revolutionary order.

The political-ideological effect of the economic disorder, of the pressure for individual survival which goes beyond the general interests as defined by the revolutionary leadership, has not been automatically dispelled by the new economic measures. Rather, it persists and may even be enhanced if a greater clarity is not achieved concerning future perspectives. A serious political consequence of this situation is that the mass organizations, fundamental components of the revolutionary forces, may tend to be "emptied" of their rank and file. On the one hand, the membership perceives that these organizations no longer represent their immediate interests; on the other hand, the class position of their members is constantly being called into question by the complex survival strategies they have been compelled to adopt.

It is necessary to return to the grassroots base, to their worldview, to their immediate needs, to their real-life behaviors, to their expectations, and to foster organizational patterns which surge from below. The revolution's current critique of the mass organizations is a key element in this process.[27] The reorganization of the structures of communication, solidarity, and organization from the local and sectoral levels is necessary to ensure that the state's economic and social policies are not designed and implemented in a vacuum. But above all, the implied alternative requires the restoration of the unity between economics and politics. The Sandinista political program proposes the democratization of power, the development of pluralist participation, and the acceptance of ideological differences within a program of national liberation. This must function not only in regard to specifically political relationships and institutions, but also *within* the realm of economic management. The political and ideological work of creating a revolutionary consciousness can be nullified if the economic alienation resulting from brutal upsets in the standard of living, without apparent logic and without a participatory social pedagogy, pressures the masses to struggle first for their immediate material survival.

The events of the last few years in Nicaragua should be taken as signs of vitality and speak well for the future of this process. The masses resisted the dictates of an economic policy which sent conflicting signals: the necessity of productive work, while unproductive activity (in the sphere of circulation) was concretely encouraged. The wary reaction of the masses to the state's pronouncements was nevertheless accompanied by their massive support for the revolutionary program in the November 1984 elections. This implies that although the Nicaraguan people are discriminating and reject slogans which conflict with their most basic interests, they are completely committed to the Sandinista project of a new society and to the anti-imperialist struggle. It is the responsibility of the state to avoid provoking unnecessarily ideological reactions contrary to the fundamental tendency of the people toward their liberation.

But what the Nicaraguan transition experience shows is that for the state's economic management to become more coherent and systematically link political and economic considerations, it is essential for the organized masses to be incorporated more actively in the participatory management of the economy. It will also be necessary for the revolution to carry out a genuine cultural revolution in social communications, based on popular wisdom and its expectations, gradually transferring scientific knowledge about reality to the masses. This in turn requires a cultural revolution within the state itself, built around an explicit strategy. The changes in state structures and policy undertaken in 1985 no doubt reflect an awareness of this need.

In summary, although they may not be easily quantifiable, the "political costs" of economic policy must be explicitly taken into consideration in economic management.[28] These costs affect the strengthening of the revolution's fundamental class base, the formation of popular power, the revolutionary relation between the state and civil society, and the coherence between individual and collective behavior and changing structures. These conditions are all essential to creating an impenetrable bloc against the war of attrition waged by imperialism. To this end, theory and research (scientific and participatory) can play a crucial role. As Cmdte. Tomás Borge recently said: "A reality that is not investigated is a reality that remains unknown. And an unknown reality is a reality that cannot be transformed. . . ."

Conclusion: On the Nature of the State in Nicaragua's Transition

In Nicaragua, the Sandinista revolution is producing economic, political, and social transformations under circumstances specific to a small peripheral agroexporting country, whose economic backwardness paralleled the political backwardness reflected in a forty-five-year dictatorship. There is a transition process from peripheral capitalism toward a social formation whose essential characteristics cannot be defined with a single term. A new socialization of the economy has taken place as well as a process of political democratization which has now entered into a phase of rapid institutionalization. There has been a drastic redefinition of the functions of the state, summed up in the phrase "regulator of the economy" in relation to material conditions. There has also been a redefinition of the national project, which is markedly anti-imperialist and oriented toward the defense of national sovereignty, as well as the satisfaction of the population's basic needs.

By its very nature, the national unity project—a condition for the efficacy of the anti-imperialist program in the present world situation—means a multiclass society, a multiparty political system, and the free expression of individual interests through organizations and the media. The formation of a social system drawn together by this program will determine to a great extent the nature of the state. The domination of the minority by the majority, as well as the ongoing building of the social consensus, contributes to the reproduction of the separation between the economic and the political which characterizes the capitalist state: political democracy and the concentration of economic power, in this case, however, in the hands of the revolutionary state.

But this separation is fictitious. Popular power cannot exist in the political realm if the alienation of the masses is reproduced in the economic process. The political and the economic realms, whether in capitalist states or those in the process of transition from capitalism, cannot be effectively separated, except in form. But neither are they the same thing. The relative weight with respect to control of the means of production by the diverse protagonists of production (Area of People's Property, private capitalism, independent producers) cannot be simply identified as a political "correlation of forces." The popular state's monopoly of force in itself gives a different content to the relations of production. Privately owned means of production are not the same thing in a context of revolutionary power, nor are wage relations. I have attempted to show that the organization of the masses cannot have a revolutionary character if not accompanied by a development of the intrinsic contradictions in civil society, and the consequent internal struggles, even under a revolutionary order that guarantees social cohesion. And this requires that the state/civil society relationship be redefined in the economic realm to decentralize power, or rather, permit its genesis under the new forms from the social bases of the revolution. The state's inherited backwardness carries such a powerful historical inertia that it could impede social development itself, strangling popular creativity. The foregoing appraisal of economic policy management during six years of transition in Nicaragua shows that the state cannot govern the economy without the active participation of civil society.

In short, state power has its limits in present-day Nicaragua. Some of these limits have been inherited from the Somoza regime, but others are derived from the resistance offered by civil society when the state's policies affect its most elemental reproduction, especially that of the masses. Resistance also arises when the state's credibility is diminished and there is an erosion of the state bureaucracy's legitimacy in running the economy. Yet the Sandinista political leadership, the FSLN, in its dealings with opposition forces, has been able to demonstrate pragmatism and skill, to the point of revising goals and objectives. This phenomenon gives a very far-reaching meaning to the 1985 rectifications in economic policy, state administration, and the mass organizations.

The process of building an effective democracy must go through a stage of growing economic democratization, which implies a genuine social revolution in the heart of civil society. This cannot be carried out exclusively from the highest state levels, without the active participation on the political stage of the autonomously organized social forces. The role of the vanguard—when it is neither mutually interdependent with the state bureaucracy nor confused with the mass organizations— is central to articulating and guaranteeing the leadership of this process. If this is achieved, then the separation between economics and politics may be gradually substituted for an integration which guarantees popular power and a social model guided by the logic of the majority.

This democratization should not be limited to worker participation in management in their centers of production. Nor should it be limited to mechanisms of political representation via periodic elections which establish the division between elected representatives and those represented. The term "participatory democracy" when used in Nicaragua has other institutional implications. It implies the creation of forums that will reflect the multiple contradictions running through society, where individual interests will converge to define the general interest in such a way that the popular classes will be the determining factor. It implies that the "peasant question," or the terms of the rural/urban relations, or the question of the bourgeoisie, or the "national (ethnic) question," be faced as national issues, with the active, direct participation of all the citizenry, and not as questions or demands of different groups before an omnipresent state. Possibly, the democratic exercise currently being carried out around the definition of a new constitution, for which genuinely open hearings have been organized, will set the pattern for a participatory mode which can be extended to other spheres of the social problematic, particularly that of the economy.[29]

To the extent that these democratic tendencies are accentuated and consolidated, it will be absurd to characterize the Nicaraguan state as "capitalist," or "populist," or much less as "Bonapartist." These features could appear from time to time in specific institutions or relations, but they would not define the character of a state in transition, the subject but also the object of transformation of the Sandinista Popular Revolution.

Notes

A preliminary version of this paper was presented at the IV Congress of Nicaraguan Social Sciences under the title "Política Económica y Revolucion Popular en Nicaragua: los costos políticos de la política económica."

1. A clear example of the latter was the FSLN's program for the November 1984 elections, which set forth in a nondemagogic manner a realistic picture of the nation's situation for the coming years.
2. By "planning" I mean a social process of collective management of the economy, in which economic agents participate under state direction. In this sense, the production of ineffective (if not unknown) documents for those affected does not mean "planning."
3. My concept of economic policy differs somewhat from the norm, which is usually limited to the state's handling of those mechanisms considered "economic" (prices, exchange rates, interest rates, currency, etc.). I also include technological policy, decapitalization laws, and others that directly affect the economic conditions of the members of the society (see Coraggio 1984).
4. My analysis focuses on state/civil society relations rather than on the triad state/party/masses since in Nicaragua there is effective multiparty competition over politics and ideology. Moreover, there is a national bourgeoisie and an important rural and urban petty bourgeoisie which can't be subsumed under the category "masses."
5. See Lichetenztejn (1981). In reality, to address economic logic is a political imperative. It is sometimes tempting to appeal to empiricist "realism," as do those who justify all economic problems citing the imperialist aggression, or those who reduce social causality to a single extraeconomic process (the war). However, it is evident that economic laws are still functioning although greatly affected by other causal factors. In this area, theory plays a fundamental role in establishing the various orders and types of determinism at each concrete juncture.
6. I will not deal here with attributes that depart from the strictly economic (gender, age, race, political ideology, religious beliefs, etc.), that are also important determining factors of economic behavior in response to a state policy, and that cannot be reduced to a class nature. On this theme see Coraggio (1985).
7. For example, it is evident that in Nicaragua, one cannot immediately identify the wage policy as an instrument directed toward the popular sectors, nor the policy toward intermediary activities as aimed at the middle-class sectors. Wages are the fundamental source of income for the middle class, and the poorest sectors of the society participate actively in "informal" intermediation. The real effect of an attack on speculation and of a revaluation of wages cannot be fully understood without taking this factor into consideration.
8. The very concept of "class struggle" must be questioned when the classes do not fit into the model embodied by this concept. The concept can be imposed upon reality, but it would be worth analyzing this question in

more depth because of its consequences for the relation between theory and practice. More comprehensive concepts, such as that of "social struggle," or a vision of social forces that includes groupings that do not fit into the schema of a society divided into classes, are an important approximation to these problems. Nevertheless, it remains to be seen how these analyses are integrated with the determinations—however incomplete they may be—of class, and the corresponding contradictions. On this theme see Núñez (1983).

The usual recourse of affirming that at this juncture the class struggle takes the form of an anti-imperialist struggle does not contribute analytically to the understanding of social contradictions, nor to orient the specific practice of distinct social agents in the revolutionary process. Everything tends to be reduced to a single principal contradiction, a mechanism which hinders "a concrete analysis of the concrete reality."

9. See "Medidas economicas forman parte de la defensa de la Patria," speech by Cmdte. Jaime Wheelock, *Barricada,* February 13, 1985. For a preliminary analysis and presentation of the measures, see *Barricada,* February 8, 1985.

10. At the end of 1979, when Cmdte. Henry Ruíz became minister of planning, it became clear that a decision had been made to make planning a central state activity. The Annual Plan for 1980 and 1981 (Nicaragua 1980; 1981) formalized this intention in official documents. But, the production of documents is not the same as the existence of a central process of economic planning. In fact, the financial system was increasingly taking on the functions of regulation and control through its allocation of foreign exchange, and through monetary and credit policy. Although it did not completely succeed, the financial system became the institution with the most substantive authority to control the Area of Public Property, the state-owned productive sector. In January 1983, the Ministry of Planning (MIPLAN) became the Secretariat of Planning, directly responsible to the Presidency of the Republic (see *Barricada,* January 8, 1985).

11. For example, the regional and sectoral Committees for Planning and Coordination, created by MIPLAN, were unable to overcome the strong institutionalist inertia of each ministry or area of state decisionmaking. In fact, the practice of planning itself contributed to its lack of legitimacy: goals were "handed down" in a manner thought of as inconsiderate by the agencies which received them; requests for information were issued whose use and destination were unclear, and which consumed efforts which the agencies would have preferred to devote to their own activities. These phenomena do not diminish MIPLAN's importance or responsibility in the management of the economy, as it participated in all the formal channels for coordinating economic policy and had the backing of a commander of the revolution and member of the FSLN National Directorate.

12. The case arose in 1981 of a state-owned livestock enterprise which produced sorghum as cattle feed. But since the consumer price for sorghum was below the price paid to the producer (the difference being a subsidy from the state marketing agency), the enterprise preferred to sell its sorghum crop and "re-buy" it, speculating on the price differential.

This action, of course, implied greater social costs with respect to transport, storage, administration, and so on.

13. More than 70 percent of the fiscal deficit in 1984 was covered through an expansion of the money supply. In February 1985 subsidies for consumer products were totally eliminated, but the subsequent skyrocketing of prices and costs made it necessary to reinstitute subsidies on some products (see Dévé and Grenier 1984).

14. See *Barricada,* December 21, 1983. On October 23 of that year the United States had invaded Grenada, and in Nicaragua it was felt that an invasion was imminent.

15. The problem of producer prices cannot be understood if seen only as a contradiction between state objectives (as regulator of the economy) and private interests. In some cases, state enterprises exerted pressure to increase prices in order to cover their deficits. Such price increases resulted in extraordinary profits by the most efficient private businesses in the same branch, as in the case of the sugar industry.

16. For the 1981–82 cycle, I calculated the following annual rates of return on variable capital invested: cotton: 24 percent; sugarcane: 52 percent; sesame: 192 percent; sorghum: 244 percent (all estimates based on average yields).

17. Without minimizing the importance of the objective factors behind the economic crisis (deteriorating terms of trade, the increasing cost of defense) we must concentrate on the subjective factors derived from an inappropriate economic policy. The February 1985 rectification points out the problems now being dealt with: elimination of subsidies on consumer goods, devaluation of the currency (maintaining a system of multiple exchange rates), and legalization of the parallel market in foreign exchange; salary adjustments aimed at maintaining salary purchasing power at 1984 levels, and increasingly linking wages to productivity; restricting public spending for social services; tax reforms aimed at reducing deficits and taxing income in the informal sector; increased interest rates (which continued to be highly prohibitive in all cases); maintenance of the profitability of private business through a policy of price adjustments to costs plus a margin of profit; price increases on imported goods via exchange rates and taxes, particularly of the goods of production; channeling of essential products to the peasantry and salaried workers in "productive" areas. But these measures, accompanied by a restricted investment plan and other measures to stimulate productivity and the rationalization of the appropriation of scarce resources (accelerated by the economic embargo subsequently imposed by the U.S. government in May 1985) cannot obtain rapid results, even though the measures moved in the right direction. In addition to high inflation (200 percent), the maintenance of the parallel foreign exchange market at a rate twelve times higher than the maximum official rate generates additional tensions leading to the "dollarization" of the economy. Relative prices are still not explicitly considered in the price-setting policy. The fact is that at present these measures are most affecting the popular sectors, for whom the salary is only one source of income, and not necessarily the most

important. The pressures to survive within the "cracks" of the formal economic system have not diminished, but have actually increased.

18. See Baumeister and Neira (this volume) for some examples of the distortion which this created with respect to class analysis.

19. As Carlos Fonseca argued, "there are those who in good faith think that it is advisable to hide revolutionary goals, and that in this they are aiding the Revolution. Experience has provided more than enough evidence to refute this point of view. . . . In order for the struggle against the Somoza dictatorship to triumph, the people's support is essential. This is practically impossible to attain if we hide our aspirations in favor of the peasantry and for the implementation of a revolutionary program of agrarian reform" (1982:35–36).

20. In fact, by 1982–83 there was a fair amount of data available pointing to the need to reorganize the focus of economic policy. This was clearly reflected in the document "Guidelines for the Economic Policy of the National Government of Reconstruction of Nicaragua" (1983–88), which was widely disseminated within and outside the nation in 1983. This document intended to issue the goals for economic growth and modify policy accordingly in order to achieve a financial adjustment along the lines of that finally adopted in 1985. During the intervening two-year period, the economic contradictions sharpened and the new measures took on the form of a *shock* policy.

21. The lack of professional and technical cadres with sufficient political clarity is a significant limitation. The revolutionary party tends to occupy the principal positions in the state apparatus, as well as in the budding mass organizations, in an effort to unify revolutionary action. But this, in turn, makes it difficult for the party to set itself up as an objective critic of state administration, as criticism could affect power positions within the party itself. As long as the mass organizations cannot develop autonomously with their own organic intellectuals they will continue to be impeded from carrying out criticism, with the additional strain that their rank and file may come to feel that their immediate demands are not being represented.

If the formation of technical and political cadres is to be a priority, we must ask what their education should consist of. Clearly necessary is the systematization of experience gained during the transition in order to overcome the inappropriate manuals focusing on the "theory of socialism." In fact, the experience of the Unidad Popular in Chile is more relevant to the Nicaraguan case than the experience of other processes qualified as socialist; see Bitar (1979).

22. The frequent FSLN reference to "phases" or "stages" is interpreted by the most politicized sectors of the bourgeoisie as meaning that their fate is sealed, and that the mixed economy is nothing more than a tactical ploy of the FSLN. While at one time this might have been true, the actual development of the revolutionary process indicates another meaning for this reference to stages, more associated with the overcoming of backwardness than with the elimination of capitalist ownership. Commander Víctor Tirado López has said, ". . . I'm asked if private enterprise is going to survive in Nicaragua. . . . (the mixed economy) is a strategic

program, not a tactical maneuver; . . . it's an emulation to see who is the most efficient, more productive, and who can resolve social problems. Therefore, the enterprises which raise their efficiency, their productivity, and help to solve the problems of backwardness, of poverty, of ignorance, are those which are going to survive, irregardless of whether they are public or private." (Transcription of the speech given by Commander Tirado in the Casa "José Benito Escobar," February 25, 1985.)

23. Despite the conviction of some state officials that the peasantry was a backward class, necessarily less efficient than state or private enterprises, practice demonstrated that the response of the peasantry to economic incentives could be superior to the business sectors and that in addition, they produced at lower costs, with less technologically intensive methods and using fewer imported products. Also, the limits of state production in this period became clear (Baumeister 1984; Wheelock 1985).

24. For example, producer prices have been continually renegotiated with the bourgeoisie, sometimes both before, during, and after the crop cycle.

25. In fact, the FSLN has made great efforts to explain the situation to the people, from the "Face the People" programs, in which cabinet officials meet with various local or sectoral groups to confront demands and engage in dialogue, to the revolutionary leaders' numerous talks. The problem is that the discourse is often not appropriate to the real receptive conditions of the masses, nor does it utilize the most efficient channels.

26. The results of a February-April 1985 poll of twenty-three Managua workplaces upheld this contention. Although all of the interviewees were participants in the Ministry of Education's adult education program, and 92 percent read the daily newspapers, 82 percent listened to radio, and 65 percent watched television, the survey revealed that 82 percent could not give an approximate percentage figure of the vote attained by the FSLN in the recent elections. This demonstrates the problems in the population's ability to handle percentages that are so widely used in explanations on the economy. A full 43 percent had no clear idea of what the APP was or anything about its nature and functions, and 37 percent had no idea at all of what the economic readjustment measures were (see Torres 1984).

27. See, for example, the address at the close of the National CDS Council by Cmdte. Leticia Herrera, "Fortalecer los CDS con nuevo estilo de conduccion," in *Barricada,* August 29, 1985.

28. See FitzGerald (1985a; 1985b) for an analysis of the economic costs of the aggression.

29. Notwithstanding the tragic conclusion of the Grenadian revolution, its experiment in the realm of popular participation in economic planning merits critical study. Torres (1984) reports that the collective discussions surrounding the 1982 Budget of the People not only forced state bureaucrats to learn to communicate—making economic concepts and problems accessible to the masses—but that as a result of the process of popular dialogue the national budget was significantly altered. Moreover, the collective decisionmaking process significantly increased productivity and strengthened efforts to fight corruption and waste.

The Making of a Mixed Economy: Class Struggle and State Policy in the Nicaragua Transition

▼▲

Eduardo Baumeister and Oscar Neira Cuadra

This essay considers the relationship between the type of capitalism inherited by the Sandinista revolution and the development initiatives carried out in its first five years. Our objective is to analyze the manner in which structural determinants condition the path of social transformation. Moreover, our concern is with how these structural determinants are perceived by different social actors, influencing the formulation of policy, rather than with the evaluation of the results of Sandinista development initiatives during the period 1979–84. The essay focuses on the articulation of distinct forms of production—state, capitalist, and peasant—in the mixed economy, and which forms have been strengthened or weakened as a result of policy interventions.

The structure of Nicaraguan society is quite different from that of Eastern Europe, the socialist countries of Asia and Africa, and nearby Cuba. At the risk of oversimplification, we can say that Nicaragua exhibits a level of commercialization and proletarization higher than that of tsarist Russia or the socialist Asiatic countries at the time of their respective revolutions. The most prominent difference between Cuba and Nicaragua is the lack of a plantation system in Nicaragua as in Cuba. What the Nicaraguan experience shares with most of the small peripheral economies in transition, including Cuba and Vietnam, is the virtual absence of an industrial base capable of industrializing agriculture.

These differences and similarities provide the framework for analyzing the various paradigms, implicit or explicit, of Nicaraguan political economy that have shaped emerging Sandinista policy initiatives. Throughout, we attempt to distinguish those results which are a product of deliberate initiatives from those which are obtained accidentally, with unpredictable or unfortunate effects. Three interconnected elements—forms of production, the emerging social forces of the revolution, and political practices—are directly related to a central

Translated by María Teresa Leite

theme of the Sandinista revolution, namely, the genesis, implementation, and transformation of a "vertical" social coalition, with a broad popular base and under revolutionary direction.

Structural Particularities

An analysis of the role of different forms of production in the transition to socialism must begin by considering the inherited social structure. Nicaragua is quite different from its neighbors in Central America (especially Honduras, El Salvador, and Guatemala), from the Caribbean countries (in particular, Cuba under Batista) and, finally, from the socialist countries of other continents.

One does not find in Nicaragua, as in other revolutionary societies, a large peasant mass, weakly linked to the market, with archaic technology. Neither does one find a large rural proletariat linked to plantation agriculture, nor haciendas or peasant communities. Rather than any single productive arrangement, small, medium, and large producers coexisted side by side, producing for export and the internal market. The majority of the Nicaraguan rural population (more than 75 percent) participated in the different markets, including the labor market. One of the unusual features of the Nicaraguan case is the early development of the credit market, and the extent to which agriculture was controlled indirectly by the banking sector, particularly as compared with other Latin American countries.[1]

Moreover, the peasantry, as other social groups, consumed both products and means of production that were wholly or in part imported. The policies of the revolution were to reinforce this high degree of integration of producers to credit, input, and product markets.

While one does find in Nicaragua uneven and unequal degrees of development between crops and regions, it appears that the degree of inequality is less than that found in other countries on the eve of revolution. Moreover, the level of inequality is quite distinct from that found in the Andes or in Guatemala, where the regional contrast between highlands and coast and peasants and capitalists is very sharp.

Taking into consideration the structural characteristics and production dynamics before 1979, Nicaragua did not exhibit the characteristics necessary for a democratic bourgeois revolution. There were no important precapitalist sectors. Moreover, the dominance of commercial and financial capital did not constitute a great obstacle to the dynamism of productive capital. Consequently, there was no need for a radical revolution to liberate the country from the chains of a precapitalist oligarchy. At the same time, the structural and political conditions to develop collective forms of production (state or cooperatives) as the primary form in the revolutionary period were not there either. The bulk of agriculture and a good part of industry was in the hands of small and medium-sized producers, including rich peasants, small landlords with capital, and the minor bourgeoisie. The other obstacle was that the peasantry could not be immediately integrated into collectivized production. There was no tradition of the peasant community upon which to build. The cooperatives have been formed primarily by peasants whose condition was closer to that of the rural proletariat (CIERA 1984).

It is important to consider the factors that engendered a significant sector of small and medium-sized producers in Nicaragua.[2] First, Nicaragua is blessed with a low population density. Maybe more important, the existence of an agricultural frontier which from the early 1940s was rapidly incorporated into production produced significant relocation of agricultural production which created favorable conditions for the development of new medium and large producers. Historically, one of the main obstacles to developing capitalist agriculture was the lack of sufficient labor. This implies that the size of enterprises producing crops which are labor intensive (like cotton and coffee) had to adapt to the availability of workers. Medium-sized farms of the coffee-growing interior regions of the country, which combined coffee production with grains and cattle, were able to attract more workers than other farms. This made possible the development of extensive medium-sized enterprises with relatively few permanent salaried workers. Large farms resembling plantations developed only in sugarcane, rice, and tobacco production, or in a few cases in the post-World War II period, as enterprises linked to an agroindustrial transformation process (cotton and coffee processing, in particular).

The currently most developed zone of the country, the north Pacific, was not incorporated into export agriculture practically until the mid-1940s. Before World War II, most coffee, cattle, and basic grain production was located in the Pacific region; several decades later it would shift to the interior regions.

These processes generated new class groupings; the generation which gave the greatest impulse to the development of coffee production and cattle breeding is practically the same one currently engaged in this activity. Thus, there could be at most two generations of coffee growers in the interior and something similar among the cotton growers of the north Pacific region.

An important sector of the peasantry experienced a similar process. For various reasons, they advanced on the agricultural frontier, changing the location of basic grain production. These were social individuals quite different from the peasantry subject to the payment of rent for access to land. They were more dynamic producers, integrated whenever possible (given road conditions) into the market. These individuals were not "land hungry," as were other sectors of the rural population. The historical demands of this group center on roads and credit.

Compared with the other Central American countries, Nicaragua's coffee production is less concentrated on haciendas, there are far fewer banana plantations, important numbers of small and medium-sized producers engage in cotton production, and basic grain production is much less centered on poorer peasants (Baumeister 1984a; 1984b).

As far as Cuba is concerned, it is important to mention the contrast in productive structures and their influence in the formation of the propertied and popular classes. These structural factors in each case influenced the creation of the sociopolitical conditions that made possible the taking of power and the construction of the new economy. There are also important differences in the dynamism of the economy of each country prior to the revolutionary victory and the international economic contexts in which the new governments had to operate.

The Cuban sugar plantations were highly controlled by foreign capital, and land was extremely concentrated, as was the economic power of the sugarmills over smaller producers; these conditions generated an important rural proletariat. In this structural setting three fundamental issues arose in the early revolutionary period: the question of independence and self-determination, the question of democracy, and the social class question, given the highly organized and combative agroindustrial proletariat (López Segrera 1985; Martínez Allier 1971).

The agrarian structure of Nicaragua did not generate anything resembling the Cuban sugar plantation and mills. Moreover, foreign investment in Nicaragua was one of the lowest in all Latin America. The presence of foreign capital was restricted to the gold mines on the Atlantic coast, and to a few industrial firms. The independence issue in Nicaragua was focused on the political control exercised by the Somoza family dictatorship. There were antagonisms, of course, related to the presence of foreign capital in trade and in finance, characteristic of any dependent nation.

The issue of democracy brought together important sectors of the anti-Somoza bourgeoisie due to political and economic contradictions. Given the small number of workers, and the fact that there were no unions or parties in which workers could organize themselves, the class issue was to be quite different in Nicaragua. The proletariat could not become the driving force of the revolution. In short, the nature of the national sovereignty problem and the degree of development of the working class are the factors which most differentiate Cuba and Nicaragua, factors reflecting structural differences.

Mention should also be made of the different economic dynamics before the revolutionary triumphs. In Cuba, sugar production had stagnated practically from the mid-1920s until the time of the revolution, except for the immediate post-World War II years (Pierre-Charles 1971). In contrast, Nicaragua had a high rate of growth in the postwar period, particularly in agriculture.[3]

We have argued that one of the basic elements characterizing Nicaraguan agriculture was the relative homogeneity among the units of production, particularly with respect to their level of participation in input, labor, and credit markets.

Nicaraguan agriculture includes diversified types of producers of whom the proportion who are also part-time wage workers is greater than in any other country that has attempted a socialist transition, with the exception of Cuba. In fact, in tsarist Russia, salaried farmworkers made up no more than 5 percent of the economically active population (EAP); in Tanzania it was less than 2 percent, and in Angola, 16 percent and Mozambique, 21 percent. In Nicaragua, agricultural wage workers represented from 30 percent to 40 percent of the labor force.[4]

The transition from capitalist to socialist agriculture in Nicaragua has to be carried out without the benefits of a large-scale capitalist economy, or even precapitalist relations (feudal, communal, or asiatic) which may favor collectivization. Rather, the transition in Nicaragua must be built on highly commercialized, small and medium-sized productive units. Nonetheless, the Sandinista revolution, and the political system now being developed, are favored by the existence of a weak bourgeoisie and a large mass of producers who are antioligarchic.

The Overpoliticization of the Mixed Economy

The form in which power was seized in 1979 has influenced the perception and practices of the revolutionary government with respect to the different groups which constitute the nation's private sector. The relationship between the state and the various groups of the private sector could be characterized as one of "overpoliticization." This is the antithesis of "economism."

An economistic interpretation would maintain that political-ideological behavior and coalitions of political parties or groups would be directly related to the economic power of the various actors. A political interpretation implicitly begins by analyzing these actors in the political arena, subsequently turning to their economic behavior. The analysis would then turn to the policies of the revolution with respect to each sector, considering who was being supported or undermined.

The issue of "overpoliticization" in the management of the mixed economy can be understood as a reading of the relative importance of certain social forces in the political arena and its correlation with real economic power. Three examples illustrate our point: the relative weight in the economy of Somoza's former enterprises; the economic importance of the private sector organized in the Higher Council of Private Enterprises (COSEP); the real economic significance of small and medium-sized producers of the private sector.

All too often it has been assumed that the organized private sector, that which has a political presence, is representative of the whole private sector. Thus, before the revolution, two forces in the economy were recognized: that of the Somozas, and that of a separate group of non-Somocista bourgeoisie.[5] Immediately after the revolutionary triumph in 1979, the emphasis shifted to an undifferentiated private sector represented by COSEP on the one hand, and the state sector on the other.

For a long time it was thought that Somoza controlled about 50 percent of the nation's production and that as a consequence of nationalization, the state sector would begin with a significant share of the country's productive base.[6] However, it is now obvious that this was not the case. Somoza controlled not 50 percent of total production, but rather, half of the resources controlled by the *large* bourgeoisie. The idea that such a high percentage of the total economy was in Somoza's hands probably came from the anti-Somoza sector of the bourgeoisie. The economic analysis was overpoliticized because it was analyzed from the standpoint of the struggle over political power. It took a while to assimilate the fact that the percentage of the economy taken over from Somoza was much lower than had been thought.

Also significant is the identification that is made between the private sector and the forces of COSEP. The idea that the private sector, organized in COSEP, was the "alter ego" of the mixed economy lasted longer than the question of the importance of Somoza's control of the economy. At first, COSEP was seen as the representative of the capitalist sector; it was only subsequently that a distinction came to be made between the leadership of COSEP, associated with the commercial sector, and the producers' associations (cotton, sorghum, rice, and coffee growers, etc.). The leadership presented itself as if it represented the interests of the entire group of producers.

In some agricultural sectors this did not pose a serious problem because the large-sized producers organized in these associations in fact constituted the bulk of the producers (as in rice and sorghum). The distribution of resources among them, their investment perspectives and political ideology were relatively homogeneous. However, as far as the three basic products of Nicaraguan agriculture are concerned (cotton, coffee, and cattle), this linear association of corporate political representation with the mass of producers generated a distorted administration of the mixed economy.

The third example is that of the small and medium-sized producers. During the first two years of the revolution they were considered to be part of the peasantry, especially important in the production of basic grains (corn and beans). But as a whole, their participation in the economy was undervalued, for they were actually contributing about 50 percent of agricultural production. Moreover, they were also important producers of agricultural exports.[7]

The recognition of the role of these producers in the economy, beyond traditional basic grain production, had to await their organization as a political force in the National Union of Farmers and Cattlemen (UNAG), and the Agrarian Reform. Also decisive in the recognition of their importance was the negative reaction of many large-sized producers to the policies of the revolution. The small and medium-sized farmers took much more positive stands with respect to these policies, differentiating them from the majority of large-sized producers of the private sector.

It is also important to take into account that small and medium-sized producers are not a homogeneous group. There were at least three subdivisions within this sector: (1) the members of the agricultural production cooperatives, with preferential access to land and machinery; (2) small producers of basic grains with difficulties in accumulating capital and a tendency toward stagnation; (3) small and medium-sized producers dedicated to export crops and the cultivation of vegetables, with a tendency toward accumulation. While the social weight of the peasantry as a whole is considerable, the economic weight with respect to production lies with this latter group.

Paradigms, Policies, and the Mixed Economy

Various paradigms with respect to economic transformation have shaped, explicitly or implicitly, the economic policies of the Sandinista revolution. These paradigms differ as to the role assigned to different economic entities, and specifically, the relative importance and priority assigned to state, cooperative, and private forms of property. The main issues concern (1) the degree to which centralized planning or the free market is to be favored; (2) whether accumulation is to take place in the public or private sector; (3) the degree of orientation toward national or international markets; and (4) whether state enterprises should be managed by the state or by the workers.

In the first place, a paradigm that emphasizes the development of the material productive forces can be distinguished. A second emphasizes recovery and expanding the economy on the existing productive structure. A third insists on increasing the power of the state in the productive realm and in its general control of the economy. A fourth paradigm emphasizes the role of small and medium-sized producers in the mixed economy. These differing emphases need not necessarily always be contradictory, since they reflect the various economic tasks of the revolution: namely, to develop the productive forces, to surpass pre-revolution levels of production, to strengthen the state, and to strengthen the nucleus of small and medium-sized agricultural and industrial producers. However, these differing emphases in practice have been contradictory at the institutional level with regard to policy.

In Nicaragua, the various state institutions have unilaterally emphasized one of the approaches mentioned above. The emphasis on increasing the productive forces has characterized the ministries with productive responsibilities, especially the Ministry of Agriculture. The emphasis on economic recovery based on the existing productive structure from the technical/productive as well as the social point of view is evident in those institutions concerned with marketing, public finance, and the broader financial system. The emphasis on the development of the state has been most important in the 1979 to 1984 period in the Ministry of Planning, which has been concerned with extending the mechanisms of direct state control over the economy. The support of small and medium-sized agricultural and industrial producers, in contrast to other positions, has crossed ministerial lines.

The "sectoralism" which this reveals within the Nicaraguan state apparatus to a large extent reflects the nature of the state in a revolutionary context. Nonetheless, it is important to point out that the Nicaraguan case differs significantly from the Chilean situation under the Popular Unity government where the tensions focused on the class struggle, disputes among the various political parties (right-wing and left-wing parties as well as within the left), and ideological confrontations.

In the Nicaraguan context, the struggle between capital and labor and confrontations between political parties, both in general and within the state apparatus, have been less significant. Ideological debates about different "interpretations" of Marxism have also not played a major role in development debates. Rather, the Sandinistas have been quite pragmatic here as in other important issues. In the case of economic policy, however, the result has been the uneven formulation and application of macroeconomic and sectoral policy.

The Emphasis on Material Productive Forces

In this paradigm, which has broad consensus in the productive ministries, emphasis is placed on the creation of a new productive apparatus, with technological levels superior to the inherited productive base. The main beneficiaries of the new investment projects would be the state enterprises, although other sectors, such as the production cooperatives, might participate as well. The high level of investment in and mechanization of agriculture in the revolutionary period reflects this emphasis. In fact, the average level of capital imports in Nicaragua has been higher than in other Central American countries during the last few years.

The Emphasis on Economic Recovery

The principal concern of those who emphasize economic recovery is increasing the short-run supply of goods and services either for the internal market or for export. Less attention is given to technological levels of production or to the relative importance of different types of producers. In order to expand output, proponents of this view have argued for expansionary credit policies, improved marketing channels, and more effective mechanisms of input distribution. Within this paradigm, maintaining the profitability of production is a paramount concern. The institutions most closely linked to this paradigm are those related to marketing, banking, and public finance. Their policy recommendations, in general, focus on productive incentives for private producers, rather than mechanisms of controlling this sector.

The Emphasis on Strengthening the State

This paradigm places greatest emphasis on the need to strengthen the economic importance of the state, arguing for greater state control over marketing, a more significant state role in direct production, and economic direction by means of centralized planning.[8] This perspective has been advanced by the Ministry of Planning, and to a much lesser degree by the productive ministries, and it is associated with a political analysis that considers the private sector to be made up of only a few large-sized producers. Thus it perpetuated the idea of the existence of only two main sectors in the Nicaraguan economy: the state sector, or area of people's property (APP), and the private sector, the latter represented by COSEP and its sectoral associations. From this it was concluded that the main and practically exclusive problem in the relationship between the state and the private sector in the economic realm was a problem of power. This analysis assumed that the private sector would modify its behavior if it were conceded morsels of political power such as protection of private property, key positions in the government, and so on. Its proponents also regarded as unacceptable economic policies that would favor this sector. Fixing prices to reflect increasing costs of production, for example, was seen as a "concession" to the private sector, which would inevitably strengthen it. In short, this was the perspective that most politicized the relationship between the state and the private sector because it associated any initiative of the state or of the private sector with the logic of political power.

This "pro-statist" perspective did not take into account two fundamental elements: (1) the actual composition of the private sector which, as we have pointed out, was quite heterogeneous and in which the large bourgeoisie was not of decisive economic importance, and (2) the low level of corporate development attained by the large bourgeoisie. Traditionally, the relationship between the Somocista state and the private sector was maintained through personal contacts. Bourgeois business associations developed only in the last years of Somoza's regime, following the First Congress of the Private Sector in 1974, called to allocate responsibility for the reconstruction of Managua after the earthquake (INDE 1974). A number of organizations were founded in March 1979, in the heat of the anti-Somocista struggle. Among them was the Union of Agricultural Producers (UPANIC), set up in large part as a result of the efforts of businessmen with close ties to the FSLN (who now have positions of responsibility in the state). In any case, the corporate groupings that existed included only the more traditional bourgeois sectors (merchants, coffee growers, cotton growers) and these never made any effort to integrate the masses of small and medium-sized producers or employers, or to represent their interests. Only after July 1979 would the bourgeois associations try to appeal to these groups.

It is interesting to observe that the "pro-statist" paradigm has its counterpart in what we will call the "ultra-privatist" paradigm, at the top level of COSEP. The participation of the COSEP leaders in the last stage of the struggle against the Somoza regime allowed them to claim for themselves a degree of representation and power that did not correspond to their real economic importance in the country, much less to their limited capacity for political mobilization. When Alfonso Robelo and Violetta Barrios de Chamorro left the Junta in May 1980, COSEP proposed a way to "overcome" the resulting political crisis: to include two of its members in the Government Junta of National Reconstruction (JGRN), with veto power; to assign to their members the ministries of Justice and Finance and the presidency of the Central Bank; and to grant them control of the national finance system (Ramírez 1983:190).

The problem of the strengthening of the state, especially with respect to control of commerce and a good deal of production, is closely related to a continuing characteristic of Nicaraguan society that has influenced the policies of the revolution. The inherited tension between productive capital and commercial-financial capital is reproduced, in the post-revolutionary period, in the relationship between the institutions directly related to productive activities and those concerned with commerce and finance. The dominant institutions are those which support the enhancement of the productive sectors, whether state or private. This is related to the nature of the coalition that overthrew Somoza and the demands articulated in the program of the Government Junta of National Reconstruction (JGRN 1979), as well as to the class and professional compositions of a good number of the intermediate- and high-ranking cadres in the economic sector. Among this group are some agrarian entrepreneurs and former managers of modern productive establishments (in sugar, intensive cattle breeding, and cotton), protagonists of the need to industrialize Nicaragua's agriculture.

The dominance of production-oriented institutions resulted, for example, in the extension of bank credit to productive sectors that previously had no access to it (with preference given to the state sector); in the subsidization of interest rates; in credit policies covering full production costs; and in the notable increase in investment in the productive sector (CIERA 1982; 1984a).

Centralized planning was seen as a mechanism of economic engineering in the sense of providing the human and material resources to the different sectors, usually known as the technical-material balance. Less attention was given to economic policies as well as to the financial, commercial, and fiscal mechanisms of regulation and management. This conception of planning, focused on the material balances between sectors, promoted an emphasis on the state sector in the institutions most closely related to national planning. These schemes are easier to apply in the state sector than in the private.

The Emphasis on Small and Medium-sized Production

The emphasis on promoting small and medium-sized production is the result of various initiatives which cross the state apparatus horizontally. Beginning in 1979, but becoming more important since 1983, these initiatives were discernible in the development of cooperatives in the agrarian reform process, as well as the encouragement of small industry and artisan production. The importance of this sector is now considerable, accounting for about 40 percent of the GNP of the country and two-thirds of productive employment.

Support to small producers has been significant in such crops as cotton, coffee, vegetables, and beans through such state policies as the lowering of land rentals, access to machinery, and access to credit. Nonetheless, this sector has received proportionately less credit compared to its contribution to the value of production, as Table 1 shows.

One of the main characteristics of this sector, independent of the not unimportant differences between small producers (peasants) and medium-sized producers (farmers or small landlords), is that it is committed to Nicaragua's future. It does not have the migration options of the large producers.

The plebian characteristics of this productive sector make them allies

Table 1
Correlation of Forces in Agriculture, 1984
(percentages)

	Land	Credit	Production
Private:			
Large bourgeoisie	13	24	25
Small & medium producers	51	22	19
Service cooperatives*	10	17	25
Production cooperatives	7	5	7
State	19	32	24
Total	100	100	100

Source: MIDINRA (1984)
*Includes small and medium producers.

of the Sandinista project. However, they are not the "classic" actors of a socialist transition, along the model of Eastern Europe or Asia. As mentioned, Nicaragua does not have the advantages of a low level of commoditization or of capitalist development in agriculture, as do the majority of countries in transition to socialism, nor has it the advantages of a deep and well-concentrated capitalist development, as was true in Cuba. Thus the question arises of how these small and medium-sized producers will be articulated in the long run, to advance in a socialist direction. It appears that these groups will survive largely with their current characteristics, implying peaceful long-term coexistence while other, deeper transformations are taking place.

From a theoretical point of view these small and medium producers are located in three modes or forms of production. One group is located within the laws of capitalist forms of production, for as "medium" producers they in fact approach small capitalists. Another group, "small" producers, more closely resemble petty commodity producers as poor or middle peasants. Finally, the production cooperatives (the CASs) represent a complex form of production where collective ownership of means of production is combined with the hiring of wage labor, the usufruct of individual land parcels, and massive state assistance in the form of access to land, credit, investment, and technical assistance.

As a result, the revolutionary transition means distinct and separate programs for each of these sectors, some of which lead to contradictions between them, such as between "medium" producers and poor peasants, and the rich peasant situated in zones of mobilized poor peasants.

State and Private Sector Relations (1980–84)

The Sandinista revolution introduced a series of changes in the pattern of economic reproduction inherited from the Somoza regime, changing its mode of operation. The creation of new forms of property through the nationalization of a good part of the modern sector of the economy, as well as through the cooperativization of small producers, did not result in the disappearance of the "private sector." Looking at the objective relationships between the so-called socialized sector of the economy and the private sector, taking into account that the latter consists of heterogeneous forms of production, we conclude that the new correlation of forces promoted by the revolution is reflected in economic policies that have prioritized the state and cooperative sectors as foci of economic development, while maintaining the private sector. The pattern of accumulation and consumption has been modified by eliminating the overexploitation of the labor force, promoting its rapid organization as workers and peasants and its ability to pressure the state at both the local and national level. Moreover, the law of value has been restricted, with state control over key sectors of the economy and the attempts at economic planning. These are clear-cut examples of the new state and its social projection, which advances the material and moral premises of the social revolution on the foundation of an essentially capitalist society.

The concentration of wealth achieved by the Somoza family made it relatively easy to create a broad public sector in Nicaragua through the nationalizations carried out immediately after the overthrow of the dictatorship. The contribution of the state in national production went from 15 percent in 1978 to 36 percent in 1980. This increase is the consequence of the appropriation of almost half of the land held in farms of more than 350 hectares (even though this represented only 20 percent of the nation's farm land), of approximately one-third of industry, and of almost all of the construction sector. The North American- and Canadian-owned mines were also expropriated with compensation. Overall, the state controlled a little more than one-fourth of all material production and almost one-half of service sector production. With the nationalization of foreign trade and banking, the new public sector that emerged after the revolution appeared equipped with strong mechanisms of economic control and a not insignificant productive capacity.

Changes in Agriculture

In the agricultural sector, along with the new state enterprises, one finds small and medium-sized producers as well as capitalist producers, as previously discussed. In the initial phase of the revolution, up until the end of 1979, rural proletarians and semiproletarians began taking over lands spontaneously, especially in the Pacific coast regions (León, Masaya, and Granada) and in the center regions of Matagalpa. These regions are basically dedicated to export production (cotton, sugarcane, and coffee). The task of what was then called the Nicaraguan Institute of Agrarian Reform (INRA) soon became to impede an uncontrolled taking over of the lands used for export crops while constituting and managing the state enterprises formed on the expropriated lands. The state also attempted to control, indirectly, the export-oriented capitalist sector through the use of credit and its monopoly over foreign trade. The immediate objective of the state was to reactivate production of traditional export crops (cotton, coffee, and sugar), which accounted for the special attention given to the large agrarian bourgeoisie. As for the state sector, it benefited from a massive injection of productive resources; for example, the majority of the nation's machinery and equipment. Investment policies were designed to dynamize the state sector so that it would have comparative advantages over the private sector.

On the other hand, the need and desire to respond to the demands of the peasantry led the government to enact a series of decrees to impede the overexploitation of workers (such as the establishment and enforcement of the minimum wage) and to reduce land rental rates. The amount of credit granted to small producers was also increased significantly, as were the prices of peasant crops. The redistribution of land under the Agrarian Reform Law began at the end of 1981, as a response to the demands of the peasants and landless workers. Beneficiaries of land redistribution, production cooperatives versus individual producers, has changed over time. Until late 1983, little land was redistributed or titled individually. Emphasis was on the effort to organize production cooperatives. After October 1983, largely as a result of the increased military attacks by the imperialists in the border regions, and with the consequent need to form a solid political alliance with the peasantry, the process of titling individuals was accelerated.

The Agrarian Reform has fundamentally altered land tenancy in Nicaragua. By the end of 1984 the state controlled 19 percent of the agricultural land and the agricultural production cooperatives controlled 7 percent, which together meant that 26 percent was in the socialized sector. The control of land by large landowners went from 36 percent in 1977 to only 13 percent in 1984.[9] Of the remaining land, 10 percent belongs to individuals grouped in service cooperatives and 51 percent is in the hands of unorganized small and medium-sized private producers; the latter are the essence of the mixed economy (see Table 1.)

The growing importance of state and cooperative property created the material conditions for central planning. Nonetheless, this has not

Table 2
Structure of Agricultural Production, 1983
(percent contribution to agricultural GDP, by crop)

Sector	State	Capitalist	Peasantry	Total
Export:	27.9	42.3	29.8	100
Cotton	23.5	50.0	26.5	100
Coffee	22.6	35.4	42.0	100
Sugarcane	48.6	39.4	12.0	100
Sesame	1.1	3.8	95.1	100
Internal Consumption	18.8	15.1	66.1	100
Sorghum	11.1	34.4	54.5	100
Rice	47.1	35.7	17.2	100
Beans	1.8	0.3	97.9	100
Corn	13.5	5.3	81.2	100
Total	24.8	32.8	42.4	100

Source: Data obtained from MIDINRA (1984).

really been realized. Up until now, the mixed economy project has resulted in relatively weak state control over the agrarian private sector and a consequent state policy to ensure the smooth articulation of the different forms of production. However, the state directly controls new investments in the agricultural sector.

Part of the planning problem is that there is not a one-to-one correspondence between the form of organization of production and product specialization, as Table 2 shows. Thus, while peasant producers dominate basic grain production they are also important producers of coffee and cotton, producing 42 percent and 27 percent, respectively, of these exports, and 95 percent of sesame production for export. Capitalist farmers produce basic grains, such as rice and sorghum, contributing from 34 percent to 36 percent of total production, while dominating export production as a whole.

In general, capitalist producers have adopted a distrustful attitude toward the revolution. The agrarian bourgeoisie is concentrated, in numbers and importance, in the production of cotton. This group's economic behavior is an indicator of the attitude they have adopted. Since 1980 the volume of their production of cotton has decreased 7 percent annually (average 1980–83).

The attitude of sorghum and cattle producers has been mixed; coffee growers have maintained their plantations but without the usual care and with no intention of expanding the area in production. Only among

Table 3
Structure of Industrial Production, 1983
(percent contribution to manufacturing GDP by sector)

Sector	State	Capitalist*	Small	Total
Food, beverages, and tobacco	34.8	48.3	16.9	100
Textile, leather, and shoes	23.1	14.3	62.6	100
Wood and furnishing	28.9	6.3	64.8	100
Paper, printing, and editorial	17.3	60.8	21.9	100
Chemical products and oil	9.3	90.0	0.7	100
Non-steel	74.3	9.4	16.3	100
Basic steel products	0.0	56.8	43.2	100
Machinery and equipment	38.5	47.2	14.3	100
Others	11.1	0.0	88.9	100
Total	27.7	49.0	23.3	100

Source: Data compiled from Ministry of Industry figures.
*All those who employ five or more workers. Small industries which employ fewer than five workers were not included in censuses before 1981, when a special survey of this group was undertaken.

sugar and rice producers does the evidence suggest cooperation with the policies of the revolution. All in all, the capitalist sector is in a sense "on hold," producing with generous credit and little of their own working capital. It is neither investing nor augmenting the area under production (except for the single private sugar plantation). Its economic logic focuses on accumulating foreign currency and the subsequent deterioration of farms and plantations. If they invest at all it is in agricultural machinery, the purchase of which is subsidized by the state.

The peasant sector has responded satisfactorily, extending the area cultivated and the production of beans and cotton. The state has steadily increased its production of all crops and has tried to make up for the lack of dynamism in areas key to domestic consumption, such as cattle and meat production. Slowly and with great difficulty, the state is beginning to produce basic grains with high technological levels.

Changes in Industry

In the industrial realm, the People's Industrial Corporation (COIP) was initially constituted in 1979 with ninety-five firms. In 1983 it accounted for 28 percent of industrial production. Small firms (with less than five employees) contribute almost as much, 23 percent; their weight is considerable, as Table 3 shows, in the garment and shoe

Table 4
Index of Industrial Production (factory price)
(1980 = 100)

Branch/sector	State Sector			Private Sector		
	1981	*1982*	*1983*	*1981*	*1982*	*1983*
Food	149	179	189	111	120	144
Beverages	94	73	78	110	116	133
Tobacco	n.d.	n.d.	n.d.	105	92	102
Textiles	156	335	411	91	6	10
Garment	237	250	486	93	76	83
Leather	267	298	159	85	91	83
Shoes	257	284	432	101	87	74
Wood	150	129	118	78	67	62
Furniture	180	156	161	100	87	89
Paper	84	90	83	148	185	213
Printing	128	161	179	138	142	158
Rubber	n.d.	n.d.	n.d.	124	124	108
Chemicals	81	120	148	97	83	99
Non-metal	108	115	162	59	21	25
Metals	97	180	233	103	37	37
Artifacts	228	230	373	110	70	79
Others	241	224	252	87	77	83
Total	116	135	164	103	92	97

Source: Data compiled from Ministry of Industry, five-year evaluation, inter-office document, 1984 (data have been rounded).
n.d.: no state production registered.

industries and in the wood and furniture industries. The capitalist sector, accounting for 49 percent of manufacturing GDP, is dominant in chemical production and in the paper and printing industry.

The transformations envisioned for the industrial sector rested upon an extremely vulnerable base. The industrial dynamism of the previous decade was related to the ephemeral development of the regional market in manufactured products. Import substitution industrialization did not result in substantially expanding manufacturing employment nor in increasing demand for local primary products. Neither did it produce the implements and equipment needed to industrialize agriculture or rural consumer goods.

The state, through its control over the allocation of foreign exchange, directly influences which manufacturing sectors can prosper. Priority has been given to petroleum refining, construction, and the food

Table 5
Global Structure of Production, 1983
(percent contribution to GDP, by form of production)

Form/sector	State	Capitalist	Small Producers	Total
Agro Exports	28	42	30	100
Domestic Consumption	19	15	66	100
Cattle	20	12	68	100
Industry	28	49	23	100
Other Material Production	90	5	5	100
Government	100	0	0	100
Commerce and Service	38	12	50	100
Total	40	29	31	100

Sources: Data compiled from Ministries of Planning, Industry, and Agrarian Reform, internal publications.

industry, while durable consumer goods and other nonbasic manufacturing (production of paint, personal hygiene items, etc.) have been discouraged.

Production in the capitalist industrial sector has been irregular and in decline, except for beverage production. This is due partly to the reorganization of the sector to respond to national needs and the decline in external loans to Nicaragua. But it is also due to decapitalization on the part of many of these businesses. On more than one occasion, workers have taken over factories to prevent their bankruptcy. Overall, many of these firms count with an obsolete productive structure which has not received adequate maintenance; the capitalist sector has not invested significantly.

The state industrial sector has attempted to respond to the new pattern of demand. This is evident in the reactivation of the food industry that includes the majority of the agroindustrial enterprises. The aim is to build a new type of agroindustrial sector, which will allow the vertical integration of agriculture and industry, with the double purpose of generating foreign exchange and foodstuffs. This subsector is increasing in weight as compared to the light consumer industry. Construction, where the state predominates, is most dynamic, since the high level of investment in the economy is accompanied by the expansion of productive capacity, along with infrastructure such as roads and buildings.

Overall, by 1983 the state controlled 40 percent of GDP, as shown in Table 5. The state was more important than the capitalist sector only in agricultural production for the internal market and cattle production and with respect to commerce and service. It surpassed the contribution of small producers only in manufacturing.

Conclusion: State and Revolution

We have argued that the formulation of state policies has been very much influenced by the analysis of the political reality of the country, which overvalued the economic influence of the most organized and active groups. There was a corresponding undervaluation of the economic influence of small and medium-sized producers who were less organized, had less access to the mass media, and less contact with the professional elite of the state.

On the other hand, the state apparatus was not able to differentiate between its sectoral activity and management of the global economy. The various ministries and institutions became the protagonists of their own projects, turning these into development initiatives for the whole economy. Lacking was any coordinated direction within the state apparatus to regulate the various activities of the private and state productive sectors.

These two points bring us back to the problem of constructing a state in the context of economic backwardness and revolutions from below. On the one hand, a political revolution based on a liberation struggle with a high degree of popular mobilization destroys the existing state apparatus, and then it must replace a good number of the intermediary bureaucrats. On the other hand, the revolutionary coalition requires that the state rapidly take over the space of the defeated alliance and at the same time begin an alternative and more complex method of economic intervention. In the case of Nicaragua, the taking over of the activities of Somoza (foreign trade, banks, confiscated companies) was relatively fast. Thus the problem of the state apparatus has been how to articulate its relation to the international market and at the same time meet the internal social demands created by this type of revolution.

This has led us to analyze the principle actors of the revolution and their role in defining the model of development. Schematically, we have distinguished the revolutionary vanguard, the masses mobilized by the revolutionary process, the inherited bureaucracy, and those economic sectors that have been thrown out of power but that still have economic influence. Each group may have its own model of development, viewing the future of the revolution with respect to the experience of other countries as reference. The question is how similar to other models theirs will be and how long it will take them to build their own model based on Nicaraguan reality.

Notes

1. The proportion of agricultural credit as a share of gross agricultural product was .35 for all of Latin America in 1973 (Ladmau and Adams 1978:43). In Nicaragua, it was as high as .64 in 1975 (our estimate, based on data of Banco Central de Nicaragua). The centralization of financial and commercial capital was partially created by the dependence of Nicaragua on the United States from the second decade of this century. At that time, the Banco Nacional of Nicaragua and its branch— Compañía Mercantil de Ultramar—were founded and were to control Nicaraguan foreign trade in subsequent decades. Later on, even though some important changes occurred, the organic separation of large producers from the banks and commercial companies was to persist. The Nicaraguan pattern thus is quite different from that in Guatemala and El Salvador where there are close vertical relationships among these entities. The three most important financial groups (those connected with Banco de America or the Pellas family, Banco Nicaraguense, and the Somoza family) in the 1960s in Nicaragua directly controlled 22 percent of the agricultural gross domestic product (GDP); 25 percent of that of industry; 35 percent of commerce; and 71 percent of construction (Strachan 1972:78).
2. This section draws on Baumeister (1984a) and Munro (1967). For the population census data see Levy (1976); on the labor force, see CIERA (1982).
3. From 1950 to 1977 agricultural production increased at an annual rate of 4.7 percent, one of the highest in all Latin America (CEPAL 1979:17).
4. Nicaraguan Population Census, 1963 and 1971; for Russia, see Shanin (1983); for Mozambique, ILO (1981:18); for Tanzania, McHenry (1979:44–5); for Angola, Guerra (1979).
5. Within the non-Somocista bourgeoisie, three financial groups can be distinguished: one related to Banco de America, one to Banco Nicaraguense, and one associated with the rest of the private sector (see Wheelock 1975; Strachan 1972).
6. North American professionals contributed to this overevaluation of the economic importance of the Somoza family. For example, Woodward reported that "it has been estimated that by 1970 they [the Somoza family] owned more than half of the agricultural production of the republic" (1976:221).
7. In 1983 small and medium producers contributed 38.7 percent of the value of agricultural exports and 69.6 percent of that oriented toward domestic consumption. They accounted for 64.3 percent of animal production, bringing their overall sectoral contribution to 54 percent. According to CIERA estimates, the state's sectoral share was 23 percent, as was that of the large private sector.
8. There is general agreement in Nicaragua of the need to strengthen the economic role of the state. There is disagreement, however, over the extent of state control. Some favor a strengthened role of the state only as the "general economic coordinator" through its control of such mecha-

nisms as external trade, finance, public expenditure, and taxation. Others would also add some state presence in direct production. The paradigm discussed here goes beyond these two positions, emphasizing the need for broader state control over means of production and the need for centralized planning.

9. The state currently controls 52 percent of the total number of farms with more than 350 hectares.

State and Society
in the Transition to Socialism:
The Theoretical Legacy

▼▲

Carollee Bengelsdorf

It is a curious paradox that the transition to socialism in the countries of the periphery has largely been measured not primarily against the experience of other like countries, but in relation to the Soviet Union. A frozen and static version of the experience of the Soviet Union has, more than any other single or particular element, determined and defined the shape and the boundaries of "actually existing socialism" (Bahro 1978) and/or clouded the common understanding of the meaning of socialism. It has structured the debates concerning the nature of the relationship between state and society during the transition, and formed the outcome of these debates. And if this "official Marxist-Leninist" version of Soviet history and reality becomes the standard, then anything other becomes a "unique experiment" or a "deviation": thus, for instance, analysts speak of the "Cuban heresy" that attempted at the end of the 1960s to simultaneously achieve socialism and communism. We are reminded of Rosa Luxemburg's prescient warning concerning the dangers of making a virtue out of necessity, of "freez[ing] into a complete theoretical system" tactics necessitated by "fatal circumstances" (1972:79).

It would seem to be far more relevant to work within another framework, one which takes cognizance of the experiences of countries in the periphery and allows these experiences to define the critical axes of comparison. And in undertaking the structuring of such a framework, by the same logic, it seems incumbent upon us to attempt to recover the theoretical parameters of the transition to socialism, for here too, the Soviet Union, in claiming for itself the legacy of the Marxist tradition concerning postcapitalist state and society, has given that tradition a particular coloring and interpretation which, at critical junctures, would seem to disguise what I will argue are its most fundamental and relevant features: thus, for instance, the popular image of the "dictatorship of the proletariat."

In this effort to reclaim the Marxist theoretical heritage concerning the relationship between postcapitalist state and society, two conclusions stand out. First, the single most important message of this heritage is the profoundly democratic thrust inherent in its vision of an entire people as subject, of a people empowered. This message is as relevant today as it was a century ago. It is a message whose diametrical opposite is the now infamous remark of former Polish leader Edward Gierek to Polish workers: "You work well, we'll govern well." And second, there is nothing in the key texts of the Marxist tradition that gives us—or by its very premises *could* give us—much of a blueprint for understanding, much less charting the transition. Indeed, the discussion of postcapitalist state and society in these texts is characterized above all by its limitations; that is, by what it does not say.

Thus, for instance, almost the entirety of our knowledge about Marx's understanding of the future society is contained, in any significant detail, in only three texts. Marx's vision remains constant in these three texts, despite the fact that one of the three, "Private Property and Communism," is among the earliest of his writings (*Economic and Philosophic Manuscripts of 1844*) while another of the three, *Critique of the Gotha Program,* is among the latest. Nor does either of these documents provide a thorough picture: on the contrary, both are really fragmentary marginal notes rather than polished pieces of work— entirely logical, as neither was intended for publication. The third text, *The Civil War in France,* is of course a finished document but one which was written very much in response to, and as a political eulogy for, the 1871 Paris Commune, and must therefore, at least in part, be understood in these terms.

Why was it that Marx had so little to say about the future shape of human society? It is by now a platitude to argue that Marx was entirely concerned with existing capitalist societies and their impending demise: thus his sketchy vision of postcapitalist society. A platitude, however, usually expresses the kernel of a truth: Marx's refusal to "compose the music of the future" (Draper 1970:305) is consistent both with his theoretical premises and with his specific political objectives. Any discussion of the future had by definition to conflict with the basic premises of his thought, which inherently denied the validity of notions rooted in the minds of individuals, rather than in actual historical circumstances. For Marx, the nature of the transition could be determined only by the specific conditions under which it is established.

There was another reason for Marx's reticence on the subject of the future society. Marx wrote and was politically active at the end of a period which had produced all sorts of schemes for socialist utopias. He was anxious, in both theoretical terms and in terms of his activities in the Workingmen's International, not to be confused with or seen in the same stream as these other socialist thinkers. Remember that Marx sought to distinguish his socialism as scientific prescription rather than a dreamer's vision: here Marx's roots in Darwinism become transparently clear.

The few images that Marx *has* given us concerning the final stage of communist society provide perhaps an additional clue to his reluctance to go into any detail: no French utopian socialist has enunciated a more romantic and idealistic picture of the future than the famous image set forth by Marx in *The German Ideology:*

> In communist society, . . . nobody has one exclusive sphere of activity but each can become accomplished in any branch he wishes, society regulates the general production and thus makes it possible for me to do one thing today and another tomorrow, to hunt in the morning, to fish in the afternoon, rear cattle in the evening, criticize after dinner, just as I have a mind, without ever becoming hunter, fisherman, shepherd or critic. (1947:22)

There is a certain irony inherent in Marx's imagery here: hunting, fishing, and critiquing are distinctly and peculiarly unindustrial pursuits. Curiously enough, most of his writing on the form and substance of communist society as such is derived, and in some cases literally taken, from the schemes set forth by the major utopian socialists.

What is clear from all his writings on the subject is that Marx saw the transition from capitalist to communist society as an unbroken process. This process is now generally broken into stages, commonly referred to as socialism and communism; Marx however never so labeled them. Rather, Marx spoke of the "first phase of communist society" (in *Critique of the Gotha Program*) or of "crude communism" (in the *1844 Manuscripts*). The description of this first stage is most fully elaborated in the Gotha critique:

> What we have to deal with here is a communist society, not as it has developed on its own foundations, but, on the contrary, as it emerges from capitalist society; which is thus in every respect, economically, morally and intellectually still stamped with the birthmarks of the old society from whose womb it emerges. . . . But these defects are inevitable in the first phase of communist society. . . . Right can never be higher than the economic structure of the society and the cultural development thereby determined. (1838:8–10)

So therefore is that state structure determined: Marx spoke about the structure of the state in the first phase of communist society as the rule, or "dictatorship of the proletariat."

The importance which Marx attaches to the concept of the dictatorship of the proletariat is nowhere more clearly indicated than in his well-known 1852 letter to Georg Weydemeyer. Here, in his attempt to summarize the historical significance of his work, Marx first clarifies that he deserved no credit for the "discovery" of classes and class struggle in modern society. Rather, he writes, "what I did that was new" was to prove:

> 1) that the existence of classes is only bound up with particular historical phases in the development of production; 2) that the class struggle necessarily leads to the dictatorship of the proletariat; 3) that this dictatorship itself only constitutes the transition to abolition of all classes and to a classless society. (Marx and Engels 1942:5)

Thus, what he calls the "dictatorship of the proletariat" seemingly stands at the heart of Marx's understanding of the evolution of history. Given this centrality, the absence of a full discussion anywhere in Marx's work of the dictatorship of the proletariat is yet another surprise.

Marx first employs the term, without any real descriptive context, in 1850 in *Class Struggles in France.* Although there are references to the concept of proletarian dictatorship in works following this, Marx does not directly employ the term again for over twenty years, until the notes he scribbled in heated reaction to the program of the German Social-Democratic Party. In what is probably the clearest statement of what he sees as the parameters of the dictatorship of the proletariat, Marx writes in the *Critique of the Gotha Program:*

> Between capitalist and communist society lies the period of the revolutionary transformation of one into the other. There corresponds to this also a political transition period in which the state can be nothing but the revolutionary dictatorship of the proletariat. (1938:18)

The phrase used by Marx, and, far more frequently, by Engels to describe the state in the period of the transition has itself, since it was first employed, given rise to an ongoing controversy concerning the major characteristics of this state. "Dictatorship," even when followed by the word "proletariat," is, as Lenin once said, "a harsh, heavy, and even bloody word" to our ears. The disagreements, of course, center upon what precisely Marx meant by "dictatorship" in this context. Hal Draper's (1962:5–71) exhaustive study of Marx's use of the term makes two things clear. First, the word "dictatorship" had a substantively different meaning in mid-nineteenth century Europe than it does now. Marx and his contemporaries' use of the word was drawn directly from its meaning in the ancient Roman Republic, where it carried a connotation of an exceptional and temporary circumstance. And second, Marx understood the "dictatorship of the proletariat" to be synonymous with his more frequently used phrase "rule of the proletariat," which for him, as he states in *The Communist Manifesto,* is synonymous with the rule "of the immense majority in the interest of that immense majority." His employment of the phrase "dictatorship of the proletariat," in both of the time periods he used it, was conditioned by attempts, in times of great popular upsurge, to form temporary and strategic political alliances with the Blanquists. For the Blanquists, dictatorship always meant the rule of a small group, a dictatorship of the "educated elite." Marx is careful to distinguish himself sharply from such a position. Indeed, he formulates the phrase "dictatorship of the proletariat" exactly to clarify the fundamental difference between his conception of dictatorship and this other conception held by the Blanquists (and by the majority of mid-nineteenth century socialists). He underlines this fundamental difference by placing the word "class" before his use of the phrase "dictatorship of the proletariat." Thus, in *Class Struggles in France* (1850), Marx writes: *"the class dictatorship* of the proletariat"—the emphasis is Marx's—is "the necessary transit point to the *abolition of class distinctions generally,* to the abolition of all the production relations on which they rest, to the abolition of all the social relations that correspond to relations of production, to the revolutionizing of all the ideas that result from these social relations" (1964:126).

We are left then with the question of the actual image and outlines, in Marx's writings, of the "class dictatorship of the proletariat." There is only one document in Marx's work that speaks to this question, by giving concrete form to his image of postcapitalist society, and it is one which must be used with great care in this context: this of course is Marx's account of the 1871 Paris Commune in *The Civil War in France.*

We must note, at the outset of this discussion, that nowhere in anything he wrote did Marx *ever* refer to the Paris Commune as the "dictatorship of the proletariat" come to life. It was Engels who made the direct connection. In his 1891 introduction to the third edition of *The Civil War in France,* Engels asks: "Do you want to know what the dictatorship looks like? Look at the Paris Commune. That was the Dictatorship of the Proletariat" (1891; in Marx and Engels 1940:22).

Marx clearly was far more reticent in this regard. The explanation of why it was that Marx could not, and did not, see the Paris Commune as the incarnation of the dictatorship of the proletariat is simple: there had not been, either in Paris or in France during 1871, a social revolution which had overthrown the capitalist order. Given this, the Paris Commune logically *could not be* the dictatorship of the proletariat. Thus in his famous 1881 letter to Domila Nieuenhuis, Marx writes, in answer to the Dutch Social Democrat's inquiry about the appropriate actions of a new socialist government once it took power, "Perhaps you will refer me to the Paris Commune, but apart from the fact that this was merely the rising of a city under exceptional conditions, the majority of the Commune was in no way socialist, nor could it be" (Marx and Engels 1942:386–87). Why then did Marx, in the final draft of *The Civil War in France,* call the Paris Commune "the political form at last discovered under which to work out the economical emancipation of labour"?

(Marx and Engels 1940:60). The most succinct answer to this is given throughout the various drafts of *The Civil War in France:* "Whatever the merits of the single measures of the Commune, its greatest measure was its own organization."[1] The Paris Commune, by its rejection of the entire apparatus of the preceding governments, set itself off from all previous social uprisings: Marx repeats this, again, through the three drafts: "the working class," he writes, "cannot simply lay hold on the ready made State machinery and wield it for their own purposes. The political instrument of their enslavement cannot serve as the political instrument of their emancipation. . . . The first condition for the hold[ing] of political power is to transform the working machinery and destroy it" (ibid.:54). The great achievement of the Paris Commune for Marx was then its destruction of what he describes in the *Civil War* drafts as the "boa constrictor," the state which had been forged in the era of absolute monarchy, and had been employed and enlarged ever since (ibid.). It is for this reason that Marx, at the same moment he speaks of the inevitable doom of the commune, writes to his friend Kugelmann: "With the struggle in Paris, the struggle of the working class against the capitalist class and its state has entered upon a new phase. Whatever the immediate results may be, a new point of departure of world historic importance has been gained" (Marx and Engels 1942:311).

When Marx begins to speak in more concrete terms about what this "new point of departure" looked like, his very phrasing gives force to Engels' comment, in an 1884 letter to Edward Bernstein, that what Marx did in *The Civil War in France* was to set forth "the unconscious tendencies of the Commune . . . to its credit as more or less conscious plans." Marx frequently employs the conditional future tense as he projects the direction in which the Paris Commune seemed almost instinctively (and in fact out of pragmatic necessity) to move. Thus "the Commune was to be a working, not parliamentary body, executive and legislative at the same time" (Marx and Engels 1940:57).

From Marx's writings about the experience of the Paris Commune, a set of "principles" giving form to the state in the period of the transition were extracted which through the medium of Lenin have found a permanent niche in the catechism of the present-day societies of actually existing socialism. These principles celebrate, above all, anti-authoritarianism and the de-institutionalization of political power: they speak of "the people acting for itself, by itself."[2] They include:

    1. the abolition of permanent, standing armies and their replacement by the armed people;
    2. the abolition of the separation of legislative and executive functions, and with this:
    3. the end of state functionarism; that is, the elimination of bureau-

cracy. All officials, including judges, were to be elected by universal suffrage;

4. constant electoral control over the entire governmental apparatus, through the constant right of recall;

5. the limitation of wages of government workers to those of workers as a whole in society;

6. the end of "parson power"; that is the complete separation of church and state. (See ibid.)

The set of principles Marx derived from the experience of the Paris Commune draws upon both the dominant and the secondary strains in his interpretation of the state. If his sketch gives a sense of the content of the class dictatorship of the proletariat, each principle also speaks to preventing the reemergence and usurpation of power by a centralized state "apparently soaring high above society" (ibid.:56) and seemingly autonomous from it: "where there were legitimate functions to fulfill, these functions were to exercised not by a body superior to the society, but by the responsible agents of society itself."[3] Thus, the commune represented, above all, the "reabsorption of the state power by society as its own living forces, instead of as forces controlling and subduing it, by the popular masses themselves, forming their own force instead of the organized force of their repression."[4]

All this, taken together, represents a conception of the political power to be exercised by the proletariat which is entirely distinct from the power which preceded it. The Paris Commune state, for Marx, is not simply a state in which the rule of one class has been supplanted by the rule of another: rather, it is a new type of state altogether. In this sense the Paris Commune did indeed indelibly stamp its imprint upon how Marx, and after him, all Marxists, thought about the essential meaning and elements of the relationship between state and society in the transition from class to classless society.

This seems to lead us directly to the one notion vis-à-vis the future with which Marx and Engels were relatively preoccupied, both before and after the Paris Commune: the inevitable disappearance or dying out of the state. Indeed, their continual return to it, in the face of their hesitancy to discuss the future, underscores the deeply anti-authoritarian impulse which characterizes their concept of postcapitalist society. The phrase so connected with Marx in this regard—the "withering away of the state"—was actually never used by Marx himself. Rather, it was Engels who in his *Anti-Duhring* and in *Socialism: Utopian and Scientific* gave currency to the specific wording "withering away." Marx himself spoke rather of the "abolition," or the "transcendence" of the bourgeois state.

The notion of doing away with the state was deeply embedded in the thought of the early utopian socialists. If Marx drew on this tradition, he also sought to distinguish his understanding of it: this is nowhere more clearly captured than in his various polemics against the anarchists. Thus, in *The Poverty of Philosophy,* Marx sets forth in essence what will be his fundamental and unbroachable disagreement with anarchism in general, whether Proudhon's or Bakunin's: the state is not the originator, but rather the expression of antagonisms in civil society, antagonisms which result from the economic organization of that society. Eliminate those antagonisms, through a social revolution which fundamentally alters this economic organization, and you eliminate the need for the state. Thus, whereas for Proudhon, and after him, Bakunin, the elimination of the state was the first order of things, for Marx and his followers, as *The Communist Manifesto* makes clear, it becomes the ultimate aim of social revolution.

But what, more correctly, does it mean to consign the state to the "scrapheap," or to the "Museum of Antiquities, by the side of the spinning wheel and the bronze axe," as Engels (1942:158) was later, so picturesquely, to write? Does everything we now connect with the state make the journey to the Museum? Do none of its functions remain in place, even if in new form? Marx himself poses this very question in his *Critique of the Gotha Program:* "The question then arises," he writes: "what transformation will the state undergo in communist society? In other words what social functions will remain in existence there that are analogous to present day functions of the state?" (1938:18). For all the reasons cited above, if he poses the question, he has not the slightest intention of answering it. But there are some suggestions, some indications which emerge from the body of his writing, that lend gray and colored tints to the black and white image of state→no state so connected to the idea of abolition, or withering away of the state. In *The Communist Manifesto,* Marx states that when in the course of development class distinctions have disappeared and all production has been concentrated in the hands of a vast association of the whole nation, the public power will lose its *political* character. The implication of this here and elsewhere is that by "political character" Marx means the repressive functions of the state, its powers of coercion. If we examine the principles he drew from the experience of the Paris Commune, this becomes clear: the organized bodies for coercion are immediately abolished, and all the capacity for force turned back over to the people as a whole. But if, as he writes in *The Civil War in France,* the merely repressive organs of the old governmental power were to be amputated, there remain "legitimate functions" which were to be "wrested from an authority usurping pre-eminence over society itself, and restored to the responsible agents of society" (Marx and Engels 1940:58–59). That is, there were legitimate, nonpolitical functions which were now to be exercised by the people as a whole, the "responsible agents of society." There is little more in the body of Marx's work which gives any further texture or image to how things would function, except perhaps in his wonderful comments scribbled in the margins of Bakunin's *Statism and Anarchy* (which is in part a diatribe against what Bakunin terms Marx's "statist socialism"). "What does it mean: the proletariat raised into the ruling class?" asks Bakunin. "Can it really be that the proletariat as a whole be at the head of the government?" Marx in his marginal scribbles, replies:

> Can it really be that in a trade union, for example, the entire union constitutes the executive committee? Will all division of labor in a factory disappear and also the various functions arising from it? And in Bakunin's construction "from the bottom up," will everybody be up at the top? Then there would be no "bottom." Will all the members of the Commune likewise administer the common interest of the Region? In this case, no difference between Commune and Region.

And in response to Bakunin's incredulous query that "there are about forty millions German. Will all forty million be members of the government?" Marx replies: "Certainly! Since the thing begins with the self-government of the Commune."

Bakunin goes on, and so does Marx: to Bakunin's charge that "by popular administration they understood administration of the people by means of a small number of representatives elected by the people," Marx replies:

> The ass! This is democratic nonsense, political windbaggery! The character of elections depends not on these designations but on the economic foundations, on the economic ties of the voters amongst one another and from the moment these functions cease being political (1) no governmental functions any longer exist; (2) the distribution of general functions takes on a business character and involves no domination; (3) elections completely lose their present political character. ("After the Revolution: Marx Debates Bakunin," in Tucker, ed. 1978:544–45)

We begin to move beyond the "dictatorship of the proletariat," the lower phase of communism, into the "realm of freedom"—full communist society: indeed, in doing so we underscore the fact that for Marx there was no demarcation that separated the two phases or froze them into discernible stages. Marx spoke only of the transition from capitalism to communism, from class to classless society.

If Marx's belief in the abolition or withering away of the state represents one of the clearest indicators of the democratic vision that informs his work, for all its attractiveness it vividly exemplifies perhaps the most fundamental weakness of the Marxist heritage concerning postcapitalist state and society. For if this theoretical heritage is profoundly democratic, it is also profoundly inadequate and contradictory, even in its own terms.

These inadequacies and contradictions center, most importantly, around the absence, in the key texts concerning the transition, of virtually any analysis or discussion, not simply of the manner in which the democratic vision would have to be mediated, but of the very need for such mediation. And this failure to consider even the need for agencies of political mediation in the transition is rooted directly in the tendency inherent in classical Marxist thought to reduce all contradictions to the category of class. This tendency determines, in critical aspects, the outlines of Marx's and Engels' vision of the transition to socialism: indeed there is perhaps no other aspect of their work as consistently and deeply infused with a class reductionist spirit. If the political arena is defined as the stage upon which one class enforces its will upon another, then the end of class domination effectively means the end of politics. The beginning of "real history" was to be marked by the reabsorption of political society by civil society. Therefore, questions of political society—of the form and nature of political institutions—are almost by definition no longer relevant. And if this was true of Marx and Engels, it is even more starkly characteristic of Lenin.

It was Lenin who more than any other person operationalized the notion of the dictatorship of the proletariat inherited from Marx, and filtered through Engels. Lenin's *State and Revolution,* the hastily drawn up "doctrinal birth certificate" of the Soviet state (Liebman 1975:193) is, in actuality, a recompilation, a simplification, and an extension on the basis of that simplification of the sketchy inherited Marxist vision of the workers' state. This seems entirely in character: for if Marx was obsessed with understanding the world in order to change it, Lenin's obsession focused above all upon the strategy for revolution itself. If Marx was a man of ideas, whose ideas impelled him to action, Lenin was, on the contrary, a man of action, who looked to ideas as justification for action.

Yet despite its simplified conceptual structure, it is above all to *State and Revolution* that Marxists look to answer the crucial question of what the workers' state will actually look like. And the answer to that question, as it emerges from *State and Revolution,* echoes what are simultaneously the most humanistic and utopian strains of the Marxist tradition and its most fundamental weaknesses.

The central thematic points of *State and Revolution* speak directly to this vision. The basis of Lenin's argument rests upon his definition of the state: here he draws upon only one strand of Marx's ambiguous legacy with regard to the state. He takes from Marx the notion of the state put forward in *The Communist Manifesto:* the state as a weapon through which the ruling class enforces its will. The state, he writes, echoing *The Communist Manifesto,* is "a special apparatus for suppression" (1932:74), a "special organization of force; the organization of violence for the suppression of some class" (ibid.:22). There is here no ambiguity, no indication of circumstances which might lead to the relative autonomy of the state, no mention of other functions that state institutions might perform.

Having established the definitional foundation of his argument, Lenin proceeds to his most central concern in *State and Revolution:* the absolute necessity that the proletariat, in carrying out its revolution, destroy completely the entire structure of the bourgeois state, rather than simply take over its machinery. Lenin takes this as the central lesson drawn by Marx from the experience of the Paris Commune: it was for this reason, at least in part, that upon his return to Russia in April of 1917, he demanded an end to all Bolshevik cooperation with the post-February order. "All revolutions which have taken place up to the present," he asserts in *State and Revolution,* "have helped to perfect the state machinery, whereas it must be shattered, broken to pieces. This conclusion is the chief and fundamental thesis in the Marxist theory of the state" (ibid.: 25). Lenin goes back again and again to this point: it is, as Lucio Colletti (1969:19) has pointed out, the basic theme of *State and Revolution.*

The nature of what Colletti calls the "power of a new type" that would replace the bourgeois state is the subject of Lenin's third major focus in *State and Revolution.* Lenin asserts, again faithfully following Marx and Engels, that it is the "dictatorship of the proletariat" that emerges as the state with the triumph of the proletarian revolution. He underscores the centrality of this concept in the Marxist tradition: perhaps leaning heavily upon Marx's letter to Weydemeyer, Lenin writes: "He who recognizes only the class struggle means to curtail Marxism—to distort it, to reduce it to something which is acceptable to the bourgeoisie. A Marxist is one who *extends* the acceptance of the class struggle to the acceptance of the *dictatorship of the proletariat*" (1932:30; emphasis in original). Lenin's understanding of the thrust of the dictatorship of the proletariat is based in an interpretation which stresses, again, the simplified Marxist definition of the state as an instrument of force, although that vision is far more tempered here than elsewhere. The dictatorship of the proletariat pictured in *State and Revolution,* although "the organization of the vanguard of the oppressed as the ruling class for the purpose of crushing the oppressors," will entail "an immense extension of democracy which for the first time becomes democracy for the poor, for the people and not democracy for the money bags" (ibid.:73). It will mean "democracy for the vast majority of the people, and suppression by force, i.e., exclusion from democracy, of the exploiters and oppressors of the people" (ibid.).

Moreover—and this is the fourth major theme of *State and Revolution*—the state that emerges with the victory of the proletarian revolution is a state that immediately begins to "wither away." It is, as Lenin variously refers to it, a "dying state," or a "nonpolitical state" (ibid.:53), or "something which is no longer really the state in the accepted sense of the word" (ibid.:37). The phrase "withering away," as we have seen, was first employed by Engels. But if Engels puts forth only a vague and generalized image of what is meant by the "withering away" of the state, Lenin goes far beyond this: he attempts to give a sense of the proportions of the process of "withering away." What is most clear—and most startling, given the traditional understanding of Leninism—in Lenin's discussion of the process of "withering away" is exactly the degree to which the state in *State and Revolution* has already withered: it is a state, as Ralph Miliband has observed, already in an "advanced state of decomposition" (1970a). This is, of course, not to say that it is a weak, powerless body: Lenin spends a significant amount of time in the text of *State and Revolution* saying nasty things about the anarchists in this connection. And although he argues firmly and repeatedly that "only communism renders the state absolutely unnecessary, for there is no one to be suppressed" (1932:75), nonetheless, it is clear—and again, startling—that for the Lenin of *State and Revolution,* the process of the state's withering away begins immediately and intensely with the proletarian accession to power.

What we have is a state which, in Lenin's understanding, like the Paris Commune, "signifies a gigantic replacement of one type of institution by others of a fundamentally different order" (ibid.:37)—a state transformed and unlike anything that has existed in the past. It is, above all, a state devoid of the principle mechanisms through which all states, in Lenin's view, and of course in Marx's understanding of the Paris Commune, had traditionally maintained their repressive functions: a standing army and a complex bureaucratic network, those "parasite(s) on the body of bourgeois society" (ibid.:26). The proletarian state is transformed from a "state of bureaucrats" into a "state of armed workers" who have organized themselves into "a militia involving the entire population" which then replaces the traditional standing army. The bureaucratic apparatus, while not altogether eliminated, is reduced to its proper position as "servants rather than masters of society," and its functions, once simplified to their proper dimensions, are taken over by the workers themselves—immediately. The specific commanding "methods of the state officials can and must begin to be replaced—immediately, within twenty-four hours—by the simple functions of 'managers' and bookkeepers, functions which are now already within the capacity of the average city dweller and can well be performed for 'workingmen's wages' " (ibid.:43). "The mass of the population rises to participation . . . in the everyday administration of affairs. Under Socialism all will take a turn in management, and will become accustomed to the idea of no managers at all" (ibid.:98).

Indeed, Lenin is speaking here not simply in normative terms: all this is not simply something which is desirable, but something which can be demonstrated, in Marxist terms, to be scientifically possible: Lenin here transposes to the political and administrative realm the Marxist analysis which says that it is capitalism itself which makes communism materially possible, by its development of the means of production to the point where abundance becomes realizable. Capitalist culture and methods of organizing work have conglomerated and "simplified [the accounting and control necessary] to the utmost, till they have become the extraordinarily simple operations of watching, recording and issuing receipts, within the reach of anybody who can read and write and knows the first four rules of arithmetic" (ibid.:84).

And again Lenin looks to the Paris Commune as the historical proof of the practicality of the idea and the possibility that it can be invoked *immediately* upon the proletarian seizure of power:

> to *break up* at once the old bureaucratic machine and to start immediately the construction of a new one which will enable us gradually to reduce all officialdom to naught—this is *no* Utopia, it is the experience of the Commune, it is the direct and urgent task of the revolutionary proletariat. (Ibid.:42)

This then brings us to the final underlying current or thread which weaves through *State and Revolution:* the notion of *unmediated class rule.* What emerges from the pamphlet is an overwhelming image of the people themselves, organized by themselves, without any intermediaries, assuming their own rule and their own defense of that rule. If this is not stated explicitly, it is *almost* so stated—anyway, it is returned to, as all the major themes are, again and again throughout the pamphlet. For all its vague sketchiness, it is a powerful and profoundly democratic image.

The radical vision and interpretation Lenin puts forth in *State and Revolution* (and in other writings and talks directly before and after November 1917) has stirred controversy on numerous planes since the day of publication. This controversy extends to the very question of why it was written in the first place. Critics of Lenin who consider themselves Marxist, as well as unsympathetic bourgeois historians, tend to see *State and Revolution* as the ultimate proof of Lenin's unprincipled opportunism. Lenin, they argue, wrote *State and Revolution* not because he believed what he wrote: much to the contrary. The real Lenin is the Lenin of *What Is to Be Done?,* a Lenin who had no faith in the masses nor in the results of any mass spontaneity, who believed in the absolute leadership of a rigid hierarchical party made up of only the most conscious members of the working class and informed by déclassé intellectuals. This Lenin was to emerge again, they argue, in full force following the Bolshevik victory: this itself is proof of the disingenuousness of *State and Revolution.*

There is, however, another view of Lenin and Leninism, and another interpretation of *State and Revolution:* it is an interpretation which sees the pamphlet in its final form as above all the reflection of the enormous revolutionary upheaval which took place in Russia during the course of 1917 (see Liebman 1975:190–205). This then becomes the source for Lenin's inversion, in *State and Revolution,* of the relationship between leadership and masses, between party and class, that he had put forward in an earlier period. Indeed, it has been argued that the model for the direct democracy of which *State and Revolution* speaks was to be found exactly in the "spectacle" of Russia from February 1917 forward. The constant dialogue—to the degree, John Reed reports, that "at every meeting attempts to limit the time of speakers were voted down" (Reed 1967), is one part of this spectacle. The unlimited and spontaneous formation of committees, or soviets, in every conceivable context—in workplaces, in the countryside, in houses, among housewives—is another part of it. All this gives support to Marc Ferro's assertion that no established authority had control, that "any delegation of power was excoriated, any authority unbearable" (1972:320). The spontaneity which marked the formation of the soviets and the cries for and attempts at workers' control echoed through every situation. Even the counterrevolution's major effort between February and November 1917, the attempted coup by General L. G. Kornilov, commander-in-chief of the Russian army, was met by a network of defense generated spontaneously: the formation of militias; the efforts of the telegraph and railroad workers to disrupt communications and transportation; the leaflets put out by printing workers—all of their own initiative—is evidence that the radicalism of the masses, from the February revolution on, far outran that of any of the political parties, the Bolsheviks included. What had in fact occurred was the very inversion of leadership and the people as a whole which Lenin was to give voice to in *State and Revolution.* Nor does *State and Revolution* stand in isolation: everything that Lenin wrote or spoke of during the period after February 1917, and in the period directly following the Bolshevik seizure of power, echoes that same voice.

State and Revolution brings up another fundamental—indeed, perhaps more profound—controversy for the Marxist tradition. For the fact is that although it remains a constant reference point for all those seeking to understand the nature of postcapitalist society, it does not in any basic way speak to the enormous and critical problems postrevolutionary society would face. This then requires of us a critical reexamination of the pamphlet and an evaluation of its weaknesses, of what it does and does *not* say about these problems.

Let us thus return to the major themes of *State and Revolution,* beginning with the fundamental structure upon which the work rests: Lenin's definition of the state. In its complete concentration upon only one strand of the Marxist concept of the state, Lenin's definition excludes reference or even allusion to the wide range of functions and mediations which the state fulfills. This reductive emphasis provides the grounds upon which *State and Revolution* can be used to justify everything the pamphlet seems to oppose. Lenin put forward what he understood to be the orthodox Marxist view of the state, as *only* an organ of repressive force used by one class against another. Yet Marx's definition, if more ambiguous, was nonetheless more complex. In *The Eighteenth Brumaire of Louis Bonaparte,* Marx develops the idea that given a certain weakness in the capacities of the bourgeoisie, the state can achieve a position of autonomy from the class whose interests it actually represents. He takes this idea one step further in *The Civil War in France,* where he writes of Napoleon's regime in mid-nineteenth-century France that "it was the only form of government possible at a time when the bourgeoisie had already lost and the working class had not yet acquired the faculty of ruling the nation" (Marx and Engels 1940:56). This phrase "ruling the nation" underscores Marx's references to continuing and "legitimate functions" seemingly to be performed by the postcapitalist state, functions which exist apart from the class struggle.

Lenin's exclusive use of the class domination model, moreover, has irretrievable implications for what we have called the central theme of *State and Revolution:* the necessity to destroy the existing state apparatus. Lenin, says Robert Daniels, "failed to grasp the basic rationale of the smashing dictum—protection of society against the dangerous independence of the state machinery—and as a result he allowed the entire program of mass control over the exercise of political power to be vitiated after his party came to power" (1953:33).

This same definitional problem besieges Lenin's very concept of the "dictatorship of the proletariat," which in fact is dealt with rather peremptorily. The definition is derived entirely through analogy to the bourgeois state, again in the limited sense in which he understood it. If the state in capitalism was the dictatorship of the bourgeoisie, then the state in the first phase of communism was therefore the dictatorship of the proletariat. Perhaps exactly because of his limited definitional base, there is, in *State and Revolution,* none of the ambiguity which characterized Marx's use of the term "dictatorship." To Lenin it is clearly an instrument for suppressing opposing classes, and despite the notion put forth in *State and Revolution* that the dictatorship of the proletariat is the most democratic of all states, since it is a "dictatorship" for the first time of the majority, there is no question of nor limits upon the repression, or as Lenin puts it, the "exclusion from democracy" of classes other than the workers and their allies.

Moreover, although Lenin speaks of "a gigantic replacement of certain institutions by institutions of a fundamentally different type," there is little in *State and Revolution* to indicate precisely what these new institutions will look like or how they will be formed. There is, to be sure, a brief reference to the soviets. And it is true that elsewhere, around the same period in which *State and Revolution* was written, he was more explicit about the centrality of the soviets as the basis upon which the new state would be constructed. Thus, in *Will the Bolsheviks Retain State Power?* he writes that the soviets provide "a bond with the people, with the majority of the people, so intimate, so indissoluble, so easily verifiable and renewable that nothing remotely like it existed in the previous state apparatus." But *State and Revolution* spends far more time denouncing parliamentarism than discussing its alternative—logical, on one level, given the fact that parliamentarism was Lenin's immediate enemy in Russia in 1917. He suggests that the "working bodies" which will replace the "talking shops" of the bourgeois parliamentarism will in fact be the soviets: "In a Socialist society," he writes, this "something in the nature of a parliament" (here he is using Kautsky's works in an ironical attack upon him) will consist of "workers' deputies" (1932:91). These workers will "break up the old bureaucratic apparatus," "shatter it to its very foundations until not one stone is left upon another," and ensure against any reemergence of bureaucratic form by remembering and acting upon the lessons of the Paris Commune: "(1) not only electiveness but instant recall; (2) payment no higher than that of ordinary workers; (3) immediate transition to a state of things when *all* fulfill the functions of control and superintendence, so that *all* become bureaucrats for a time, and no one, therefore, can become a bureaucrat" (ibid.:92; emphasis in original).

The problem is that the formula has never proven sufficient: the vast bureaucratic apparatus that has come to characterize many of the states of "actually existing socialism" was already apparent in the brief years between the Bolshevik accession to power and Lenin's death in 1924. And, in truth, this was as inexplicable to Lenin as it was to his followers. By the time of his death, Lenin was forced to admit that Russia was a "socialist state with a bureaucratic deformation." But the truth is that, given his formulas, Lenin never fully understood the nature and sources of the mushrooming Soviet bureaucracy. He tended to see it as an inheritance from the past, as the persistence of old forms, as the result of a failure to "shatter" all of these forms to their "very foundations, until not one stone is left upon another."

A discussion of enduring bureaucracy leads us directly into an examination of what we have cited as the fourth major theme of *State and Revolution:* the withering away of the state. Lenin, it will be remembered, argued in *State and Revolution* that the state begins to wither *immediately* upon the workers' accession to power. Yet we hear him, as early as 1918, asserting that "for the present, we stand unconditionally for the state." It is true that, in one sense, this statement does not contradict *State and Revolution,* since Lenin saw the need for a strong postrevolutionary state power to carry on the task of repression of opponents. But this state, as it is envisioned in *State and Revolution,* has been transformed: it is no longer a state in its usual sense, according to Lenin, but a state in which the workers, armed, are themselves the power. And it becomes only too clear, particularly in the aftermath of the Civil War, that this state of armed workers, directly empowered, is not the state that came into existence.

Further, the unmediated class rule that echoes forth from the pages of *State and Revolution* is clouded immediately, before and particularly after the Bolshevik seizure of power, by an element which Lenin refers to only obliquely and in passing in the pamphlet: this element is, of course, the party. The omission in *State and Revolution* of any discussion of the party—an element so central to Lenin's thought and work—ranks as probably the most startling aspect of the pamphlet. There are by generous count exactly three possible references to the party in the text of *State and Revolution,* and only one of these, even ambiguously, speaks to its relationship to, or role in, the dictatorship of the proletariat.

The question of exactly *why* Lenin so totally ignores the party in *State and Revolution,* and basically in all his work of this period, is a difficult one to answer: it evokes the controversy concerning Lenin's opportunism discussed earlier. But there is another possible explanation—again emerging from the actual historical moment in Russia during which *State and Revolution* was written. It was Lenin's historical greatness to recognize that it was not any party which was calling the dice in Russia in 1917. It was the people who were the most radical force in Russia and 1917 was their triumph: the Bolsheviks gained power only because, under enormous prodding from their leader, they recognized this and went along with it. Yet, it remains nonetheless true that the entire question of political leadership—the existence of leadership, its role, its relationship to the population as a whole—is left undealt with in *State and Revolution.* And this is a crucial—perhaps in the light of history, *the* crucial—question.

We are faced finally with the question, why? Why did Lenin's radical vision in *State and Revolution* fade? We can perhaps attribute it entirely to the horrible and devastating reality which the Soviet Union faced in the months and years after October: herein lies, certainly, a part of the answer. For within that reality was contained the basis for the destruction of any possibility of the democratic rule envisioned in *State and Revolution*. "Leninism," as Ralph Miliband has written, "comes to power under conditions which were as unfavorable as they could possibly be." Or we can conclude, with Miliband, that even without taking the historical reality of the post-1917 Soviet Union into account, Lenin's vision in *State and Revolution* is "not a viable state for the morrow of the revolution." Miliband traces the core of *State and Revolution*'s fateful heritage to its failure to come to any kind of terms at all with the question of political mediation. Dictatorship, "even in the most favorable circumstances," he argues, "is unrealizable without political mediation," despite the theme of unmediated class rule which permeates *State and Revolution*. This theme allows Lenin to avoid discussion of the difficult and vital problem of the form this mediation will take. If, for instance, the form is single party rule—and, indeed, that is of course exactly what form it took in Russia after 1921—then this rule "postulates an individed, revolutionary proletarian will of which it is the natural expression." But, argues Miliband, this is hardly a "reasonable postulate upon which to rest the 'dictatorship of the proletariat.' In no society, however constituted, is there an individed, single popular will. This is precisely why the problem of political mediation arises in the first place." Thus, he asserts, the radical democratic vision of *State and Revolution* may be "just so much hot air . . . unless adequate provision is made for *alternate* channels of expression and political articulation (1970a:85–87).

What then can we say about the legacy which Marx, Engels, and Lenin leave to those who followed them concerning the postcapitalist state? Clearly, history has evolved in directions which neither Marx nor the Lenin of *State and Revolution* could or did foresee. The fact that socialist revolution was not a worldwide occurrence, and that socialist revolutions have occurred largely in countries of the periphery— countries characterized by economic underdevelopment and threatened, in some cases intensively, by the most powerful forces of imperialism—must, of necessity, determine a very different relationship between state and society in the transition to socialism in these countries. The tasks of the state in production, in exchange, and in defense against external and internal aggression, in this context, take on a different color.

But the interaction of these realities—underdevelopment and external threat—overpowering as they are, cannot by itself explain the present condition of the socialist project in the majority of countries defining themselves as socialist today. Any understanding of that condition also must take cognizance of a theoretical legacy which, as noted, is at its very core contradictory. It carries with it, on the one hand, a central commitment to a profoundly democratic vision, in the sense of a people empowered, of a society which has reabsorbed into itself the authority which formerly stood above it. And this holds true, as Miliband has argued, "not only in relation to a distant communist society, but also to the period of transition which is to preceed it" (1965:293). And at the same time, this legacy is characterized by its failure to recognize that institutions would be needed during the transition to give form to the democratic impulse and upsurge.

That Marx and Lenin give us no detailed description of what these institutions might look like is hardly strange. It would be simply ridiculous to ask of them, or of their work, specific formulas to guide a history whose unfolding they would not know. Indeed, the attempts by certain of the countries of actually existing socialism to justify actions taken on the basis of specific words of Marx or of Lenin regarding the "dictatorship of the proletariat" are often little more than ludicrous. However, that Marx, and following him in an even more severe and ultimately more damaging form, Lenin, fail to take cognizance of the fact that such agencies of mediation would be essential in the transition to socialism, is another issue. What makes this failure critical, what makes it reverberate through the whole history of actually existing socialism, is that what they did put forth has been enshrined, in distorted form, as a functioning system, a perfectly adequate model, a "ready-made formula," as Luxemburg labeled it. It has been treated as such in many of the states of actually existing socialism ever since. Thus, ironically, the theoretical legacy of classical Marxist thought concerning the transition to socialism has been twisted in the service of unraveling the fabric of socialism and democracy. It has come to serve as the underpinning of models for the "proper" construction of socialism which are fundamentally authoritarian and therefore the negation of the democratic vision which is at the heart of the Marxist concept of the realization of socialism.

Amilcar Cabral once wrote of the "weapon of theory"; in so doing he recovered, in essence, the importance of theory and the relevance of the Marxist concept of praxis for third world struggles (1969:73–90). For people, or countries, which claim to be socialist in the Marxist tradition, theory cannot be an abstraction or an after the fact justification; it is the outcome and one of the principal guides to practice. And if this is true, then the distance at which theory lags behind practice— behind history, in effect—in the societies of actually existing socialism is stark and frightening. I would argue that no arena of Marxist thought has remained as underdeveloped and at least partly as a consequence, as stultified and stultifying, as distorted and distortable. The history of socialism in this century serves to underline the critical need for a reengagement with this theoretical heritage. And it is exactly the democratic vision that informed this heritage, that gave it sustenance, which must define the terrain for such a reengagement. For this belief in popular participation and popular rule retains the most profound relevance for all those who seek, concretely, to realize the socialist project.

Notes

1. Karl Marx, "The Civil War in France" (first draft), in Hal Draper, ed., *Karl Marx and Frederick Engels: Writings on the Paris Commune* (New York: Monthly Review Press, 1971), p. 153.
2. Ibid., p. 130.
3. Ibid. (second draft), p. 200.
4. Ibid. (first draft), p. 152.

The Role of Ideology
in the Transition to Socialism
▼▲

John S. Saul

What is ideology? The question was made concrete for me when in 1981–82 I taught in Maputo, Mozambique, in the FRELIMO Party School and in the Faculty of Marxism-Leninism at the University of Eduardo Mondlane, both institutions functioning under the auspices of the Department of Ideological Work of the country's ruling party, FRELIMO.[1] In such a context "ideological work" meant refining the insights FRELIMO had developed during the period of its armed struggle against Portuguese colonialism and the early postindependence years, both as a guide to practice and as a framework for pedagogy in the political education of cadres and general public alike. FRELIMO grasped, as other revolutionary socialists in small peripheral countries have done, that merely learning by a process of trial and error in the course of elaborating its socialist practice was not enough. The party saw that for socialists the need to wed theory to practice is no mere cliché, that it is through the struggle to clarify and advance the theoretical basis of their efforts that socialists become ever more *self-conscious* agents of change, conscious both of the full implications of their own practice and of the cumulative wisdom of those who have struggled for socialist advance throughout the world.

Like most revolutionary socialists in small peripheral countries FRELIMO sought to ground its "ideological work" so defined on the terrain of the Marxist tradition. A wise choice, given the strength of that tradition in helping to structure an understanding of capitalist imperialism as a global economic and military system, of society as a nexus of class struggle, and of politics as a focus of such struggle with its own peculiar imperatives and opportunities. A wise choice but not, however, an entirely straightforward one, for "the Marxist tradition" is by no means single voiced. It is no accident that Marx himself asserted on one occasion that he was in fact no "Marxist," if that latter term were understood to embrace those who tried to cast and defend his theories in a rigid manner. Closer to our own time Henrí Lefebvre has commented on "the fierce struggle inside . . . Marxism between dog-matism and the critique of dogmatism." Lefebvre pointed out:

> This struggle is not over; it goes bitterly on. Dogmatism is strong, it can call on the force of authority, of the state and its institutions. Moreover, it has advantages: it is simple and easily taught; it steers clear of complex problems, this being precisely the aim and meaning of dogmatism; it gives its adherents a feeling of both vigorous affirmation and security. (1968:13)

For "dogmatism," read "ideology." But here the term "ideology" is used with a quite different connotation than that intended by FRELIMO in the above-mentioned phrase "ideological work"! In fact, there are two different concepts of ideology at work within the Marxist tradition. Attempting briefly to clarify the distinction between them can provide us with a useful entry point for discovering both the strengths and the weaknesses of the Marxist tradition as a guide for revolutionary practice.

Perhaps the most characteristic definition of the concept of "ideology" found in Marx and Engels' own writing is a negative or pejorative one. According to Raymond Williams, "this sense of ideology as illusion, false consciousness, unreality, upside-down reality, is pre-dominant in their work" (1976:128). Another writer has characterized this view as one which sees ideology as "a distortion of thought which stems from, and conceals, social contradictions":

> . . . in effect, as long as men, because of their limited material mode of activity are unable to solve these contradictions in practice, they tend to project them in ideological forms of consciousness, that is to say, in purely mental or discursive solutions which effectively conceal or misrepresent the existence and character of these contradictions. By concealing contra-dictions the ideological distortion contributes to their reproduction and therefore serves the interest of the ruling class. (Larrain 1983:218–19)

Such writings as *The German Ideology* and the chapter in *Capital* on "commodity fetishism" document this view of the function of ideology especially within the capitalist mode of production. By this definition, ideology, as an inevitably distorted perception, is at the opposite end of the spectrum from scientific understanding.

There is an alternative, more positive (or at least neutral) definition of ideology within the Marxist tradition, however, one which even Marx himself seemed to fall back upon occasionally. Thus, a classic citation finds him making a distinction "between the material transfor-mation of the economic conditions of production . . . and the legal, political, religious, aesthetic or philosophic—in short, ideological—forms in which men become conscious of this conflict and fight it out" (1859; in Tucker 1978:5). As Raymond Williams comments, "This sense of ideology as a set of ideas which arise from a given set of

214 John S. Saul

material interests . . . is very difficult to reconcile with the sense of
ideology as mere illusion" (1976:129). And when this second definition
is further elaborated upon by Lenin, ideology is seen "no longer (as) a
necessary distortion which conceals contradictions but becomes a
neutral concept referring to the political consciousness of classes,
including the proletarian class" (Larrain 1983:22).[2] "Bourgeois ideology" can, in short, confront "proletarian ideology," and while it is the
case that "bourgeois ideology" will have many of the attributes of
ideology as pejoratively defined, this is not necessarily true of proletarian ideology. Indeed, the latter will approximate, rather than contradict,
scientific understanding—because it has no vested interest in masking
the truth. Lucio Colletti, who has argued this case convincingly,
summarizes the point as follows: "Marxism is therefore science. It is an
analytical reconstruction of the way in which the mechanisms of
capitalist reproduction work. On the other hand, as well as being a
science, Marxism is a revolutionary ideology. It is an analysis of reality
from the standpoint of the working class" (1972:235–36). Clearly, this
is the sense in which Mozambicans have come to use the term "ideology" (as in "Department of Ideological Work"), as being coextensive
with a genuinely scientific social science, coextensive with revolutionary theory.
   Are there circumstances in which Marxism, an ideology in this
positive sense, might become, in any of its variants, an ideology in the
negative sense? Indeed there are. The classic case is that of the Soviet
Union in the Stalin period, when Marxism/Marxism-Leninism was
frozen into a mold that had more to do with rationalizing and legitimating
the Stalinist dictatorship than providing the popular classes with the
tools of a liberating science. Moreover, even though "official Marxism-
Leninism" of the Soviet variety has changed somewhat since Stalin's
day, it has never recovered from that deformation; indeed, it continues
to be reproduced in a similar form because, "by concealing contradictions" within "actually existing socialisms," it "contributes to their
reproduction" (and even, some would argue, "serves the interest of the
ruling class" in these so-called socialist countries). If this is true, even in
part, the point is also relevant to the attempted transition to socialism
by small peripheral countries. For the brand of Marxism most readily
available to these latter is precisely this "frozen" variant, proffered by
the "Eastern allies" of fledgling socialisms in the form of multitudinous
textbooks, teachers, and ideological advisers.
   No doubt the acceptance of such Marxism is facilitated in the third
world by an awareness of the historic role of its main protagonists in the
global anti-imperialist struggle (in particular Russia, with its Bolshevik
revolution of 1917) and by their apparent success in overcoming some
aspects of underdevelopment: often, too, these allies gain credibility

from having played a valued support role in the original struggle under consideration, to win its independence and/or to carry through its revolution. But we must not ignore the possibility that a "frozen Marxism" will be welcomed because of, not in spite of, its weaknesses, these dovetailing all too neatly with—and helping to rationalize—weaknesses in the socialist practice of the peripheral countries themselves. Under such circumstances the chief function of Marxism may prove, once again, to be the concealing of contradictions rather than their exposure. And there are other variants of Marxism which we can identify as prone to becoming ideological in this pejorative sense (what I have elsewhere [Saul 1984] called "populist Marxism," for example). I will explore these possibilities in what follows, but the importance of the struggle for ideological clarity in the small peripheral countries—and especially the "ideological class struggle" which manifests itself on the terrain of Marxism itself—should already be apparent.

Marxism

We must be circumspect, however. It is all too easy to label the variants of Marxism with which one disagrees as "mere ideology" and the formulations one finds most illuminating as the "true Marxism." Yet the debate is not an entirely arbitrary one. Some definitions of Marxism do advance both an understanding of the world and a liberating social practice more effectively than others which, reshaped in their essentials by deeper social currents (class formation and the like), tend to function as ideologies in the pejorative sense. We cannot avoid making such distinctions. At the same time we must also admit that even the most dogmatic versions of Marxism tend to be merely one-sided presentations of what are, nonetheless, very real tensions within Marxism. And these tensions are not easily resolved by even the most judicious practitioner or theorist. Although the "ideological class struggle" referred to above is unavoidable, there is also obviously room for honest disagreement among Marxists on such questions.

A detour across the minefield of the Marxist tradition is clearly in order. We must specify with care the areas of tension, for only when we do so will we be able to identify the manner in which Marxism can lose its way. We can begin with what is perhaps the most paradoxical (dialectical?) formulation in the Marxist canon: "Man makes his own history, but he does not make it under conditions of his own choosing." This citation juxtaposes "man" (sic) as active agent of history to "man" as an element in the historical process whose actions are predetermined by broader socioeconomic forces. These emphases, if polarized as alternatives rather than held in creative tension, give rise to formulations which have been characterized in the Marxist argot as, on the one hand, erring toward "voluntarism" and, on the other hand, erring toward "determinism." Each extreme in turn has both a methodological and a practical implication.

Marx himself did hold these two emphases together, although some have argued that his work showed a shifting balance between them over time. Thus his early work may have tended more to emphasize "man" as an active agent overcoming his own alienation (even if, from very early on, this process was seen as being profoundly conditioned by historical context and possibility), while his later work may more strongly have emphasized "men," concrete and historical, as actors whose possibilities for self-realization were tightly delimited by the existing level of socioeconomic development. Nonetheless, Marx held firmly to *both* aspects of the Marxian paradox quoted earlier, something his successors have often been much less successful in doing.

First, let us consider the methodological implications of the failure to do so. Thus those whose Marxism has tended to lay maximum emphasis upon the ineluctable movement of history have also been those who have given pride of place to a "scientific" understanding of that movement. However, in this formulation science has sometimes come much closer to "scientism," producing, at the extreme, the attempt to ground (and give added resonance to) inevitable laws of history in equally inevitable laws said to be characteristic of all natural phenomena (the "dialectics of nature"). Unfortunately, such an attempt has all too often lent to Marxian materialism a metaphysical, even quasi-religious, air, while also giving rise to a pseudo-science of rigid and abstract inevitabilities rather than a scientific method geared to examining hypotheses, detecting tendencies, and illuminating cases.

At the other pole of the intra-Marxist debate lies a "critical Marxism" which, in its focus on the centrality of conscious human agency in the historical process and on the releasing of human energies, effectively critiques much of what passes for science under such rubrics as "dialectical materialism," while also challenging any glibly deterministic reading of Marxism. Yet this emphasis in turn runs the risk of focusing too exclusively on subjective, cultural barriers to class consciousness and losing sight, in an "idealist" manner, of the great "objective" and "determining" sea-changes occurring in the production process (economic crisis, class polarization, etc.).

The latter formulation also risks linking itself *in practice* to a "voluntarist," even adventurist, underestimation of the constraints upon socialist creativity, to the notion that, in Marx's mordant phrase (when criticizing Bakunin), *"will,* not economic conditions, is the foundation of (the) social revolution." Exclusive reliance on political solutions (e.g., "mobilization") to what are necessarily far more complex socioeconomic challenges can then be a temptation, as can the danger that revolutionaries will seek to run ahead of historical possibility in a potentially self-defeating way. Yet breaking with fatalism is also crucially necessary, not least when capitalism is comprehended in its global dimensions by Marxists in the small peripheral countries of the third world. These Marxists have then begun to focus creatively on (1) the possible revolutionary vocation of peasantries and of the "worker-peasant alliance" in furthering socialist advance, and (2) the potential importance of anti-imperialist nationalism as a complement to a class-based consciousness in making a revolution or in underwriting postrevolutionary development efforts in their countries.

The "realism" of a more economistic approach has a contribution to make here, of course; it offers a kind of vaccination against adventurism and a warning against any underestimation of the barriers that "historical backwardness" can present to socialist advance in third world settings. Yet such emphases can easily give way to their own brand of dogmatism. Take, for example, the various extreme and Eurocentric versions of Trotskyism that come close to suggesting that the absence of a fully developed working class disqualifies third world settings, virtually by definition, from the socialist realm. Take, too, the conclusions of some "world system" theorists who see global capitalism as more or less a closed system, impervious to third world socialist assertions, or those of writers like Bill Warren who deploy an overstated model of the universal and continuing development potential of that same global capitalism in order to denigrate alternative socialist projects (Warren 1980). Equally negative can be the impact of a rather different brand of economism: the tendency, most marked in Stalinist formulations, to redefine the transition to socialism in the postrevolutionary period almost exclusively in terms of the pace of expansion of the forces of production, other dimensions of what might be thought to be implied in the idea of transition (class struggle, for example, or democratization) then being assigned a distinctly secondary status.

Several related problems have by now been hinted at. The more "scientific" reading of Marxism emphasizes the shaping force of the production process (its structure and level of development) and/or its associated class structure. But, as noted, it is quite easy for this reading of Marx to turn deterministic in much too rigid a manner, to become "economistic" or "class reductionist." Engels wrestled with precisely these dangers in a series of well-known letters, admitting, on one occasion, that

> Marx and I are ourselves partly to blame for the fact that the younger people sometimes lay more stress on the economic side that is due it. We had to emphasize the main principle *vis-à-vis* our adversaries, who denied it, and we had not always the time, the place or the opportunity to allow the other elements involved in the interaction to come into their rights. (1890; in Tucker 1978:762).[3]

This clearly is complex terrain for Marxists, and neither their theory nor their practice has always stood the test of clarity and relevance in this regard. Nonetheless, a Marxism fully attuned to the question of consciousness has stood the best chance of keeping alive a sense of the dialectical tension between production process-cum-class determinations on the one hand and such variables (cultural/"ideological" but also material) as nation, ethnic group and region, race and gender on the other. And the need to do so is at least as relevant in third world settings as elsewhere.

Either pole of the economistic-voluntaristic dichotomy can also lead to the blurring of another important tension within Marxism, what we have come to think of as the relationship between *vanguard* and *mass action*. Marx made it clear that the active agent of revolutionary change must be the collective laborer. While he saw the role of communists to be that of a catalyst of that collective laborer's self-activity as a class, he tended not to contemplate the possibility that any very dramatic contradiction could arise between party and class; though not precisely a "revolutionary fatalist" he was nonetheless remarkably confident that capitalism was creating its own gravediggers in the form of a proletariat which could come to consciousness as a class-for-itself reasonably expeditiously. Latter-day Marxists, both in the third world and in more advanced capitalist settings, have had to face up to a more complex reality, however: there is a pressing need for leadership in order to transcend the existing limitations upon spontaneous class action and to facilitate and focus revolutionary class consciousness. Yet the temptations for such leadership to substitute itself for the agency of popular classes in negative ways is also one of "actually existing socialism's" most evident characteristics.

Marxists of more determinist persuasion can find ample rationalization for this trend within the logic of their theory: their Marxist commitments (including their privileged scientific insights) make them "vanguards of the proletariat" almost by definition, and make their governments, after establishing state control of the economy and thereby eliminating classes (sic), "dictatorships of the proletariat." Similarly, some "voluntarists" (though this is very far from begin true of all variants of "critical Marxism") can begin, self-righteously, to make a virtue of the necessity they feel to force the pace of history; socialist democracy can, once again, be the first casualty. Whatever the diverse roots of such formulations, the fact remains that it is around the theme of leadership and democracy that a particularly crucial tension within Marxism can be seen to surface. Nor is it a tension, a contradiction, that can be resolved, once and for all, in some definitive manner, either in theory or in practice. Indeed, the need to resolve it positively— deepening the democratic activity of the popular classes even as leadership is pointing the way forward—represents an on-going, continually renewed, challenge within the transition to socialism. In fact, it virtually defines the most crucial political process within that transition.

Marxism as Ideology

These tensions on the terrain of the Marxist tradition are real, then: Marxism as science vs. Marxism as critique; economism vs. voluntarism; reductionism vs. "culturism" (for want of a better term); leadership vs. mass action. The great strength of the Marxist tradition is that, at its best, it forces Marxists to live self-consciously on the knife edge of these contradictions, to conceive reality not in terms of "either–or" but dialectically. Unfortunately, this is far more easily said than done and, as hinted earlier, such as been the trajectory of twentieth-century socialist practice that much of the adventure of the dialectic implicit in these pairings has been lost. Here, we must look more carefully at how Marxism itself has tended historically to freeze up and become "ideological" in the negative sense of that term. As was suggested earlier, the trajectory of the Soviet revolution has been crucially important in this regard.

Tendencies toward "fatalism" were already present in the Marxism of the Second International, of course (e.g., Karl Kautsky, the Mensheviks), as was, at the other extreme, the kind of moralizing voluntarism represented by Eduard Bernstein. The Bolsheviks lived the relevant tensions or contradictions within Marxism in a much more self-conscious and creative manner. In fact, the situation in Russia forced them to do so. Although there was an active proletariat there—it was to be the single most important actor in the making of the Russian revolution—it nonetheless remained small and afloat in a sea of peasant production and underdevelopment. Lenin, Trotsky, and others debated whether Russian conditions made feasible a socialist revolution and even when events and their deep commitment to radical change pushed them forward they continued to look to a revolution in the more advanced capitalist centers as necessary to provide the elbow room they thought postrevolutionary Russia required. Indeed, they very much feared the probable costs of having to go it alone.

The Bolsheviks' dialectical sensibility proved to be an invaluable resource, however. Thus the critical/voluntarist strand in their thinking was sufficiently alive to force them to begin (though only to begin) to examine such matters as the role of the peasantry within a worker-peasant alliance and, in the first years of the Comintern, to contemplate the global revolutionary significance of anti-imperialist nationalism. Yet their simultaneous sensitivity to the fact of Russia's economic backwardness and the "unripeness" of conditions there also served to give a measured tone to certain of their postrevolutionary development strategies. Hence Lenin's profound concern with "educational work"— in "our insufficiently cultured country" the "political and social revolution preceded the cultural revolution, that very cultural revolution which nevertheless now confronts us" (in Tucker 1975:712–13); hence his ability to conceive and to implement the New Economic Policy (NEP) as a subtle and legitimate tactical adjustment in policy rather than as the strategic retreat some of his critics interpreted it as being.

Yet pushing back the boundaries of "objective" constraints while treating such constraints with absolute seriousness proved a difficult balance to maintain. Moreover, it has been argued, notably by Corrigan, Ramsay, and Sayer (1978), that from the outset the Bolshevik project carried some of the seeds of its own demise (and of the counterbalancing of its "many emancipatory qualities") in its too exclusive preoccupation with the technological side of the development challenge it faced; it had begun too onesidedly to privilege the development of the forces of production over and above a concern with the character of the social relations of production within that classic Marxian couplet. Even if these were merely "tendencies" within Bolshevik Marxism, these authors argue, they did help set the stage for a much more full-blown economistic turn within Soviet Marxism under the aegis of Stalin.

Before looking at this latter phase, we must take note of another tension within Marxism that the Bolsheviks sought valiantly to straddle, albeit with mixed results. Lenin, like Marx before him, insisted that he was no Jacobin, no Blanquist, and that the dominated classes must make their own revolution, build their own socialism. Yet within the Marxist tradition there is an eloquent strand of criticism—from such stalwarts as Rosa Luxemburg and the Council Communists, for example—of various Leninist formulations and Leninist practices for their undemocratic implications in the political realm. Of course, as I have argued elsewhere (Saul 1985), one does not even have to leave the terrain of Lenin's own thought—a simple juxtaposition of *What Is to Be Done?* and *The State and Revolution* would be instructive enough in this respect—to get a sense of the real tensions between the legitimate claims of leadership on the one hand and mass action on the other which he was prepared to acknowledge and to struggle to reconcile.[4] Not that Lenin ever resolved this tension, either in theory or in practice, entirely effectively. But he did continue to agonize over it right up to the moment of his death. With Stalin, however, the sense of any such tension virtually disappeared.

Numerous writers have analyzed the crystallization of Stalinist Marxism, tracing its weaknesses to its roots in the paradoxical realities of the Soviet Union itself. Charles Bettelheim has characterized the society that emerged in Russia in the 1930s as being marked by "the complete defeat of the private bourgeoisie, the numerical increase of the Soviet proletariat, the modernization of the economy, and a tremendous industrial advance, which contributed to the advance of forces fighting for socialism throughout the world." At the same time, he notes, "the worker-peasant alliance was gravely weakened, the industrial development of the Soviet Union became more and more one-sided, and the primacy accorded to technology tended to strengthen the role played by technicians and by the administrative and economic apparatuses, and even by the apparatus of repression" (1978:594).[5]

I have already suggested the extent to which these latter emphases dovetailed with a Marxism that reduced the notion of socialist transition to one coterminous with the expansion of the forces of production. As Bettelheim has documented, this formulation went hand in glove with a downplaying of the possibility that to change production relations might itself actually help "ensure, under certain circumstances, the development of the productive forces." It also meant factoring out any necessity for class struggle in the context of transition. So much for empowering the workers—in genuine "soviets"—at the base of the production process, or empowering peasantry (this latter seen instead as being primarily a manipulable source of the surpluses necessary to the maximization of accumulation). So much, more generally, for a perspective which valued the empowering of the popular classes within all relevant social institutions so as to permit them to safeguard effectively their class interests over and against the dangers inherent in a crystallization of bureaucratic power.[6]

Small wonder that many have found the most important key to explaining the character of the Marxism favored by Soviet leaders to lie precisely in the kind of relationship that came to exist between the Bolshevik party and the popular classes, a relationship of "revolution from above." Not only did the implied narrowing of the definition of "socialist power" to one coterminous with state planning tend to fetishize the notion of planning and to overstate its incompatibility with such tactics as, say, the measured utilization of market mechanisms. More important, by unproblematically identifying the state which does such planning with "the dictatorship of the proletariat" it helped deflect attention away from the question of genuinely institutionalizing the power of the popular classes. The possibility of any very meaningful contradiction between leadership and mass, party and class, began to be defined away by theoretical fiat, a clear example of Marxism as comfortable "dogmatism" in the sense indicated by Lefebvre. What was emerging on the ideological plane, then, was a "contradictory reality in which a constant struggle went on between revolutionary Marxist theory . . . and various ideological currents which were alien to Marxism—parodying it, because they often borrowed its 'terminology' " (Bettelheim 1978:501).

What of the first principles underlying such "dogmatism"? Certainly one must be cautious about seeing in Stalinist Marxism a more systematic and coherent intellectual project than in fact existed. It is true, as suggested earlier, that a particularly "mechanical" materialism did begin to find its way into the theoretical formulations of the period, one that, in deducing historical materialism from dialectical materialism, tended, as Z. A. Jordan notes, to substitute "a one-sided causal dependence of man upon his environment for the Marxian conception of interaction and mutual modification of the one by the other" (1967:363). This approach was used, Jordan continues, "to show, however erroneously, that the policies of the Party were not arbitrary decisions of individuals; being an application of scientific knowledge, they constituted an integral part of it" (ibid.:364)! Small wonder that it is this "scientific" outlook which continues to buttress the official version of Marxism-Leninism to be found in most "actually-existing socialist regimes" to the present day. But equally evident in Stalinist Marxism were extremely voluntarist (some might say idealist) emphases, according to which political ideas could mobilize the masses to heroic feats and thus force the pace of development (ibid.:363–64).

This is a familiar enough contradiction to be sure, yet what was distinctive about the Stalinist ideological mix was that these two emphases were no longer held together in creative tension. Instead, they existed as the opposite poles of unpredictable ideological oscillations, serving to rationalize policies—either by giving pseudo-scientific status to ongoing party programs on the one hand or by legitimating dramatic breaks with the party line on the other—chosen quite opportunistically as circumstances and the demands of power dictated. Slowly but surely, by this and other means, Marxism as the ideology (in the positive sense) of the proletariat was being transformed into Marxism as a dominant ideology (in the negative sense) in the service of the Soviet state.

Appropriate Marxism

Soviet Marxism encapsulates both the strengths and the weaknesses of the Bolshevik tradition, although in its most fully codified, post-Stalinist form the weaknesses far outweigh the strengths.[7] Moreover, as noted, it has tended to be this latter brand of Marxism which, for good reasons and bad, has provided much of the framework for the most prominent expressions of the Marxist tradition in small peripheral countries. Needless to say, third world revolutionaries draw on their

own experience and on their own reading of the Marxist canon—
including the diverse and dissident voices which that canon houses—in
defining their ideologies. Yet the sheer visibility—and apparent success—of the Soviet variant lends it special prominence. Moreover, as I
have noted, this is not a strictly intellectual exercise. Marxisms which
are less than creative can mesh all too readily with *raison d'état* and
with the interests (class or otherwise) of bureaucratic strata, party
hacks, and chauvinistic males, among others. It therefore behooves us
to ask just what kind of ideological creativity—and what kind of
ideological class struggle!—seems to be most appropriate to socialist
development in the small peripheral countries.

"Ideological Work"

Most difficult to realize, most difficult even to conceptualize, is the
clarification of theoretical first principles. Sometimes, too, such an
exercise can seem an academic luxury to revolutionaries under pressure, to revolutionaries in a hurry. Yet the most dedicated of third
world revolutionaries have often seen quite clearly that the textbook
Marxism available to them—and also being preferred to their younger
cadres-in-training in party schools and in the educational system more
generally—does not quite work. As Samora Machel of Mozambique
once put the point:

> Marxism-Leninism sprang up among us as the product of our struggle and
> of the debates over ideas within FRELIMO itself. To underestimate this
> fact is to deprive Marxism-Leninism of the vital force which it possesses in
> Mozambique, it is to reduce it to clichés and abstract stereotypes, to
> pale copies of realities beyond our borders. "Historical materialism" must
> be studies with reference to the realities of Mozambican society and to the
> specific circumstances of its historical evolution. . . . [Such studies] are
> not to be made in an abstract manner, independently of Mozambican
> reality, or by treating Mozambican reality with merely passing references.[8]

Innovation has followed such pronouncements, though even then it has
tended to be innovation which seeks, the latter part of this quotation
from Machel may suggest, to counter the formidable abstractness of
much of what passes for Marxism-Leninism primarily by complementing it with more concrete materials about the specific country and by
making it more "applied." Less frequent has been a critique that traces
that very abstractness to the mechanical, onesided, and lifeless (undialectical) manner in which so much "dialectical-cum-historical materialism" seeks to explain social interconnections in the first place.

Yet only a tough-minded confrontation with the dialectical complexity of the central Marxian paradox referred to earlier ("Man makes
his own history but . . .) will suffice. For without that the dialectical
mainspring of Marxism—the tense interchange between human self-

224 John S. Saul

activity on the one hand and historically determined socioeconomic constraints on the other—will be broken. At that point, as with Stalinist Marxism, a quite mechanical materialism and a rather narrow economic determinism can carry the day "philosophically"—the dialectic, for example, now transformed into a mere human reflex of some more general law of nature. As for "self-activity": if, from time to time, it springs to the fore it will do so quite arbitrarily as a kind of opportunistic voluntarism on the part, more often than not, of the leadership stratum only. And once this has happened historical experience suggests that all the other creative tensions that serve to push Marxist theory and practice forward will begin to atrophy. It thus behooves third world Marxists to keep their definition of the Marxist tradition as open as possible, to appropriate Marxism as a science, but one which interrogates reality, reexamines hypotheses, a science which lives. They must, in short, ask the "big questions" for themselves.

Democratization

Certainly a more coherent—if problematic—sense of the importance of human self-activity seems to be necessary if democratization is to be the crucial consideration it should be for Marxists. In contrast, a more mechanical materialism has tended to fit all too neatly with authoritarian practices—practices which are no less authoritarian for being done "in the name of socialism." Of course, third world socialists have been justifiably suspicious of much of the democratic-cum-human rights discourse which has been directed at (and even against) them, seeing it as redolent with bourgeois mystification and manipulation. They have also harbored suspicions about various democratic discourses on the left, including that of a "new left" which they often feel to be willfully naive and/or unduly schematic in its thinking about such questions. They see this "new left" as ignoring precisely the simultaneity of the claims that both leadership and mass action have to a revolutionary's attention, see it, in short, as being undialectical in its own right. Indeed, under the conditions of economic crisis and imperialist intervention in which third world Marxists more often than not find themselves, claims made on behalf of "leadership" and strong organization will seem doubly attractive.

Small wonder that the elements of Lenin's organizational preoccupations that have passed over into official "Marxism-Leninism" make the latter's formulations so often appear commonsensical to revolutionaries in small peripheral countries. Yet, as we have seen, the good reasons for a certain kind of top-down "Leninism" can easily turn themselves into bad ones, permitting leaders to overemphasize the "centralism" half of their "democratic centralism," to too glibly charge their critics with "populism," and to turn their own democratic rhetoric into mere "terminology." The result? In few aspirant socialist countries can one find the degree of openness of discussion, expression, and action—in the media, the arts, the political arena—that one suspects is necessary to sustain full socialist creativity, even granting the very hard conditions faced by these various countries.

One must immediately add that these latter kinds of judgments are notoriously difficult to make. Finding the means of institutionalizing the most efficacious "political mediation of revolutionary power" (in Ralph Miliband's phrase) is a real challenge (1970b:313). I have mentioned some of the voices within the Marxist tradition—voices all too often held out of earshot—which could complement official "Marxism-Leninism" in this respect. Moreover, innovative attempts in the under-developed countries themselves—albeit marked by widely varying degrees of success—have ranged from Mao Tsetung's Cultural Revolution to Samora Machel's "political and organizational offensive" against bureaucratization and corruption, and the Sandinistas' distinctive brand of alliance politics. In any case our present task is not to give advice on such matters, but rather to point toward the kinds of ideological preoccupations which might help to keep the search for real "political mediation" alive.

Class Struggle

Not surprisingly, within the framework of a rigid quasi-Marxism the deemphasis on democratization goes hand in hand with an avoidance of any very concrete discussion of the imperatives of class struggle during the socialist transition process. Yet democratization is no mere luxury: historical experience suggests that unless the popular classes are progressively empowered, at an ever higher level of consciousness, to defend their class interests in the socialist project, there is every likelihood that the project which ostensibly is theirs will be hijacked, and warped to serve the narrower interests of privileged strata who come to command the centers of power and decisionmaking. Not that Marxism, in general terms, is weak in the area of class analysis. Indeed, it is precisely the fact that it places class analysis front and center that has recommended it to third world revolutionaries. At the same time, it is no coincidence that the canon of Soviet Marxism is strikingly underdeveloped precisely with reference to the class analysis of the transition process.

There are theoretical as well as practical reasons for this weakness. As seen, a simplistic (and economistic) identification of socialism with the bare fact of state predominance within the economy helps facilitate the preemption of class analysis. And this is readily reinforced, in turn, by a rigidly stagist theory of inevitable (and irreversible) progression from feudalism to capitalism to socialism to communism. Moreover, the terms of an alternative, more open and problematic, analysis of the range of social development possible in a postrevolutionary situation are not so easy to come by, as a growing literature on the subject will testify. Yet third world countries can ill afford to permit their own seduction by comforting formulas that theorize away the realities of stratification. There are just too many ways in which ostensibly socialist revolutions can become bureaucratized, top-heavy, heavy-handed—in turn permitting the loss of most of their socialist dynamic.

Fortunately, such issues are not entirely profane knowledge in the small peripheral countries, as my own experience in Mozambique has proven to me. And there are other issues of class analysis to which third world Marxists have had to remain alert. Thus, the discussion of the Soviet Union above pinpointed a further danger—a brand of Marxism which is so sensitive to Marx's legitimately strong focus upon the crucial importance of the proletariat that it underemphasizes the full significance of later attempts to positively evaluate the potential revolutionary role of the peasantry in positive terms. Not that Marx was deaf to such concerns himself. Recall that in the very text in which he despairs most memorably about the peasantry, likening it, in terms of its potential for class consciousness, to a "sack of potatoes," he speaks of possible circumstances in which "the French peasant parts with his belief in his small holding" and "the proletarian revolution obtains that chorus without which its solo song in all peasant nations becomes a swan song" (1852, in Tucker 1978:614). Even more germane to the problematic of socialist construction is a remark in his criticism of Bakunin:

> . . . either the peasantry hinders every workers' revolution and causes it to fail, as it has done in France up till now; or the proletariat (for the landowning peasant does not belong to the proletariat and even when his own position causes him to belong to it, he does not *think* he belongs to it) must as a government inaugurate measures which directly improve the situation of the peasant and which thus win him for the revolution; measures which in essence facilitate the transition from private to collective property in land so that the peasant himself is converted for economic reasons. (quoted in McLellan 1971:210)

In contrast, revolutionary Marxists have often turned with suspicion, in postrevolutionary settings, upon the very peasantry which formed their chief political base during the making of the original revolution, undermining rather than deepening the terms of the worker-peasant alliance in a frenzy of accumulation and/or "proletarian messianism." And even where peasants have been taken more seriously, they have sometimes been characterized much too broadly by that very term "peasants," rather than being seen as "peasantries" specified in particulars important to policymaking by their concrete local circumstances. Marxism is nothing if it is not an *applied* science, and it therefore requires a capacity to work close up—in a virtually anthropological manner. Unless great care is taken, its sweeping historical preoccupations and global pretensions can overwhelm this capacity.

Non-Class Forms of Domination

The energetic movements for national, racial, and gender liberation of recent decades have prompted an increasingly serious discussion regarding the primacy of class struggle. Erik Olin Wright has argued, with some reason, that the latter emphasis remains correct owing to the fact that a tendency toward transformation of the class structure is inherent in the very process of economic development (in the development of the productive forces), providing class relations with an "internal logic of development" denied to other forms of domination. "The apparent symmetry in the relationship between class and gender or class and race, therefore, is disrupted by the developmental tendencies of class relations. No such developmental trajectory has been persuasively argued for other forms of domination" (1983:24). Despite the strength of this argument, however, it can easily become reductionist. And this may be a particularly costly danger in third world settings where racial and national oppression have been so much a part of the overarching structure against which revolutionaries have rebelled; moreover, these realities have affected, often crucially, the discourses that have shaped people's resistance to oppression. Of course, third world revolutionaries have already made signal contributions to reclaiming such realities on behalf of Marxist theory and practice. But a continuing challenge remains.[9]

Recent third world experience makes clear that ethnic subnationalisms can also have a vigorous vitality, focusing cultural preoccupations and intensely lived histories (in addition to their more negative attributes of being subject to manipulation by counterrevolutionary forces, both external and indigenous). Revolutionaries yield to the temptation to bulldoze over these realities as, say, manifestations of "false consciousness" only at considerable peril. Even more serious questions are at stake in the sphere of gender oppression and gender consciousness. The emancipation of women is perforce a key ingredient of any genuinely liberatory project, not least in small peripheral countries where the potent combination of unenlightened traditional and colonial practices (sometimes reinforced by religious imperatives) has had a particularly crippling impact on women. Yet weaknesses of Marxist theory in this sphere, weaknesses which are only very slowly being confronted in all parts of the world, have tended to mesh all too comfortably with the corporate interests of men (even ostensibly revolutionary men) to narrow the scope of what are deemed to be legitimate claims in this sphere—even in postrevolutionary settings.

One other controversial issue might be raised here. Marx was certainly an atheist and a principled materialist. This is probably true of a majority of Marxists. Yet the claims of Marxist materialism—especially when set in terms of the dogmatic and ultimately unprovable "first principles" of dialectical materialism—can also be cast so broadly as to constrain revolutionary progress. For "materialism" remains a hypothesis, close to a faith principle in its own right; except in its more messianic manifestations it need not constrain revolutionaries from dealing flexibly with manifestations of the religious impulse in their societies. If there is a real "opiate" intertwined with that impulse it lies principally in the (negative) ideological practices of various institutions (churches and the like), practices which in turn reflect the maneuverings of privileged classes and groups. In confronting these latter there seems less need for Marxists to paint themselves into a narrow ideological corner and withdraw (often at very great potential cost) from dialogue with believers than an unduly rigid Marxism might apply.

Economic Strategy

I have mentioned the fixation with "accumulation" and "planning" that determinist and centralizing definitions of Marxism can facilitate, a fixation which culminated, in the Soviet Union in the 1930s, in "the Stalinist solution": extreme centralization, an emphasis upon "primitive socialist accumulation" at the expense of the peasantry and in the interests of heavy industry, and the priority given to state farms in the rural sector. Ideological class struggle must also focus on the onesided premises—and vested interests—which can cluster around this agenda. For an alternative to the "primitive socialist accumulation" model does exist—one which shifts the emphasis to urban-rural exchanges as the principal means of driving the economy forward. The accumulation process could then be carried forward precisely by finding outlets for industrial production in meeting the growing requirements, the needs of the mass of the population. The key to "expanded reproduction" would then lie in the exchanges suggested above, with food and raw materials moving to the cities and consumer goods and producer goods (including such modest items as scythes, plows, hoes, axes, and so on) moving to the countryside. Moreover, accumulation—collective saving geared to investment—could then be seen as being drawn essentially, if not exclusively, from an expanding economic pool, rather than, of necessity, merely being squeezed from the population.

Here revolutionaries in small peripheral countries could draw upon alternative formulations to the Stalinist one within the Marxist tradition; in this case, for example, upon the promise of the Soviet Union's New Economic Policy before the false polarization of the industrialization debate and its brutal resolution by Stalin. As I have argued elsewhere (Saul 1985; Saul 1983), such a "socialism of expanded reproduction" would make the betterment of the people's lot a short-term rather than long-term prospect, offering in this way a much sounder basis for an effective, rather than merely rhetorical, alliance of workers and peasants. It would also offer, in all probability, a much sounder basis for a democratic road to revolutionary socialism.

It does so, in part, by taking the peasantry seriously (something Stalinoid Marxism has had grave difficulties in doing). Taking the peasantry seriously might also involve reaffirming the virtues of cooperativization of the peasantry, rather than subordinating this to a onesided emphasis upon state farms (these latter too often privileged merely because capital intensive—the "productive forces" argument again—or "more proletarian"). Of course, a freshly innovative Marxism would want to view such cooperativization less romantically than has sometimes been the case, casting programs in terms much closer to the spirit of Lenin than of Stalin, to Lenin's sense that the virtues of cooperativization would have to prove themselves on the terrain of the NEP: "We must win the competition against the ordinary shop assistant, the ordinary capitalist, the merchant who will go to the peasant without arguing about communism. . . . Either we pass this test in competition with private capital or we fail completely" (quoted in Bettelheim 1978:35).

Needless to say, the precise role to be assigned to the market—with all its inherent dangers (class formation and the like)—presents another difficult question. Yet we need not go as far as Alec Nove (1983) who now argues that there is a very positive role indeed to be played by the market in the transition to socialism, to admit that the question must remain open. By closing it off revolutionaries could, once again, disarm themselves with "terminology," making it difficult to think through the most realistic and effective mechanisms of socialist planning. Closing off the question also makes it difficult to conceive of the ways in which, in a hostile environment, necessary compromises might be made with capitalist actors, both local and international, while still safeguarding those features of the development effort which strengthen the long-term socialist project. These are, in fact, some of the most serious considerations which confront socialist planners in such countries as Mozambique and Nicaragua. And generally these planners have found little which is of help to them on such matters in conventional Marxist-Leninist manuals. Reconceptualizing the terms of economic strategy is one more area, therefore, where real theoretical creativity is essential in postrevolutionary societies.

This essay has attempted, in brief compass, to explore issues that only a book would suffice to cover. But it may at least have served to remind the reader how crucial a part of the effort to construct socialism in small peripheral countries is the attempt to prevent Marxist ideology from turning "ideological" in the negative sense and to permit Marxism to illuminate rather than obscure the challenges involved. To return to the words of Lefebvre with which we began: "the fierce struggle inside Marxism between dogmatism and the critique of dogmatism . . . is not over; it goes bitterly on." And it is important.

Notes

1. I have elaborated on the Mozambican experience in ways relevant to the present paper in Saul (1985) and Saul, ed. (1985:ch. 2).

2. Gramsci also worked with the neutral definition of ideology, viewing it as "the terrain on which men move, acquire consciousness, struggle, etc." He also enriched the concept by seeing an "organic ideology" as "a conception of the world that is implicitly manifest in art, in law, in economic activity and in all manifestations of individual and collective life" and as a conception which structures the "hegemony" of the dominant class.

3. Engels continued in the same letter: "What these gentlemen all lack is dialectics. They always see only here cause, there effect. That this is a hollow abstraction, that such metaphysical polar opposites exist in the real world only during crises, while the whole vast process goes on in the form of interaction—though of very unequal forces, the economic movement being by far the strongest, most primeval, most decisive—that here everything is relative and nothing absolute—this they never begin to see."

4. See, on this subject, Antonio Carlo, "Lenin on the Party," *Telos* 17 (Fall 1973): 2–40.

5. Chapter 3 of section 4 of this book, entitled "The Bolshevik Ideological Formation and Its Transformation," is particularly useful as regards this theme.

6. Simultaneously, the narrowing of the definition of human emancipation inherent in an increasingly economistic Soviet Marxism also helped to narrow the manner of posing those important "cultural" questions referred to earlier. The quest for women's emancipation, for example, tended to be deflated into some function of equality in the production process narrowly defined, rather than obliging an even more fundamental confrontation with gender inequality.

7. This can be seen, for example, in *The Fundamentals of Marxism-Leninism,* a widely used Soviet handbook.

8. Samora Machel, "Dominar a Ciencia e Arte Militares Para Defender Conquistas da Revolucao," speech in Nampula on the opening of the Military School and printed in *25 de Septembro* 88 (December 1979).

Ideology and Revolutionary Politics
in Transitional Societies
▼▲
Orlando Núñez Soto

In the construction of a revolutionary society, human begins intervene in history, making economic transformation possible and making themselves the key factor in such transformation. This essay will explore the potential and limitations of these interventions in the political sphere in revolutionary peripheral societies, where conscious actions must compensate for the limitations imposed by economic conditions.

Any revolutionary project must deal with both objective conditions—the economic and material needs of transformation—and subjective conditions—the relationship between historical consciousness and revolutionary action. While the focus here is on the subjective conditions, particularly the role of revolutionary action, this is not to emphasize one set of revolutionary conditions over another, in either the objective or the subjective sphere. While economic laws and the reality of history's great socioeconomic changes operate in the first sphere, the motives and prefigurations from which revolutionary action springs operate in the second.

In most peripheral economies, agroexport capitalism has generated a process of concentration of trade, finance, and production, which in turn proletarianizes the masses, lending these countries an often explosive social dynamic. In this process, conflicts between concentration and dispersion, proletarianization and "peasantization," growth and underdevelopment, and the economy's capitalization and decapitalization are fought out. It is this raw material which a revolutionary project must deal with once it has seized power. However, making a revolution does not mean accepting society just as it is; the task is to discover its tendencies and to dedicate oneself to creating a new order.

Aside from the inherited structure of agroexport capitalism, two other factors condition most revolutions in peripheral societies: (1) dependence on the world capitalist market, and (2) confrontation with

Translated by Helen Banberger

U.S. imperialism. The process of transition is an effort to deal with all of these factors, to use the recently conquered political power to negate the previous order, and to establish conditions for the development of socialism.

Even when the struggle for a transition to socialism starts as one principally against external forces, it requires an internal process of proletarianization, not only of the working class but of society as a whole. Here the concept of proletarianization refers to the very creation of the working class as the historical subject of the revolution and the generation of the economic conditions needed for its development, a process which necessarily begins in the political sphere. I will argue that a proletarian project is indispensable for breaking with capitalism and building an alternative society. The main difference between revolutions in the developed and underdeveloped countries is that in the former, the revolutions can begin under conditions of advanced proletarianization, whereas in the latter the process of proletarianization is still one of the main ideological, political, social, and economic tasks.

The Dialectic Totality of the Revolution

Any revolutionary analysis must look at two main relationships (1) the state of the material forces of production and how they shape social relations, and (2) the relationship of revolutionary ideology to political practice. These two relationships can and must interact in any revolutionary situation: to remain in the first would imply reducing Marxism to a means of interpretation and passive theory—waiting, as Fidel Castro would say, to see capitalism's coffin pass by—while concerning ourselves only with the second would imply reducing revolution to actions of volition and a technique for taking power.

An understanding of the relationship of ideology and practice requires us to look at subjective conditions, that is, the relationship between the revolutionary ideology that motivates action and the political practice that initiates transformation and later continues intervening in the class struggle from a position of power. However, ideology contains both the manifestations of the objective contradiction and the manifestations of the contradiction between consciousness and action. Ideology is here defined as that sphere of knowledge and set of beliefs that organize the resolve and condition the behavior of class forces around a political practice that advocates a certain social project.

Religion and traditional values, philosophy, sociology, and the other social sciences, as well as the sciences of production and reproduction, have nourished the ideological sphere in different ways in different periods of time. In all known systems and classes, a newly emerging ideology nourishes the most progressive and revolutionary ideas, values, and knowledge, questioning and advancing reality. But after a certain period of time, this same ideology can become a restraining force, trying to justify its existence and holding back the development of society. That is why today especially, while the bourgeoisie maintains its social consciousness with false ideological representations, the working class and all those sectors that adopt the proletarian project must turn to the scientific knowledge of history.

In the same way, political practice concretely carries out the tendency of historical movement. It simultaneously becomes the objective and subjective expression of the projects of change. By political practice is meant all organization and conscious mobilizations of classes and class forces in relation to political power, aimed at satisfying humanity's material and spiritual needs during every stage of development. Thus, the concept of political practice includes all rebellions, insurrections, or revolutions that struggle against exploitation and oppression in all their forms. Without a conscious and participatory component, political practice ends in the world of alienation.

Conscious political practice in revolutionary societies should create situations that favor creativity and the development of human potential—from the collective administration of the economy and of political decisionmaking (political power), to the collectivization of daily life and the elimination of classes, the state, and the family. Ultimately, the postulates of revolution are found in the conditions of production and reproduction of life, since to live, as Marx correctly pointed out, we have to produce and relate to others in a specific manner.

After a revolution has occurred, the operation of the superstructure, consciousness, and action on the economic base and on society gains more relevance than before. Because of the importance of ideology in the revolutionary process, the implementation of economic measures during the transition should not be discussed apart from political tasks and measures. Once the revolution has taken power, political practice becomes political and political-economic practice. In this regard the revolutionary project must simultaneously affect consciousness and action through the following steps:

—collectivization of the means of production and exchange;

—democratization and proletarianization not only of the working class but also of society as a whole (political power and daily life);

—planned growth and development of the economy;

—hegemony of the strategic interests of the working class and the government of society through science and creative labor;

—decommoditization of production and consumption;

—decommoditization of culture and love; reaffirmation of values of cooperation and solidarity;

—workers' administration of and social control over the distribution of the surplus; and

—direct participation of all sectors of society—women, youth, children, the elderly, ethnic groups, artists and professionals, and so on—in the resolution of their own problems.

Thus we are discussing not only expropriating power and the means of production from the previous regime but also of ideologically strengthening the universal values of liberty, justice, and happiness; of scientifically taking charge of myth, faith, imagination, and audacity; of recovering the collective consciousness that was alienated under the previous systems; and of avoiding, by all means possible, the reduction of the tasks of transition to statism and economic planning.

In the peripheral economies of the third world, the revolutionary project must simultaneously carry out a multitude of different tasks: it must overthrow the bourgeoisie's political and military power, neutralize imperialist intervention, and move the rest of society, particularly the petty bourgeoisie, toward the historical project of socialism. Once power has been won and consolidated, transition in these countries must be accomplished through the development of the material productive forces, transformation of the social relations of production, and a progressive change in the social consciousness of the workers.

Thus the subjective becomes the objective not only when it is embodied in the masses revolutionizing reality, but also when it is converted into political-economic measures aimed at developing the material and social base of the revolutionary project. This happens when ideology is nourished by science, when consciousness extends itself into revolutionary action, and science extends itself into productive techniques; in other words, when science is transformed into reality through people's power, economic development, and the transformation of daily life to the benefit of the workers.

One of the most significant contributions of modern revolutions has been to reveal that the political-ideological factor is a lever for undertaking transformations of the economic and social structure. Conscious of the breadth that the technical-productive factors have for historical transformations (e.g., the agricultural and industrial revolution of the developed countries), I will here highlight the role that political revolution can play in underdeveloped societies to reach these same transformations.

A revolutionary project in power can carry out some of the changes that the developed countries achieved through economic evolution, such as the elimination of rent, of landlords and usurers, of bank capital, nationalization of the banks and of trade, concentration of property and production, the material and political development of the proletariat, the raising of the worker's standard of living, and so on. These are precisely the steps that should be taken to liberate and develop the productive forces, which are being not only blocked but also destroyed by the counterrevolutionary forces.

Some of the measures can be accomplished through decrees. But often a revolution in power does not possess sufficient strength to implement these measures; political power is found to be insufficient and suffers from a lack of ideological development among the masses to support the process and continue struggling against the adverse forces. This is not an attempt to take recourse in the importance of the subjective factor, or to be an apologist for revolutions that are carried out from the top down. But it is intended to show the role that the economic policies of the state play in the class struggle, how they support and complement the role of the masses in the revolution. As Bettelheim (1978) has noted: "Every policy affecting the conditions of production and change equally affects class relations: they also constitute, therefore, an intervention in the class struggle."

Until now, the bourgeoisie has often understood much better than the socialists the relationship between ideology, political action, and the material forces of production. The great advance in the productive forces of capital since the fifteenth and sixteenth centuries, as well as the development of capitalist relations of production at the moment of feudal breakdown, did not prevent the bourgeoisie from applying itself systematically to the task of seizing power, precisely in order to drive forward a historical process that had already been initiated in favor of its class. All these advances and victories were accompanied, preceded, and continued by an ideological and political revolution that had as its objective the drawing in of the other social sectors, including workers, peasants, women, and youth. The goal was to implant bourgeois ideas and political practices in the heart of the other social classes. For this reason, proletarianization means for us not only the objective process of collectivization, but also the spread of socialism to the rest of the population. Proletarianization is analogous to the bourgeoisification that occurred in an earlier era.

The Orthodox View of Transitional Societies

Over the years debate on the revolutionary strategies for transitional societies has been hindered by the belief that the direction of revolutions is determined by existing social and economic forces. Latin American Marxist analyses have tended to focus on the role the material productive forces play in provoking great changes in history. This has often resulted in economic reductionism and political abstentionism, stemming from the tendency of revolutionary analysts to apply the same theoretical analysis to revolutionary situations that they have used for understanding capitalist societies. They analyze the social and economic structures and then assert that these determine what type of revolutionary state can, or cannot, emerge. In a schematic fashion, they proclaim that one class will be ascendant in the new state, and that it will dominate all other sectors and impose its ideas and ideology on them.

In actuality, the revolution runs the inverse course. It starts at the bottom with the growing political conscientization of the exploited classes interacting with the revolutionary vanguard. Once these classes have attained power, the social relations of production that sustained the previous dominated classes are altered, and the revolution can begin the task of developing the productive forces that had been blocked.

Revolutionaries cannot and should not wait for the forces of economic production to advance by themselves; that would be to postpone the revolution indefinitely. This is not to say that we should ignore existing economic conditions; but the path for unleashing the revolution will always come from the political sphere, from overcoming ideological underdevelopment and social alienation.

On another level, the confusion of political revolution with the transformation of the mode of production has led to orthodoxy and economic and social reductionism; the proletarian character of revolutionary struggle is not accepted by some unless it exists under conditions of developed capitalism and has the exclusive participation of the workers. These analysts forget that in every political revolution, the class that gains power and exercises hegemony over the revolutionary project has to use all the social forces available to it in order to be able to hold power. This was true in the case of the bourgeois political revolutions in Western Europe, where even though the bourgeoisie was a minority, it managed to incite the whole nation against feudal power and emerged triumphant.

Once the revolutionary consciousness of the popular classes reaches a certain level of social and historical awareness, the task of the revolutionary can be none other than to be the vanguard of all the collective movements until hegemony is won for all existing grassroots movements, be they peasant, craft, feminist, ethnic, youth, or even religious. In the concrete case of Nicaragua, it is clear that the Sandinista Front represents not just the proletariat, but several distinct social sectors with revolutionary consciousness, and bent on creating a new order.

Who Takes Power?

In the analysis of revolutions the nature of the class that takes power has often been confused. The general belief is that it is the dominated class (i.e., the proletariat) that becomes the new ruling class. But this is a dogmatic view of history. In general, class struggle in all known class systems does not result in the conquering of power by the previously dominated class but rather in the emergence of a third class, which held a secondary position in the previous system. This third class stands out as the class which plays the most revolutionary role after the break with the previous system.

The emergence of this new revolutionary class has occurred historically in every major social transformation. Facing the contradiction between slaveowners and slaves, the feudal lords inherited power; facing the contradiction between the lords and the serfs, the bourgeoisie were those who finally imposed themselves. Today, facing the contradiction between the agrarian bourgeoisie and the working class allied with the popular sectors, we necessarily are witnessing a metamorphosis of the previously dominated classes: the peasants are being transformed into members of cooperatives, the workers into free workers, and the petty bourgeoisie into a proletarianized petty bourgeoisie.

Thus the historical project of the revolution imposes itself on the immediate interests of the dominators and the dominated, and radically transforms them both. Once the revolution has gained state power, the revolutionary process tends to alter social and economic conditions, and with that the social sectors that supported the revolution tend to disappear. It would be absurd to do the opposite, to perpetrate the previous situation, leaving intact the social sectors that had fought precisely to transform society and to transform themselves.

The state recognizes and develops the interests of a new revolutionary class—its social base—but more importantly it represents the interests of the project as a whole, even if this conflicts with the particular interests of the groups which constitute the revolutionary class it represents. This is how the capitalist state, the most developed of all the forms of the state, operates. It obeys the rationality of capital to a greater degree than the particular interests of individual capitalists. As Engels pointed out: "the modern state, again, is only the organization that bourgeois society takes on in order to support the external conditions of the capitalist mode of production against the encroachments as well of the workers as of individual capitalists" (1970:145). To want to make a political revolution only with the dominated class, or only around the interests of that class, is to lose historical perspective of the struggle. That approach would allow the bourgeoisie to win over

the remaining social sectors, and limit the development and transformation of the potentially revolutionary classes.

The same error that orthodox analysts make before the political
revolution is made by heterodox analysts after the political revolution.
They both disqualify the movement as proletarian because its social
composition is hybrid or heterogeneous, or because the proletariat
itself is not directly running the government. They see revolution as
nothing more than one class taking and exercising political power,
forgetting that the revolution is the realization of a social project that is
most certainly led by the interests of one class, but with the participation of the other dominated social sectors.

The reductionism of orthodox analysts proclaims that revolution
cannot take place without the exclusive participation of the proletariat,
while the heterodox position holds that revolution is no longer made by
the proletariat, but by the people. The first school tells us that it is no
longer possible to make revolution in small peripheral countries, while
the latter makes every possible effort to demonstrate that these revolutions are not proletarian. The nearsightedness of the first view lies in
not seeing the popular in the proletarian and that of the second, in not
seeing the proletarian in the popular. In both cases—though for
different reasons—the analysis denies the possibility of making proletarian revolutions in third world countries.

Another position related to the orthodox school denies the feasibility and viability of the revolutionary project by not seeing its immediate
realization; proponents confuse their idealistic desires with what is the
actual unfolding of the historic project. Often they will focus on the
nonproletarian nature of the government, forgetting that every dominant class delegates the execution or administration of power to a
specialized sector, which is often not of the same social class. It is not
the class background of government officials that determines the class
character of the state or of the revolution, in the same way as it was not
the class background of the combatants that determined the class
character of the insurrectionary movement.

What can be proletarianized is not the state administrative apparatus,
but the policies and measures that the state implements. Material
limitations must be recognized, but some measures can be implemented that will help overcome the limitations of the past and prepare
conditions for the future. Clearly economic policy is one important way
that class hegemony is exercised by the superstructure. While limited
nationalization and planning may be the only steps taken during the
early process of transition, it is critical that even these measures
respond to the common interests of the dominant sectors—the workers
or other popular sectors. This can occur even though the men and
women charged with administration are not proletarian or involved in
direct production.

The Proletarian Character of the Revolution

Since capitalist society obviously does not disappear once a revolution occurs, it is important to try to define the class character of the revolution, particularly during the period of transition.

The struggle against the established order initially takes the form of questioning the entire dominant bloc—the bourgeoisie, landowners, shopkeepers, creditors, usurers, merchants, and so on. This bloc must be confronted by the greatest number of social forces possible. For that reason, the character of the revolution cannot be anything but popular, and the new political power has to represent the whole of the popular interests, even though the direction or tendency of the historical movement can only be of a proletarian character since the working class is the class with the greatest possible commitment.

As regards one class having the ability to represent the totality of national and popular interests, the bourgeoisie did this during the inception of its revolution. The fact that the working class is the only class in capitalist society capable of representing the historic interests of the movement is demonstrated by its being the only class among the direct producers with experience in social production and organization—including the bourgeoisie—and with greater objective interests in socializing production, distribution, and daily life.

In the underdeveloped countries, the objective necessity of revolution is highlighted by the reactionary character of the ruling classes, specifically by their inability to develop the productive forces by means of national capital alone, thus contributing to their abdication in favor of imperialist capital. Given this situation, only a socialist or proletarian project can simultaneously represent the interests of the working class and the other popular classes, and develop the productive forces, overcoming the contradictions of the capitalist structure.

In sum, the working class cannot successfully complete the political revolution when faced with indifference or lack of confluence of other social forces. Second, political power that fails to represent popular interests in general cannot be legitimized. And third, only proletarian ideology can represent and unite the heterogeneous interests of each and every one of the popular classes at the same time as it unites the interests of the historical movement as a whole.

The proletarian character of the revolutionary project in the social and political spheres is shaped by several factors: first, under agroexport capitalism, which is predominant in underdeveloped and peripheral economies, struggles and rebellions can only be against the owners, usurer loanmakers, speculators, and the bourgeoisie. In general, it is a struggle against the defensive political and economic regime of capitalism and imperialism. Second, the rejection and questioning of the existing situation is not the heritage of the working class, but of the entire people—workers, peasants, and the petty bourgeoisie in general, as well as all existing patriotic and anti-imperialist forces.

Third, the revolutionary struggle against the reigning order may take on a democratic and nationalist character, or it may acquire a socialist character, that is, a proletarian character in the historical sense. The second path implies two considerations: (1) a conscious political-ideological project must be embodied in the masses, whose goal should be the destruction of the ruling political system (bourgeois and pro-imperialist), and (2) a socioeconomic project of collectivization and proletarianization of the new society and the new economy must be undertaken.

The true base of this socioeconomic project is found: (1) in the economic, political, and ideological conditions of the different popular sectors, principally, in the objective conditions of the urban working class and the agricultural class—including seasonal farm workers—and the struggle of these sectors to unionize (strikes, demonstrations, organizing campaigns, and other collective and participatory activities); (b) in the collective land takeovers by the peasantry as well as their struggles to organize and mobilize themselves around their interests, confronting the landowners and the local and national authorities; (c) in the collective mobilizations of the inhabitants of the neighborhoods around social demands challenging the political regime (water, electricity, taxes, justice, freedom, etc.); (d) in the organization and collective mobilization of students around democratic demands (including solidarity with the working and peasant classes); and (e) in the demands of the ethnic, national, youth, feminist, and other movements.

In small peripheral societies the entire population does not belong to the working class, nor is it concentrated in the urban areas. The productive forces retain their precapitalist features (wooden hoes and animal power in agriculture, low technology in manufacturing). However, the bourgeoisie can hardly continue developing the productive forces, since it is aligned with imperialism and must move against the interests of the workers. It is driven to repress any show of protest by the working class or of any other popular sector.

Once we have disqualified the bourgeoisie, no other class—with the exception of the working class—can lead the socialization of production in the economic sphere. (This is not the case for socializing consumption, food supplies, health care, and education as well as political and cultural power.) It is in the working class that the immediate interests against the dominant class (the bourgeoisie) coincide most with the strategic interests of proletarianizing itself and all of society, as well as socializing the economy.

The working class can encounter contradictions in trying to make its own immediate interests coincide with those of the rest of the popular sectors. Economic and political conditions make it difficult to carry out proletarianization on a general level. But if successful the proletariat can change from being a working class that shares work with the other classes to a proletariat that is the historical subject that universally inherits the previous system.

In the revolutionary project, the defense of the immediate interests of the working class is no more revolutionary than the defense of the interests of any other popular class. What truly makes the working class revolutionary—the same as any other historical subject—is the defense of the interests of the social project as a whole. The revolution's popular and proletarian character—before and after taking political power—lies in the participation of all the dominated social sectors in the process of proletarianization.

Forging Class Alliances in Transitional Societies

By no means does the political and military defeat of the bourgeoisie and the conquest of political power by the proletarian project end the need to organize society. The fact that imperialism continues to sustain the forces that try to reimpose the old bourgeois project makes it imperative to move the proletarian project forward. The need to know who and what will guarantee the movement and the revolutionary continuation of the entire process arises immediately. One should not look exclusively to the superstructure, to the good will of the leaders or governing officials. Rather, it is the social and material base on which the project is based that will shape the direction of the revolution.

As regards the prevailing social base in the process of transition in the peripheral societies, it appears that once the bourgeoisie has been dismissed as the leading political class the internal struggle between the socialist project and the efforts to restore the bourgeois system is manifest in the conduct of two forces that are still economically separate: the working class and its historical project on the one hand, and a residual bloc or third social force (the petty bourgeoisie) on the other. The latter is composed of both economic groups (peasants, artisans, and merchants) and technical-ideological groups (professionals, technicians, government officials, administrators, students, nonproductive salaried workers in general, etc.). Involved in this struggle also are special movements (youth, student, feminist, pacifist, religious, ethnic, or cultural movements) formed under the previous systems that are motivated ideologically to favor the immediate interests of their particular group.

All of these social forces may persist on a popular level and either form strategic alliances (worker-peasant) in favor of the proletarian project, or contribute to restraining the project or even play a counterrevolutionary role. It is worth noting that this "residual" sector may be in the majority in small peripheral societies. But even more important than its numbers is the fact that its character and attitudes can pose problems for the revolutionary process. As Marx pointed out: "In countries where modern civilization has become fully developed, a new class of petty bourgeois has been formed, fluctuating between proletariat and bourgeoisie, and ever renewing itself as a supplementary part of bourgeois society" (1964:45). We could add that if this class is not won over politically by the proletarian project, it will undoubtedly be won over by the bourgeoisie, which has been less than scrupulous when choosing its allies. In small peripheral countries this class—whether in the city or in the country—constitutes the main social force, and to ignore it becomes a serious mistake.

The "residual" sector of peasants, artisans, and merchants tends to confront the revolutionary project in the sphere of production and distribution. This conflict may be resolved in favor of the narrow interests of the petty bourgeoisie—through privatization and commercialization—or it can be resolved in favor of the proletarian project through socialization and planning. On the other hand, for the sector of what I have called the technical and ideological third force (Núñez 1984), the confrontation occurs on the plane of economic and social organization and the administration of society (business and the state), as well as in the fields of culture and daily life. This contradiction manifests itself as a struggle between the centralization and specialization of power and the alienation of daily cultural life on the one hand, and democratization, socialization, and social liberation on the other. These contradictions are transcended by the development of the material productive forces and the political development of the working class.

In the case of the first group, the productive petty bourgeoisie, its proletarianization and elimination can only be attained through the implementation of a series of measures that favor the socialization of the economy. This class is the most difficult of the ideological sectors, since its neutralization can be achieved only through the development of material and ideological ties with the working class, through its participation in economic and political administration, and finally through the elimination of the social division of labor.

Under these conditions, the vanguard of the movement and the revolutionary state will feel and express the pressure exerted not only by the bourgeoisie's residual influence (political as well as economic) but also from the immediate interests of the working class and the petty bourgeoisie. The advantages of the working class lie in its being the only class whose strategic interests coincide with the project's historical interests (the socialization of production and of social life), while it is also the class with the most resistance and experience in organic political practice. On the other hand, the advantages of the technical-ideological petty bourgeoisie lie in its being a sector (the intellectuals) with a relatively high degree of access to culture and a great deal of experience in administration and organization in the economic and political spheres, precisely because they had been linked in various ways to the previous dominant classes. Finally, the productive petty bourgeoisie's advantage lies in their commercial relations in a market that still favors them.

Thus, while the worker-peasant alliance constitutes a great advance for the economic development of the proletarian project in a strict sense, the support that the entire petty bourgeoisie can give to the revolutionary movement has deep significance for the maintenance and the political and social development of people's power (just as occurred during the political revolution). In small peripheral countries, the poor peasantry can be a good ally of the working class, not only due to the conditions of misery in which it lives but also because it is somewhat proletarianized. On the other hand, the medium and rich peasantry can turn into an advocate for reprivatization and an opponent of socialization.

After taking power, the proletarian project confronts the resentment of the displaced classes, who are supported by imperialism and who seek to drag sectors of the petty bourgeoisie to their ranks by any means possible. The displaced classes will capitalize on these petty bourgeois sectors following the first difficulties the revolution experiences, such as economic blockades, shortages, restriction of certain privileges, and so on. Structural advances made by the revolution may also attack the immediate interests of these sectors: socialization, control of the economy, and the prioritization given to fulfilling basic needs that do not always benefit all of society. From that point of view, the policies undertaken by the revolution to win over those sectors can add to a delay in socialization. Measures such as the maintenance of privileges, the granting of land or credit to the peasants, artisans, and merchants will continue privatizing or commercializing the economy. This very contradiction, which is manifest in the economic sphere, is also seen in the ideological sphere, where the petty bourgeoisie—intellectuals among them—often shows itself to be a better defender of the values of the capitalist system than the bourgeoisie itself.

Thus while either group of the petty bourgeoisie can be the proletariat's best ally they can also be the proletarian project's main enemy. Given the fact that during the stage of transition, political and administrative activities are still largely separate from the tasks of production, and therefore necessarily in the hands of specialized sectors, the particular development of the working class takes a back burner to ensuring that the proletarian ideology develops as the dominant ideology of all society, not only in its own sphere, but also within the petty bourgeoisie. Similarly, it is in the interests of the proletarian project that mechanisms of participation be developed to guarantee the representation of the popular sectors in the political and economic administration of society.

In sum, the revolution starts with the defeat of bourgeois power by a revolutionary project embodied in the people's will to liberation, and led by a vanguard with a socialist leadership. Thereafter people's power must be consolidated in order to advance the revolution. This occurs through raising socialist consciousness and the concrete building of people's power, accompanied by measures that eliminate bourgeois hegemony through the formation of new values. Mass mobilizations are undertaken to counteract individual attitudes and behavior in an educational way, and at the same time to exercise forms of consultation and popular administration. Finally, a third movement is aimed at transforming capitalist relations of production and building relations of cooperation and solidarity.

Civil Society vs. Political Society

Besides the direct struggle between the interests of the opposed classes, a vertical contradiction may also manifest itself between civil society (social classes) and political society (the state and the party). The first emphasizes the demands for the masses' immediate needs; the latter emphasizes the movement as a whole. Thus the class struggle will be expressed as the struggle between two projects: the bourgeois project supported by U.S. imperialism, and the proletarian project supported by the progressive and socialist peoples and governments. Before and after taking power, the role of the vanguard was not to split society into two separate poles but rather to carry the struggle between the two projects to all possible arenas: workers, peasants, students, young people, women, the religious and ethnic communities, and diplomatic and cultural circles. The vanguard had to bring the class struggle and the revolutionary message to those sectors traditionally considered to be reactionary, that is, to regard every possible political and ideological arena as a battlefield.

If it is true that the objective conditions already existed for making a political revolution, it is also true that the objective conditions make the already difficult road of social revolution even more difficult. Thus another of the experiences of transition in the peripheral economies is the gap between realizing the political revolution and realizing the social revolution.

During the transition period, the revolutionary leadership will oscillate between maintaining and defending its power and advancing and carrying out the revolutionary project. Sometimes, the national and international correlation of forces will make the defense of power a priority, slowing the project's advance. For example, land may be granted to individual peasants to gain their support, even though this holds back collectivization. Economic surpluses may be distributed to satisfy needs and meet the demands of the masses even though it reduces investment and future growth. In other instances, resources may have to be prioritized for the military, thereby reducing investments in health care, education, and so on.

The tasks of growth, development, and economic transformation have the social objective of increasing economic proletarianization through the agrarian reform, the agricultural and industrial revolutions, and the socialization of production. At the same time the revolution eliminates the petty bourgeoisie's material and social base, collectivizes the peasantry and small industry, and links the ideological sectors with the activities of production and reproduction through which the working class develops. The strengthening of the working class and the proletarianization of all workers is no longer aimed at perpetuating their conditions of existence but rather at transforming all salaried workers into freely associated workers. While communism presupposes a society without classes, socialism in the underdeveloped countries contributes to that goal, paradoxically strengthening not only proletarianization as a whole but also its historical subject, the working class and its allies as the proletariat.

If we start from the postulate that the social subject of every revolution has been composed of the popular classes, then the historical subject is the class that embodies the movement as a whole in a given moment, while the political subject is the class that synthesizes and leads that movement. In capitalist society the historical subject (the bourgeoisie) had the advantage of making the interests of its project coincide with the immediate interests of its agents (the individual bourgeoisie). An additional advantage was the fact that society had already previously developed a private structure of commercial relations, in which competition between capitalists favored the development of the system.

In the transitional society, by contrast, the revolutionary project depends upon the historical subject (the proletariat) being able to subordinate its immediate needs to the interests of the project. In the previous society if the bourgeois dedicated himself to doing his job well, he strengthened himself and, simultaneously, the system. But now if the worker is interested only in carrying out his or her individual job, this results in alienation and compromises the future of the class. The worker's struggle is not to affirm his or her individual class status but rather to stop being that class, to eliminate the class as such and to eliminate the rest of the classes. Liberation in this case is defined by what it is not, that is, by its negation and future affirmation. Previously, society produced more for individuals than individuals did for their society; now individuals must counteract and produce more for their society instead of accepting its terms. But precisely because the task consists of changing this limitation the worker is an actor and a conscious author of history. In changing their conditions of being they will be able to change and liberate themselves, while simultaneously changing and liberating the society in which they live.

If the worker's daily work does not form part of socialist relations of production, if the management is divorced from worker participation, how can a symbiosis be achieved between individual and class interests? The agencies of mediation must be workers' control boards, neighborhood committees, or any other organisms of planning, participation, or direct local rule by people's power. These can be set up despite the fact that until the social division of labor has been overcome, representation must be centralized in order to deal with the overall process of social management. But this superstructure will be able to assist the proletarian project only if it responds to the base and carries out those measures that favor the historical project of the freely associated workers.

The Centrality of Participatory Democracy

In the struggle between the proletarian project and the old order, major obstacles can be overcome through the practice of participatory democracy. By participatory democracy is meant all those forms through which the working class and the popular sectors participate in the socialist project. They can exercise political and economic power in many different ways: for example, through the territorial militias, unions and cooperatives, workers' control councils in the centers of production, defense committees in the neighborhoods, the mass organizations (workers, peasants, inhabitants of the neighborhood or communities, women, youth, students), voluntary work brigades, or cultural brigades.

Participatory democracy implies a political division of labor among the vanguard, the state, and the masses. The vanguard is the party of revolutionaries, regardless of their class origin; that is, people who have a strong revolutionary ideology and are the activists in participatory democracy. These revolutionaries organize the project during the insurrectionary and transitional phases and mediate between theory and practice and between the present and the future. The party is a workers' party in the strict political sense, since the ideology that cements it is proletarian ideology; it represents the interests of the workers, peasants, and remaining social sectors (in that order) at the same time as it represents the interests of the movement as a whole.

The masses are organized according to their immediate interests, which gradually begin to coincide with the general interests of the revolutionary project. They have as many organizations as concrete particularities, even though these may be contradictory between the different classes. The vanguard will nourish itself from the organized masses (unions, guilds, neighborhood associations, etc.) for its membership and also for the form and content that the struggle and revolutionary practice will assume. So that this symbiosis will be possible, the workers in general have to appropriate the project for themselves, not only in terms of ideology but also in the basic practical and concrete tasks of formulating opinions, participating in the decisionmaking process, and directly or indirectly managing the institutions of power, the economy, and of culture. They will have increasingly greater control over a process where individual interests gradually begin to coincide with collective interests.

The state lies between the party and the masses and its task is to devise policies that express the masses' immediate interests and the project's general interests. The state is a combined form of dictatorship and democracy: intransigent toward those who oppose or endanger the proletarian project, but democratic in implementing that project. Its challenge is to transform the dictatorship into hegemony, to govern with increasing consensus until people's power is fully realized.

Thus a false dilemma is posed by the assertion that the revolution realizes its tasks either by means of a dictatorship of the proletariat or by a proletarian democracy. One should remember that the concept of the dictatorship of the proletariat is based on the existing broad alliance of popular sectors. As Lenin stated in 1919: "The dictatorship of the proletariat is a specific form of class alliance between the proletariat, the vanguard of the working people, and the numerous non-proletarian strata of the working people (petty bourgeoisie, small proprietors, peasants, intelligensia, etc.) or the majority of these strata, an alliance against capital, an alliance whose aim is the complete overthrow of capital, complete suppression the resistance offered by the bourgeoisie as well as of attempts at restoration on its part, an alliance for the final establishment and consolidation of socialism" (1960/70:380).

The chain of dictatorship-democracy-hegemony is an integral process that will advance with the development and transformation of the economy, with the hegemonic growth of the working class, with the scientific and cultural ideologization of the proletarian population, and through the daily exercise of participatory democracy. The greatest obstacles to this process will continue to be imperialism and underdevelopment while its greatest allies will continue to be conscious, imaginative, and bold belligerence and a militant and democratic practice. Economic conditions will persist as limitations, but the political conditions will provide the potential for transcending economic limitations.

Participatory democracy is not only a means of legitimizing and guaranteeing the defense of the project: it is also the continuation of the political revolution in the search for one of socialism's substantive goals—the building of people's power. If the insurrection is born of a parallel people's power, then participatory democracy represents the development of this same people's power in civil society. Unlike representative democracy, participatory democracy—which can also include elections and a representative parliament—is part of the revolutionary project that strives to eliminate the isolation and the competitive lack of communication between people. It is a permanent attitude that develops in the society's centers of production and reproduction. It simultaneously nourishes itself from and generates proletarian and revolutionary ideology. Being a political activity, it also contributes to solving economic problems.

Faced with many contradictions in revolutionary society—between the classes that still exist, between these classes and the political parties, as well as between the political parties and the state—participatory democracy is a guarantee benefiting people's power, a form of collectivization of production, reproduction, and daily life. In sum, it makes possible the implementation of a social project that will slowly begin to eliminate the social division of labor and the consequent economic and political alienation that has accumulated.

The struggle against the previous regime, imperialism, and underdevelopment, is a great one, one that has required revolutionary societies such as Cuba, Vietnam, or Nicaragua to arm their populations, ideologically and militarily, in order to defend their independence and their revolutions. Adversity has not stopped us from prioritizing basic consumer goods when distributing what little there is. It has not stopped us from freely and critically organizing and discussing our achievements, problems, and dreams, and from practicing direct and indirect administration in the factories, fields, neighborhoods, and throughout the nation. In other words, we are not backing down on our principles. We continue to deepen the revolution by advancing the proletarian ideology that is embodied in the people and by engaging in revolutionary and participatory practice.

The Politics of Transition
▼▲
Richard R. Fagen

> On January 1, 1959, many people
> thought they had stepped into a world
> of riches. What they had really done
> was to win the opportunity to start
> creating—in the midst of underdevel-
> opment, poverty, ignorance, and mis-
> ery—the wealth and well-being of the
> future.
> —Fidel Castro, on January 1, 1969,
> 10th anniversary of the triumph of the
> Cuban revolution

In the twentieth century, all nationally based experiments in the
transition to socialism have taken place in the context of inherited
structures of underdevelopment. The pattern of domestic production
and international exchange, the manner in which labor is organized and
exploited, the sociogeography of cities and countryside, the class
structure itself, and much more reflect in very direct and dramatic ways
these inherited structures. And if the history of revolutionary movements in this century teaches any consistent lesson, it is that these old
structures do not quickly or easily yield to new ones.

At first glance it would seem that of all the elements of this
inheritance, the old political structures are most easily vanquished. The
tsar and his decadent court, the Portuguese (or British, or French)
colonialists, Somoza and his brutal *Guardia* are all swept away by
massive uprisings and insurrectional activity. Overnight, new leaders
occupy the centers of power. The masses assume a new historical role.
The nation is born or reborn, clothed in newly cut and highly legitimate
institutional garb. Free at last!

But in the cold light of historical analysis, it becomes clear that politics
are not so easily transformed. True, the political architecture can be

changed more easily than economic or cultural structures, but the legacy of the past continues to condition the politics of the present in profound ways.

In part this is because of the intimate relationship between economics and politics: all economic transitions imply profound political transitions, if only because economic transitions reorganize and redistribute power, and power is the coin of political transactions. And since the economy is transformed slowly, and only with great difficulty, it follows that the new politics is halting, imperfect, and conflictual. In fact, some contributors to this volume would go one step further and argue that politics is primary in the overall process of transition. In this view, the economic transition is seen as limited not only by obvious material factors (scarce resources, low level of development of the forces of production), but also by essentially political variables such as the degree of popular mobilization and related changes in consciousness. And since the material conditions are impossible to overcome in the short or even medium run, politics are (and ought to be) in command during the transitional period.

Perhaps the most telling illustration of this complex interaction is the Cuban case. One of the most striking features of the Cuban revolution is how successful it has been *despite* its very mediocre economic performance (understood in conventional growth-oriented terms). Politics, broadly defined, has everything to do with this success, and economics very little (Fagen 1969; Mesa-Lago 1981; Brundenius 1984; Halebsky and Kirk 1985). The Cuban revolution has survived and even prospered in adversity because the integrative and mobilizational politics of the regime have given second, third, and even tenth chances to a revolutionary state which has, in general, managed the economy poorly—with the exception of winning large amounts of aid from the Soviet Union. The example should not, however, be read in reverse. It is not an argument for ignoring economic performance. Rather, the Cuban case, generalized to the extent possible, suggests that with dynamic and innovative political practices, economic blows (both those that are inevitable and those that are self-inflicted) can be softened and absorbed.

In sum, progress in the transition can be made even in what appear to be unfavorable objective circumstances. This requires, however, that the politics of the transition be seen not as superstructural, but rather as the necessary foundation and sustaining framework on which a new economic base must be constructed. But to make this assertion is simply to state the problem, not to analyze it. Thus, in what follows, we will examine some of the specific ways in which the politics of the transition are themselves transitional—affected by the past, vexed, incomplete, and at times seemingly in contradiction to what some would claim is rational or necessary in the economic sphere.

The Assumption of Power and the New State

The organizational chart drawn on Monday morning—after Sunday's victory—shows that the revolutionaries have taken the "commanding heights" of the political system ("revolutionaries" is simply shorthand for those who were victorious in the struggle for power that initiated the transition). Executive organs, the military, foreign policy, the planning system (such as it is), and key elements of the cultural system (such as public education) are all directed by revolutionary elites. Thus, in the cases which this essay addresses, the organizational chart of power in the transitional political system looks more like Nicaragua under the Sandinistas than like Chile under Allende.

Even this formal seizure of power, and the occupation of its commanding heights are, however, incomplete in a number of ways. In the first place, many second- and third-level positions in the state apparatus (and occasionally even some top positions of a more technocratic sort) are occupied by persons not closely identified with and not committed to a thoroughgoing transition. Scarcity of qualified cadres and a need to keep lines of communication open to "other sectors" dictate this mixed staffing of the state apparatus. In general, at least at the outset, the government is neither totally "revolutionary" *nor* very "expert."

Outside the state apparatus, the consolidation of power is also not as thoroughgoing as it might seem. The unity and euphoria of the post-victory honeymoon temporarily disguise fundamental weaknesses in the revolutionary organization itself. The struggle against the oppressor regime is often not led by a political party, but rather by a revolutionary organization of a political-military sort (26th of July Movement, Sandinista National Liberation Front). Although well prepared to wage war (or lead a clandestine struggle), this organization is not similarly prepared to govern and to oversee the development process.

The transitional tasks of consolidation, mobilization, and coordination call for strong party organization and linked mass organizations. But although these structures are desperately needed from the outset, they usually do not exist except in embryonic form. Typically, the transition begins with revolutionary organizations that look more like the Sandinista National Liberation Front (FSLN) of 1979 than the Chinese Communist Party of 1948. And even where effective party structures predate liberation, they are deeply shaped by the exigencies of war and oppositional politics rather than by the politics of governing. Furthermore, in conditions of social backwardness, low literacy, poor intra- and interregional transport and communications, the rapid extension of party structures would be difficult under the best of circumstances. And the transition seldom takes place under such mythical "best of circumstances."

If the postvictory honeymoon disguises certain weaknesses in party organization and party-related structures, it also tends to mask the continuing strength of the opposition. The formal seizure of power seldom fully destroys or completely immobilizes old contenders for power—even those most closely identified with the *ancien régime*. Even if such contenders are temporarily rendered impotent at the moment of revolutionary triumph, the dynamics of transition provide new opportunities for their remobilization. Frequently supported by external forces, they continue to contest directly for power, often through armed struggle. In time they may be fully discredited and militarily defeated (Cuba), but typically, in the early years of transition, their challenges are real and costly (Nicaragua, Angola, Zimbabwe). Necessarily, then, the politics of the transition becomes, in substantial measure, a politics of (armed) defense.

In fact, appearances to the contrary, in the period immediately following the victory there is no such thing as a fully articulated "transitional state." There is only the old state apparatus, captured and partially restaffed by the revolutionaries, plus a political-military organization (often extremely popular and sometimes well organized) that exercises state power in the name of reconstituting the nation and directing development to benefit the less privileged (what has been called in Nicaragua the "logic of the majority"). The transitional state, in both its constitutional and organizational manifestations, is still to be created.

The organizational side of this process can be seen very clearly in the Cuban case. At first, after 1959, there was an extended period of direct rule by the leaders of the 26th of July Movement (with support from some other political organizations). Then, during the second half of the 1960s, there was a rather tumultuous period of construction and reconstruction of what eventually came to be called the Communist Party of Cuba (not to be confused with the PSP or "old" Communist Party). In the 1970s there was a flurry of experimentation with local elections and governmental restructuring (*poder popular*). And later in the decade, economic reforms were coupled to significant administrative decentralization (Harnecker 1980; *Cuban Studies* 1976).

As the Nicaraguan case suggests, however, what is ultimately at stake is much more than the particular institutional forms by which power will be articulated and disciplined, or planning will be rationalized and coordinated. The basic rules of the political game itself—who will be allowed to contend, under what conditions, with what possibilities of winning, with control over what domains of life—are not defined at the outset. Nor, as we have repeatedly seen, are they automatically embodied in the practice of any given institution. "Committees for defense of the revolution" can be simple administrative organs of the state or party apparatuses, or they can be the seedbeds of local, decentralized power. What is under dispute is nothing less than the real meaning of "the constitution": What does "pluralism" mean in practice? What are the rights and obligations of citizens? In what ways can (and should) a triumphant revolutionary elite be held accountable to the population at large? Such questions are not settled when the old political garbage is swept aside. Nor can they be settled quickly, easily, or without close attention to the legacy of the past and the challenges of the present and future.

Politics and Economics

At the outset we noted that all economic transitions imply profound political transformations. This is so vast a topic that it cannot be elaborated in systematic fashion here (but see Horvat 1982; Nove 1983; Albert and Hahnel 1981). It is important, however, to illustrate more specifically what is meant by this generalization, and the kinds of tensions and contradictions that derive from the political nature of the economic transition. As a starting point, consider two propositions which appear to be widely valid for the experiments under consideration. The first emphasizes that the small peripheral economy in transition must fundamentally rely on raw or semiprocessed commodity exports to lend dynamic to the economy and permit capital accumulation. The second suggests that a key aspect of the economic strategy must be an increasing supply of basic needs for the majority of the population. This is seen as politically necessary to ensure popular support, and what might be called functionally necessary to ensure the reproduction of the labor force (FitzGerald 1985c). Although the theoretical status of these two propositions is different (the first is a characterization of a structural feature of the economy, and the second is both a normative and a functional statement), both point to the interconnectedness of politics and economics. This can be seen more concretely with respect to five issues.

Private Capital and the Export Sector

Except in somewhat special cases such as the Cuban, private capital will continue to be involved in production for export in the economies under consideration. This may take forms as diverse as Gulf Oil in Angola, or small, medium, and even large cotton and coffee producers in Nicaragua. But in all such cases, the following paradox is present to a greater or lesser degree: *private capital is proportionally more important in the economic sphere than it can be allowed to be in the political sphere.* Thus, there emerges a disjunction between economic power (defined as the capacity to withhold or reduce critical investment and production) and political power (defined as control over key decisional structures). *Homo economicus bourgeois* is told that he will no longer be allowed to be *homo politicus,* at least in the way and to the extent that he was before.

This is an anomalous and basically unstable situation, different from the relationship of economics to politics that prevails in more classic socialist and capitalist social formations. Many treatments of the deceptively simple concept of the "mixed economy" gloss over this reality, pointing out that Sweden and a number of other countries also have "mixed economies"—and function politically without undue strains. What they overlook is that Sweden (or Brazil for that matter) is not a small peripheral economy undergoing a transition to socialism. The anomaly is not created by the mere fact of a high level of public investment or even substantial state ownership. Rather, it comes into play when those who direct a revolutionary development effort insist that the new politics shall not reflect the geography of property in the ways typically found in peripheral capitalism.

Labor and the Export Sector

Given the structural characteristics of the small peripheral economy, accumulation is particularly vulnerable to threats to the flow of foreign exchange. In Chile, for example, the anti-Popular Unity activities and strikes of copper workers were extremely damaging to the Allende government—as well as a classic example of the problems that can arise when export activities generate a labor aristocracy linked to transnational corporations (Stallings 1978; Fleet 1985). Not only was a significant fraction (approximately 30 percent) of organized labor affiliated with the opposition Christian Democratic Party, but the degree of unionization was significantly higher in the export sector than in the rest of the economy.

Even in cases where labor in the export sector is much less "aristocratic" and much more closely integrated into the transitional process, the political-economic equation remains delicately balanced: on the one hand, the export sector must remain competitive in international markets that are not of the small country's making. Wages must thus remain roughly in line with wages in societies having little or no commitment to the welfare of the popular classes (at least in cases where production technologies are roughly equivalent). On the other hand, the material benefits delivered to labor in the export sector must be sufficient (or sufficiently admixed with rising political consciousness) to avoid replays of the Chilean scenario.

This situation illustrates very clearly the close and often uneasy relationship between the tight constraints on economic change and the more open character of *lo político*. International patterns of production and exchange, as well as the local development of the forces of production, set rather sharp limits to the wage structure in the export sector. But marginal decisions within those limits—and particularly decisions to violate the limits—are not economic in nature. And above all, the creation of a level of popular consciousness which enables the workforce to understand and live within these limits is not an economic task.

It is thus not surprising that within the heart of the revolutionary movement itself there should be sharp disagreements with respect to proper policies in this and other areas. A cadre with front-line economic responsibilities will naturally gravitate toward positions which "make sense" in terms of the balance sheet of costs and prices—however those are determined. A cadre with primarily political responsibilities will necessarily weight mobilizational and legitimacy criteria more heavily. In the worst of cases, the former will come to consider the latter an unbridled romantic and a voluntarist, while the latter will (at least *sotto voce*) accuse the former of dogmatism and economic determinism. Such ideological disputes are not simply a matter of bad faith or ignorance (often defined as "incorrect reading of the classics"). Rather, they mirror the concrete situation in which the small transitional economy finds itself in today's world.

Money Income and Inflation

A high proportion of the households in the transitional society is intimately and ineluctably linked to the money economy. This does not mean that an equally high proportion of the economically active population is basically wage earners, much less classic proletarians. It simply means that household consumption (particularly outside of food for some of the rural population) is largely a function of available cash or credit. Whether that cash comes from selling homemade or homegrown goods in a local market, from picking cotton, or from tending a lathe is less important *politically* than the actual number of pounds and pesos available at the end of the week and the relative purchasing power of those coins and bills.

The level of inflation (more specifically, the real purchasing power of the popular classes, since they are least able to buffer themselves against rising prices) thus becomes a crucial political issue in the transition, even if planners do not originally perceive it as such. This is particularly the case with basic commodities and services (foodstuffs, fuel, clothing, mass transportation) that are very widely purchased and used. There is a point, not quantifiable, when grumbling about the price of rice and beans or a bus ticket ceases to be a "harmless" expression of discontent, and passes into the realm of a politically explosive issue.

Again, because of the expressed commitment of the revolutionary leadership to the welfare of the popular classes, the threshold where grumbling crystalizes into basic discontent must be taken very seriously. It is not sufficient to point out that this situation will of course be exploited (even perhaps partially caused) by opponents of the transition. This only underscores the essentially political nature of the issue of inflation.

Monetary Wages and Social Wages

For a variety of reasons (not the least of which is the difficulty of increasing the flow of money income to the popular classes), great emphasis is given in the transition to what are sometimes called social wages: improved working conditions, schooling, health, housing, and recreational facilities. The analysis of benefits of this sort is itself underdeveloped. Some are true collective benefits, some quite individual, some extremely costly, others capable of being generated by mobilizational efforts in which the chief input is labor (and often un- or underutilized labor at that). Furthermore, different benefits have quite different consequences of an integrative and/or participatory sort.

Despite these differences, however, several hypotheses are worth pursuing. First, at least at early stages of the transition, most persons (and households) would prefer an increase in their real monetary income to an increase in their nonmonetary benefits (with the almost universal exception of medical benefits, and perhaps literacy and schooling). Second, even in cases where nonremunerated labor can be mobilized in significant amounts, the actual cost (training, local and imported components, etc.) of the social wage is likely to tax the real economic possibilities of the society (the Cubans, for example, did not move massively in the housing field until more than a dozen years after the triumph of the revolution). Thus there are strict economic limits to the kind and amount of social wage that can be paid. Third, the mobilizational and integrative effects of these efforts tend to be exaggerated and even mystified. The highly successful literacy campaigns of Cuba and Nicaragua are the exceptions that prove the rule. The literacy model cannot easily be repeated in other domains of social and economic activity. You cannot have a "potable water" campaign or a "cotton picking" campaign with the same personal/psychological/political and resource-generating features of a literacy campaign.

Finally, there is no guarantee that an increased flow of monetary income to households will be spent in ways as directly conducive to social benefits as would the same capital invested directly by the state in the benefits themselves. The literature on development is replete with dramatic stories of "misspent" income in both capitalist and noncapitalist settings. In Ghana, for example, in the period immediately after independence, serious attempts were made to return more of the money earned by cocoa exports directly to the producers. According to one detailed study, much of this additional money was spent on elaborate funerals, litigation, and travel around the country to visit medicine men and shrines (Field 1960). In a very different setting, on January 2, 1980, when presenting Nicaragua's first national plan for economic development, Cmdte. Henry Ruíz cautioned his audience against undue pressure on wages, adding: "Brother workers and peasants, it will be necessary for you to make adequate use of what salary you have this year, meeting your family responsibilities and not spending your money on unnecessary things. Begging your pardon, but you will have to get drunk less and dedicate more of your salary to your family" (Government of Nicaragua 1980:8). There thus remains a very strong collective and developmental argument in favor of making tough decisions not to "give in" to the wage pressures posited in the first hypothesis, and, instead, to press ahead with elements of the social wage even though many, if given the choice, would prefer to have a bit more individual income.[1]

Employment and Unemployment

The more fully the money economy has permeated the society, the more politically unacceptable even a relatively low level of unemployment becomes. This is why policies of (sometimes artificially constructed) full employment make so much sense at the outset of the transition, even though they may violate economic rationality, and often have to be partially revoked at a later date. Again, the history of the Cuban revolution is instructive: for more than a decade there was—both officially and in practice—no significant unemployment in Cuba. Of course, bureaucracies and factories were sometimes over-staffed, out-migration created real shortages of professional and skilled labor, and so forth. But in effect all those who wanted to work—and some who did not—were employed. Only in the 1970s, when the economy was reorganized and "rationalized," did unemployment appear. Cynics would say that it was present all along. It is more accurate to say that at the outset the Cubans (wisely) decided that the political and social costs of open unemployment were greater than the economic costs of full employment.

The above, of course, simplifies an immensely complicated set of trade-offs and constraints. Nevertheless, it is essential to view the question of employment and unemployment as a political issue, not simply as a point (or points) on a graph where curves cross. The commitment to the popular classes and the "logic of the majority" embody the right to work as a priority element. Jobs for everyone and the satisfaction of basic needs are inseparable. Again, the search for political solutions to what seem to be economic impossibilities is central to the drama of the struggle for socialism.

Democracy and the Transition to Socialism

Much is made, by both the friends and the enemies of various countries embarked on a transition to socialism, of the question of democracy. Without wishing to enter into a book-length debate about the meaning and possibilities of democracy, we are on fairly safe ground in suggesting three constituent elements of a working definition.

Democracy is a system of governance in which

(1) there is *effective participation* by individuals and groups in the decisions that most affect their lives;

(2) there is a *system of accountability* whereby the behavior of leaders and officials can be monitored, judged, and—if necessary—changed by those who are subject to their authority;

(3) there is *political equality* (in the sense of equality before the law, equal opportunity to participate in the political process, etc.).

This definition, like all of its genre, is an idealization.[2] Nowhere, in any actual system, would we find perfectly working processes of participation, accountability, or equality. But it does give guidelines for thinking about the question of democracy in ways not immediately tied to concrete institutions such as elections, party systems, and so forth.

The definition does not, however, despite its usefulness, suggest the living reality in which the question of democracy is raised in a transitional society. Above all, this is a reality of conflict—between classes, social groups, different parts of the state apparatus, and even among revolutionaries themselves. Additionally, it is a context of multiple emergencies—military, economic, and organizational. Differing versions of what a transition to socialism ought to be vie with each other, and previously powerful groups contest nothing less than the legitimacy of the goal itself.[3]

At the moment of triumph over the oppressive state (dictator, white minority, colonial power), the grant of authority given to the liberators and to the organization which embodies the liberation struggle is both very broadly based and essentially unquestioned—one might even say unexamined. But time and circumstance erode this grant in two ways.

First, the class nature of the measures taken by the revolutionary government necessarily intensifies the antagonisms of those in whose favor the revolution is *not* being made. If there is a logic of the majority, there is also a political logic of the minority, and that logic is nonparticipatory, obstructionist, and potentially subversive. There is thus an objective and inevitable basis for conflict. The "anti-Somoza" or the "anti-Portuguese" coalition breaks up. The honeymoon is over.

Second, the inevitable economic difficulties (admixed with mismanagement, political mistakes, and sabotage by those who are intransigently opposed to change) erode the unquestioning quality of the grant of authority previously given by the popular classes. "What's in it for us?" becomes the day-to-day legitimacy-challenging question of the popular classes. For those who are actually benefitting in material terms in a very palpable way (medical care, schooling, land, increased real purchasing power), the answer is not far to seek. For those highly integrated into the transitional process through neighborhood, class, and other mass organizations, increased consciousness may well offset lack of short-run material benefits. But for many other citizens, neither material benefits nor increased consciousness are produced in sufficient quantity to prevent an erosion of legitimacy. Although this erosion is not inevitable, it is highly probable given the political-economic circumstances of societies in transition.

Furthermore, in the worst of cases, the race between the growth of material benefits and consciousness on the one hand and the erosion of legitimacy on the other leads to increased levels of repression. The "less-legitimate-then-previously" state begins to substitute more restrictive practices (*mano dura*) for the cooperation that its previous level of legitimacy elicited. Although restrictions on liberal freedoms (press, assembly, etc.) are usually the tendencies most noted by outsiders and the local bourgeoisie, increased activity (often harsh and arbitrary) of the state security forces signals the changes most palpably felt among the popular classes.

In addition to these class-based sources of conflict, there are others engendered by tribal, ethnic, religious, and regional identifications. This cultural and regional tapestry changes slowly—and at times even more slowly when under political and economic pressures orchestrated by "outsiders." This situation presents a special challenge for the politics of transition. On one level, these politics must be *integrative*. Citizens of the most diverse backgrounds and beliefs must increasingly come to view themselves as—first of all—Nicaraguans, Angolans, or Mozambicans. Although the word is not often used, the transition must be a process generating *patriotism*. The *patria* must become a primordial identification along with (but not necessarily instead of) tribal, ethnic, religious, and other identifications. As history suggests, this is no easy task.

On the other hand, what appears as the politics of integration when viewed from the center is often experienced as an assault on local autonomy, religious freedoms, or immemorial lifeways by those being "integrated." How quickly and effectively these state-society conflicts are seized upon by enemies of the revolutionary government is well illustrated by the Miskito Indian situation on Nicaragua's Atlantic coast and by a host of African cases. It is thus by no means a simple matter to ensure that the inevitable conflicts of class are not joined to the "unnecessary" and often violent conflicts of tribe, ethnicity, religion, and region.

In this conflictual context, the question of democracy in the transition is raised most urgently at the multiple points where dissent is (or would be) expressed.[4] In fact, in transitional situations even more dramatically than elsewhere, there is a fundamental constitutional and institutional dilemma: *silencing dissent (or even attempting to intimidate dissenters) is costly, at times counterproductive, and—in the eyes of many, at home and abroad—morally unacceptable. But allowing the full range of classical liberal freedoms during the transitional period runs the risk of tipping the balance in favor of those who do not want any basic changes at all—in short jeopardizing the entire effort.*[5] Thus, for those committed to democracy, the key question is not the abstract issue of how much dissent will be allowed, but rather what forms and channels of dissent are most compatible with the construction of a working consensus supportive of a new political-economic order. Note that this is not the way the issue would be formulated in the well-established industrialized democracies.

Historically, in transitional situations in the third world, the question of forms and channels of dissent has most frequently been answered in antidemocratic fashion. In the early 1960s, Tanzania's Julius Nyerere spoke for many when he said flatly: "This [national development] calls for the maximum united effort by the whole country if it is to succeed. *There can be no room for difference or division*" (1962:186, emphasis in original). Slightly earlier, in Ghana, Kwame Nkrumah had stated a somewhat different version of the same idea, different only in that he saw the period of nondemocratic practices as limited—although he never discussed the limits: "even a system based on social justice and a democratic constitution may need backing up, during the period following independence, by emergency measures of a totalitarian kind. Without discipline true freedom cannot survive" (1957:x).

Nor are such arguments limited to the past. In general, in developmental situations there exists a powerful pull toward the centralization of decisionmaking and authoritarian practice. The rationalities and realities are familiar: a firm hand at the helm as we sail through stormy seas; a necessary period of tutelage while the masses learn the skill and discipline needed to participate more fully in the management of their lives and labors. Mass organizations are charged with implementing state policies rather than representing the interests of their constituents to the state. Thinly staffed national ministries attempt to administer programs that are beyond their human and material resources. Yet devolving some of these responsibilities to local groups is certainly not a solution that springs automatically to the bureaucratic mind. Leaders, many schooled for years in military discipline, turn easily to command models to solve obdurate developmental problems—as if the citizens were troops, and developmental obstacles were forts to be stormed.[6]

However, as suggested by other essays in this volume, there are powerful counterarguments as well, much more strongly supported both empirically and politically in the 1980s than they were in the 1960s. Some are functionalist: vigorous criticism is needed to control bureaucratic tendencies and abuses; real changes in consciousness cannot be coerced—they must be cultured in an ambience of open discussion; the voices of the discontented must be heard—only then will leaders know the realities of the problems at hand. Other counterarguments are closer to conventional liberal discourse: the state does not have the right to supress individual expressions of opinion or group advocacy; without oppositional rights to organize and contend for power *at the top* of the political hierarchy, leadership cannot be held accountable to the masses in whose name it ostensibly rules.

Thus the contest is joined. Powerful traditions, arguments, and urgent realities pull toward a nondemocratic system of conflict management in the context of the transition to socialism. Eloquent voices and increasingly persuasive arguments pull in a more democratic direction. And it is by no means clear, either globally or in most individual cases, which tendency is now winning.

It is also not clear what particular institutional forms an appropriate democratic practice might take. Elements of representative democracy and multiparty contestation? Vigorous intraparty competition of the sort envisioned by Lenin and others at certain points in their writings—but never practiced in the Soviet Union (or elsewhere) except very briefly? Mass organizations wholly autonomous from the state? Private ownership of the mass media? State ownership of media with guaranteed access? The list is very long.

What is already clear, however, is that the answers to these and other questions will ultimately not be found in texts, old or new. They will be hammered out in practice, just as bourgeois democracy in Europe and America developed in a highly conflictual manner as a response to pressures and problems that in turn were rooted in the maturation of capitalism over several centuries. So too in the small peripheral nations now experimenting with transitions to socialism: if there is to be a democratic practice associated with socialism in the periphery in the coming decades, it will issue from the concrete circumstances in which today's societies in transition find themselves. Inventing and perfecting that democratic practice will take decades, it will certainly be conflictual, and its ultimate success is far from guaranteed. But without such practice, the liberation promised by the revolution will at best be incomplete and at worst degenerate into new forms of tyrannical rule.

Notes

This essay is based on work supported by the National Science Foundation under Grant No. SES-8120619. Any opinions, findings, and conclusions or recommendations expressed are those of the author and do not necessarily reflect the views of the National Science Foundation. The author wishes to thank Marcia Rivera-Quintero, Carmen Diana Deere, and Michael Lowy for their helpful comments.

1. Some reportage and scholarship on the problem of "misspent" income in developmental settings is badly tainted by racism and cultural chauvinism (the "natives" refuse to behave like their more modern "betters" say they should). But there is no question that (a) the replacement of what is degrading and destructive in the old way of life is essential if the new social order is going to be more humane and egalitarian, (b) determining and preserving what is meaningful and worth defending in traditional culture and lifeways are difficult whenever change is rapid, and (c) hard choices have to be made regarding the extent to which the spending of income will be left to individual choice when culture and the market continue to produce (formally or informally) socially destructive commodities (drugs, prostitution, gambling) in a context of scarcity of basic needs. Few have treated these issues more literately and insightfully than Trotsky (1973) in the essays known collectively as "Problems of Everyday Life."
2. Note that the definition does not include "civil liberties," "a free press," or other such "Bill of Rights" elements. I regard these as instrumental aspects of democracy—necessary conditions or institutions (in most instances) for effective participation, accountability, and equality to take place. They are operational, not definitional aspects of democracy. They reenter the discussion of conflict, dissent, and emergency which follows.
3. In the classic Weberian formulation (compatible with at least some Marxist interpretations), legitimacy derives from a "grant of authority" given by followers to their leaders (or the ruled to their rulers). Weber identified three types of authority: charismatic, traditional, and rational-legal (1947:324–86). The revolutionary/collective bases of authority (and thus legitimacy) in most postvictory cases of transition are not captured by the Weberian categories. See also Antonio Gramsci's discussion of hegemony and counterhegemony (Gramsci 1971).
4. It is precisely on this topic that liberal and right-wing critics of politics in the societies in transition gain their most sympathetic national and international audiences. Given the continuing quasi-hegemony of liberal political thought in centers of world opinion, socialist experiments in these societies are particularly vulnerable to charges that dissenters are being silenced.

5. This dilemma is present in one form or another in the theory and practice of all modern states. For example, the civil-libertarian Supreme Court justice William O. Douglas, in defending the rights of the U.S. Communist Party to advocate and organize, said:

    > In days of trouble and confusion, when bread lines were long, when the unemployed walked the streets, when people were starving, the advocates of a short-cut by revolution might have a chance to gain adherents. But today there are no such conditions. The country is not in despair. . . . *Some nations less resilient than the United States, where illiteracy is high and where democratic traditions are only budding, might have to take drastic steps and jail these men for merely speaking their creed.* But in America they are miserable merchants of unwanted ideas; their wares remain unsold. The fact that their ideas are abhorrent does not make them powerful.
    > (William O. Douglas, Dennis v. U.S., 341 U.s. 494, 1951, pp. 588–89, emphasis added.)

6. In such circumstances the attractiveness of the Leninist/Stalinist model of political organization and highly centralized single-party dominance is understandable—even when the model fails to function as predicted. For a useful analysis of the economic shortcomings of the centralized, single-party model, see Nove (1983).

Mass Organization, Party, and State: Democracy in the Transition to Socialism
▼▲

Michael Lowy

What lessons can be learned about the problems of democracy in the transition to socialism based on the experiences of the small peripheral countries? What difficulties, errors, or objective contradictions have blocked the development of democracy in the majority of these countries? What type of relationships between the revolutionary party and the mass organizations guarantees effective participation of the workers in transition? How can the bureaucratic degeneration of revolutionary power and the transformation of the state into an authoritarian apparatus separated from the people be avoided? What are the main positive advances that have been attained in the small peripheral countries in transition to socialism, from the point of view of revolutionary democracy? Without attempting to fully answer this set of questions, I will set forth some working hypotheses, based upon the Marxist conception of the dialectic between democracy and socialism.

Democracy is not a problem of "political form" or institutional "superstructure": it is the *very content* of socialism as a social formation in which workers and peasants, young people, women, that is, the people, effectively exercise power and democratically determine the purpose of production, the distribution of the means of production, and the allocation of the product.

In *The Communist Manifesto,* Marx wrote that "all previous historical movements were movements of minorities, or in the interests of minorities. The proletarian movement is the self-conscious, independent movement of the immense majority in the interest of the immense majority" (1964:22). What does the term "independent movement" mean for Marx? It means that the proletariat has to liberate itself: only by its own autonomous action as a class, by its own revolutionary practice, can workers understand the need for a radical change of social conditions and effectively implement this change.

Translated by Ricky Weiss

While the metaphysical materialism of the Enlightenment (which was taken up by the Jacobins of 1793) holds that human beings are the product of circumstance and that society can only be transformed by a force external to the *social mechanism,* by a force raised *above socie-ty*—an enlightened despot, supreme legislator, or revolutionary elite—Marx proclaimed in his "Theses on Feuerbach" (which is the seed of a new conception of the world) that change in social circumstances and human self-transformation coincide in *revolutionary praxis.*

The idea of revolutionary praxis—which radically distinguishes Marx's materialism from all previous forms—is the theoretical foundation of the Marxist conception of *self-emancipation of the proletariat through revolution.* The coincidence between the changes of social circumstance and human circumstance means that in the course of the revolutionary struggle and the process of construction of the new society, the proletariat transforms itself, raises its consciousness and its solidarity, and creates a "new human being." As Marx emphasized in *The German Ideology* (1846):

> For the production of this communist consciousness on a mass scale and for the success of the cause itself, the alteration of men on a mass scale is required. This can only take place in a practical movement, in a *revolution.* A revolution is necessary, therefore, not only because the ruling class cannot be overthrown in any other way, but also because the class overthrowing it can succeed only by revolution in getting rid of all the traditional muck and become capable of establishing society anew. (1947:94–95)

In other words, the only authentic liberation is *self-emancipation;* without workers' self-education by their own experience—that is, without effective *democracy*—it is not possible to advance along the road of transition to socialism. No Infallible Helmsman, no Supreme Chief can liberate the people; emancipation of the workers will be the work of the workers themselves. Democracy, therefore, is an essential characteristic of the process of the construction of socialism, of the process of the emancipation of working people from all forms of exploitation, oppression, or alienation.

Of all the twentieth-century Marxist revolutionaries, Rosa Luxemburg, founder of the German Communist Party who was assassinated by the counterrevolution in January 1919, set forth in the clearest and most incisive manner the importance of democracy in the construction of socialism. In a pamphlet written in 1918, she wrote:

> Freedom only for the supporters of the government, only for the members of one party—however numerous they may be—is no freedom at all. Freedom is always and exclusively freedom for the one who thinks differently. . . . Socialism in life demands a complete spiritual transforma-

tion in the masses degraded by centuries of bourgeois class rule. Social instinct in place of egotistical ones, mass initiative in place of inertia, idealism which conquers all suffering, etc., etc. . . . The only way to a rebirth of this is the school of public life itself, the most unlimited, the broadest democracy and public opinion. . . . Without general elections, without unrestricted freedom of press and assembly, without a free struggle of opinion, life dies out in every public institution, becomes a mere semblance of life, in which only the bureaucracy remains as the active element. . . . (The aim of the proletariat is) by conquering political power, to create a socialist democracy to replace bourgeois democracy—not to eliminate democracy altogether. But socialist democracy is not something which begins only in the promised land after the foundations of socialist economy are created. . . . It begins at the very moment of the seizure of power by the socialist party. It is the same thing as the dictatorship of the proletariat. Yes, dictatorship! But this dictatorship consists in the *manner of applying democracy,* not in its *elimination,* in energetic, resolute attacks upon the well-entrenched rights and economic relationships of bourgeois society, without which a socialist transformation cannot be accomplished. But this dictatorship must be the work of the *class,* and not a little leading minority in the name of the class—that is, it must proceed step by step out of the active participation of the masses; it must be under their direct influence, subjected to the control of complete public activity; it must arise out of the growing political training of the people (1972:245–49).

Are these principles applicable to third world nations today? How are the political problems of the transition to socialism in small peripheral economies concretely set forth?

The Party and the State in the Transition

Let me begin with the principle that without *revolution,* that is, without the destruction by popular insurgency of the bourgeois state's repressive apparatus, its repressive bureaucratic structures, it is not possible to begin the transition to socialism. The expropriation of large landholders, multinational enterprises, and capitalists takes place over months or even years; but the indispensable starting point is a popular armed rebellion that breaks with the oligarchical/capitalist state's police-military system and constructs a new type of state in its stead, supported by its revolutionary army and a militia made up by workers, peasants, and the masses. This has been the experience of Nicaragua and Cuba and all of the third world countries in transition to socialism. Any attempt to initiate a process of transition within the framework of the bourgeois state, with its repressive structures intact, can only lead to the defeat of the workers: the tragic experience of Chile in 1973 categorically confirmed this. Socialist democracy is not an "extension" of bourgeois democracy (in which the instruments of true power remain in the hands of the dominant class), but rather, begins with the liquidation of the bourgeois state's repressive structures and the establishment of a power of a different nature, organically linked to the armed working class.

If revolution is the democratic expression of the people's aspirations, how can the continuity of democracy under the revolutionary power in transition to socialism be assured? In third world countries, and particularly in the small peripheral economies, economic, social, and political conditions provide huge obstacles to the development of socialist democracy. The lack of resources, underdevelopment, insufficient technically qualified personnel, and the absence of democratic traditions objectively exert pressure toward bureaucratization; that is, the creation of a layer of functionaries, administrators, and managers who authoritatively monopolize economic planning and political and military power, excluding the people from decisionmaking and appropriating material privileges for themselves. Neither imperialist intervention nor counterrevolutionary sabotage favors democratic liberties or pluralism. An ideological factor must be added to these objective ones: the influence of the authoritarian models for the construction of socialism.

To date, all of the postrevolutionary states in the small peripheral economies of the third world have experienced lesser or greater degrees of bureaucratization and the effective democratic participation of workers has been limited, in the best of cases, to local levels of power. It is necessary to recognize the positive value of certain experiences, such as popular power in Cuba, but also to bear in mind their limitations.

The absence of democracy in the heart of a revolutionary party or in a country's political life leads, sooner or later, to the bureaucratization of the state. In its most degenerated forms, this means the creation of a social layer of bureaucrats with its own interests, different from those of the proletariat; the concentration of all power in the hands of one individual (the "cult of personality"); police repression of any divergent opinions; the absence of any possibility for the people to exercise control over their leaders. The People's Republic of Korea is an example of this type of development. Its economic success and high level of industrialization are undeniable, but the state resembles a hereditary monarchy (Kim Il Sing has named his son as successor) more than a socialist democracy.

Closer to us, the tragic example of Grenada demonstrates the terrible consequences of the absence of socialist democracy. Due to the absence of democratic structures within the New Jewel Movement

(NJM) which would have permitted the party's base to control its director, a small sectarian, bureaucratic, and authoritarian fraction apparently succeeded in gaining hegemony in the leadership bodies, eliminating Maurice Bishop, despite the fact that he had the support of the majority of the party militants. The same occurred at the state level: the absence of effective democratic instruments permitted this fraction to control the state apparatus and the armed forces, removing from power the leaders recognized by Grenada's popular classes. With the assassination of Maurice Bishop and his colleagues, the regime lost its popular base and conditions were created for the imperialist intervention and the crushing of the revolutionary experience.

It is important to draw lessons from these tragic events, which demonstrate that socialist democracy is not a luxury or a "concession to the petty bourgeoisie," but rather, that it may become the very condition for the survival of the revolution in its confrontation with imperialism.

The Cuban revolution has tried from the outset to combat the threat of bureaucratic degeneration. In his celebrated speech of March 26, 1962, Fidel condemned the attempt by a sectarian and bureaucratic fraction of Stalinist formation (Anibal Escalante and friends) to transform the Integrated Revolutionary Organization (ORI) into an apparatus isolated from the masses, a party of submissive and docile people. Che Guevara, in his speech before the members of the State Security Department on May 18, 1962, spoke along these same lines:

> We have gone along that road, which has been called sectarian, but which is much more than sectarian and stupid: (it is) the road of separation from the masses . . . the road of suppression of criticism. Not only suppression of criticism by those who have the legitimate power to do so—the people—but also the suppression of critical vigilance by the party apparatus, which became an executor, and by doing so, lost its characteristics of vigilance. . . . All this establishes a lesson we must learn and, moreover, establishes a great truth—that security bodies, whatever type they be, must be under the people's control. . . . (1970:487–88)

Several years later, *Granma,* the official newspaper of the new Communist Party of Cuba, published an article in which it warned, with scientific depth and in a critical spirit, against the danger of bureaucracy:

> When the revolution triumphs and management of the economy passes into the hands of the state, the bureaucracy intervenes in the management of production, in the control and government of the country's human and material resources. . . . This apparatus has a specific relation with the means of production, different from the rest of the population, that can convert bureaucratic positions into places of accommodation, stagnation, or privilege. Here is the deepest and most important problem in the struggle against bureaucratism!

What happens if the party organism submerges itself in this bureaucratic slumber? A special layer with ambitions of perpetuity consolidates itself in the state's administration and management and in its political direction; a layer that increasingly distances itself from the masses, divorces itself from useful and productive work, and from those who perform that work; it converts itself into a privileged body unable to make the people advance, unable to develop the people's consciousness toward superior levels. And when this happens, the construction of socialism and communism is forgone.

The struggle against bureaucratism constitutes a true revolution within the revolution, as much for its own importance as for the strength it is now gathering. (It is) possibly the revolution that has not yet been made in any other place. . . . It will be a long struggle (and) we cannot be careless for even a single minute; but we will foil the danger posed by a special layer within our revolutionary society, we will raise against it the creation of a new man, and victory will be ours.

For that, it is necessary to raise the consciousness of our entire people. Only with a broad and deep consciousness in the young cadres and workers in general can we win this decisive battle; that is, carry out the revolution that has not yet taken place: the antibureaucratic revolution.[1]

The antibureaucratic revolution did not take place in Cuba, but some important measures were taken in the struggle against bureaucratization. In 1962 the party was reorganized, permitting workers to elect from among themselves those whom they considered worthy of being part of the vanguard. Assemblies were created in workplaces, permitting workers to organize the distribution of certain consumer goods. Between 1963 and 1966 a public and open discussion was held on the differences of opinion concerning the methods of economic management (the role of the law of value in socialist planning, material or moral incentives, etc.), on the methods of teaching Marxism (using Soviet manuals or the works of Marx, Engels, and Lenin themselves). A far-reaching popular consultation was carried out on the country's major legal reforms: the judicial reform of 1973, the family code of 1974, and the new Constitution in 1976. But the key question of democratic participation of the masses in the state had not been resolved. Beginning in 1975, a new and original solution, without precedents in any other state in transition, was to be implemented: popular power.

The essential principle of popular power is that all production or service units which supply goods or services to the community should be under that community's management and control. This meant that schools, medical centers, stores, eating places, factories, movie theaters, entertainment centers, and so on were all to be managed by the community in each location. Only those units and fields of activity that served the entire country were to be controlled on a national level: the merchant marine fleet, heavy industry, the banks, the fishing industry, the railroad; the other activities were to be under municipal or provincial management. Popular power is delegated in a pyramid-like structure: the population of a local community elects its delegates to a municipal assembly; the municipal assemblies elect provincial assemblies, and these, in turn, elect the National Assembly.

Every two and a half years the population elects its representatives (a total of 10,735 delegates) to the 169 municipal assemblies of popular power. The delegates have to periodically "account" to the population through accountability assemblies, and these have the power to remove any delegate who proves to be bureaucratic or corrupt.

Through popular power decisions have been decentralized, collective solutions have replaced administrative solutions, and the spontaneous creativity of the masses has been stimulated. Popular power allows the Cuban people to take local and immediate problems into their own hands through the municipal assemblies. With this, they have managed to halt bureaucratic tendencies at a local level, that is, in the domain of daily life, in which the masses rightly show a great sensitivity. The people have concretely demonstrated their support for the revolution by actively participating in the community management of activities and services. Popular power in Cuba represents a real democratic advance in the transition to socialism and an example that should be carefully studied (see Casal 1975).

But the system has obvious limits that make its democratic breadth relative. In the absence of political pluralism, of different points of view in a discussion, or of different parties that compete in the elections of delegates, the masses do not have the power of *decision* between alternative economic or political policies. The result is that the popular base has very little real control on the provincial and especially on the *national* levels of power (the National Assembly, Council of State, and Council of Ministers). The problem is not so much the predominance of party members (or of the Communist Youth) in the popular power bodies (75.2 percent in the local assemblies and 96.7 percent in the National Assembly) but rather, the fact that the masses have no possibility to choose from among different proposals presented by various parties or various tendencies within the same party. The one-party system and the party's monolithic internal structure are the principal limitations on socialist democracy in Cuban popular power.

How can these bureaucratic and authoritarian (to a certain point, unavoidable) tendencies be neutralized and conditions favorable to socialist democracy be created? It is not a matter of formulating a universal model; there are no universal models for the transition to socialism outside of each country's concrete circumstances. What can be proposed here are some suggestions, some working hypotheses in response to this decisive question based on concrete experiences (positive or negative) or the societies in transition in third world countries.

The *revolutionary party* is indispensable in order to advance the process of the transition to socialism; it should be composed of the working class's most conscious sectors, those most prepared to struggle and sacrifice themselves on the battlefields, to assume the most difficult and dangerous tasks. Obviously, the revolutionary party struggles for hegemony, to win the role of the leader recognized by the masses. But it should never impose its monopoly on political life by administrative or, even worse, by repressive methods. The one-party system—predominant, so far, in the states in transition—is the direct source of bureaucratization and a decisive obstacle to effective democracy.

Moving from the law of profits and capitalist competition to a socialist logic and the people's support of a *collective* program (and not of individual profit) is not possible if each worker does not feel he or she is an active participant in *collective decisions, co-responsible* for the policy adopted. Political pluralism—that is, the free organization of all political parties that *respect revolutionary legality*—is not a concession to the bourgeoisie, but rather the condition for the existence of a real political life, a real confrontation of points of view and the possibility of a real *decision* by workers on matters essential to the country's economic, social, and political life.

It must be remembered that for several years in the Soviet Union under Lenin, political pluralism existed in the soviets with the effective participation of the Mensheviks, left-wing social revolutionaries, anarchists, and so on. Lenin, Trotsky, and the Bolshevik leaders seemed to consider pluralism as a normal aspect of the dictatorship of the proletariat.

Today, the example of Nicaragua demonstrates that the deepening of the revolution and its defense against the imperialist and counterrevolutionary enemy is perfectly compatible with political pluralism; that is, with the free organization of all currents that do not advocate violence against Sandinista power.

Political pluralism implies freedom of expression and freedom of the press. It is undeniable that reactionary bourgeois ideology does not disappear after the revolutionary triumph and maintains its influence over sectors of the population. But it is a grave error to believe that it should be fought with administrative or repressive methods. Historical experience demonstrates that repression of bourgeois opinions and ideologies is ineffective. On the contrary, in the long run those methods ultimately reinforce reactionary ideas. The only effective way to eliminate the persistence of these ideologies in sectors of the working class is through (1) the creation of objective conditions in which the material roots of their propagation (ignorance, illiteracy, cultural backwardness, bureaucracy) are eradicated; and (2) the unceasing struggle against these ideas in the ideological and political arena.

In other words, reactionary arguments and ideas must be answered with revolutionary arguments and ideas; counterrevolutionary acts of violence must be responded to with the iron fist of revolutionary power, with the violence of the armed workers.

Only those who do not have confidence in the superiority of socialist and revolutionary ideas, nor in the proletariat and the workers, fear open ideological confrontation with bourgeois and reactionary ideologies when the proletariat is in power. This confrontation is the sole means by which the working class can ideologically educate itself and free itself from the influence of bourgeois ideas.

Marxism, which represents critical thought *par excellence,* can only develop in an atmosphere of broad freedom of discussion, of constant confrontation with other currents of thought, that is, in an atmosphere of ideological and cultural pluralism. Any attempt to administratively impose an ideological monopoly of Marxism (or, even worse, of a particular interpretation of Marxism), repressing other currents of thought, can only lead to the degeneration of Marxism itself and its transformation into a state's official doctrine or religion.

For the revolutionary party to be able to play its role of the leading force recognized by the masses, it is important that it constitute an example of internal democracy by holding regular congresses in which different points of view can be expressed, including those organized in tendencies. We should not forget that in the Bolshevik Party of Lenin's era, not only did the free expression of divergencies exist—in the time of the Brest-Litovsk treaties, for a while Lenin himself was in the minority of the party's leadership bodies (1918)—but (at least until 1921) so too did the possibility of forming tendencies (Alexandra Kollontai's worker opposition, Vladmir Smirnov's Democratic Centralists, etc.).

The Role of Mass Organizations in the Transition

If the revolutionary party represents the most conscious and active vanguard, the *mass organizations* have the role of mobilizing the broadest popular sectors around their immediate interests. The revolutionary party must struggle to gain hegemony in those organizations, but respect the plurality of opinions within them and their *autonomy* in relation to the party and the state. If the mass organizations become a mere instrument of the state, or a mechanical "transmission belt" of the party, they will be transformed into a bureaucratic apparatus without popular credibility and without effective democratic content.

The *unions*—worker and peasant—take on new functions in the transition to socialism, but it is important that they continue to defend the workers' immediate interests. The fact that a revolutionary power exists, a power representing the workers, does not mean that the unions do not need to defend their class. In the discussion on the unions in the USSR between 1920 and 1922, Lenin insisted on this point:

> It was natural for us to write about the workers' state in 1917; but those who now ask, "Why protect, against whom protect the working class, there is no bourgeoisie now, the state is a workers' state," commit an obvious mistake. Not altogether a workers' state; that is the whole point. . . . It is evident from our Party programme . . . that our state is a workers' state with bureaucratic distortions. . . . Here you have, then, the reality of the transition. . . . Our present state is such that the entirely organised proletariat must protect itself, and we must utilise these workers' organisations for the purpose of protecting the workers from their own state and in order that the workers may protect our state. (1937:8–10)

Lenin set forth the need for union action not only against capitalist property-holders (permitted under the New Economic Policy), but also in the state enterprises: "Therefore, it is undoubtedly the duty of the trade unions in regard to the state enterprises as well, to protect the class interests of the proletariat and the working masses against their employers" (1960/70; vol. 42:376). He concluded, therefore, that "the Communist Party, the Soviet government and the trade unions must never forget and must never conceal from the workers and the mass of the working people that the strike-based struggle in a state where the proletariat holds political power can be explained and justified only by the bureaucratic distortions of the proletarian state" (ibid.:377).

In the great majority of the countries in transition to socialism, union autonomy and independence from the state was not maintained and thus unions ended up being transformed into mere intermediaries between management and workers. In Poland, this led the workers to organize their own unions outside of the framework of the official union.

In an analysis of unions in Cuba in 1961, Che Guevara stated that the unions had to assume "the defense of the working class's specific and immediate interests at the level of the enterprise or factory. The establishment of the socialist system does not eliminate contradictions but rather, modifies the way to resolve them. The union must act in particular when the pressing needs of the worker masses at their work places are unknown" (1970:124). Unions in Cuba had experienced a certain stagnation and bureaucratization until the union structures were reactivated and democratized during the thirteenth Confederation of Cuban Workers Congress in 1973.

That does not mean that the unions in transition to socialism have to limit themselves to economic claims: it is fundamental that they participate in the construction of socialism, in the defense of the revolution, in the socialist education of the workers. But these tasks can by accomplished only if the unions have the confidence of the worker and peasant masses, if they are the democratic expression of these masses, and if they independently defend the immediate and concrete aspirations of the masses.

Organizing the population by neighborhoods is an original form of popular organization that appeared in the Latin American revolutions and that has been very successful. Cuba's Committees in Defense of the Revolution (CDRs) and Nicaragua's Sandinista Defense Committees (CDSs) have managed to organize and mobilize the masses more effectively and more broadly than any other institution. These have allowed extensive sectors of the population to actively participate in the revolution's concrete tasks in their neighborhoods: defending against counterrevolutionary sabotage, distributing rationed goods, taking part in health or education campaigns, and so on.

Authoritarian, repressive, bureaucratic tendencies may inevitably appear within these mass organizations, with very negative consequences. Problems of this type arose for the Cuban CDRs in 1962. According to Che Guevara, "The Defense Committees, for example, an institution that emerged in the heat of popular vigilance and represented the desire of the people to defend their Revolution, were transformed into dens of opportunism. They became organizations in antipathy to the people. Today, I believe it can be very rightly said that the CDRs are in antipathy to the people; they have taken a series of arbitrary measures. . ." (1970:487). The Cuban CDRs have tried to overcome those errors, but these are dangers that threaten a mass organization when it is not effectively and democratically controlled by its members.

Another decisively important mass organization for third world societies in transition to socialism is an *autonomous women's movement*. Only such an organization, which struggles without making concessions on any of women's specific interests, can guarantee the participation by half of the population in the transition process, and move toward the abolition of patriarchal oppression—two processes which are intimately linked. Centuries of oppression and discrimination have tried to reduce women to a passive condition. Women's emancipation, the rupture of that oppressive patriarchal system, is the condition for the release of the formidable energy of women, particularly working-class women, for the revolution and the construction of socialism. In the same way that unions must defend workers from the bureaucratic deformations of state institutions, the women's organization must defend women against the inevitable patriarchal deformations of those same institutions.

The issue of the *state* is obviously at the crux of a democratic transition to socialism. State economic planning, indispensable for the transition, simultaneously creates favorable conditions for the authoritarian bureaucratization of decisions. It is important to try to overcome the false dilemma (which is found in many countries in the transition to socialism) between accepting the laws of the market (the so-called market socialism of Yugoslavia) and the bureaucratic/centralist conception of planning, with a technocratic apparatus that monopolizes decisionmaking without consulting the workers (as in Poland). The fetishism of commodities and *the fetishism of the state* must be replaced by what constitutes the political essence of the transition to socialism: the effective democratic control by the workers of overall economic and social life.

How can the "spontaneous" tendency toward bureaucratization be neutralized? The only way to do this is through active participation of the people in all levels of state activity.

First, on the economic level, self-management must be fought for through factory councils and worker assemblies. Che Guevara wrote in 1961:

> The production assembly encompasses all the workers in a factory who, democratically assembled, present their points of view on the progress of the industry and the plan. The production assembly represents a type of legislative body that judges the task itself and that of all the employees and workers. There, criticism and self-criticism must reign as arms of socialist education. This model permits managers to be educated in the school of critical analysis of their own tasks before the plenum of the workers and the latter, in effective control of management (1970:131).

In these assemblies it is also necessary to discuss the central economic plan's general propositions while they are being prepared, so that planners can know the worker's opinions on the key planning issues: production priorities, ways of distributing scarce goods, and so on.

Naturally, worker self-management of enterprises, schools, hospitals, and the like must be coordinated with the municipal power (council), responsible for managing all the local enterprises, as well as with the general economic plan.

Second, on the military level, worker, peasant, and popular militias must be formed alongside the revolutionary army—in which relations between officers and soldiers should be egalitarian and fraternal, without the military authoritarianism of traditional armies. The example of the Cuban revolution illustrates the decisive importance of these militias in the defending of the revolutionary process and its defense against imperialism and the counterrevolution (Bay of Pigs). The same occurs in Nicaragua, where the militias, as the *armed people,* play an essential role in the defense of the Sandinista revolution, a role that cannot be replaced by the regular armed forces. To the degree that the militia units bring together groups of neighbors from the same neighborhood or village, they are strengthened by personal bonds of confidence and solidarity, which raise their morale and combativity.

Third, on the political level itself, in addition to local popular power, which is the concrete foundation of any authentic democratization, it is important that the people be able to elect a National Assembly by free, direct, and universal suffrage; this implies, as we have seen, political pluralism, that is, the recognition of all parties that respect revolutionary legality.

In a country that has experienced an authentic popular revolution, these elections will undoubtedly result in the triumph of the political forces that have directed the workers' and people's insurrection and that are set up at the forefront of the process of the transition to socialism. The example of Nicaragua demonstrates that it is possible and correct for a revolutionary power to organize general elections with a truly democratic and open nature. The Nicaraguan elections of 1984, unprecedented in the history of other countries in transition to socialism, will be an historic landmark on the people's road toward socialist democracy. Nonetheless, the election of a national assembly based on party representation meant that the mass organizations lost their right to direct representation in a legislative body, until 1984, the Council of State.

An hypothesis that requires consideration is that it perhaps may be necessary to elect a *second assembly,* constituted of delegates from all the country's mass organizations. This "workers' assembly" would have the task of *controlling* or *complementing* the National Assembly's activities. This would permit the mass organizations, representing the most active part of the working class, to directly influence the country's political and economic policies.

Representative democracy's values and institutions have been conquered by popular struggle but used as instruments by the bourgeoisie. Socialist revolution must reclaim these conquests, *integrating and overcoming* representative democracy. Periodic elections of a National Assembly are insufficient to assure the people's effective participation in decisionmaking and economic political management. Participatory democracy includes the mechanisms of representation but, going far beyond its limits, surmounts its partial nature. It creates new structures and institutions, organically linked to the people's *daily life,* and ensures their *ongoing participation* in all levels of economic and political power. Mass organizations (unions, women's organizations, youth organizations, etc.), local committees in defense of the revolution, factory councils (or rural cooperatives), popular militias, and the National Assembly appear as *complementary forms* of the exercise of popular power, whose unity brings about the full richness of participatory democracy. It is not a matter of establishing a static, institutional model but rather, of finding the concrete forms that will permit the working class to make major decisions at any given moment as they defend their revolution from imperialist aggression. Historical experience seems to indicate that representative democracy and direct democracy are two essential, irreplaceable, and complementary dimensions of popular power.

Undoubtedly, one of the most complex problems is the democratization of economic planning. An essential piece of the process of the transition to socialism, planning calls for a large specialized and centralized technical apparatus with political authority. How can its bureaucratization be avoided? Although there is no miraculous recipe, two concrete proposals can be made: (1) A public, democratic discussion of the plan's priorities and objectives should be held in local councils and committees, mass organizations, and the National Assembly (or workers' assembly). The vanguard party brings to this discussion concrete proposals that try to integrate each popular sector's interests, harmonizing them with the revolutionary program—that is, with the common historic interests of the exploited and oppressed. After an open, pluralist debate by all political and social forces, the decision on the plan's features will be the democratic expression of the majority of the working class. (2) Control mechanisms should be placed on the planning institutions by the popular organizations and committees.

In addition to the democratization of the party, the mass organizations, and the state, the struggle against bureaucratization has another fundamental aspect: the absence of material privileges, either direct (salary) or indirect (cars, housing, special stores), for the party and state's leaders and political cadres. Privileges of this type, which are found in the majority of the countries in transition to socialism, decisively favor the consolidation of the bureaucracy as a social category with its own interests, different from those of the workers. These are the professional dangers of power that the old-time Bolshevik Christian Rakovsky referred to in 1928; when the division of work and the specialization of leadership bring privileges, this leads to an organic differentiation. The *functional* differentiation becomes a *social* one, and the bureaucracy objectively and subjectively, materially and morally, becomes a consolidated social layer separated from the workers. The postrevolutionary power runs the danger of being transformed from a workers' state with bureaucratic deformations (Lenin's definition of the USSR in 1922), into a bureaucratic state with proletarian-communist remains (see Rakovsky 1980:126–30).[2]

It is useful in this context to recall the principle that Marx put forth in his writings on the Paris Commune: an official or leader's salary (or standard of living) must not be higher than that of a worker (1940:57).

Some aspects of this program of socialist democracy have been implemented in certain small peripheral economies in transition to socialism (particularly in Cuba), but with many limitations and contradictions. Sandinista Nicaragua is a formidable laboratory of social revolution. Despite the terrible conditions of the struggle against imperialism and its counterrevolutionary agents, it is undoubtedly today the most advanced experience of democratic transition to socialism.

Obviously, the Sandinista revolution's priorities are concrete and urgent: to do away with hunger, unemployment, epidemic sickness, and illiteracy; to arm the people to defend their revolution against imperialism and its Somocista agents; to raise the population's levels of nutrition and health; to guarantee schools for the children; and to increase production of grains and basic goods. But experience demonstrates that it is precisely with democratic methods that the broadest strata of the working class are mobilized to perform these tasks and advance the revolution toward socialism.

It is true that during the first years after the triumph of the insurrection some errors were committed: prohibition of strikes, jailing of militants of small left-wing groups, authoritarian behavior toward the Miskitos, and so on. But those errors have been gradually overcome and currently, despite the imperialist and counterrevolutionary aggression—which, as in any country at war, inevitably imposes limits on freedom of expression—*there is more democracy in Sandinista Nicaragua than in any other state in transition to socialism.* This is seen not only on the level of democratic liberties—relative freedom of press and organization—and political pluralism, with the possibility for opposition parties (left, center, or right) to effectively participate in elections, but also in the significant degree of autonomy that the mass organizations have, and their capacity to take initiatives independent from the state.

Obviously, there are still many problems to resolve: democratization of the FSLN structure itself, effective participation by workers in the management of production centers, democratization of economic planning, and so on. But Nicaragua will undoubtedly open a new chapter in the history of the transition to socialism in the small peripheral economies: for the first time, the deepening of the revolutionary process has not led to a growing degree of authoritarianism but, on the contrary, to a widening of democratic space and liberties.

Sandinista popular power has put into practice the golden rule of revolutionary democracy: reactionary arguments must be answered with revolutionary arguments; the contras' crimes and sabotage must be responded to with the people's organized force, the Sandinista army and militia. The revolutionary arguments triumphed in the November 1984 elections: despite a campaign by the proimperialist sector of the dominant classes—led by the Higher Council of Private Enterprise (COSEP) and the parties organized in the Democratic Coordinating Committee (CDN)—to boycott the elections, the political hegemony of the Sandinista Front has been legitimized by universal suffrage in the first truly democratic and pluralist election in Nicaragua's history.

The possibility of restrictions on democracy in the future, under the pressures of war as well as of the authoritarian models of bureaucratic socialism, cannot be dismissed. But this is not an inevitable fatality: if Sandinista Nicaragua continues and deepens the path it has been on thus far, it will be transformed into a model of worldwide historic importance of democratic and revolutionary transition to socialism.

Notes

1. "La lucha contra el burocratismo: tarea decisiva," Editorial from weekly supplement of *Granma*, 5–12 March, 1967 in *Lecturas de Filosofía* (Havana: Instituto del Libro, 1968), Vol. II, pp. 644–47.
2. This concept was formulated by Rakovsky to define Stalin's regime.

Mobilization Without Emancipation?
Women's Interests, State, and Revolution
▼▲
Maxine Molyneux

After several decades in which socialist revolution was seen as advancing the cause of women's emancipation, a more pessimistic view has emerged about the capacity of socialist governments to fulfill their commitment to women's emancipation.[1] Critics point out that not only does gender inequality still persist in these states but that in some ways women could be considered to be worse off than they were before the revolution. Far from having been "emancipated" as official pronouncements sometimes claim, women's workload has often increased and there has been no substantial redefinition of the relations between the sexes. To the traditional roles of housewife and mother have been added those of full-time wage worker and political activist, while the provision of childcare facilities remains inadequate. As one Soviet woman recently summed it up: "If this is emancipation, then I'm against it" (Hansson and Liden 1983).

The negative image of socialist states in this regard is reinforced by their failure to establish anything near sexual parity in the organs of political power and by the absence of real popular democracy. The conventional explanations of these shortcomings, at least in the poorer states, in terms of resource scarcity, international pressure, underdevelopment, or the "weight of tradition," are greeted with increasing skepticism; a feminist writer recently expressed an emerging consensus when she wrote: "if a country can eliminate the tsetse fly, it can get an equal number of men and women on its politburo" (quoted in MacKinnon 1982).[2]

An even more negative view of the record of socialist states sees them as representing merely another form of patriarchal domination. It suggests that the "revolutionary equality" commonly claimed as the experience of men and women fighters in battle is replaced in the postrevolutionary period by the status quo ante with men in the positions of power. As the all-male leadership grows increasingly unconcerned about advancing women's interests, it appears that women's sacrifices in the struggle for a better society have gone unrewarded by those whom they helped to bring to power. Women, like the working class in another conception, appear to have been "sold out," only in this case, not by a "new bureaucratic bourgeoisie," but by a more pervasive and at the same time analytically elusive entity: "the patriarchy."[3]

This essay discusses the proposition that women's interests are not served by socialist revolutions. It does so by examining how women are affected by government policies in the aftermath of a successful revolutionary seizure of power in which they participated on a mass scale. It considers these wider questions in the context of the Nicaraguan revolution and its progress since the seizure of state power by the Sandinistas in July 1979. The first part reviews some of the theoretical questions raised by this debate, particularly the matter of "women's interests"; in the second, the policies which the FSLN has adopted in relation to women are described and interpreted in order to see whether, and if so how far, women's interests are represented within the Sandinista state.

Women in existing socialist countries certainly have not achieved full equality, let alone emancipation. But the argument set forth here takes issue with the view that women's interests have been denied representation or have been deliberately marginalized through the operations of "patriarchy."[4] Male power, whether institutionalized or interpersonal, and the essentialist or naturalist arguments which legitimize it, do play a part in the explanation of women's continuing subordination after revolutionary upheavals; but the importance of such factors should not be exaggerated. Nor should the achievements of these revolutions be underestimated, or the real material constraints that they have faced be left out of account. To recognize the importance of these constraints is not to provide an apologia for the failings of postrevolutionary society but to establish more realistic parameters for comprehending the underlying and persistent causes of gender inequality.

The central concern of this discussion, which much of this debate ultimately depends upon, is the concept of "women's interests." Most feminist critiques of socialist regimes rest on an implicit or explicit assumption that there is a given entity, "women's interests," which is ignored or overridden by policymakers. However, this assumption must be examined rather than simply taken for granted, for the question of these interests is far more complex than is frequently assumed. As the problems of deploying any theory of interest in the analysis of postrevolutionary situations are considerable, the following discussion must be considered as exploratory rather than conclusive, as opening up debate rather than attempting closure. This is especially so in the case of third world revolutions such as Nicaragua's which afford no simple conclusions because of the severe pressure they are under, the short span of the revolutionary governments, and the resulting unevenness of their records, especially in relation to women.

Most women have benefited in some way from the substantial advances made by revolutionary governments in the area of social policy and welfare. All women have seen some improvement in their legal rights through the enforcement of the equal pay and labor laws and through reforms designed to tackle discrimination in the family. Nonetheless, despite these undeniable advances, it remains true that relatively little is done to dismantle other mechanisms through which women's subordination per se is reproduced in the economy and in society in general, and many of men's privileges over women remain. Does this mean, then, that women's interests have not, after all, been adequately represented within the state?

Conceptualizing Women's Interests

The political pertinence of the issue of whether states, revolutionary or otherwise, are successful in securing the interests of social groups and classes is generally considered to be twofold. First, it is supposed to enable prediction or at least political calculation about a given government's capacity to maintain the support of the groups it claims to represent. Second, it is assumed that the nature of the state can be deduced from the interests it is seen to be advancing.[5] Thus the proposition that a state is a "worker's state," capitalist state, or even a "patriarchal state" is commonly tested by investigating how a particular class or group has fared under the government in question.

However, when we try to deploy similar criteria in the case of women a number of problems arise. If, for example, we conclude that because revolutionary governments seem to have done relatively little to remove the means by which gender subordination is reproduced, that women's interests have not been represented in the state and hence women are likely to turn against it, we are making a number of assumptions: that gender interests are the equivalent of "women's interests," that gender should be privileged as the principal determinant of women's interests, and that women's subjectivity, real or potential, is also structured uniquely through gender effects. It is also supposed by extension that women have certain common interests by virtue of their gender, and that these interests are primary for women. It follows then that trans-class unity among women is to some degree given by this communality of interests.[6]

Yet while it is true that at a certain level of abstraction women can be said to have some interests in common, there is no consensus over what these are or how they are to be formulated. This is in part because there is no theoretically adequate and universally applicable causal explanation of women's subordination from which a general account of women's interests can be derived. Women's oppression is recognized as being multicausal in origin and mediated through a variety of different structures, mechanisms, and levels, which may vary considerably across space and time. There is therefore continuing debate over the appropriate site of feminist struggle and over whether it is more important to focus attempts at change on objective or subjective elements, on structures or on men, on laws and institutions or on interpersonal power relations—or on all of them simultaneously. Since a general conception of interests (one which has political validity) must be derived from a theory of how the subordination of a determinate social category is secured, and supposes some notion of structural determinacy, it is difficult to see how it would overcome the two most salient and intractable features of women's oppression—its multicausal nature, and the extreme variability of its forms across class and nation. These factors vitiate attempts to speak *without qualification* of a unitary category "women" with a set of already constituted interests that are common to it. A theory of interests that is applicable to the debate about women's capacity to struggle for, and benefit from, social change, must begin by recognizing difference rather than assuming homogeneity.

It is clear from the extensive feminist literature on women's oppression that a number of different conceptions prevail of what women's interests are, and that these in turn rest, implicitly or explicitly, upon different theories of the causes of gender inequality. For the purpose of clarifying the issues discussed here, three conceptions of women's interests that are frequently conflated will be delineated. These are (1) "women's interests"; (2) strategic gender interests; and (3) practical gender interests.

Although present in much political and theoretical discourse, the concept of *women's interests* is, for the reasons given above, a highly contentious one. Because women are positioned within their societies through a variety of different means—among them class, ethnicity, and gender—the interests which they have as a group are similarly shaped in complex and sometimes conflicting ways. It is therefore difficult, if not impossible, to generalize about "the interests of women." Instead, we need to specify how the various categories of women might be affected differently, and act differently on account of the particularities of their social positioning and their chosen identities. However, this is not to deny that women may have certain general interests in common. These can be called gender interests to differentiate them from the false homogeneity imposed by the notion of "women's interests."

Gender interests are those that women (or men, for that matter) may develop by virtue of their social positioning through gender attributes. Gender interests can be either strategic or practical, each being derived in a different way and each involving different implications for women's subjectivity. Strategic interests are derived in the first instance deductively, i.e., from the analysis of women's subordination and from the formulation of an alternative, more satisfactory set of arrangements to those that exist. These ethical and theoretical criteria assist in the formulation of strategic objectives to overcome women's subordination, such as the abolition of the sexual division of labor, the alleviation of the burden of domestic labor and childcare, the removal of institutionalized forms of discrimination, the establishment of political equality, freedom of choice over childbearing, and the adoption of adequate measures against male violence and control over women. These constitute what might be called strategic gender interests, and are the ones most frequently considered by feminists as women's "real" interests. The demands that are formulated on this basis are usually termed "feminist," as is the level of consciousness required to struggle effectively for them.[7]

Practical gender interests are given inductively and arise from the concrete conditions of women's positioning by virtue of their gender within the division of labor. In contrast to strategic gender interests, practical gender interests are formulated by the women themselves who are within these positions rather than through external interventions. Practical interests are usually a response to an immediate perceived need and they do not generally entail a strategic goal such as women's emancipation or gender equality. Analyses of female collective action frequently deploy this conception of interests to explain the dynamic and goals of women's participation in social action. For example, it has been argued that by virtue of their place within the sexual division of labor, as those primarily responsible for their households' daily welfare, women have a special interest in domestic provision and public welfare (Kaplan 1982; Hufton 1971). When governments fail to provide these basic needs women withdraw their support; when the livelihood of their families, especially their children, is threatened, it is women who form the phalanxes of bread rioters, demonstrators, and petitioners. It is clear from this example, however, that gender and class are closely intertwined; it is, for obvious reasons, usually poor women who are so readily mobilized by economic necessity. Practical interests, therefore, cannot be assumed to be innocent of class effects. Moreover, these practical interests do not in themselves challenge the prevailing forms of gender subordination, even though they arise directly out of them. An appreciation of this is vital in understanding the capacity or failure of states or organizations to win the loyalty and support of women.

This raises the question of the pertinence of these ways of conceptualizing interests for an understanding of women's consciousness. This is a complex matter that cannot be explored in detail here, but three initial points can be made. First, the relationship between what we have called strategic gender interests and women's recognition of them and desire to realize them cannot be assumed. Even the "lowest common denominator" of interests that might seem uncontentious and of universal applicability (e.g., complete equality with men, control over reproduction, and greater personal autonomy and independence from men) are not readily accepted by all women. This is not just because of "false consciousness," as is frequently supposed, although this can be a factor, but because such changes realized in a piecemeal fashion could threaten the short-term practical interests of some women, or entail a cost in the form of a loss of forms of protection which is not then compensated for. Thus the formulation of strategic interests can be effective as a form of intervention only when full account is taken of these practical interests. Indeed, it is the politicization of these practical interests and their transformation into strategic interests that women can identify with and support which constitutes a central aspect of feminist political practice.

Second, and following on from the first, the way in which interests are formulated, whether by women or political organizations, will vary considerably across space and time and may be shaped in different ways by prevailing political and discursive influences. This is important to bear in mind when considering the problem of internationalism and the limits and possibilities of cross-cultural solidarity. And finally, since "women's interests" are significantly broader than gender interests, and are shaped to a considerable degree by class factors, women's unity and cohesion on gender issues cannot be assumed. While gender issues can form the basis of unity around a common program, such unity has to be constructed; it is never given. Moreover, even when unity exists, it is always conditional, and the historical record suggests that it tends to collapse under the pressure of acute class conflict. Unity is also threatened by differences of race, ethnicity, and nationality. It is therefore difficult to argue, as some feminists have done, that gender issues are primary for women at all times.[8]

This general problem of the conditionality of women's unity and the fact that gender issues are not necessarily primary is nowhere more clearly illustrated than by the example of revolutionary upheaval. In such situations, gender issues are frequently displaced by class conflict, and this is principally because although women may suffer discrimination on the basis of gender and may be aware that they do, they nonetheless suffer differentially according to their social class. These differences crucially affect attitudes toward revolutionary change, especially if this is in the direction of socialism. This does not mean that because gender interests are an insufficient basis for unity among women in the context of class polarization, they disappear. Rather, they become more specifically attached to, and defined by, social class.

These, then, are the different ways in which the question of women's interests can be addressed. An awareness of the complex issues involved serves to guard against any simple treatment of the question of whether a state is or is not acting in the "interests of women," that is, whether all or any of these interests are represented within the state. Before any analysis can be attempted it is first necessary to specify in what sense the term "interest" is being deployed. As suggested earlier, a state may gain the support of women by satisfying either their immediate practical demands or certain class interests, or both. It may do this without advancing their strategic interests at all. However, the claims of such a state to be supporting women's *emancipation* could not be substantiated merely on the evidence that it maintained women's support on the basis of representing some of their more practical or class interests. With these distinctions in mind, we can turn to the Nicaraguan revolution, and consider how the Sandinistas have formulated women's interests, and how women have fared under their rule.

The Nicaraguan Revolution

The Nicaraguan revolution represents an extreme case of the problems of constructing a socialist society in the face of poverty and underdevelopment, counterrevolution and external intervention. It could therefore be seen as an exceptional case, and its usefulness as an example consequently limited. Yet while the Sandinistas face a particularly severe constellation of negative circumstances, most socialist revolutions have encountered difficulties of a similar kind and even of degree. One has only to think of the encirclement and internal disruption by enemy forces which the Bolsheviks faced after 1917, or the conditions of dire scarcity prevailing in postrevolutionary Mozambique, China, or South Yemen, or the blockade of poor nations such as Cuba, or the devastation through war wreaked on Vietnam, to realize that such conditions are more common than not in the attempts to build socialist societies.

Yet the fact that Nicaragua shares certain circumstances with the states referred to above does not imply that it belongs to the category of revolutions that these countries represent. The latter were, or became, for the most part avowedly communist in their political ideology, and anticapitalist in their economic practice, moving rapidly to place their main resources under state control. Most also aligned themselves directly with the Soviet Union, or at least maintained a distance from the NATO bloc of countries in their foreign affairs. All of them are one-party states in which dissent is allowed little, if any, free expression.

By contrast, the forces which overthrew Anastasio Somoza in July of 1979 distinguished themselves by their commitment to a socialism based on the principles of mixed economy, nonalignment, and political pluralism. Political opposition was allowed to operate within certain clearly defined limits, and 60 percent of the economy remained in private hands, despite the nationalization of Somocista assets. The concept of "Sandinismo" promised to produce a different kind of socialism, one that consolidated the revolutionary overthrow of the old regime through the creation of a new army and its control of other organs of state power, but was more democratic, independent, and "moderate" than many other third world socialisms had been. Through its triumph and its commitment to socialist pluralism, Nicaragua became a symbol of hope to socialists, not only in Latin America, but across the world. It was this, perhaps, rather than its "communism" which accounted for the ferocity and determination of the Reagan administration's efforts to bring the process to an end.[9]

The Nicaraguan revolution also gave hope to those who supported women's liberation, for here too, the Sandinistas were full of promise. The revolution occurred in the period after the upsurge of the "new feminism" of the late 1960s, at a time when Latin American women were mobilizing around feminist demands in such countries as Mexico, Peru, and Brazil. The Sandinistas' awareness of the limitations of orthodox Marxism encouraged some to believe that a space would be allowed for the development of new social movements such as feminism. Some members of the leadership seemed aware of the importance of women's liberation and of the need for it in Nicaragua. The early issues of the women's organization's newsletter, *Somos AMNLAE,* contained articles about feminist issues and engaged with some of the ongoing debates within Western feminism. Unlike many of its counterparts elsewhere, the revolutionary party, the Sandinista Front (FSLN), did not denounce feminism as a "counterrevolutionary diversion," and some women officials had even gone on record expressing enthusiasm for feminist ideals.

In practical terms, too, there was promise: the FSLN had shown itself capable of mobilizing many thousands of women in support of its struggle. It had done this partly through the Association of Women Confronting the National Problem (AMPRONAC), an organization that combined a commitment to overthrow the Somoza regime with that of struggling for women's equality. At its peak in 1979, two years after it was founded, AMPRONAC had attracted over 8,000 members. Feminist observers noted the high level of participation of women in the ranks of the combat forces, epitomized in Dora Maria Téllez' role as "Commander Two" in the seizure of the Presidential Palace by the guerrillas in 1978, and they debated how the Sandinista commitment to women's equality would be realized if they triumphed.

Once the Sandinistas were in power, these hopes were not disappointed. Only weeks after the triumph, article 30 of Decree Number 48 banned the media's exploitation of women as sex objects, and women FSLN cadres found themselves in senior positions in the newly established state as ministers, vice-ministers, and regional party coordinators. In September AMPRONAC was transformed into the Luisa Amanda Espinosa Association of Nicaraguan Women (AMNLAE) to advance the cause of women's emancipation and carry through the program of revolutionary transformation. Public meetings were adorned with the slogan "No revolution without women's emancipation: no emancipation without revolution." The scene seemed to be set fair for an imaginative and distinctive strategy for women's emancipation in Nicaragua.

But after the first few years in power the FSLN's image abroad began to lose some of its distinctive appeal. The combined pressures of economic scarcity, counterrevolution, and military threat were taking their toll on the Sandinista experiment in economic and political pluralism, placing at risk the ideals it sought to defend. In the face of mounting pressure from U.S.-backed counterrevolutionaries in 1982, a further casualty of these difficulties appeared to be the Sandinista commitment to the emancipation of women. AMNLAE reduced its public identification with "feminism" and spoke increasingly of the need to promote women's interests in the context of the wider struggle. At its Constitutive Assembly at the end of 1981 it had defined its role as enabling women to integrate themselves as a decisive force in the revolution. Indeed, AMNLAE's first priority was given as "defense of the revolution." But it was only in 1982, as the crisis deepened and the country went onto a war footing, that the priority really did become (as it had to) the revolution's survival, with all efforts directed to military defense. AMNLAE became actively involved in recruiting women into the army and militia. Under such circumstances it is hardly surprising that the efforts to promote women's emancipation were scaled down or redefined. Emancipation was to come about as a by-product of making and defining the revolution. Yet, even before the crisis deepened little had been achieved to tangibly improve the position of women, and FSLN cadres considered that progress in this area was necessarily limited. In the first major speech on women's status since the overthrow, in October 1984, the minister of defense, Tomás Borge, acknowledged that while certain important advances had been made, "all of us have to honestly admit that we haven't confronted the struggle for women's liberation with the same courage and decisiveness [as shown in the liberation struggle]. . . . From the point of view of daily exertion, women remain fundamentally in the same conditions as in the past."[10] Is it the case then that women's specific interests have not been adequately represented in Sandinista policies?

Sandinista Policy with Regard to Women

As a socialist organization, the FSLN both in and out of power recognized women's oppression as something that had to be overcome in the creation of a new society. It gave support to the principle of gender equality as part of its endorsement of the socialist ideal of social equality for all. The FSLN 1969 program promised that "the Sandinista people's revolution will abolish the odious discrimination that women have been subjected to compared with men" and "will establish economic, political, and cultural equality between women and men." This commitment was enshrined a decade later within the Estatuto Fundamental, the embryonic constitution that proclaimed "the unconditional equality of all Nicaraguans without distinction of race, nationality, creed, or sex." It went further in pledging the state to "remove by all means available" the obstacles to achieving it! Thus the juridical context was set for future legislative and policy measures aimed at securing some of the conditions enabling this equality to be achieved.

Most contemporary states have enshrined within their constitutions or equivalents some phrase that opposes discrimination on the grounds of race, sex, or creed. What distinguishes socialist states as diverse as Sweden, Vietnam, and the USSR is their recognition of the specificity of women's oppression and their support for measures that combine a concern to promote equality with a desire to remove some of the obstacles to achieving it. Some of the strategic interests of women are therefore recognized and, in theory, are to be advanced as part of the process of socialist transformation. In its essentials, the FSLN's theoretical and practical approach to women's emancipation bears some resemblance to that found in those state socialist countries that espouse Marxist theory, among them Cuba, South Yemen, Albania, Eastern Europe, the USSR, and Mozambique. These countries share an approach that links gender oppression to class oppression and believe women's emancipation can be achieved only with the creation of a new, socialist society and with the further development of the productive capacity of the economy. In the meantime, however, measures can be taken to alleviate the considerable inequalities between the sexes and begin what Borge referred to as the task of "humanizing life and improving the quality and content of human relations."

According to official views and party documents this involves implementing the principles of the classic socialist guidelines for the emancipation of women as formulated by the Bolsheviks and broadly adhered to ever since by socialist states.[11] Some of these guidelines have been incorporated into AMNLAE's official program, which lists its main goals as (1) defending the revolution; (2) promoting women's political and ideological awareness and advancing their social, political, and economic participation in the revolution; (3) combatting legal and other institutional inequalities; (4) promoting women's cultural and technical advancement and entry into areas of employment traditionally reserved for men, combined with opposition to discrimination in employment; (5) fostering respect for domestic labor and organizing childcare services for working women; and (6) creating and sustaining links of international solidarity. The 1969 program of the FSLN also made special mention of eliminating prostitution and other "social vices," helping the abandoned working mother, and protecting the illegitimate child. Each of these issues has been addressed in subsequent legislation and social policy. There is also official concern with allowing greater freedom of choice to women in the matter of childbearing, by making contraception more widely available and by not prosecuting those who carry out abortions.

Although these goals, if realized, would be insufficient on their own to achieve the complete emancipation of women, based as they are on a somewhat narrow definition of gender interests, they nevertheless embody some strategic concerns, in that they are directed toward eliminating some of the fundamental inequalities between the sexes. However, progress in Nicaragua has so far been uneven. There is official support for the implementation of the full program, but only some of the guidelines have been translated into policy and then only with limited effect. Employment opportunities in the formal sector have been slightly expanded but remain restricted both in number and scope. Most Nicaraguan women continue to eke out a living as petty commodity producers, small-scale traders, or house servants, remaining at the bottom of the income structure. The socialization of childcare and domestic labor has affected only a minority of women: according to the Oficina de Mujer, which coordinates the activities of AMNLAE with the FSLN, by mid-1984, forty-three childcare centers were able to absorb around 4,000 children, and further expansion was not envisaged because of mounting financial difficulties, caused by the contra war.

The embryonic Family Law, the *Ley de Alimentos,* passed by the Council of State at the end of 1982, aimed to establish a more democratic, egalitarian, and mutually responsible family, but it was not taken up by the executive and public discussion of the issues it raised all but ceased in 1983. The greatest benefits that women received were from the welfare programs and from certain areas of legal reform. They also felt the impact of change in the realm of political mobilization in which they played an increasingly active part. Despite these advances it was evident that the gap between intention and realization with regard to these policies was considerable.

Beyond the obvious problem of lack of time there are three other considerations which must be given due weight in any assessment of this record. The first concerns the practical limitations, which restricted the state's capacity for social transformation; the second involves factors of a general political kind; and the third concerns the nature of the policies themselves and the way in which the Sandinistas' commitment to women's emancipation was formulated. All of these issues have to be taken into account when assessing the position of women in postrevolutionary Nicaragua and other societies in transition, for they help to explain why social policy initiatives to improve the position of women have been diluted, and why governments in these countries have on occasion adopted different priorities, sometimes ones which are at variance with the goals of emancipating women.

The problems of material scarcity in an underdeveloped economy, or the toll exacted by military aggression, do not require extensive discussion here. Details can be found elsewhere of the perilous state of the Nicaraguan economy, the ravages of war and natural disasters, the effect of the contras and U.S. pressure, and the size of the external debt. What is most striking in all of this was the government's success in shielding the population from the effects of these difficulties throughout 1982 and much of 1983. However, the combined effects of material scarcity and the destabilization efforts of internal and external forces limited the available resources, which had to both satisfy the military requirements of the state and be allocated to long-term economic programs, short-term consumer needs, and the popular expectation to expand social services. It is not difficult to see how these factors reduced the scope of planning objectives, channeling scarce resources of both a financial and technical kind, as well as human potential, away from social programs into national defense and economic development.

If these two factors, scarcity and threat, explain the restrictions placed on the funding available for such projects as building and staffing nurseries, and expanding female employment, they also go some way toward explaining why the emancipation of women, except within a rather narrow interpretation of the term, was not considered a priority.

Even where the resource base existed, the government still faced problems of implementation in the form of political opposition to some of the proposed reforms. The Nicaraguan revolution is a clear illustration of the truism that the acquisition of state power does not confer on governments absolute power either in formulation or implementation of policies, even when they might have widespread popular support. The 1973 overthrow of Salvador Allende in Chile was a dramatic demonstration of the ever-present threat of counterrevolution and of the diversity of sites within the state and civil society through which it can be organized.

The Sandinistas were in a stronger position internally than the government of Popular Unity in Chile even if they faced a more determined threat from the United States and its allies in the region. They dismantled Somoza's repressive apparatus, replacing it with their own military and police forces, and established control over a number of state and government institutions. In the six years since the fall of Somoza, the revolutionary government also succeeded in consolidating its power base through the establishment of the "mass organizations," the popular defense committees, the militia, and the revolutionary party, the FSLN. Moreover, the opposition, both civilian and military, was unable to offer a credible alternative, in part because of its links to the United States and with the Somocistas.

Despite the strategic and political advantages that accrued to the Sandinistas as a result of these transformations of the state and its institutions, the government did not feel obliged to seek the elimination of the opposition. The constitutional commitment to the principles of economic and political pluralism allowed a space, albeit a restricted one, from which opposition forces could operate. The FSLN attempted to maintain, as far as the situation permitted, a broad multiclass base of support. It tried to win over a sector of the capitalist class, and on the whole it sought to maintain a conciliatory attitude toward its opponents, sometimes in the face of considerable provocation. The opposition therefore had the right to make its views heard and could organize to protect its interests, providing these did not jeopardize the government's overall survival or place the interests of the majority at risk. When these interests were considered threatened, the Sandinistas intervened. The State of Emergency declared in 1982, and again in 1985, allowed the state to curb some of the opposition's activities and imposed censorship on the main opposition paper, *La Prensa*. By international standards, these moves were moderate ones, especially given the conditions of war which prevailed from 1983 onward. Moreover, the government lifted the State of Emergency to allow for the preparations of the late-1984 elections, and the opposition was encouraged to contest them.

The commitment to allow dissent, and opposition parties and press, represents an important principle of socialist democracy. Too many socialist countries have interpreted socialism as merely the socialization of the economy and have failed to implement the other side of the equation—the democratization of political power. But in this, the

Sandinistas at least have tried harder than most. However, as with most attempts at compromise, there has been a price: the commitment to "pluralism" and to maintaining the support or at least neutrality of the capitalist class had as one of its necessary effects the imposition of certain limits on the transformative capacity of the state in some areas of policy. This was especially clear with regard to the government's program to improve the position of women.

The maintenance of a sizable private sector (78 percent of industry, 60 percent of commerce, 76 percent of agriculture) and the granting of a measure of autonomy to it, allowed some employers, especially those in the smaller nonunionized enterprises, to evade legislation designed to protect and improve the working conditions of women, as well as to pursue discriminatory employment policies. The same was true of that major employer of women, the service sector, whether public or private. But an even more intractable form of opposition to government policies, and one which offered the most sustained resistance to Sandinista policies, was the Catholic church, dominated as it was by conservatives hostile to the legacy of Medellín. The church's extensive institutional presence, forms of organization, access to the media (it had its own radio station), and base within a substantial section of the population made it a formidable opponent. In the areas directly concerned with women its impact on slowing reform was considerable. Conservative clergy have actively opposed educational and family reforms, enforced bans on weekend work (which made it difficult for voluntary labor schemes to achieve much), opposed the conscription of women, and have been enthusiastic advocates of traditional family life and the division of labor that characterizes it.[12] The conservative wing of the church opposed divorce reform and urged adherence to the papal encyclical which states that it is sinful to employ "unnatural" methods of birth control. It has also opposed the legalization of abortion, forcing thousands of women to remain in the hands of back street practitioners.[13] This problem of vigorous religious opposition is not characteristic of socialist states. Most of these states preemptively bring the clergy and their resources under state control and discourage traditional religious practices. In extreme cases, as in Albania and during the period of Stalin's rule in the Soviet Union, religion was severely dealt with. Even today religion is virtually outlawed in Albania. In this, as in other things, the FSLN has shown considerable moderation.

Yet what was a positive feature of the Sandinista revolution, its democratic commitment, did have the effect of diluting policy measures and weakening the government's capacity for implementation. It is therefore erroneous to imagine that just because a state might have a coherent set of policies and a unifying ideology that it has the capacity to be fully effective in social policy terms. It should be clear that the most favored solution historically is a problematic one to say the least: the subjugation of the opposition and the strengthening of the state.

A second political factor of a very different kind, but equally crucial to the success or failure of government policies, is that of the population's degree of support for, or resistance to, such policies. As far as changes in the position of women are concerned, the Sandinistas were limited in what they could do both by the conservative hold of the Catholic church and by the relatively small social base of support for feminism. There was no history of a popular and militant feminism in Nicaragua with the result that the Sandinistas had to contend with deeply entrenched *machista* attitudes and considerable hostility among much of the population to the idea of women's emancipation.

Nevertheless, the revolutionary war provided the initial context for the weakening of the traditional stereotypes and conventions, and it was on this basis that the Sandinistas began to build popular support for AMNLAE's campaigns. These tended to be successful when sufficient time and energy were devoted to explaining the objectives and learning from the women's responses, that is, creating and reproducing an organic link between the organization and the people it was representing, a process which at its best amounted to synthesizing the practical and strategic aspects of women's interests. Yet, as we shall see shortly, the campaigns suffered from a number of familiar limitations, including the fact that they were directed mostly at women and did not seek to make radical changes in the attitudes and behavior of men. As the tensions of the war mounted, there was pressure on AMNLAE from some sections of the FSLN to abandon the more feminist themes in the belief that they would alienate popular support. How far this was a risk, however, could not be established in the absence of extensive research into both attitudes and concrete conditions to establish the likely effects of the proposed reforms.

Only in this context is it relevant to discuss the third factor that accounts for the limited achievements of the Sandinista record on women: their conception of the place of women's emancipation within the overall context of their priorities. It is clear that the FSLN was able to implement only those parts of the programs for women's emancipation that coincided with its general goals, enjoyed popular support, and were realizable without arousing strong opposition. The policies from which women derived some benefit were pursued principally because they fulfilled some wider goal or goals, whether these were social welfare, development, social equality, or political mobilization in defense of the revolution. That is in effect what the Sandinistas meant by the need to locate women's emancipation within the overall struggle for social reform, and latterly of survival against intensifying external pressure.

This kind of qualified support for women's emancipation is found in most of the states that have pursued socialist development policies. Indeed, the guidelines that form the basis of socialist programs for women's emancipation (discussed earlier) all have universalistic as well as particularistic goals, in which the former is the justification for the latter. Thus, women's emancipation is not just dependent on the realization of the wider goals but is pursued insofar as it *contributes to the realization* of those goals. There is therefore a unity of purpose between the goals of women's emancipation and the developmental and social goals of revolutionary states.[14]

Revolutionary governments tend to see the importance of reforming the position of women in the first period of social and economic transformation in terms of helping to accomplish at least three goals: (1) to extend the base of the government's political support; (2) to increase the size or quality of the active labor force; and (3) to help harness the family more securely to the process of social reproduction. The first aim, to expand or maintain the power base of the state, is pursued by attempting to draw women into the new political organizations, such as the women's youth, and labor unions, the party, and neighborhood associations. There is a frequently expressed fear that unless women are politicized they may not cooperate with the process of social transformation. Women are seen as potentially and actually more conservative than men by virtue of their place within the social division of labor, that is, as primarily located outside the sphere of production. More positively they are also regarded as crucial agents of revolutionary change, whose radicalization challenges ancient customs and privileges within the family and has important effects on the next generation through the impact on their children. In Soviet Central Asia in the 1920s, where there was virtually no industrial working class, Bolshevik strategists directed their campaigns at women because they were considered the most oppressed social category. In general, the political mobilization of women supposes some attempt to persuade them that their interests as well as more universal concerns (national, humanitarian, etc.) are represented by the state.[15]

The second way in which the mobilization of women is regarded as a necessary part of the overall strategy is more directly relevant to the economy. The education of women and their entry into the paid labor force increases and improves the available labor supply, which is a necessary concomitant of any successful development program. In most underdeveloped countries women form only a small percentage of the economically active population and while the figures tend to conceal the real extent of women's involvement by registering mainly formal rather than informal activities, the work they do is frequently unpaid and underproductive, confined to family concerns in workshops or in the fields, and subject to the authority of male kin. Government policies have therefore emphasized the need for both education and a restructuring of employment to make better use of the work capacities of the female population. This is bolstered theoretically by Engels' argument concerning the emancipatory effect on women of entering employment.

The third aim is to bring the family more into line with planning objectives and to place it at the center of initiatives aimed at social reconstruction. Postrevolutionary governments regard women as key levers in harnessing the family more securely to state goals, whether these be of an economic or an ideological kind. The prerevolutionary family has to be restructured to make it more compatible with the developmental goals of revolutionary governments. Once this has been accomplished, the reformed family is expected to function as an important agent of socialization, inculcating the new revolutionary values into the next generation. Women are seen as crucial in both of these processes.

Although these three considerations are shared by most socialist states, the peculiar circumstances of Nicaragua's transition have determined the relative emphasis placed on these policy objectives, and have shaped the state's capacity to implement them for the reasons described earlier. For example, in Nicaragua there is no absolute shortage of labor, nor is production being greatly expanded. There is as yet therefore no urgent requirement for women to enter paid employment despite some expansion in state sector demand. Initially women were called upon to supply a considerable amount of voluntary labor as health workers and teachers in the popular campaigns (health in 1981, literacy in 1982). But there was no strong material incentive to provide widespread nursery care while the economy did not depend upon a mass influx of female labor. Moreover, since most urban women worked in the informal sector, it was assumed that a substantial percentage of these jobs were compatible with their domestic responsibilities. This attitude might be expected to change if there is a significant escalation of military activities, necessitating the entry of women into jobs vacated by men serving in the armed forces.[16]

As noted earlier, the emphasis of the government was on two other strategies, those of legal reform and political mobilization. The new laws regarding the family were designed both to strengthen the institution, promoting greater family cohesion, and to remove the gender inequalities which prevailed. The high rate of male desertion, migrancy, and serial polygamy left large numbers of women as the sole providers for their children: according to the Oficina de la Mujer and the central planning agency (MIPLAN) 34 percent of Nicaraguan households were female-headed and 60 percent in Managua, a factor which contributed directly to the high incidence of female poverty. The 1982 Ley de Alimentos made all adult members of the family, on a three generation basis, legally liable for maintaining the family unit, which meant also taking a share in the household tasks. In addition to these changes, the health and safety provisions of women workers were improved, while new legislation (Decrees 573 and 538) gave rural women workers an entitlement to their own wages to redress a situation in which a family wage was conventionally paid to the male head of the household.

As far as the political mobilization of women was concerned, by 1984 there were more women mobilized than at any time since the months leading up to the triumph. According to the Oficina de la Mujer, AMNLAE claimed a card-carrying membership of 85,000, and women made up 22 percent of the FSLN's membership and over one third of the leadership. Women's participation in the other mass organizations and in the organs of popular defense also expanded with the deepening of the crisis. Around half of the members of the Sandinista Defense Committees, a type of neighborhood association, were women, and women made up a similar proportion of the militia.

These then, were the areas in which the greatest advances were registered in relation to achieving policy objectives which concerned women *as such*. Yet more women benefited, and benefited more, from the implementation of measures designed to secure general objectives. Chief among these was welfare.

A detailed analysis of the impact of Sandinista social policies is beyond the scope of this discussion.[17] Instead, I will briefly summarize some of the main conclusions in relation to the issues raised earlier by considering the effects of the reforms in terms of the three categories of interest outlined at the beginning.

If we disaggregate the concept of "women's interests" and consider how different categories of women fared since 1979, it is clear that the majority of women in Nicaragua were positively affected by the government's redistribution policies. This is so even though fundamental structures of gender inequality were not dismantled. In keeping with the socialist character of the government, policies were targeted in favor of the poorest sections of the population and focused on basic needs provision in the areas of health, housing, education, and food subsidies. In the short span of only five years the Sandinistas reduced the illiteracy rate from over 50 percent to 13 percent, doubled the number of educational establishments, increased school enrollment, eradicated a number of mortal diseases, provided the population with basic health care services, and achieved more in their housing program than Somoza had in his entire period of rule (Walker 1985). In addition, the land reform canceled peasants' debts and gave thousands of rural workers secure jobs on the state farms and cooperatives or their own parcels of land (Deere 1983; CIERA 1984). These policies have been of vital importance in gaining the support of poor women. According to government statistics, women form over 60 percent of the poorest Nicaraguans; in the poorest category in Managua (incomes less than 600 córdobas per month) there are 354 women for each 100 men.[18] It is these women, by virtue of their *class* position, who have been the direct beneficiaries of Sandinista redistributive efforts, as have their male counterparts. But by the same token, it is obvious that not all women were to benefit from these programs; women whose economic interests lay in areas adversely affected by Sandinista economic policies (imports, luxury goods, etc.) suffered some financial loss, as did most women from the privileged classes as a result of higher taxation. It is also the case that while poor women benefited from the welfare provisions, they were also the most vulnerable to the pressures of economic constraints and especially to shortages in basic provisions.

In terms of *practical* gender interests these redistributive policies also had gender as well as class effects. By virtue of their place within the sexual division of labor, women are disproportionately responsible for childcare and family health, and they are particularly concerned with housing and food provision. The policy measures directed at alleviating the situation in these areas, not surprisingly, elicited a positive response from the women affected by them as borne out by the available research into the popularity of the government. Many of the campaigns mounted by the women's organization, AMNLAE, were directed at resolving some of the practical problems women faced, as exemplified by their mother and child health care program, or by their campaign aimed at encouraging women to conserve domestic resources to make the family income stretch further and thus avoid pressure building up over wage demands or shortages.[19] A feature of this kind of campaign is its recognition of women's practical interests, but in accepting the division of labor and women's subordination within it, it may entail a denial of their strategic interests. This is the problem with many women's organizations in the socialist bloc.

With respect to strategic interests, the acid test, so to speak, of whether women's emancipation was on the political agenda or not, the progress which was made was modest but significant. Legal reform, especially in the area of the family, confronted the issue of relations between the sexes and of male privilege, by attempting to end a situation in which most men were able to evade responsibility for the welfare of their families while retaining sole legal rights to the children. Through the provisions of the new laws, women acquired custody rights and men became liable for a contribution to household and childcare maintenance, in cases where paternity was acknowledged. This contribution could be made in cash, in kind, or in the form of services. The meetings called to discuss these reforms also enabled the issue of domestic labor to be politicized in the discussions of the need to share this work equally among all members of the family. The land reform program tackled the problem of rural women's invisibility by encouraging their participation and leadership in cooperatives and by giving them wages for their work and titles to land. There was also an effort to establish childcare agencies such as nurseries, preschool services, and the like. Some attempts were made to challenge female stereotypes, not just through outlawing the exploitation of women in the media, but also by promoting some women to positions of responsibility and emphasizing the importance of women in the militia and reserve battalions.[20] And finally, there was a sustained effort to mobilize women around their own needs through the women's organization, and there was discussion of some of the questions of strategic interest, although this has been sporadic and controversial. In these respects Nicaragua is fairly typical of other countries in the socialist periphery.

To sum up, we can see that it is difficult to discuss socialist revolutions in terms of an undifferentiated conception of women's interests and even more difficult to conclude that these interests have not been represented in state policymaking. The Sandinista record on women is certainly uneven, and it is as yet too early to make any final assessment of it, especially while it confronts increasing political, economic, and military pressures. Nonetheless, it is clear that the Sandinistas have gone further than most Latin American governments (except Cuba) in recognizing both the strategic and practical interests of women and have brought about substantial improvements in the lives of many of the most deprived. When AMNLAE stated that its priority is defense of the revolution because the latter provides the necessary condition for realizing a program for women's emancipation—it was, with certain qualifications, correct.

Yet these qualifications remain important, and they have a significance which goes beyond the Sandinista revolution to the wider question of the relationship between socialism and feminism. Three of these, which are general to socialist states, can be listed here in summary form.

The first is that although strategic gender interests are recognized in the official theory and program of women's emancipation, they nonetheless remain rather narrowly defined because they are based on the privileging of economic criteria. Feminist theories of sexual oppression, or the critique of the family or of male power, have had little impact on official thinking, and indeed are sometimes suppressed as being too radical and too threatening to popular solidarity.[21] There is a need for greater discussion and debate around these questions both among the people and within the organs of political power, so that the issue of women's emancipation remains alive and open, and does not become entombed within official doctrine.

The second issue concerns the relationship that is established by planners between the goal of women's emancipation and other goals, such as economic development, that have priority. It is not the *linkage* itself that constitutes the problem—principles such as social equality and women's emancipation can be realized only within determinate conditions of existence. So linking the program for women's emancipation to these wider goals need not necessarily be a cause for concern because these wider goals may constitute the preconditions for realizing the principles. The question is rather the nature of the links: are gender interests *articulated into* a wider strategy of economic development, for example, or are they irretrievably *subordinated to it?* In the first case we would expect gender interests to be recognized as being specific and irreducible, and requiring something more for their realization than is generally provided for in the pursuit of the wider goals. Thus, when it is not possible to pursue a full program for women's emancipation this can be explained and debated. The goal can be left on the agenda, and every effort made to pursue it within the existing constraints. In the latter case, the specificity of gender interests is likely to be denied or its overall importance minimized. The issues are trivialized or buried; the program for women's emancipation remains one conceived in terms of how functional it is for achieving the wider goals of the state. It is difficult to say how these issues will be resolved in Nicaragua in the long run. For the moment, the intense pressures that the Sandinistas are under make it difficult to resist the pattern which has emerged elsewhere in the socialist bloc of countries, that of subordination rather than linkage or articulation.

And this raises the third general issue, which is that of political guarantees. For if gender interests are to be realized only within the context of wider considerations, it is essential that the political institutions charged with representing these interests have the means to prevent their being submerged altogether and action on them being indefinitely postponed. Women's organizations, the official representatives of women's interests, should not conform to Lenin's conception of mass organizations as mere "transmission belts of the party." Rather, they must enjoy a certain independence and exercise power and influence over party policy, albeit within certain necessary constraints. In other words, the issue of gender interests and their means of representation cannot be resolved in the absence of a discussion of socialist democracy and the forms of the state appropriate to the transition to socialism; it is a question therefore not just of *what* interests are represented in the state, but ultimately and crucially, of *how* they are represented.

Notes

This article is based on research carried out in Nicaragua with the help of the Nuffield Foundation. It is part of on-going research into state policies, women, and the family in postrevolutionary societies. Many thanks to the readers of an earlier version of this text, especially to Ted (E.) Benton and Hermione Harris. An earlier version was published in *Feminist Studies,* Spring 1985 and a shorter version appeared in *Critical Social Policy* 10, Summer 1984.

1. The term "socialist" is used here for the sake of brevity. In relation to most of these states, some qualification is required along the lines suggested by Rudolf Bahro ("actually existing socialism"), for the reasons he advanced in his book *The Alternative in Eastern Europe* (1978). Others have not reached the level of economic socialization that qualifies them for inclusion in this category.

2. For critical discussions of the record of socialist states, see, among others Markus (1976) and Stacey (1983).

3. This position is a logical extrapolation of its premises, and is one frequently expressed at meetings and discussions within the women's liberation movement. However there does not exist, to my knowledge, any written theoretical elaboration of it.

4. There are differing definitions of the term "patriarchy" but most agree that it describes a power relation existing between the sexes, exercised by men over women, and institutionalized within various social relations and practices among which can be instanced the law, the family, and education.

5. There is a third usage of the term "interest" found in Marxist writing which explains collective action in terms of some intrinsic property of the actors and/or the relations within which they are inscribed. Thus, class struggle is ultimately explained as an effect of the relations of production. This conception has been shown to rest on essentialist assumptions and provides an inadequate account of social action. For a critique of this notion see Benton (1982) and Hindess (1982).

6. Zillah Eisenstein, editor of *Capitalist Patriarchy* (1979), has produced a sophisticated version of the argument that women constitute a "sexual class" and that for women, gender issues are primary. See Eisenstein (1984).

7. It is precisely around these issues, which also have an ethical significance, that the theoretical and political debate must focus. The list of strategic gender interests noted here is not exhaustive but is merely exemplary.

8. This is the position of some radical feminist groups in Europe.

9. One of the best accounts of the Reagan administration's policy of destabilizing and attempting to overthrow the Sandinistas is by Nairn (1984).

10. Borge's speech was delivered on the occasion of the fifth anniversary of AMNLAE. It was published in *Barricada,* October 4, 1982, and is available in translation from Pathfinder Press.

11. These were laid down at the 1921 Comintern Congress and stressed five main goals: to encourage the entry of women into wage labor; socialize domestic labor and childcare; provide juridical equality; greater protec-

tion for mothers and the family; and the mobilization of women into political activity and public administration. See Jancar (1978).

12. Substantial numbers of women were in favor of conscription and bitterly resented the Council of State's 1983 decision to exempt women. AMNLAE fought a popular campaign to revoke the decision which resulted in women having the right to volunteer.

13. In 1981 one Managua hospital was admitting an average of twelve women a day as a result of illegal abortions. The main maternity hospital there records four to five admissions weekly of women following abortions. In press reports in 1982 the number of abortions was said to be rising (quoted in Deighton et al. 1983), while a study reported in November 1985 that during the period from March 1983 to June 1985 in one hospital alone, 8,752 abortions were attended, that is, an average of ten per day (*Barricada,* November 19, 1985).

14. For a fuller discussion of socialist policies with regard to women and the family see Molyneux (1981).

15. This has to be compared and contrasted with many nationalist movements that call for the sacrifice of women's interests (and those of other oppressed groups) in the interests of the nation.

16. In agriculture this is already evident. In some of the regions most affected by the war (Matagalpa, Jinotega), where male conscription is high, women had by February 1984 come to represent as much as 40 percent of the workforce. (Author's interview with Magda Enriquez, a member of AMNLAE's national directorate, March 1984).

17. For a fuller account of Sandinista social policies see Walker, ed. (1982) and for their policies on women see my article in the same volume.

18. Unpublished data from the Instituto Nacional de Estadisticas y Censos, Managua, December 1981.

19. AMNLAE argued that the implications of women conserving resources under a socialist government are radically different from those under capitalism because the beneficiaries are the people in the first case and private interests in the second.

20. Although there are no women in the nine-member Junta which constitutes the FSLN leadership, the Vice President of the Council of State was a woman and women assumed many key positions in the party at the regional level. On three occasions after 1979 women filled ministerial posts.

War, Popular Participation, and Transition to Socialism: The Case of Nicaragua

▼▲

Peter E. Marchetti, S. J.

> The generations that successfully
> make the transition to socialist so-
> ciety are going to smile when they
> read the descriptions of Marx,
> Engels, and Lenin about how to
> make it, that is, if they are generous.
> —a political cadre of a
>   communist party, 1981

Socialism is young. Despite the intentions of socialism to integrate theory and practice, there is little correspondence between the theoretical guidelines of Marxism-Leninism concerning the transition to socialism and its contemporary practice. Moreover, the appearance of the socialist formation in the capitalist periphery instead of at its center has thoroughly bedeviled efforts to compare contemporary socialism with the classical texts. Although the pace of the consolidation of socialism may ultimately be much quicker than the nine centuries of the transition to capitalism, socialism is now in its youth. As a mode of production, it is undergoing its period of trial-and-error experimentation, of progress and failures. The words of the communist political cadre cited above alert us (a) to the fact that the period of socialist transition is indeed lengthy, and (b) to the danger of believing that there are theoretical-political recipes for this transition.

As Lenin noted, and as the experience of over seventy years of transition has confirmed, there are two steps in the transition to socialism: the most difficult is not the first, overthrowing the old dominant classes, but rather the second, which Lenin defined as attaining "the regulation of production by the worker"; for this it was necessary to destroy the inherited social relations that work actively

---

Translated by Ricky Weiss

against the creation of socialism. These pages are intended to contribute to the current debate over popular participation in societies in transition toward a socialist economy and to submit this "second step" to analysis—with particular reference to the experience of Nicaragua.

The "second step toward socialism" is, however, never taken in a vacuum. From 1917 to the 1979 triumph of the Sandinista revolution in Nicaragua, it has always taken place in the context of imperialist military aggression against socialist revolutions. Yet this should not preclude progress toward socialist goals. One of the most common errors in criticizing the transition to socialism is to present the phenomenon of socialist militarization as contradictory to the growth of popular and democratic participation. The first step in the analysis of socialist transition is to recognize that socialism develops in dialectic with its imperialist enemy and that the first phase of this dialectic is military, not only before taking power, but especially afterward, when new social institutions must be built in the midst of a protracted war.

Wartime is obviously not the most propitious moment in which to develop popular participation and democracy. This is increasingly true today, as imperialists learn their lessons from popular tactics, making their counterrevolutionary operations more effective. A good dose of Vietnamese guerrilla strategy has been incorporated into this new counterrevolutionary warfare. Since its costly defeat in Vietnam, U.S. imperialism has preferred a low profile, or *low intensity war,* that uses a fraction of the peasant population—normally that most isolated from national infrastructure and revolutionary programs—against the revolutionary process. The twin aims of the low intensity war are the economic and social attrition of the revolutionary project in the mid-term, and the creation of the diplomatic conditions for involving puppet nations as proxies in the long-term project of military destabilization. Today, the Reagan administration is financing guerrilla wars in Central America, several African countries, Afghanistan, and Southeast Asia. War, then, is the context in which socialism is born and must develop. It has to be taken into account for any serious analysis of popular participation in the young socialist societies of the third world.

Aggression, economic pressures from the capitalist bloc, the slow unfolding and, at times, reversal of the socialist revolution on the international level, and finally, the backwardness of the productive forces are undoubtedly the principal barriers to the full development of popular participation during the transition to socialism. However, those who emphasize only these factors do nothing more than lament the people's misfortunes and condemn the enemy's practice. Lament and condemnation are characteristic of theories that rationalize the slowness of the transition toward participatory socialism in terms of the existence of a series of historical factors that have prevented the precise application of "true Marxist-Leninist thought." The more lamentable the transition in terms of participation, the more sacred become the texts that are said to contain the correct path.

This essay will thus attempt to analyze a series of issues within the revolution in the context of the war against imperialist aggression. The reader may rightly object that the issues of popular participation outlined herein are problems of the socialist transition whether or not the economy is a war economy and that the war only exacerbates the tensions and limits the options. In the abstract this is certainly true, but the problem is that we do not have a case of socialist transition where imperialist aggression and war have not played a major role. Social scientists must take full account of military matters or else our critique of the transition will remain hopelessly "ivory tower." War is, if you want, the particular light in which the entire mode of production (third world socialism) is bathed and therefore understood. This essay is a first and necessarily preliminary attempt to take the fact of war seriously.

Popular Participation in the Vision of Critical Marxism: The Subjective Factor

The term "popular participation" carries an emotional impact that is as strong as it is imprecise, due to its easy relevance for every social project, whether progressive or reactionary. Its use thus calls for a clear definition. This essay will follow sociologists Pearse and Steifel in defining popular participation as "the organized efforts to increase the control over resources and regulating institutions by groups and movements of workers and peasants previously excluded from such control" (1979:80–108). In the first moments, popular participation has to do with the art of armed insurrection; after taking power through armed struggle or within a government that is attempting to prepare the path for the transition, "popular participation" has to do with the *continuation of the class struggle under new conditions*. Participation and power are not "things" but rather relationships among classes or a particular correlation of social forces. In other words, the mere presence of progressive forces in a government does not mean that the working class has gained power, but simply that it has entered upon a new phase of its struggle. Here, I will at the outset separate this concept from any type of Stalinist thought which proclaims the *disappearance* of the class struggle and *identifies* the proletariat with its vanguard.

To overcome Stalinist obscurantism is to recognize that one of the internal contradictions of the transition process is the gap between popular revolutionary movements and their subsequent institutionalization; between the practice of the masses and the practice of their vanguard party; between the workers' and peasants' ideology and that of their representatives in the new state institutions. A basic proposition of critical Marxism is to recognize the existence of this gap.

The fundamental questions then become: What happens to the class struggle when the guerrilla soldiers must professionalize themselves in the tasks of production, education, health, and the like? What happens to the class struggle when revolutionary parties are no longer in the opposition but, on the contrary, have the responsibility for creating and governing the new society? And what happens within the revolutionary organization as it has to professionalize its army while at the same time managing the entire society in the face of economic, diplomatic, and military pressure? Taking the second step toward socialism depends largely on this transition between the popular insurrection movement and the national organization of revolutionary power. While this link between popular participation and institutionalization is seen more clearly in the first years of a revolution, it is a central and permanent dialectic of the transition toward a new society.

Another central hypothesis in critical Marxist thought is that the critique of the praxis of institutionalizing popular movements can contribute something to the search for a socialist formation that favors mass participation in the humanization of work, in the transformation of the old division of labor, in the cultural revolution, in changing patterns of consumption, in forming small circles of workers with multiple goals (management, political education, communication, recreation), and in creating what Che Guevara called (six years into the Cuban revolution) "the institutionalization of the Revolution that has still not been attained" (1970:375).

While bourgeois thought characterizes popular participation in terms of free economic competition and the existence of parliamentary structures, and power elite theory conceptualizes participation as dependent on the development of the productive forces and organizational capacity, the Marxist perspective prioritizes equality as key for participation and conceptualizes participation as a subjective factor that permits human potential to be realized.[1]

Within Marxism, a critical current maintains that the principal obstacle to the development of a truly democratic socialism lies not in the backwardness of the productive forces with its series of problems, such as the level of educational inequality, but rather in *the division of labor* that has remained essentially capitalist in form and reproduces itself in political and ideological relationships in such a way that the economic logic continues to privilege individual interests over communal ones.[2]

Che Guevara represents this critical line, which maintains that revolutionizing the social relations of production should be a permanent component of the revolutionary praxis during the transition. In his view, the victories of the socialist movement in the capitalist periphery owe much more to the subjective factor than Marx could have imagined (ibid.:371–72).

The fact that the economic structure prevents the people from consciously grasping and feeling the very contradictions of capitalism means that the road to socialism is not an easy one, that "the new society in formation has to compete very hard with the past," and that the battle against the past has to be based on consciousness, on subjective aspirations: "We must create the man of the twenty-first century, although that is still very much an unsystematized, subjective aspiration" (ibid.:371–79).

Guevera's criticism of using "the worn weapons bequeathed to us by capitalism" (that is, what is on hand when the transition begins: commodity forms, profit maximization, individual motivation), lies in the fact that this old political economy and its tools carry within themselves a subjective poison from the past (ibid.:372–78). We now know (after Guevara's experiment) that the tools inherited from the past cannot be replaced overnight. For this very reason, it is all the more necessary to accentuate the subjective factor in the early years of the transition.

In contrast to theories based on the primacy of the development of the productive forces during the transition, Che set forth the need to base the transition on two fundamental pillars: "the formation of the new man and the development of the technology. . . . In order to construct communism, the new man must be made simultaneously with the material base" (ibid.:372).

The creation of this so-called new man demands, if it is to be more than just rhetoric, major changes in the social relations of production, especially the elimination of the division of labor between routine manual labor and administrative, intellectual work. As Rudolf Bahro points out: "The essence of actually existing socialism is conceived as one of socialization in the alienated form of a stratification, this being based on a traditional division of labour, which has not yet been driven to the critical point at which it topples over" (1978:13–14). During the transition "the old division of labor" must be understood very concretely. Is the agrarian reform program imposed from above by urban bureaucrats or do peasant communities have a say in defining its character? How much freedom do neighborhood organizations have in defining their needs? Or are they merely "alienated labor" for the party's political program?

One of the great traps in underdeveloped societies is the milieu of social relationships, in which it is hard to distinguish between "friendly favors" and "the commoditization of human life." As a result, the state bureaucracy can appear as revolutionary, just, and egalitarian simply

because it is impersonal. The fervor for creating a bureaucratic apparatus and for multiplying the paperwork on the part of revolutionaries for
middle-class backgrounds is understandable, but often it becomes a
substitute for the principal task of the ideological struggle, subjective
encouragement, and the promotion of popular participation among the
masses through very concrete, base-level programs. The desk is easier
than the hard life in a poor neighborhood, or even worse, in the
countryside. In the eagerness to create the apparatus, whose very
existence seems to guarantee that change is taking place, the old
divisions of labor are left without any major modifications.

It was precisely the old division of labor that Guevara wanted to
break, and this was why he insisted on moral and material incentives
and on simultaneous advances in *participation* and in *training.* His
definition of training as participation in management (ibid.:375), and
that of participation as political, technical, and ideological education,
are very different from Bukharin's theory, which expected that the
expansion of educational opportunities was going to result in "an overproduction of agitators and cadres who will question the stability of the
elites" (Marchetti 1975:104). Bukharin proposed the following: education first and then question the hierarchies of power defined by levels
of training. For Guevara, the two processes were parallel.

Carrying out the Marxist ideal of the humanization of work demands
more than just questioning the division of labor; it means creating in the
workplace what the Sandinista revolution calls workers' circles, what
Bahro calls autonomous personal communication groups, and what
Unger (1977) calls organic groups, so that the individual feels more
fulfilled. These are groups with multiple goals (education, management, recreation) in which the division of labor is broken down through
personal communication and collective effort. They are groups in
which the members of the vanguard become a part of the local
community and in which the party member has to carry within himself
or herself the gap between the vanguard and local interests as a personal
tension. Without personal communication the subjective factor with-
ers, and there is no transition. The ethos of the old Marxism with all its
impersonality even now raises in me a doubt about airing such issues in
a discussion of transition to socialism. Yet the glaring need for militants
who can establish profound levels of communication with workers and
peasants drives me to run the risk of seeming ridiculous: "Let me tell
you, at the risk of sounding ridiculous, that the true revolutionary is
guided by profound feelings of love. It is impossible to imagine an
authentic revolutionary without this quality" (Guevara 1970:382).

Without a place in revolutionary strategy for ideological struggle, for
capturing the energy of the subjective and personal aspirations in the
hearts of workers and peasants, it is doubtful whether socialism will be

able to overcome the existing contradiction between socialized means of production and individualized means of motivation. Only the direct and conscious praxis of the vanguard and the masses can produce the type of institutionalization of popular participation envisaged by Guevara. It cannot be the fruit of nonhuman factors such as the inexorable development of the productive forces.

What does all this have to do with war? And with the hard problems facing the transition in the periphery? This perspective of critical Marxism was not born out of reaction against European Marxism but rather out of the lived practice of transition in the third world. Critical Marxism is born amidst the lived experience of imperialist aggression rather than out of some sort of rapprochement between the social democrats and the Leninists.

It cannot be denied that the subjective factor played an enormous role in the consolidation of socialism in Cuba or that anti-imperialist consciousness and nationalism have been the motors of change in all the processes of national liberation in the contemporary third world. Anti-imperialist ideology, however, is too thin to carry the entire weight of the new consciousness necessary for socialism to work. In Nicaragua, the grinding pressure of the U.S.-backed contra war forced the Sandinistas to turn the 1984 elections into a massive mobilization of FSLN members among the masses in order to strengthen mass consciousness. Although some Sandinistas and many foreign observers thought the elections were an export product aimed at social-democratic Europe, the increased contact of party militants with the masses in the home-to-home visits became a deadly serious project of incorporating the people's subjective desire for elections into an enriched anti-imperialist consciousness and into a new maturity of knowing that voting Sandinista would not mean an improved standard of living, but only national dignity and democratic pride in their war against the U.S. government's aggression.[3] Similarly, after the elections, an economic insurrection was proclaimed by the Sandinista vanguard as a way of coupling the needs of a war economy with all the subjective values and habits of cooperation that the word "insurrection" evokes in Nicaragua.

The truth is that small third world nations, when they are faced with imperialist aggression, have no significant economic, technological, or financial resources on which to rely. The only option they possess is the subjective factor: ideological mobilization. For countless centuries reactionaries have carefully "worked the human soul." In Europe that task was held to be so tainted by those who struggled to hold onto the past that Marxists naively hoped that the whole concern would wither away with the development of the forces of production. Not only has this strategy allowed the reactionaries to establish serious barricades in the human soul against the socialist project but it has meant that socialist revolution in the capitalist periphery has had to proceed in giving emphasis to the subjective factor with little or no theoretical guidelines.

War, then, has been the midwife of critical Marxism, but it goes without saying that the ideological austerity of wartime nationalism, the ethos of sacrifice for the future generation, and so on, needs to be enriched even more radically than the Sandinistas have done up to this point. Marxism needs to work seriously on the subjective side, the human soul, the whole complex of motivation.

Popular participation and its institutionalization in the context of war and the transition to socialism confront three problems: (a) the role of the vanguard and whom it represents; (b) the role of the state; and (c) the question of revolutionary alliances and styles of transition. Each of these must be dealt with separately.

The Role of the Vanguard

Perhaps the most acute problem facing the vanguard of the working class is that its political-military victory has taken place in countries where its principal base (the industrial working class) is a minority. In conditions of dependent underdevelopment, the principal social force is not the working class but the peasantry, and this compels the working class and its party to tie themselves to the rest of society in their new role as the *leading social force.* As Bettleheim points out, a dual problem exist here:

> The problem here presented is twofold—that of the contradiction between the massive presence of nonproletarian and democratic character of the ruling power, and that of *the correct handling of this contradiction.* ... This contradiction is more or less acute depending on the characteristics of the ideological and political leadership exercised by the proletariat and its party over the popular masses themselves. (1975a:100)

The essence of the problem is the following: on the one hand there exists the Charybdis of integrating the nonproletarian forces fully within the transition and running the risk that these will indelibly mark the process with their rural backwardness and their petty capitalism. On the other hand there is the Scylla of not including the peasantry and the urban middle sectors in the revolution and running the risk of losing the masses' voluntary support and with it the vanguard's leadership role.[4] Bettleheim pronounces the correct treatment of the contradiction between the dominant social force and the leading social force, namely: "Ensure the party's leadership role, which can only be developed to the extent to which the proletarian party places its trust in the popular masses, and thus permits them, through their own experience, to put themselves increasingly under the party's guidance" (1975a).

But what looks so easy in print always turns out to be difficult in revolutionary practice. The problems that arose between the party and the peasantry in the USSR need no commentary. Before analyzing similar problems in Nicaragua, we need to look more carefully at the question of who is the leading force in the revolutions taking place on the periphery of the international capitalist system. The question of what social force will be the leading force in the transition to socialism (in the institutionalization of participation) is not rhetorical in the context of Africa, Central America, and the Caribbean. In the Russian revolution, there was no doubt that the industrial working class was the leading force. This was not the case in Nicaragua. Moreover, it appears that the urban working class will not be the spearhead of the revolution in El Salvador or Guatemala. The divergence with respect to the Russian model can be found in what Orlando Núñez points out about the configuration of social classes in the small and dependent countries of the Caribbean Basin:

> In our societies long subject to imperialism, the development of the proletariat is greatly disproportionate to that of capitalism. And although I agree that the importance of the proletarian project cannot be measured in quantitative terms (just as it could not be for the bourgeois project), it is also true that the proletarian project cannot exist only in the heads of the intellectuals. (1980:142)

As in tsarist Russia, the peasantry and the agricultural proletariat of Nicaragua together comprise the largest social force numerically, accounting for over 50 percent of the economically active population (EAP). Nicaragua's industrial and manufacturing working class makes up less than 15 percent of the EAP while the informal service sector involves nearly 33 percent of the population. The main difference with Russia lies in the praxis of the social classes. In Russia, the insurrection was born within large industry and overflowed the factory walls in order to occupy political power. In Nicaragua, a vast alliance of popular sectors that found their central axis in what Núñez calls *the third social force* was responsible for toppling the Somoza dictatorship:

> The importance of the sectors considered in this work as the revolution's third force in the national liberation movements (apart from full-time workers and peasants), did not appear only in the Cuba of the 1950s, but in all the countries subject to imperialism where the overabundance of commercial capital and the intermediary state, as the principle motors of capitalism, have produced a service sector so gigantic that day by day an expanding proletarianized mass finds itself unable to be organically integrated into capital's productive sphere and must peddle its goods and services on the streets. (Ibid.:143)

Thus in the neocolonial countries the principal contradiction between capital and labor is not expressed exclusively in terms of the conflict between worker and employer, but also emerges between the intermediary state and the unemployed of the cities, the urban and rural artisans and merchants, public employees, small business people, journalists, professors and teachers, and youth.

In Nicaragua, the political vanguard was able to articulate and unite the struggle of a broad-based front against the dictatorship. The massive front was constituted by (a) peasants and workers, (b) young people, (c) the urban middle class, (d) the unemployed and underemployed of the informal service sector, and (e) the vanguard itself, which, in an alliance with the bourgeois opposition, successfully overthrew the dictatorship. This broad-based social movement, and not the working class, was the leading force of the Nicaraguan revolution. Therefore, the mechanical identification of the historical subject of the revolution (the proletariat) with the political subject (the political organization of workers) does not work in Nicaragua, nor in many other countries in the region.

As Núñez points out:

> If the time dedicated to proletarian labor is less each year, if the level of underemployment grows over the course of that same year, and if the majority of a society's individuals is increasingly unable to integrate itself into the system, then the revolution cannot hold onto the illusion of waiting for the emergence of a complete army of workers attired in their proletarian uniforms before attempting to take power in favor of proletarian interests. (Ibid.:155)

The synthesis of the objective and historic conditions in these countries of the capitalist periphery has been to lessen the weight of the proletariat in the balance of social forces. This constitutes the objective base for explaining how power has been taken by various anti-imperialist national liberation movements without the proletariat as a leading force. It is precisely because the old formula has lost its validity that the question arises of who will be the leading force after the victory and during the transition period.[5]

All this takes on more importance and complexity in the context of the Caribbean Basin. In 1980, the Cuban Communist Party recognized a new formula for the taking of power: instead of the industrial proletariat and its political representative, the Leninist party, power is taken by the coupling of a loosely knit broad front of popular organizations (students, teachers, neighborhoods, women, trade unions, religious groups) with a highly disciplined and conscious armed organization of rural and urban guerrillas. In Nicaragua, the Sandinista National Liberation Front (FSLN) was not organized as a political party before the national insurrection of 1979 and serious work on creating party organization in the Sandinista movement did not begin until two years after the fall of Somoza's regime.

As is well known, power is not "a thing" that falls from the rotten tree of the old society into the hands of the vanguard, but a *relationship,* a correlation between the different social forces. The question, then, is: Which of the social forces that made up the broad-based social movement which overthrew the dictatorship will be able to determine the shifts occurring among the different social forces?

The third force, lodged as it is in the public and commercial sectors, is the popular sector with the most education, with a virtual monopoly on technical skills, and often with the most access to the political vanguard. Despite the fact that it represents only a third of the economically active population, the third force is a strong candidate for becoming the leading force in these small revolutionary societies. Although what Sandino said is true, "that only the peasants and workers will go on to the end," it appears that in Nicaragua and in other revolutionary movements in the area, the worker-peasant alliance (the first and second forces) will have to walk for a good while hand-in-hand with the third social force.

At the Tricontinental Conference of Havana in 1966, Amilcar Cabral pointed out that in neocolonial countries

> events have shown that the only social sector capable of being aware of the reality of imperialist domination and of directing the state apparatus inherited from this domination is the native petty bourgeoisie. . . . We will see that this specific inevitability in our situation constitutes one of the weaknesses of the national liberation movement. (1979:108)

The inevitability Cabral referred to is this: given the social and material formation of these countries and their peculiar insertion into the international market, they must depend on this third social force or, as was the case in Cuba, pay the high social cost of creating it once again after rolling it under the wheels of the peasant-worker alliance.

Núñez' theory about the third social force is more comprehensive than Cabral's regarding the petty bourgeoisie, because among the nonproletarian forces in many third world countries, the urban poor and the masses of young people constitute a more numerous force with greater revolutionary potential than the petty bourgeoisie per se. A Filipino author wrote once: "The third world is a teenager with a gun in his hand," a description proved true by the objective and subjective conditions in Nicaragua. In 1979, 67 percent of the total population was under twenty-four years old; 59 percent was under twenty years old, which was by far the most combative age group in the struggle against Somoza. During the insurrection, the National Guard identified youth as its principal enemy; it was virtually a crime to be between the ages of eleven and twenty. Young people, acting as a unique component of the revolutionary forces, played a major role in the insurrection and turned their crime into victory. After the insurrection, and even more so after the second great mobilization of youth, the literacy campaign, it was said that at the dinner tables of the bourgeoisie and petty bourgeoisie the revolutionary perspective of the FSLN and the suffering of Nicaragua's peasants made itself present through the experiences of those families' children.

When class suicide is spoken of, the possibilities are certainly greater among the ranks of young people. The old tactical vision of dividing and conquering the middle classes through providing material benefits to certain strata and not others could perhaps be modified with a program to win over the middle sectors using age as a criteria, given the extraordinary and *growing* weight of youth in the society of small peripheral countries. The case of Chile gives clear testimony to the weakness of the economistic tactic of dividing and conquering the petty bourgeoisie through its stomach. Its appetite, when tied to a consumer mentality, is insatiable and takes as a guide those who consume the most, namely the bourgeoisie. Committing suicide as a class to consume more is an absolute contradiction in terms.

To speak of sacrificing one's own class interests to take on the values of the proletariat calls for a response to the question: What for? Fifty thousand young people died for a reason: freedom. They did not die for the freedom that would one day appear at the end of a transition period, but for the immediate freedom present during the struggle itself. To join the insurrection was to gain freedom from all the family controls which had been used to prepare docile subjects for Somoza and for imperialism.

Death was mixed with joy, a reality that is hard for the bourgeoisie and the positivists to grasp intellectually. And it is here that a new path opens up during the transition period: win over the young people and a small part of the petty bourgeoisie by offering them what the capitalist regime never offered—the freedom of, and complete participation in, a new project of society, the core of which turns on the subjective factor and increased human responsibility. In this way, "abundance is created with consciousness instead of waiting for the development of abundance to create consciousness," to use the words of Fidel Castro. Núñez states:

> Proletarianized young people led by a revolutionary organization can contribute to universal revolutionary culture to help history take steps that the bourgeoisie has been unable to implement. But this time, everything will be different, even the tasks themselves take on a new nature when carried out by different subjects. (1980:156)

Although the third force and youth are strong candidates for the leading force in the transition, the most reasonable answer to our query is that there is no *single* leading force. This in turn means that the vanguard leadership will have a heightened importance in the transitional period.

Núñez, however, leaves us with two questions with regard to this participatory utopia for the youth of the third world. In the first place, what steps will be taken? The bourgeoisie has been incapable of creating a proletariat: therefore, we have a revolution in search of a proletariat. The great masses of young people will be the source from which that new proletariat and its project will be molded.

Second, what type of proletariat will be created in the transition period? If it is a patient and alienated proletariat, like the working class of capitalist systems that has to wait to participate for two generations, until the productive forces have developed, it can be expected that young people and the entire third force will take a position of class resistance instead of sacrificing their interests. No young person today is going to die for a boring job in a factory or in a public office. On the other hand, if youth are allowed the freedom to become educated and participate in the creation of the new proletariat, young people can sacrifice their interests for a project of self-liberation. They will seek the ideal of a free worker with full rights to participate and manage his or her workplace. (I am speaking of course of technical and political management, and not of economic self-management.)

Antonio Gramsci wrote somewhere, in an era much less favorable to the development of the subjective factor, that it is not the economic structure but the interpretation of that structure that ultimately determines political action. Marxists such as Rudolf Bahro, calling attention in their analyses to the "growing role of the subjective factor," propose "*a cultural revolution* in the truest sense of the term: a *transformation of the entire subjective form of life* of the masses" (1978:257; emphasis in original). In the very center of that revolution Bahro proposes the immediate goal of overcoming the capitalist division of labor, which means not only opening the process to a certain degree of chaos and delay in the pace of accumulation, but also placing the participation of the masses as one of the revolution's true priorities.

Marx noted that it is impossible "to make mere will power the motor of the revolution." Revolutionary morale, however, is not purely epiphenomenal, nor is it connected exclusively to the development of productive structures. It is based on the nature of man; the species is made for the kingdom of freedom and has to share to survive. Socialization and freedom now motivate directly without being mediated by elite policymakers.

Leading a victorious revolution to strengthen the interests and values

316   Peter E. Marchetti, S.J.

of a proletariat that is not yet prepared for the transformation that is
needed, is how Núñez characterizes the Nicaraguan process
(1980:152–57). This presupposes that the proletariat exists as a moral
potential in human nature and an ideal sought by the movement when it
has not been formed by the historical process. If that possibility does
not exist in human nature outside of the socioeconomic moment, then
the vanguard project of supporting the development of the proletariat
in these countries is pure voluntarism. Marx's faith in the creativity of
the bourgeoisie to give birth to a historical redeeming force in the
proletariat has not taken place either in advanced capitalist countries or
in the third world. It seems that the revolutionary proletariat will be the
object of human search and revolutionary practice based on the
growing subjective factor and the new morale of cultural revolution.
The leading social force will give us the answer as a realization of the
human potential in the road that stretches out before us. This is the
great challenge of the revolution in countries subject to imperialism
and the great hope of a more fertile transition period in terms of
popular participation.

As mentioned earlier, war is not only the context in which the
transition takes place but is rather the crucial factor determining: (a) the
development of the vanguard as a political organization; (b) the type of
proletariat and proletarian project being forged during the early years
of the transition; and (c) the whole future of increased popular participation and heightened stress on the subjective factor.

In short, the army, not the factory, is the primary school of socialist
politics. Not only is the lived experience of the early vanguard leadership that of an urban or rural guerrilla force, but the second generation
of leaders, the whole third force, and the masses of youth have as their
principle tutor the war effort against imperialist aggression. The code
for socialist participation, learned through the organizational structure
of the army, will be the model for the future society because the heroes
of the war are destined to occupy the leadership posts (top and middle
level) after the peace is won. Thus, to the extent that the socialist army
remains conventional in its organization and ideology, one can expect
little transformation in the social relations of production and lower
levels of popular participation in the new society.

Breaking through the boredom and separation from the civilian
population inherent in conventional military discipline will be crucial
not only for the future of the socialist project but more immediately for
the participation and support of the noncombatant population, especially in those areas where imperialist aggression has focused the
terrorism of the low intensity war.

In Nicaragua, the pressure of having to rapidly build and expand the
military forces, both in the urban (because of a possible massive U.S.

invasion) and in the rural areas (in order to confront the low intensity war) has made it very difficult to move very far beyond conventional military organization. In terms of ideological preparation, however, the revolution has dedicated its most talented people to the task of creating consciousness among the rank and file. As the war against the contra has worn on, nonconventional military styles are being developed and increased involvement of the troops in the economic and social problems of the peasantry are being stressed. Under the blast of war, civilian politics and participatory style seem out of place, but this is precisely the crucible in which they must come to life. In a small country such as Nicaragua the relationship between the troops and civilians is crucial and as visible as what is behind the shop glass window. The way the civilian population responds to the economic hardships of the war depends to a great extent on what they see in that window.

Similarly, the decision of the Sandinista leadership to create a party organization came to a great extent as a response to the appearance of the counterrevolutionary bands and the development of the Reagan administration's military strategy for Central America in late 1981 and early 1982. If on the one hand the necessity of fighting a defensive war against U.S. aggression while simultaneously attempting to maintain the economy called forth a greater centralization of power in the vanguard's political structure, the very polyvalency of the class structure and the need to respond to several distinct social forces vying with each other for the position of leading force (the third force, the working class, the peasantry, and even the small and medium bourgeoisie) has on the other hand forced the vanguard into new styles of leadership.

The demands on a vanguard organization in the peculiar configuration of social forces in Nicaragua and many other small dependent nations demands a high degree of flexibility and above all the creative capacity to penetrate and absorb the demands of the grassroots of the various social forces so that these same social forces put themselves increasingly under the leadership of the vanguard. The most serious problem of the imperialist aggression for the vanguard is the temptation to blame all the problems and even its own errors on "the imperialist enemy and its lackeys." In the final analysis, the possibility of institutionalizing popular participation in the midst of a war depends above all on the humility of the vanguard, and on its capacity for self-criticism, for recognizing errors, for asking forgiveness of the people, and for returning to the masses over and over again to relearn the lesson of socialism.

The possibility of effective intervention by a vanguard, of correct guidance in the midst of contradictions, and of a just policy that comes from the real historical movement depends on that vanguard's capacity for self-criticism and the popular organizations' capacity for criticizing

318 Peter E. Marchetti, S.J.

the vanguard. Self-criticism by the vanguard in regard to its limitations is the real base from which Lenin's ideal—that the party take on the role of its own opposition—can be realized. Here also lies the potential for the mass organizations to constitute a center of participation and power complementary to that of the state.

One of the great limitations on the vanguard in its task of guiding the state structures in the transition period is the fact that a large percentage of the new cadres is recruited from the ranks of state functionaries. That is, the party in control of the state is narcissistically nourished by the state itself. These bureaucratic origins mark the party with a great deal of fear about taking risks and of making changes. The question posed by Cienfuegos, Pereira, and other leaders of the Cuban revolution with regard to this problem is the following: Why do we generate so many cadres who always want to be in the center of the table where there is no possibility of either making a mistake or of advancing the revolution?

It is possible that the overproduction of cadres who prefer the security of the center of the table comes not only from an overidentification of the party with the state apparatus, but also from a theoretical deficiency of Marxism that has had repercussions in the theory of vanguardism. We are referring to the *Marxist concept of human beings as essentially free from limitations.* In a famous passage of his manuscript on communism, Marx admits that he cannot prove his proposition (that humans are essentially unlimited) but also adds that the opposite position cannot be proved either. Marx chose to suppress the concern over the limitations of the human race (the question of sin and God) in order to save time in the theoretical-practical task of liberation from capitalist structures. It was a practical, not a theoretical, choice. This idea of human beings without limitations is sometimes translated in the theory of vanguardism into the position that the vanguard cannot err in the movement toward socialism. From here, revolutionary voluntarism is stained with the image of the political cadre who has no limitations and, above all, does not make fundamental errors.

It is easy to see why people prefer to be close to the center of the revolutionary table; that is, better to wait than to take the risk of failure, because the vanguard is the correct line of historical development which will be implemented sooner or later. I want to propose the need to open a debate and a profound discussion on the *tactical utility* of the idea of human beings without limitations, because it blocks the development of revolutionary criticism, which is the source of potential increase in popular participation during the transition period. Marx's idea of saving time with his epistemological decision has resulted in a delay of perhaps decades in finding new formulas of transition with high levels of mass participation.

It is obvious that in all revolutionary processes the war of aggression lowers the vanguard's capacity for self-criticism. Nicaragua is no exception. In war, the fundamental psychological impulse is to blame the enemy and cover up one's own mistakes. Intense ideological energy is needed to overcome this problem.

The State and Popular Participation

The economic conditions and political traditions existing in countries subject to imperialism are not only incapable of eliminating the deeply rooted economic underdevelopment and political dependence, but represent a force capable of corrupting and deflecting the initiatives of progressive forces. This is why we must insist that the transition to socialism always be closely tied to the creation of a strong revolutionary state. Bahro has pointed to this in discussing the possibility of transformation in conditions of underdevelopment:

> The only alternative here is a bureaucracy, civilian or military, whose members are corruptible chiefly through their power over the process of transformation itself. The discipline of obedience to instructions, which can only be made effective with a despotism of some kind or other, is the surest guarantee that the progressive interests will carry the day, in the actions of individual officials who are personally rooted in the old structures by a thousand threads. Party centres such as Lenin and Mao Tse-tung [who] were able to forge for their future bureaucracies, are up till now still unparalleled prototypes of a discipline not rooted only in terror, and which therefore proves extraordinarily fruitful. (1978:130)

Change is simply not going to be pleasant, and some level of state coercion will always be necessary, even in the new vanguard model being developed in small countries such as Nicaragua.

In the transition period itself two fundamental dichotomies exist. The first, which everyone acknowledges, is between capital and labor. The second, which must be acknowledged for any objective analysis of the institutionalization of participation, can be expressed this way: "People and functionaries—this is the unavoidable dichotomy of every proto-socialist society. It is the most important 'contradiction' among the people" (ibid.: 241–42). Bahro's message, in summary, is the inevitability that to one degree or another, the transformation project occurs against the will of the people. This is where we find, beyond all moralisms, the material base of bureaucratic deformations. Lenin expressed this problem with much realism, accepting Bukharin's criticism that the worker-peasant state was really a worker-peasant conflict: "In the first place, our state is not really a workers' state, but a workers' and peasants' state. And from this follow many things. . . . It is evident from our Party programme . . . that our state is a workers' state with bureaucratic distortions" (1937:9).

In the small countries subject to imperialism in our region, where the third force and not the industrial proletariat has played a key role in the insurrection and is the force that will manipulate the gears of state power in the initial moments of transition, it is even more essential to recognize the class character of the state. The consciousness that progressive forces are seeking a social formation which will support their revolutionary ideal must have as a coaxiom an increased concern over the correlation of forces between cadres of the petty bourgeoisie and of the worker-peasant alliance in the state apparatus.

Given the inevitability of bureaucratic growth during the transition, debate should not center on anarchic vs. statist conceptions, but rather about how to defend the vitality of the popular movement against bureaucratic deformation and how to control the state. The two traditional positions in this debate were those of Trotsky and Lenin. Trotsky maintained that the masses did not need unions and mass organizations to defend themselves against the state after the triumph, since the state was a workers' state. Lenin, on the other hand, argued that unions were an essential weapon so that the masses could defend themselves from the state, precisely to continue being the material base of that state.

The problem today is really how to implement Lenin's position, the failure to do so having produced the well-known relationship between the state and the party. The solution to bureaucratic deformations of state power and corruption has been *"to construct an additional bureaucracy over and above the state apparatus in the form of the party apparatus"* (Bahro 1978:243; emphasis in original). The politbureau is, in fact, the group that grows out of the need to coordinate the military effort and the state in time of tension and war.

The historical problem in terms of participation is that this apparatus and its function of control have been placed above the state, but are still connected to the sphere of the state. The debate today should focus on the advantages and disadvantages of placing that control function of the bureaucracy in the hands of party cadres whose full-time work is educating and forming mass organizations. The control of the state should come from below and not from above. The advantages of this solution are obvious in terms of popular participation. But there are the disadvantages that this new power (this people's-bureau) will probably have an impact on the quality of the party cadres in the state. The disadvantage is, in the final analysis, the problem of two centers of power.[6]

The bureaucratic apparatus will always resist political control from above or from below with all the complex strength of passive aggression, that is, with the weapon of laziness. Bureaucratic laziness, as a moral characteristic, has a socioeconomic base and comes from the reciprocal effect of the abandonment of coercion proper to capitalist society on the one hand, and, on the other, the dissipation of personal initiative in the general bureaucratic cohesion of a socialist society in development. As Bahro says, "It is no accident that the officials have the ironic motto: 'Everything works by itself' " (1978:235). Another disadvantage is that when the party apparatus is placed above the state, the administrative structures of the state tend to become a screen between the political power of the party and the popular masses. As Bettleheim points out:

> Due to this [screen], from the moment that the bases of the party are blocked from direct access to leadership, the leaders are not well aware of what is really happening in the country, in particular what is happening in the rural areas nor, of course, what is happening right within the state apparatus. (1975a)

How has the Sandinista revolution confronted these old dilemmas of state power and popular participation in the transition to socialism? And how has the dynamic of the war affected the outcome of those dilemmas?

In Nicaragua there is a saying among party members who realistically recognize the problem of power: "The logic of power is terrible." This realism has meant that revolutionary leaders have sought to limit the abuses of power, with traditional forms of bourgeois democracy as well as with new experiments in the executive branch and with popular power.

In both spheres the war has played a crucial role. The fact that the Nicaraguan transition is taking place within the U.S. sphere of influence at a moment of heightened U.S. international aggressiveness has meant that the Nicaraguan revolution has had to seek significant international diplomatic and economic support in Western Europe and key capitalist nations in Latin America. The incorporation of national elections within the transition to socialism was not only a promise made by the Sandinistas to their people in 1979 but an absolutely essential ingredient for obtaining that international support. Similarly, the desire of the Sandinistas for a nonaligned international position is at once an authentic and unchangeable patriotic stance as well as the only realistic position given the military context in which the revolution has had to develop.

Within the executive branch, the nonexistence of a revolutionary party at the time power was taken and its relative weakness even after five years of revolutionary process have allowed new models of administration and popular participation to develop. The style of collective and democratic leadership within the vanguard (nine commandantes), the lack of clarity as to which of the social forces is really the leading force, and the nature of the alliance with the private sector have resulted in the vitality of three fundamental political forces: the state, the party, and the mass organizations. The massive nature of the popular insurrection in Nicaragua is another factor that explains the effective separation between those three political forces.

Perhaps the mere *formality* of the separation and the balance of powers in bourgeois democracy (judicial, legislative, and executive branches) is what explains to some degree the failure of the parliamentary model in regard to popular participation. In Sandinista practice in Nicaragua, not only does the threefold division of powers exist, but there also exists *an effective division within the executive branch*— between the state, the party, and the mass organizations. Perhaps this division will end up being a more effective guarantee for the limitation of state power than the more formal guarantees of bourgeois democracy. The uniqueness of the experience of transition in Nicaragua before the war created a new dynamic which was the participatory space created by the tensions between these three political forces. As the Instituto Histórico Centroamericano (IHCA 1984) has argued in a detailed and chronological fashion, the impact of the war of aggression has meant a gradual weakening of the popular organizations in comparison with the growth of state power and party organization, particularly in the military sphere.

The mass organizations in Nicaragua have always had a *double character.* On the one hand, the political activists of the vanguard used the popular organizations as "seed beds" for combatants in the struggle against Somoza and later for political cadres in the state and the army. On the other hand, the popular organizations were born of and became powerful through the political activity of oppressed social forces concerned with solutions for their immediate needs. The defense of one's country is always the most immediate need and with the growing weight of the war the equilibrium of the mass organizations' dual character shifted heavily in favor of the "seed bed of the vanguard" concept.

We would also argue that the party organization has become increasingly identified with the state as the war has forced Nicaragua to integrate much of the state's efforts around the work of the Ministry of Defense. Thus, the power of Sandinistas' people's-bureau has suffered as a result of U.S. military aggression. This does not mean, however, that the Sandinista revolution has fallen into the scheme of a one-party state. As the war has progressed, an increasing number of the more experienced militants have been dedicated full time to the defense effort while the state is increasingly in the hands of those with less experience as Sandinistas. Thus, even though the tension between party and state has lessened it is still strong enough that many expect that the new legislative forum produced by the 1984 elections will be a stage for the public expression of that tension.

Another cause for the decline in the power and participation of the popular organizations and the slowdown of mass mobilization in the civil and economic sphere has been the need to maintain the alliance with the private sector vis-à-vis foreign aggression. The FSLN has had to limit the mobilization of workers and peasants in order to preserve that alliance. In the final analysis, however, it is the war and the inability of the FSLN to maintain a rhythm of reproduction of sufficient new cadres to attend to the needs of both civilian and military mobilization that explain the shift in the constellation of political forces today in Nicaragua. The rate of reproduction of political activists is at the heart of the participation issue because without real popular participation you can't develop new activists and without activists it is extremely difficult to expand real participation.

Revolutionary Alliances, War, and New Styles of Vanguard Leadership

In examining the first two problems of participation, we have tried to indicate the way in which the peculiar class structure of the small nations in capitalism's periphery and the military dialectic between socialist revolution and imperialist reaction act as twin midwives assisting the appearance of new styles of vanguard leadership and of new strategies in the transition to socialism. This becomes all the more clear if we turn our attention to the question of transition and revolutionary alliances.

In small peripheral countries there is no clear leading force and no potential for a single center of organizational power in the transition. This context either leads to futile attempts by the vanguard to use the old model of dictatorship of the proletariat and to its subsequent loss of popular support (as has happened in many African countries) or to the vision of the revolution as a series of alliances with the varied social, cultural, and ideological forces at work in the revolutionary society. The *sine qua non* for this system of alliances and the participation of the varied nonproletarian forces is a strong revolutionary army and a vanguard leadership capable of using the subjective factor in ideological struggle to mobilize the soul of the people.

The Nicaraguan revolution exploded in the urban sector due to the hyperurbanization of the Somocista model of development (CIERA 1984b), and the youthful third revolutionary force played a key role not only in the insurrection but in government programs after the fall of the dictatorship. Although the Sandinista revolution is urban based, it has had to advance through five key revolutionary alliances: (a) with the indigenous populations of the Atlantic coast; (b) with the peasantry; (c) with the churches; (d) with women; and (e) with the private sector.

It is indeed interesting that the fury of the imperialist, military, and

324   Peter E. Marchetti, S.J.

ideological aggression against the Sandinista revolution has in fact been
focused on these five revolutionary alliances. The U.S. administration,
if it can not destabilize the new Nicaraguan government, at minimum is
prepared to ensure that these revolutionary alliances be broken and
that the new type of socialism and vanguard leadership style developing
in Nicaragua be thwarted.

The Alliance with the Indigenous Peoples

The earliest efforts of the U.S. administration in armed counterrevolutionary activity took place among the Miskito indigenous population in northern Zelaya province. This military intervention only
intensified the difficulties faced by any country in solving what is called
"the national question"; indeed, it can be argued that it was contra
support that put this question on the agenda. War and the forced
relocation of thousands of Miskitos seriously weakened the potential
for a revolutionary alliance with indigenous peoples of the Atlantic
coast. Throughout the period 1982–84, the revolution continued to try
to recoup this lost potential through its policies of humane prisons,
massive pardons, and amnesty for those who had been swayed by
imperialist propaganda—some even taking up arms. In late 1984,
through increased activism at the grassroots of the Miskito, Rama, and
Suma communities, and increased stress on the subjective factor and on
the desires of the peoples and their religious representatives for
autonomy, the revolution developed its project for the autonomy of
the peoples of the Atlantic coast, which during 1985 began to restore
the alliance with the indigenous peoples.

During 1985, the Sandinistas entered into negotiations with armed
bands of Miskitos at the local level. In many areas there were as many as
ten meetings. As a result of these meetings, called *Rondas,* the
Sandinistas sent doctors, food, and medical supplies to the Miskito
guerrillas as a way of arriving at a local ceasefire agreement. The
Miskito military leaders responded positively, since they themselves
and their social base were experiencing much hunger and shortages of
medicine. At the beginning, the Sandinista military were taking food
upstream to their Miskito enemies. The main contra force, the National
Democratic Front (FDN), lacking the Miskitos' close ties to the civilian
population, not only would not accept such negotiations but began
attacking the Sandinista boats. At the next *Ronda* the Sandinistas
demanded that the Miskito leaders come to the cities unarmed to get
supplies for their people. The Miskitos accepted. The type of negotiations between the Sandinistas and the grassroots of the Miskito movement were on bread-and-butter issues and the ceasefire agreements
allow hope for not only a satisfactory but a highly creative solution to
the national question. The imperialist aggression weakened the alliance, but in a very real sense it was the challenge of the same war that

obliged the vanguard to take bolder and more creative steps to solve the problems of the Atlantic region.

The Alliance with the Peasantry

From March 1983 to the present, the contra war has been centered in the mountainous interior of Nicaragua that stretches from the Honduran border in the north all the way to Costa Rica. The 1980 report of the Rome-based International Fund for Agricultural Development indicated the immense efforts of the Sandinista agrarian program to benefit the peasantry through a new credit policy, control of land rents, and restriction of commercial usury through 1979 and 1980. Even without land reform (which was forestalled to solidify the alliance with the private sector), the peasantry responded positively to the new government and the cooperative movement expanded rapidly, especially in the interior mountainous region. Nevertheless, the Rome report warned that without land reform and increased support of the poor peasantry the worker-peasant alliance was in danger of slipping into an alliance between petty bourgeois producers and the urban middle strata.

The very history of the country's underdevelopment made it much more difficult to create an alliance with the peasantry in the interior mountains. The few Sandinista cadres who knew the mountains were lost in the sea of urban combatants who were rather prejudiced against "backward peasantry."[7] The peasants in the mountains wanted individual land parcels, and the urban militants wanted production coops with modern and collective administrative arrangements. The result was that most of the actual land transfers to peasants took place in the Pacific region and not in the interior regions or along the agricultural frontier. Moreover, long-term investment projects in agriculture were centered in the state sector and the allocation of scarce foreign currency favored the urban areas and the modernized agricultural sector, be it state or private. The weakening of the worker-peasant alliance in economic terms allowed the counterrevolution to gain a certain amount of passive support from the peasantry. Moreover, the war in the mountains seriously accentuated the shortages of the type of inputs and consumer goods needed by the peasantry. Above all, the shortage of militants capable of understanding "the ideological world of the peasantry" limited the levels of popular participation in local peasant communities. Since the local community is the only point of political reference for the peasantry, the alliance was seriously weakened. Although the profound contradiction between city and countryside, a product of the country's historical development, has been intensified by the war, it is the challenge of the war itself that now forces the resolution of that contradiction. In 1985 the revolution began giving priority to individual land distribution and to allocating foreign currency for obtaining peasant inputs and consumer goods. More and more of the country's highly qualified militants were being assigned to the political and ideological struggle in the countryside.

The Alliance with the Churches

Despite the revolution's unique openness to the religious sector and the high level of religious freedom permitted both within the society and within the vanguard, the inevitable tensions between church and state have been as prominent in the international press as have the tensions with the indigenous populations. Moreover, the weakness of the alliance with the churches has had primarily an ideological impact on the national population, creating confusion, particularly among the peasantry. Even though the majority of clerics are favorable to the revolution, the symbolic impact of certain conservative religious leaders has been enormous. The proimperialist forces and even the U.S. Pentagon by its own admission consider this sphere of the struggle against the Sandinista revolution to be crucial. The lack of support of these conservative religious figures for national defense has created problems for the revolution among some sectors of the populace, who resist the national draft.

The response of the revolution to this type of imperialist intervention in national affairs has been twofold. First, the vanguard has gone out of its way to control public expression of the ideological perspective on religion of its nontheist members without restricting their personal liberties in any way. This has allowed the vanguard to gain much political support through more tactful handling of church-state tensions. For example, the government in its initial reporting on Miguel Obando y Bravo's first mass as Cardinal in Miami with the leaders of the counterrevolution refrained from editorial comments, simply laying out the facts. This sophisticated treatment successfully exposed the imperialist tactic, avoided making Obando a victim of yet another government attack, and won increased support for the revolution on the part of liberal church leaders and other believers who had been doubtful about the Cardinal's political stance. In addition, the identification of conservative church ideology with gruesome acts of counter-revolutionary terrorism is beginning to turn the population against the overpoliticization of church authority.

The Alliance with Women

The overall impact of the Reagan administration's low-intensity war of attrition falls most heavily on the women of Nicaragua, because it is they who suffer most from economic restrictions and from the costs of the war on their husbands and sons. Here the ideological struggle has been particularly intense. The importance given to Nicaraguan women in the war propaganda, the high visibility of women in key leadership posts within the revolution, and several laws that have benefited urban women in particular have been able to fend off the combined religious, economic, and military ideology of conservative forces in the new Nicaragua. It is nevertheless true, as Molyneux points out at length in this volume, that much more needs to be done in solidifying the revolutionary alliance with women.

The Alliance with the Private Sector

Surprisingly, the alliance that has been least affected by the war of aggression has been that with the private sector. When the popular movement controls the armed forces, the alliance with sectors of the bourgeoisie, if correctly handled, can organize their participation in the revolution in ways that prove beneficial to the poor majorities. In a sense, it is a matter of imitating in an inverse fashion the traditional strategy of the entrepreneurial classes: keep the workers and peasants alive enough to advance the interest of capitalist growth. In Nicaragua, popular control over finances and international trade has reduced the agroexporting bourgeoisie to a "merely administrative bourgeoisie." In short, a very low level of capitalist reproduction has been permitted in order to profit from the entrepreneurial, technical, and administrative capacity of the old dominant classes. The richest of Nicaragua's entrepreneurial class have accepted the cut in their profit margins as long as the revolution offers half of the pie to them. The financial security of this very reduced number of capitalists gives them a greater ability to resist the lures of the counterrevolutionary political line of disinvestment. Many of the next echelon of entrepreneurs (less than 3 percent of the whole class) have quit producing, left the country, and/or support the counterrevolution. The vast majority of the entrepreneurial class (the so-called *chapiolla* bourgeoisie) had been excluded from participation in the Somoza development model and have accepted the alliance with the Sandinista revolution.

In the country's mountainous interior regions, the vanguard correctly analyzed the high levels of dependence of workers and poor peasants upon this *chapiolla* bourgeoisie that produces much of Nicaragua's coffee, cattle, and dairy products. The relative poverty of these small entrepreneurs and their closeness to their workers gives their paternalism real vitality, especially in the agrarian frontier areas. When the revolution captures the support of this back-country entrepreneurial group, they also gain the support of their workers and the poor peasants who work the land of this group. In line with this analysis, more representation and participation was given to the petty bourgeois and rich peasants in UNAG (National Union of Farmers and Cattlemen) without excluding middle and poor peasants. The success of this alliance with the private sector can be evaluated in terms of continuously expanding agricultural output between 1980 and 1983 (a first in a revolutionary context), by the inability of the counterrevolutionaries to interrupt the coffee harvest of 1984, by the negative response of entrepreneurs to the contra efforts to interrupt the flow of milk and cheese to the cities, and by the inability of the contra to occupy even a small rural city during the past five years.

The war has affected this class and this alliance basically through the shortage of labor resources, due to the numbers of young workers and peasants involved in combat. Moreover, the alliance has been weakened most through lack of attention to maintaining the equilibrium of certain macroeconomic mechanisms that have traditionally tied the city and the countryside to each other. The attempt of the revolution to control rural commercial profits through its state distribution enterprises ENABAS (agricultural goods) and MICOIN (industrial goods) was successful in the first moment at eliminating the power of the rural merchant but did not succeed in replacing the role played by private enterprise in the countryside. The merchant was the fluid that oiled the exchange of agricultural goods for the basic industrial goods needed by peasants. That exchange is the material base not only of the worker-peasant alliance but also of the alliance with the private entrepreneurial sector in the countryside. Moreover, an imbalance favoring allocation of foreign currency to intensive capital investment rather than to extensive, simple technology-based development not only affected the peasantry adversely but also weakened the revolution's alliance with the back-country entrepreneurs. Throughout late 1984 and 1985, the revolution attempted to reestablish formal private commerce and recover a proper balance in its investment scheme. That readjustment as well as the other readjustments in all five alliances has flowed primarily out the revolution's primary concern for defense against U.S. military aggression.

Conclusion: The Importance of Macro Processes and the Struggle for the Soul of the Masses

In these reflections on socialist democracy I have tried to underline how the class structure of small countries on the capitalist periphery and the struggle against the imperialist war of aggression combine to produce new styles of vanguard leadership and new strategies in the transition to socialism. I have argued that the old models of the industrial proletariat as the leading force and the vanguard as the political representative of the dictatorship of the proletariat are not valid in transition to socialism in small nations on the periphery. The periphery is characterized by a revolution of *combined social forces* in which the vanguard must play the difficult role of structuring the revolution as a series of alliances with these varied social and ideological forces. The vision of revolution as a series of alliances goes hand in hand with a style of vanguard leadership rooted in *hegemonic alliances* (the third problem) rather than in "dictatorial control over the nonproletarian forces." In this developing strategy of transition in the periphery, there really is no leading force (the first problem) and no single center of organizational power (the second problem).

In the new style of transition the subjective factor must play a much more prominent role. The older ideology of the industrial proletariat as the secure, positivistic, and material base of the transition must give way to increasingly sophisticated ideological struggle aimed at increasing popular participation of all the different social forces within the construction of the new society and in the fashioning of the proletarian project through human creativity. Success in the military struggle against foreign aggression is the *sine qua non* of the new hegemonic style of leadership. Thus a central conviction of these reflections is that an analysis of popular participation in socialist transition should begin at the military crossroads. Other points of departure run the double risk of idealizing and/or moralizing to nations that suffer from extended foreign military aggression and economic boycotts.

During the first five years of the Sandinista revolution, the judicial forms of socialist production have not been made into any kind of fetish. The alliance with the national bourgeoisie was controlled through mechanisms operating in the spheres of finance and international commerce. I regard the attention given to the macrodynamic of the foreign sector over all other forms of production (whether capitalist or socialist) as a highly creative contribution to the strategy of transition. On the other hand, I view the management of the macroeconomic dynamics of urban-rural exchange and the balance between intensive and extensive investment strategies as a major weakness affecting the process of popular participation in the new Nicaragua.[8] These macroeconomic dynamics condition the quality of direction of the vanguard, the success of alliances, and the development of the class struggle during the transition more than the imposition of socialist forms of production or the maintenance of certain private production forms within the revolution. If we get stuck on the question of what is "the correct form of production" or of "what type of cooperative is more socialist" and forget about the macroeconomic mechanisms, the popular participation needed to advance the transition will be lost.

The development of popular participation depends to a large extent on the subjective, moral, and ideological quality of the members of the vanguard. Popular mobilization demands above all political cadres capable of striking up friendships with the workers, peasants, and workers in the tertiary sector, capable of understanding the ideological world of the masses and launching processes of political conversion among them. In short, it is necessary to win the soul of the masses, particularly in times of economic crisis and during a war of attrition. It is as necessary to concentrate on the subjective and moral behavior of the representatives of the revolution as it is to control the macroeconomic dynamics.

Frequently, the socialization of the means of production is conceived as a necessary step in order to forge the new revolutionary morality. What I have argued here is that the effective socialization, control, and administration of the means of production by workers (the second step toward socialism) will be more the product of the moral and subjective commitment of party members and their agile control of macroeconomic mechanisms than the cause of that commitment and sophistication.

Notes

This article is a reformulation of a series of reflections for a Latin American debate organized by United Nations Research in Social Development (UNRISD).

1. For a typical example of bourgeois thought on participation see Dahl (1967). For a summarized introduction to power elite theory see Mills (1967).
2. That is, private property continues to exist with regard to the real appropriation of surplus value, although it has disappeared in judicial terms.
3. Other contributions to this volume explain in depth the compatibility of elections within the process of popular participation and transition to socialism.
4. In spite of its level of abstraction, the most synthetic description of the leadership role of the vanguard that I know is by Bettleheim: "The most that the vanguard can accomplish is an effective intervention in the historical movement through its leadership role." An effective intervention is a "correct orientation amidst the contradictions that helps the popular classes act upon those contradictions through a correct political line, a line that is based on the real movement of masses and takes into account their potentialities" (Bettelheim 1976).
5. Some participants in the UNRISD debate have indicated that the myth of the need for proletarian leadership is one of the most serious obstacles to popular participation in third world transitional states.
6. The possibility of a people's bureau will mean that the party allows a certain tension among cadres in the state and cadres in mass organizations.
7. For an analysis of the urban phenomenon, its connection with Nicaragua's agricultural model, and historical roots of the judgment about the peasantry's backwardness, see CIERA (1984b).
8. For a more thorough analysis of the impact of intensive vs. extensive investment strategies on the size of the domestic market and on the possibilities of national accumulation, see Marchetti (1984).

▼Bibliography▲

Abate, Alula, and Tesfayi Teklu. 1982. "Land Reform and Peasant Associations in Ethiopia: A Case of Study of Two Widely Differing Regions." In Amit Bhaduri and M. A. Rahman, eds., *Studies in Rural Participation.* New Delhi: Oxford Publication Co.

Albert, Michael, and Albert Hanhel. 1981. *Socialism Today and Tomorrow.* Boston: South End Press.

Amaro, Nelson, and Carmelo Mesa-Lago. 1971. "Inequality and Classes." In Carmelo Mesa Lago, ed., *Revolutionary Change in Cuba.* Pittsburgh: University of Pittsburgh Press.

Amin, Samir. 1977. "Self-Reliance and the New Economic Order," *Monthly Review* 29, no. 3.

———. 1976. *Unequal Development.* New York: Monthly Review Press.

———. 1974. "Accumulation and Development: A Theoretical Model," *Review of African Political Economy* 1.

——— et al. 1982. *Dynamics of Global Crisis.* New York: Monthly Review Press.

Angola, Government of. *Textes et Legendes, Services Officels Anglois.* Paris: n.d.

Aricó, José. 1980. *Marx y America Latina.* Mexico: Alianza Editorial Mexicana.

Bahro, Rudolph. 1978. *The Alternative in Eastern Europe.* London: New Left Books.

Balta, Paul, and Claudine Rulleau. 1978. *La Strategie de Baumediene.* Paris: Sinbad.

Baron, S. H. 1963. *Plekhanov.* Stanford, CA: Stanford University Press.

Barker, Jonathan. 1979. "The Debate of Rural Socialism in Tanzania." In B. U. Mwansasu and C. Pratt, *Toward Socialism in Tanzania.* Toronto: University of Toronto Press.

Baumeister, Eduardo. 1984a. "Estructura y Reforma Agraria en el Proceso Sandinista," *Desarrollo Economico* 24, no. 94.

———. 1984b. "La Significación de los Medianos Productores en el Agro Nicaraguense." Paper presented to the Seminar on "Medium-sized Producers in Latin America," FAO and the Center for Latin American Studies, Cambridge, MA.

———. 1982. "Notas para la Discusion de la Cuestion Agraria en Nicaragua," III Congress of the Nicaraguan Association of Social Scientists (ANICS).

Bekele, Dawit. 1982. "Peasant Associations and Agrarian Reform in Ethiopia," *IDS Bulletin* 3, no. 4.

Benjamin, Medea, Joseph Collins, and Michael Scott. 1984. *No Free Lunch: Food and Revolution in Cuba Today.* San Francisco: Institute for Food and Development Policy.

Benton Edward. 1982. "Realism, Power and Objective Interests." In Keith Graham, ed. *New Perspectives in Political Philosophy.* Cambridge: University Press.

Bettelheim, Charles. 1978. *Class Struggles in the USSR: Second Period: 1923–1930.* New York: Monthly Review Press.

———. 1976. *Class Struggles in the USSR: First Period: 1917–1923.* New York: Monthly Review Press.

———. 1975a. *Economic Calculation and Forms of Property.* New York: Monthly Review Press.

———. 1975b. *The Transition to Socialist Economy.* Hassocks: Harvester.

Bhaduri, Amit, and M. Rahman. 1982. "Agricultural Cooperatives and Peasant Participation in the Socialist Republic of Vietnam." In Amit Bhaduri and M. A. Rahman, eds., *Studies in Rural Participation.* New Delhi: Oxford Publication Co.

Bitar, Sergio. 1979. *Transición, socialismo y democracia. La experiencia chilena.* Mexico: Siglo XXI.

Blackstock, Paul W., and B. F. Hoselitz. 1952. *The Russian Menace to Europe—by Karl Marx and F. Engels.* Glencoe, IL: Free Press.

Blair, Thomas L. 1969. *Land to Those Who Till It.* New York: Doubleday.

Blasier, Cole. 1971. "The Elimination of the United States Influence." In Carmelo Mesa-Lago, ed., *Revolutionary Change in Cuba.* Pittsburgh: University of Pittsburgh Press.

Bogomolov, O. 1983. *Socialist Countries in the International Division of Labor.* Moscow: Progress Publishers.

Boorstein, Edward. 1968. *The Economic Transformation of Cuba: A First-Hand Account.* New York: Monthly Review Press.

Braun, O. 1975. *Imperialismo y Comercio Internacional.* Buenos Aires: Siglo XXI.

Brundenius, Claes. 1984a. "Estructura y Reforma Agraria en el Proceso Sandinista," *Desarrollo Economico* 24.

———. 1984b. "La Significacion de los Medianos Productores en el Agro Nicaraguense." Paper presented to the Seminar on "Medium-sized Producers in Latin America," FAO and Latin American Studies, Cambridge, MA.

———. 1983. *Revolutionary Cuba: The Challenge of Economic Growth with Equity.* Boulder: Westview Press.

Bukharin, Nikolai. 1979. *The Politics and Economics of the Transition Period.* London: Routledge and Kegan Paul.

Burbach, Roger, and Patricia Flynn, eds. 1984. *The Politics of Intervention: The United States in Central America.* New York: Monthly Review Press.

Caballero, José María. 1984. "Unequal Pricing and Unequal Exchange between the Peasant and Capitalist Economies," *Cambridge Journal of Economics* 8, no. 4.

Cabral, Amilcar. 1978. *Unity and Struggle: Speeches and Writings of Amilcar Cabral.* New York: Monthly Review Press.

———. 1969. "The Weapon of Theory." In *Revolution in Guinea.* New York: Monthy Review Press.

Carr, E. H. 1972. *The Bolshevik Revolution 1917–1923,* Vol. II. London Macmillan.

Carciofi, R. 1983. "Cuba in the Seventies." In Gordon White et al., eds., *Revolutionary Socialist Development in the Third World.* Lexington: University of Kentucky Press.

Casal, Lourdes. 1975. "On Popular Power: The Organization of the Cuban State During the Period of Transition," *Latin American Perspectives* 2, no. 4.

Castro, Fidel. 1983. *La Crisis economica y social del mundo. Sus repercusiones en los paises subdesarrollados, sus perspectivas sombrias y la necesidad de luchar si queremos vivir.* Havana: Oficina de Publicaciones del Consejo de Estada.

Centro de Estudos Africanos (CEA). 1980. *A Transformacao da Agricultura Familiar na Provincia Nampula.* Maputo: Eduardo Mondlane University.

CEPAL. 1979. *America Latina en el Umbral de los Anos 80.* Chile: CEPAL.

CIERA. 1985. *Informe Anual 1984.* Managua: CIERA.

———. 1984a. *Informe Anual 1983.* Managua: CIERA.

———. 1984b. *Managua es Nicaragua.* Managua: CIERA.

———. 1984c. *La Mujer en las Cooperativas Agropecuarias en Nicaragua.* Managua: CIERA.

———. 1982. *Mano de Obra de Algodón y Café.* Managua: CIERA.

———. 1980. *Capitalismo Agrario 1950–1979.* Managua: CIERA.

Clark, Edmund W. 1978. *Socialist Development and Public Investment in Tanzania.* Toronto: University of Toronto Press.

Cohen, John. 1984. "Agrarian Reform in Ethiopia: The Situation on the Eve of the Revolution's 10th Anniversary." Harvard Institute for International Development, Discussion Paper No. 164.

Colletti, Lucio. 1972. "Marxism: Science or Revolution?" In *From Rousseau to Lenin.* New York: Monthly Review Press.

———. 1969. "Power and Democracy in Socialist Society," *New Left Review* 56 (July/August).

Conroy, Michael. 1985. "External Dependence, External Assistance, and Economic Aggression against Nicaragua," *Latin American Perspectives* 12, no. 2.

Corragio, José Luis. 1985. *Nicaragua: Revolución y Democracia.* Mexico: Editorial Linea.

———. 1984. "Estado, politica economica y transición en Centroamerica," *Estudios Sociales Centroamericanos* (San Jose), January-April.

Corrigan, Phillip, Harvie Ramsay, and Derek Sayer. 1978. *Socialist Construction and Marxist Theory: Bolshevism and Its Critique.* New York: Monthly Review Press.

Coulson, Andrew. 1982. *Tanzania: A Political Economy.* Oxford: Clarendon Press.

Cuban Studies/Estudios Cubanos. 1979. "Cuba: The Institutionalization of the Revolution," *Cuban Studies* 6, nos. 1 & 2.

Dahl, Ronald. 1967. *Pluralist Democracy in the United States: Conflict and Consent.* Chicago: Rand.

Danaher, Kevin. 1985. *The Political Economy of U.S. Policy Towards South Africa.* Boulder: Westview Press.

Daniels, Robert. 1953. "The State and Revolution: A Case Study in the Genesis and Transformation of Communist Ideology," *The American, Slavic and East European Review* 12 (February).

Davidson, Basil. 1981. "Angola: An End and a Beginning." In David Wiley and Allan Isaacman, eds., *Southern Africa: Economy and Liberation.* East Lansing: Michigan State University Press.

Deere, Carmen Diana. 1985. "Rural Women and Agrarian Reform in Peru, Chile, and Cuba." In June Nash and Helen Safa, eds., *Women and Change in Latin America.* New York: Bergin and Garvey.

———. 1983. "Cooperative Development and Women's Participation in the Nicaraguan Agrarian Reform," *American Journal of Agricultural Economics* (December).

——— and Peter Marchetti, S. J. 1981. "The Worker-Peasant Alliance in the First Year of the Nicaraguan Agrarian Reform," *Latin American Perspectives* 8, no. 2.

———, Peter Marchetti, S. J., and Nola Reinhardt. 1985. "The Peasantry and the Development of Sandinista Agrarian Policy, 1979–1984," *Latin American Research Review* 20, no. 3.

Deighton, Jane, et al. 1983. *Sweet Ramparts: Women in Revolutionary Nicaragua.* London: War On Want.

Desfosses, Helen, and Jacques Levesque, eds. 1975. *Socialism in the Third World.* New York: Praeger.

Dévé, Frederico y Phillipe Grenier. 1984. *Precios y subsidios de los granos basicos en Nicaragua.* Managua: MIDINRA/PAN.

Díaz-Alejandro, Carlos. 1978. "Delinking North and South: Unshackled or Unhinged?" In A. Fishlow et al., *Rich and Poor Nations in the World Economy.* New York: McGraw-Hill.

Dizard, John. 1980. "Why Bankers Fear the Nicaraguan Solution," *Institutional Investor* (July).

Dobb, Maurice. 1970. *Welfare Economics and the Economics of Socialism.* Cambridge: University Press.

Draper, Hal. 1970. "The Death of the State in Marx and Engels," *Socialist Register.* London: Merlin Press.

———. 1962. "Marx and the Dictatorship of the Proletariat," *Cahiers L'Institut de Science Economique Applique: Etudes de Marxologie.* Series S, no. 6 (September).

Dunman, Jack. 1975. *Agriculture: Capitalist and Socialist.* Atlantic Highlands, NJ: Humanities Press.

Eckstein, Susan. 1981. "The Socialist Transformation of Cuban Agriculture: Domestic and International Constraints," *Social Problems* 29, no. 2.

————. 1980. "Capitalist Constraints on Cuban Socialist Development." *Comparative Politics* 12, no. 3.

Eisenstein, Zillah. 1984. *Feminism and Sexual Equality*. New York: Monthly Review Press.

————. 1979. *Capitalist Patriarchy and the Case for Socialist Feminism*. New York: Monthly Review Press.

Ellis, Frank. "Prices and the Transformation of Peasant Agriculture: The Tanzanian Case," *IDS Bulletin* 13, no. 4.

Ellman, Michael. 1979. *Socialist Planning*. Cambridge: University Press.

————. 1975. "Did the Agricultural Surplus Provide the Resources for the Increase in Investment in the USSR During the First Five Year Plan?" *The Economic Journal* 85:844–63.

————. 1973. *Planning Problems in the USSR*. Cambridge: University Press.

Engels, Friedrich. 1955. *The Peasant Question in France and Germany*. Moscow: Progress Publishers.

————. 1942. *The Origin of the Family, Private Property, and the State*. New York: International Publishers.

————. 1892. "Socialism: Utopian and Scientific." In Karl Marx and Friedrich Engels. *Selected Works*. Moscow: Progress Publishers, 1970.

Evers, Tilman. 1979. *El Estado en la periferia capitalista*. Mexico: Siglo XXI.

Fagen, Richard R. 1969. *The Transformation of Political Culture in Cuba*. Stanford: Stanford University Press.

Feinberg, Richard. 1983. *The Intemperate Zone: The Third World Challenge to U.S. Foreign Policy*. New York: W. W. Norton.

Feis, Herbert. 1965. *The Diplomacy of the Dollar*. Garden City, NY: Anchor Books.

Ferro, Marc. 1972. *The Russian Revolution of February 1917*. London: Routledge and Kegan Paul.

FitzGerald, E. V. K. 1985a. "La economía nacional en 1985. La transición como coyuntura." Paper presented to the IV Congreso Nicaraguense de Ciencias Sociales "Han Gutiérrez Ávendaño." Managua, mimeo.

————. 1985b. "Una evaluación del costo económico de la agresión del gobierno estadounidense contra el pueblo de Nicaragua." Paper presented to the Latin American Studies Association (LASA) meetings, Albuquerque, NM.

————. 1985c. "The Problem of Balance in the Peripheral Socialist Economy: A Conceptual Note," *World Development* 13, no. 1.

Fleet, Michael. 1985. *The Rise and Fall of Chilean Christian Democracy*. Princeton: Princeton University Press.

Fonseca, Carlos. 1982. *Obras*. Tomo I: *Bajo la Bandera del Sandinismo*. Managua: Editorial Nueva Nicaragua.

Forbes Magazine. 1984. "The 100 Largest U.S. Multinationals," July 2, pp. 129–33.

Gomez, Orlando. 1983. *De la Finca Individual a la Cooperativa Agropecuaria*. Havana: Editora Politica.

Gordon, Alec. 1981. "North Vietnam's Collectivization Campaigns: Class Struggle, Production, and Middle-Peasant Problem," *Journal of Contemporary Asia* 11, no. 1.

————. 1978. "The Role of Class Struggle in North Vietnam," *Monthly Review,* January.

Gramsci, Antonio. 1971. *Selections from the Prison Notebooks.* New York: International Publishers.

Griffith-Jones, Stephany. 1981. *The Role of Finance in the Transition to Socialism.* New York: Allanheld.

Guardia, Alexis. 1979. "Structural Transformations in Chile's Economy and Its System of External Economic Relations." In S. Sideri, ed., *Chile 1970– 1973: Economic Development and Its International Setting.* The Hague: Nijhoff.

Guerra, Henrique. 1979. *Angola: Estructura Economics e Classes Sociales.* Lisbon: Edicoes 70.

Guevara, Ernesto Che. 1970. *Obras 1957–1967.* Havana: Casa de las Americas.

————, E. Mandel, C. Bettelheim, et al. 1968. *La Economía Socialista: el Gran Debate.* Barcelona: Nova Terra.

Haimson, Leopold H. 1961. *The Russian Marxists and the Origins of Bolshevism.* Cambridge, MA: Harvard University Press.

Halebsky, Sandor, and John Kirk, eds. 1985. *Cuba, 25 Years of Revolution: 1959–1984.* New York: Praeger.

Halliday, Fred. 1983. "The People's Democratic Republic of Yemen: The 'Cuban Path' in Arabia." In Gordon White et al., eds., *Revolutionary Socialist Development in the Third World.* Lexington: University of Kentucky Press.

————. 1978. "Yemen's Unfinished Revolution," *MERIP* 81.

————, and Maxine Molyneux. 1982. *The Ethiopian Revolution.* London: Verso Books.

Hanlon, Joseph. 1984. *Mozambique: The Revolution Under Fire.* London: Zed Press.

Hansson, Carola, and K. Liden. 1983. *Moscow Women.* New York: Pantheon.

Harnecker, Marta. 1980. *Cuba: Dictatorship or Democracy?* Westport, CT: Lawrence Hill.

Harris, John. 1983. "Tanzania's Performance in Meeting Basic Human Needs: The International Context." Boston University African Studies Working Paper #82.

Harris, Laurence. 1980. "Agricultural Coops and Development Policy in Mozambique," *Journal of Peasant Studies* 7, no. 3.

Harris, Richard, and Carlos M. Vilas. 1985. *Nicaragua: A Revolution Under Siege.* London: Zed Press.

Havens, Eugene A. 1980. "Rural Change," Working Paper No. 3, Human Resources for Rural Development in the Syrian Arab Republic, Land Tenure Center, University of Wisconsin, Madison.

Herrera, Leticia. 1985. "Fortalecer los CDS con nuevo estilo do conduccion," *Barricada,* April 29.

Hiebert, Murray. 1984. "Contracting in Vietnam: More Rice, New Problems," *Indochina Issues,* no. 48.

Hindess, Barry. 1982. "Power, Interests and the Outcome of Struggles," *Sociology* 16, no. 4.

————, and Paul Hirst. 1975. *Precapitalist Modes of Production.* London: Routledge and Kegan Paul.

Holmquist, Frank. 1983. "Correspondent's Report: Tanzania's Retreat from Statism in the Countryside," *Africa Today* 30, no. 4.

Horvat, Branko. 1982. *The Political Economy of Socialism.* Armonk, NY: M. E. Sharpe.

Huberman, Leo, and Paul Sweezy. 1969. *Socialism in Cuba.* New York: Monthly Review Press.

Hufton, Olwen. 1971. "Women in Revolution 1789–1796," *Past and Present* 53.

Hyden, Goran. 1980. *Beyond Ujamaa in Tanzania.* Berkeley: University of California Press.

ILO. 1981. *Growth and Distribution: The Case of Mozambique.* World Employment Program, Research Working Paper. Geneva: ILO.

INDE. 1974. *Primer Congreso de la Iniciativa Privada.* Managua: Inde.

Instituto Historico Centroamerica. 1985. "The Right of the Poor: The Defense of their Unique Revolution—Five Years of the Sandinista Process." *ENVIO,* July.

Institute of Development Studies (IDS). 1982. "Agriculture, the Peasantry and Socialist Development," *Bulletin* 13, no. 4.

International Monetary Fund. 1982. *Direction of Trade Statistics, Yearbook.* Washington, DC: IMF.

Irvin, George. 1983. "Nicaragua: Establishing the State and the Center of Accumulation." *Cambridge Journal of Economics* 7, no. 2.

Isaacman, Allan. 1985. "After the Nkomati Accord," *Africa Report* (January-February).

————, and Barbara Isaacman. 1984. *Mozambique from Colonialism to Revolution, 1900–82.* Boulder: Westview Press.

Ismael, Tareq. 1982. "The People's Democratic Republic of Yemen." In Bogdan Szajkowski, ed., *Marxist Government in the Third World.* Lexington: University of Kentucky Press.

Jameson, Kenneth P., and Charles K. Wilber, eds. 1981. "Socialist Models of Development," *World Development,* 9, no. 9.

Jancar, Barbara. 1978. *Women Under Communism.* Baltimore: Johns Hopkins University Press.

Jordan, Z. A. 1967. *The Evolution of Dialetical Materialism.* London: Macmillan.

Josephs, Paul. 1981. *Cracks in the Empire.* Boston: South End Press.

Kalecki, Michal. 1976. *Essays on Developing Economies.* Hassock: Harvester Press.

————. 1972. *Essays on the Growth of Socialist and Mixed Economies.* Cambridge: University Press.

Kaplan, Irving. 1979. *Angola: A Country Study.* Washington, DC: American University.

————. 1978. *Tanzania: A Country Study.* Washington, DC: American University.

Kaplan, Temma. 1982. "Female Consciousness and Collective Action: The Case of Barcelona 1910–1918," *Signs* (Spring).

Kifle, Henock. 1983. "State Farms and the Socialist Transformation of Agriculture—A Comparative Analysis." Paper prepared for the FAO Workshop on "The Transformation of Agrarian Systems in Centrally Planned Economies of Africa." Arusha, Tanzania, October.

Klare, Michael T. 1984. *American Arms Supermarket.* Austin: University of Texas Press.

Kofi, Tetteh A. 1981. "Prospects and Problems on the Transition from Agrarianism to Socialism: The Case of Angola, Guinea-Bissau and Mozambique," *World Development* 9, nos. 9/10:851–70.

Laclau, Ernesto. 1977. "Feudalism and Capitalism in Latin America." In *Politics and Ideology in Marxist Theory.* London: New Left Books.

Ladman, Jerry, and Dale Adams. 1978. "The Rural Poor and the Recent Performance of Formal Rural Financial Markets in the Dominican Republic," *Canadian Journal of Agricultural Economics* 26, no. 1.

Larrain, Jorge. 1983. "Ideology." In Tom Bottomore, ed., *A Dictionary of Marxist Thought.* Oxford: Blackwell.

Leca, Jean. 1975. "Algerian Socialism: Nationalism, Industrialization and State Building." In Helen Defosses and Jacques Levesque, eds., *Socialism in the Third World.* New York: Praeger.

Lê Châu. 1967. *Del Feudalismo al Socialismo: La Economia de Viet-Nam del Norte.* Mexico: Siglo XXI.

Lefebvre, Henri. 1968. *Dialectical Materialism.* London: Jonathan Cape.

Legum, Colin, ed. 1984. *Africa Contemporary Record, 1982–83.* New York: Holmes and Meier.

Lenin, V. I. 1971. *Alliance of the Working Class and the Peasantry.* Moscow: Progress Publishers.

———. 1960/70. *Collected Works.* Moscow: Progress Publishers.

———. 1937. "Trade Unions and Mistakes of Trotsky." In *Selected Works.* Vol. 9. New York: International Publishers.

———. 1932. *State and Revolution.* London: International Publishers.

LeoGrande, William. 1984. *Central America and the Polls.* Washington, DC: Washington Office on Latin America.

Levine, Norman. 1982. "The Ideology of Anti-Bolshevism." *Journal of Peasant Studies* 9/10:155–85.

———. 1968. *Russian Peasants and Soviet Power.* Evanston: Northwestern University Press.

Levy, P. 1976. *Notas Geográficas y Económicas sobre la República de Nicaragua.* Managua: Banco de America.

Lichentenztejn, Samuel. 1981. "Crisis, politica economica y alternativas politicas." In *America Latina 80: Democracia y Movimiento Popular.* Lima: DESCO.

Liebman, Marcel. 1975. *Leninism Under Lenin.* London: Jonathan Cape.

The Literary Digest 42, no. 4 (January 22, 1927).

Lopez Segrera, Francisco. 1985. *Raíces Históricas de la Revolución Cubana.* Mexico: UAS Eds.

Luxemburg, Rosa. 1972. *The Russian Revolution.* Ann Arbor: University of Michigan Press.

———. 1972. "The Russian Revolution, 1918." In R. Looker, ed., *Selected Political Writings.* London: Jonathan Cape.

MacEwan, Arthur. 1981. *Revolution and Economic Development in Cuba.* London: Macmillan.

MacKinnon, Catherine. 1982. "Feminism, Marxism, Method and the State: An Agenda for Theory," *Signs* (Spring).

Maeda, J. "Peasant Organization and Participation in Tanzania." In Amit Bhaduri and M. A. Rahman, *Studies in Rural Participation.* New Delhi: Oxford Publication Co.

Mandel, Ernest. 1962. *Marxist Economic Theory.* New York: Monthly Review Press.

Marchetti, Peter, S. J. 1984. "Consumo Basico y Reforma Agraria," *Encuentro,* no. 19 (July).

———. 1975. "Worker Participation and Class Conflict." Ph.D. diss., New Haven, Yale University.

Markus, Maria. 1976. "Women and Work: Emancipation at a Dead End." In A. Hegedus, et al., eds., *The Humanism of Socialism.* London: Alison and Busby.

Martinez Allier, Juan. 1971. *Cuba: Economía y Sociedad.* Paris: Ruedo Ibérico.

Marx, Karl. 1978. "Class Struggles in France," and "Theses on Feuerbach." In Robert Tucker, ed., *The Marx-Engels Reader.* New York: W. W. Norton.

———. 1973. *Capital,* Vols. I, III. New York: International Publishers.

———. 1964. *The Communist Manifesto.* New York: Monthly Review Press.

———. 1947. *The German Ideology.* New York: International Publishers.

———. 1938. *Critique of the Gotha Programme.* New York: International Publishers.

———, and Friedrich Engels. 1942. *The Selected Correspondence of Karl Marx and Friedrich Engels.* New York: International Publishers.

———. 1940. *The Civil War in France: The Paris Commune.* New York: International Publishers.

Maxfield, Sylvia. 1982. "The Debt Trap Revisited: Nicaragua and the International Banks." Paper presented at the Mid-West Political Science Association Annual Meeting, Milwaukee.

McHenry, Dean. 1979. *Tanzania's Ujamaa Villages: The Implementation of a Rural Development Strategy.* Berkeley: University of California.

McLellan, David. 1971. *The Thought of Karl Marx.* London: Macmillan.

Mesa-Lago, Carmelo. 1981. *The Economy of Socialist Cuba: A Two-Decade Appraisal.* Albuquerque: University of New Mexico Press.

———. 1982. "The Economy: Caution, Fragility, and Resilient Ideology." In Jorge Dominguez, ed., *Cuba, Internal and International Affairs.* Beverly Hills: Sage Publications.

Meyer, Arno. 1967. *Politics and Diplomacy of Peacemaking: Containment and Counterrevolution at Versailles, 1918–1919.* New York: Alfred A. Knopf.

MIDINRA. 1984. "Informe de la Gestion Estatal de MIDINRA," *Revolucion y Desarollo,* no. 1.

———. 1982. *Marco Juridico de la Reforma Agraria Nicaraguense.* Managua: CIERA.

Miliband, Ralph. 1970a. "Lenin's 'The State and Revolution'," *The Socialist Register.* London: Merlin Press.

————. 1970b. "The State and Revolution," *Monthly Review* 21, no. 11 (April).

Millar, James. 1974. "Mass Collectivization and the Contribution of Soviet Agriculture to the First Five-Year Plan," *Slavic Review* 33, no. 4:750–66.

Mills, C. Wright. 1967. "The Structure of Power in American Society." In I. L. Horowitz, ed., *The Collected Essays of C. Wright Mills.* New York: Oxford University Press.

Mittelman, James. 1981. *Underdevelopment and the Transition to Socialism: Mozambique and Tanzania.* New York: Academic Press.

Moise, Edwin E. 1976. "Land Reform and Land Reform Errors in North Vietnam," *Pacific Affairs,* 41, no. 1.

Molyneux, Maxine. 1981. "Women's Emancipation Under Socialism: A Model for the Third World?" *World Development* 19, no. 9/10. Also in *Monthly Review* 34, no. 3 (July 1982).

Morris, Roger. 1977. *Uncertain Greatness: Henry Kissinger and American Foreign Policy.* New York: Harper & Row.

Munro, Dana Gardner. 1967. *Five Republics of Central America.* New York: Russell & Russell.

NACLA. 1973. *New Chile.* Berkeley: NACLA.

Nairn, Allan. 1984. "Endgame," *NACLA* XVIII, no. 3 (May/June).

Nairn, Tom. 1975. "The Modern Janus," *New Left Review* 94 (November-December).

National Security Council. 1975. "A Report to the National Security Council by the Executive Secretary in United States Objectives and Programs for National Security," April 14, 1950, *Naval War College Review* 27 (May-June).

Navarro, Vincent. 1985. "The Road Ahead," *Monthly Review* 37, no. 3 (July-August).

Nicaragua, Government of. 1981. *Programa económica de austeridad y eficiencia.* Managua.

————. 1980a. *Programa de Reactivación económica en beneficio del pueblo.* Managua.

————. 1980b. "Exposición de Comandante Henry Ruíz, Ministro de Planificación Nacional," mimeo issued by the Press and Publication Office.

Nkrumah, Kwame. 1957. *Ghana: The Autobiography of Kwame Nkrumah.* Edinburgh: Thomas Nelson.

Nove, Alec. 1983. *The Economics of Feasible Socialism.* London: Allen and Unwin.

————. 1982. *An Economic History of the U.S.S.R.* New York: Penguin.

Núñez Soto, Orlando. 1983. *Fuerzas clasistas de la Revolución Popular Sandinista.* Managua: SISRA.

————. 1981. "The Third Social Force in National Liberation Movements," *Latin American Perspectives* 8, no. 2 (Spring 1981).

Nuti, Domenico Mario. 1979. "The Contradictions of Socialist Economies: A Marxist Interpretation," *Socialist Register.* London: Merlin Press.

Nyerere, Julius. 1962. "One Party Rule," *Atlas* (Review of the World Press).

Nyrop, Richard, et al. 1972. *Area Handbook for the Yemens.* Washington, DC: American University.

O'Connor, James. 1970. *The Origins of Socialism in Cuba.* Ithaca: Cornell University Press.

OECD. 1985. *Geographical Distribution of Financial Flows to Developing Countries, 1980–83.* Paris: OECD.

———. 1983. *Geographical Distribution of Financial Flows to Developing Countries, 1978–81.* Paris: OECD.

———. 1973. *Geographical Distribution of Financial Flows to Developing Countries, 1971–77.* Paris: OECD.

Ortega, Marvin. 1985. "Workers' Participation in the Management of the Agro-Enterprises of the APP," *Latin American Perspectives* 12, no. 2.

Owen, Launcelot A. 1963. *The Russian Peasant Movement, 1906–1917.* Rep. ed. New York: Russell.

Over, A. M., Jr. 1983. *On the Care and Feeding of a Gift Horse.* Boston University African Studies Center Working Paper #89.

Payer, Cheryl. 1982a. *Tanzania and the World Bank.* Bergen, Norway: Christian Michelsen Institute.

———. 1982b. *The World Bank: A Critical Analysis.* New York: Monthly Review Press.

———. 1974. *The Debt Trap.* New York: Monthly Review Press.

Pearse, A. and Steifel. 1979. "Participation Popular: Un enforque de investigacion." *Socialismo y Participation,* no. 9.

Petras, James, and Morris Morley. 1975. *The United States and Chile: Imperialism and the Overthrow of the Allende Government.* New York: Monthly Review Press.

Pfeiffer, Karen. 1981a. "Algeria's Agrarian Transformation," *Merip Reports* 99:6–14.

———. 1981b. "Agrarian Reform and Development of Capitalist Agriculture in Algeria." Ph.D. diss. Washington, DC, American University.

Pierre-Charles, Gerard. 1971. *Origenes de la Revolucion Cubana.* Mexico: Siglo XXI.

Pollitt, Brian. 1982. "The Transition to Socialist Agriculture in Cuba: Some Salient Features." *IDS Bulletin* 3, no. 4:12–22.

Portes, Alejandro. 1979. "Internal and External Balance in a Centrally Planned Economy," *Journal of Comparative Economics.*

Preobrazhensky, Evgeny. 1965. *The New Economics.* Oxford: Oxford University Press (originally published in Moscow in 1926).

Rakovsy, C. 1980. "The Professional Dangers of Power" (1928). In *Selected Writings on Opposition in the USSR 1923–30.* London: Allison & Busby.

Ramirez, Sergio. 1983. *El Alba de Oro.* Mexico: Siglo XXI.

Reed, John. 1967. *Ten Days That Shook the World.* New York: International Publishers.

Rodriquez, Carlos Rafael. 1983. *Letra con Filo.* Havana: Editorial Ciencias Sociales.

———. 1967. *Cuba en Transito al Socialismo, 1959–63.* Mexico: Siglo XXI.

———. 1965. "The Cuban Revolution and the Peasantry," *World Marxist Review* 8.

Roesch, Otto. 1984. "Peasants and Collective Agriculture in Mozambique," mimeo, University of Toronto.

Rosberg, Carl G., and Thomas M. Callaghy, eds. 1979. *Socialism in Sub-Saharan Africa.* Berkeley: University of California Press.

Rowthorn, Bob. 1980. *Capitalism, Conflict and Inflation: Essays in Political Economy.* Atlantic Highlands; NJ: Humanities Press.

Rudebeck, Lars. 1979. "Socialist-Oriented Development in Guinea-Bissau." In Carl G. Rosberg and Thomas M. Callaghy, eds., *Socialism in Sub-Saharan Africa.* Berkeley: University of California Press.

Rumantsiev, A. M. 1973. *Economia Politica del Socialismo.* Moscow: Progress Publishers.

Sanders, Jerry W. 1983. *Peddlers of Crisis: The Committee on the Present Danger and the Politics of Containment.* Boston: South End Press.

Saul, John S. 1985. "Ideology in Africa: Decomposition and Recomposition." In Gwendolen M. Carter and Patrick O'Meara, eds., *African Independence: The First Twenty-five Years.* Bloomington: Indiana University Press.

———. 1984. "Development Studies for Social Change in Southern Africa," *Review* 8, no. 2 (Fall):173–96.

———, ed. 1985. *A Difficult Road: The Transition to Socialism in Mozambique.* New York: Monthly Review Press.

———. 1983. *Marxismo-Leninismo no Contexto Mocambicano.* Maputo.

Schmidt, Patrick. 1983. "Foreign Investment in Cuba: A Preliminary Analysis of Cuba's New Joint Venture Law," *Law and Policy in International Business* 15, no. 2.

Shanin, Teodor. 1972. *The Awkward Class.* New York: Oxford University Press.

———, ed. 1983. *Late Marx and the Russian Road.* New York: Monthly Review Press.

Sholk, Richard, and Sylvia Maxfield. 1985. "U.S. Financial Aggression Against Nicaragua." In Thomas Walker, ed., *Nicaragua in Revolution,* 2nd ed. New York: Praeger.

Singh, Agit. 1983. *Tanzania and the International Monetary Fund.* Cambridge: Department of Applied Economics.

Smith, Tony. 1975. "The Political and Economic Ambitions of Algeria's Land Reform," *The Middle East Journal* 29, no. 3:259–78.

Somerville, Keith. 1984. "The USSR and Southern Africa Since 1976," *Journal of Modern African Studies* 22, no. 1.

Stacey, Judith. 1983. *Patriarchy and Socialist Revolution in China.* Berkeley: University of California Press.

Stallings, Barbara. 1982. "Euromarkets, Third World Countries, and the International Political Economy." In H. Makler et al., eds., *The New International Economy.* London: Sage Publications.

———. 1978. *Class Conflict and Economic Development in Chile, 1958–1973.* Stanford: Stanford University Press.

Steedman, Ian. 1977. *Marx after Sraffa.* London: New Left Books.

———, ed. 1970. *Fundamental Issues in Trade Theory.* London: Macmillan.

Strachan, H. 1972. "The Role of the Business Group in Economic Development: The Case of Nicaragua." Ph.D. diss. Cambridge, MA, Harvard University.

Sutton, Keith. 1978. "The Progress of Algeria's Agrarian Reform and Its Settlement Implications," *The Maghreb Review* 3 (January-April):10–16.

Szajkowski, Bogdan, ed. 1981. *Marxist Governments: A World Survey*. Vol. 1. New York: St. Martin's Press.

Szentes, Tamas. 1971. *The Political Economy of Underdevelopment*. Budapest: Akademiai Kiado.

Thomas, Clive. 1974. *Socialism and Transformation: The Economics of the Transition to Socialism*. New York: Monthly Review Press.

Torres, Rosa María. 1984. *Educación y democracia en la Granada Revolucionaria*. Cuadernos de Pensamiento Propio, Serie Ensayos, No. 8, Managua: INIES.

Trotsky, Leon. 1975. *Problems of Everyday Life, and Other Writings on Culture and Science*. New York: Pathfinder Press.

Tucker, Robert C., ed. 1978. *The Marx-Engels Reader*. New York: Norton.

———. 1975. *The Lenin Anthology*. New York: Norton.

Unger, Robert Mangabiera. 1977. *Knowledge and Politics*. New York: Free Press.

U.S. Congress. 1982. Joint Economic Committee. *Cuba Faces the 1980s*. Washington, DC: GPO.

U.S. Congress. 1974. *United States and Chile During the Allende Years, 1970–73*. Hearing before the Subcommittee on Inter-American Affairs of the Foreign Affairs Committee, U.S. House of Representatives.

Urdang, Stephanie. 1984. "The Last Transition? Women and Development in Mozambique," *Review of African Political Economy* 27/28.

Valdes Paz, J. 1980. "La Pequeña Producción Agricola en Cuba," *Ciencias Sociales* 19-20:91–106.

Von Freyhold, Michaela. 1979. *Ujamaa Villages in Tanzania: Analysis of a Social Experiment*. New York: Monthly Review Press.

Vickerman, Andrew. 1982. "Collectivization in the Democratic Republic of Vietnam, 1960–66: A Comment," *Journal of Contemporary Asia* 12, no. 4.

Vilas, Carlos M. 1986. *The Sandinista Revolution*. New York: Monthly Review Press.

———. 1985. "Nicaragua año V: transformaciones y tensiones en la economía," CIDCA.

Walker, Thomas, ed. 1985. *Nicaragua in Revolution*, 2nd ed. New York: Praeger.

———. 1982. *Nicaragua: The First Five Years*. New York: Praeger.

Warren, Bill. 1980. *Imperialism: Pioneer of Capitalism*. London: New Left Books.

Weber, Max. 1947. *The Theory of Social and Economic Organization*. Glencoe, IL: Free Press.

Weinert, Richard. 1981. "Nicaragua's Debt Renegotiation," *Cambridge Journal of Economics* 5, no. 2.

Weissman, Stephen R. 1974. *American Foreign Policy in the Congo, 1960–64*. Ithaca, NY: Cornell University Press.

Wheelock, Jaime. 1984. *Entre la Crisis y la Agresión: la Reforma Agraria Sandinista*. Managua: Editorial Nueva Nicaragua.

White, Christine Pelzer. 1983. "Debates in Vietnamese Development Policy." In Gordon White et al., eds., *Revolutionary Socialist Development in the Third World*. Lexington: University of Kentucky Press.

————. 1982. "Socialist Transformation of Agriculture and Gender Relations: The Vietnamese Case," *IDS Bulletin* 13, no. 4.

————, and Elizabeth Kroll. 1985. "Agriculture in Socialist Development," *World Development* 13, no. 1.

Wiegersma, Nancy. 1983a. "Regional Differences in Socialist Transformation in Vietnam," *Economic Forum* 14 (Summer).

————. 1983b. "Women, National Liberation and Socialism in Vietnam." Paper presented at the American Social Science Association Conference, San Francisco, California.

Wiles, Peter, ed. 1982. *The New Communist Third World*. New York: St. Martin's Press.

Williams, Raymond. 1976. *Keywords*. London: Fontana/Croom Helm.

Wolf, Eric. 1969. *Peasant Wars of the Twentieth Century*. New York: Harper & Row.

Wolfers, Michael, and Jane Bergerol. 1983. *Angola in the Front Line*. London: Zed Press.

Wolpe, Harold. 1980. *The Articulation of the Modes of Production*. London: Routledge and Kegan Paul.

Woodward, Ralph. 1976. *Central America: A Nation Divided*. New York: Oxford University Press.

World Development. 1981. Special issue on "Socialism and Development," 9, nos. 9/10.

————. 1985. Special Issue on "Agriculture in Socialist Development," 13, no. 1.

Wright, Eric Olin. 1983. "Giddens' Critique of Marxism," *New Left Review* 138 (March-April).

Wuyts, Marc. 1981. "The Mechanization of Present Day Mozambican Agriculture," *Development and Change* 12, no. 1.

————. n.d. "Money in the Context of Socialist Transition: A Case Study of Mozambican Experience," unpub. ms.

Zafiris, Nicos. 1982. "The People's Republic of Mozambique: Pragmatic Socialism." In Peter Wiles, ed., *The New Communist Third World*. New York: St. Martin Press.

▼Notes on Contributors▲

Eduardo Baumeister, an Argentinian sociologist, is a researcher at CIERA in Managua and a professor at CIERA's training school. He is the author of numerous articles on the Nicaraguan agrarian reform and state agricultural policy.

Carollee Bengelsdorf is an associate professor of politics and feminist studies at Hampshire College in Massachusetts. Her work has centered on the questions of democracy and socialism in theory and practice. She has carried out extensive research on Cuba.

Roger Burbach, director of the Center for the Study of the Americas (CENSA), is co-editor (with Patricia Flynn) of *The Politics of Intervention* and *Agribusiness in the Americas*. He is currently editor of CENSA's *Strategic Reports*.

José Luis Coraggio, an Argentinian economist, is research director of the Program on "The Popular Project and Social Transition" at CRIES in Managua. He is author of *Nicaragua: Revolución y Democracia* (1985) and of numerous articles on regional planning in Latin America.

Carmen Diana Deere is an associate professor of economics at the University of Massachusetts, Amherst. She has been an adviser to the Rural Women's Research group at CIERA in Nicaragua and has written numerous articles on the Nicaraguan agrarian reform and on rural women in Latin America. She is currently a member of the Executive Council of the Latin American Studies Association.

Richard R. Fagen is a professor of political science and Gildred Professor of Latin American Studies at Stanford University. His most recent book (edited with Olga Pellicer) is *The Future of Central America: Policy Choices for the U.S. and Mexico* (1983). In 1975 he was president of the Latin American Studies Association.

E.V.K. FitzGerald is a professor of economic development, Institute of Social Studies. The Hague, Holland. Since 1979 he has served as economic adviser to the Nicaraguan government, first with the Ministry of Planning and then the Office of the Presidency. He has written extensively on the economic problems of transition.

Michael Lowy is research director of the sociological section of the French National Center for Scientific Research (CNRS) and Lecturer at the Ecole des Hautes Etudes en Sciences Sociales in Paris, France. His most recent publications include *The Politics of Uneven and Combined Development, The Theory of Permanent Revolution* (1981) and *El Marxismo en America Latina, de 1909 a nuestros dias* (1982).

Peter E. Marchetti, a Jesuit priest and sociologist, is director of research and graduate studies at the Central American University (UCA) in Managua. From 1980 to 1985 he was an adviser to CIERA and currently works with the Central American Historical Institute. He is the author of numerous articles on agrarian reform and peasant organization in Nicaragua, Chile, and the Dominican Republic.

Maxine Molyneux is a lecturer in sociology at Essex University, England. She is the author of numerous articles on women in socialism, *State Policies and the Position of Women Workers in the People's Democratic Republic of Yemen* (1981), and co-author (with Fred Halliday) of *The Ethiopian Revolution* (1982).

Oscar Neira Cuadra, a Nicaraguan economist, is coordinator of research at CIERA and a professor at CIERA's training school. He is a member of the editorial group of *Revolución y Desarollo* (MIDINRA) and writes on macro-economic development issues.

Orlando Núñez Soto is director of CIERA. A Nicaraguan political sociologist trained at the Sorbonne, he has written extensively on the social movements of the Nicaraguan revolution. He is director of the editorial group of *Revolución y Desarollo* (MIDINRA).

John S. Saul is professor of social sciences at Atkinson College, York University, Toronto. He taught at the University of Dar es Salaam, Tanzania, for seven years and, more recently, in Mozambique at the FRELIMO Party School and at the University of Eduardo Mondlane. He is the editor of *A Difficult Road: The Transition to Socialism in Mozambique* (1985) and author of *South Africa: Apartheid and After* (1986).

Barbara Stallings is associate professor and director of the Ibero-American Studies Program at the University of Wisconsin-Madison. She is the author of *Class Conflict and Economic Development in Chile, 1958–73* (1978) and a forthcoming book on international finance in Latin America.

▾Index ▴

Accumulation, in transition model, 17–18, 30, 34, 46–50
Actually existing socialism: compared with transitional societies, 18; and financing of transitional societies, 25, 67, 69, 74; global system and, 12; impact of war and imperialism on, 24; as model for transitional societies, 10, 16–17, 21–22; self-reliant development strategy and, 55; and transfer of technology, 49. *See also under specific countries*
Africa, U.S. imperialism and, 80–81. *See also* Mozambique; Tanzania
Agrarian reform during transition, 16, 97–100; in Nicaragua, 157–58, 171, 183–85, 297–98; and Russian revolution, 102–6; and worker-peasant participation, 24, 137–39. *See also* Agricultural production cooperatives; Collectivization of peasantry; Land distribution; State farms
Agricultural production cooperatives, 104–5, 113–14, 117–37, 173
Agroexport capitalism, impact on transition, 113–14, 231
Algeria, 11, 107, 108, 109, 115–16, 124–26
Angola, 82–83, 86–88, 106, 116–17, 129–30, 253
Anti-intervention movement, 90–92, 94, 96

Bilateral government loans, 59–61, 66, 68, 71, 72–73
Bourgeois democracy, 99–100, 172–73, 266–67, 276
Bourgeois ideology, 271–72
Bureaucracy, 16, 22, 24, 207–10, 267, 270–72, 274, 275, 319–23

Capital goods, 34–35, 54–55, 56
Capitalist countries, 9–10, 15; cultural dominance of, 12; division of labor inherited from, 306–7; measure of value in, 39; relationship between economics and politics in, 143; transitional societies and, 14, 15, 65, 66. *See also* Global capitalism; Imperialism
Capitalist sector in transitional societies, 19–21, 30–31, 32, 45, 47, 51, 148–50
Carter administration, 83–84, 86, 89
Catholic church, in Nicaragua, 293
Centralized planning, 10, 20–22, 24, 31, 43–46, 51, 64, 67, 180–81, 185, 221. *See also* Bureaucracy; State sector
Chile, Popular Unity government in, 11, 26, 68–69, 251, 254, 266–67, 292, 314
China, 12. *See also* Actually existing socialism
CIA, 82–83, 87, 88
Class consciousness, 216, 218

Class struggle, 225–27, 244–46; democracy and, 258–59; and economic policy, 158–60, 178, 228–30; national unity and, 23; and non-class forms of domination, 227–28; and relation of economics to politics, 156–58; war and, 306. *See also* Revolutionary alliances; State-private sector relations in Nicaragua

Collectivization of peasantry, 119–37; and inherited social structures, 172–73; and production cooperatives, 24; resistance by petty producers, 33; in Soviet Union, 105–6. *See also* Peasantry

Cuba, 11, 80; agrarian reform in, 106, 108; and Angola, 87; assumption of power and organization of new state, 252; collectivization of peasantry, 109, 111–13, 133–36; direct foreign investment in, 65; economy, compared with Nicaraguan economy, 171; external financing, 63–74; full employment in, 257–58; and global system, 11; neighborhood organizations in, 274; popular power in, 269–79; revolution, 63–64, 250, 312; role of militias in, 275; struggle against bureaucracy in, 268–70; U.S. perception of, 26; unions in, 273

Defense, in transitional model, 50–52, 57, 64, 128, 149, 288. *See also* Military mobilization; War and popular participation

Democracy, in transition model, 15, 21–23, 258–62, 264–79; and autonomous women's movements, 274–75; central planning and, 24; centrality of, 246–48; class composition of vanguard and, 22–23; and class struggle, 258–59; in Cuba, 268–70; and elections, 276; forms of agricultural production and, 24; impact of war on, 25, 275–76; and Marxist theory, 21, 224–25, 264–66; and neighborhood organizations, 274; in Nicaragua, 165, 174, 278–79, 292–93; and relationship of state to class forces, 23–24; and role of mass organizations, 272–79; and state-party relations, 266–72; and tensions between vanguard and mass, 22–23; and tribal, ethnic, religious and regional differences, 259–60; and unions, 273–74. *See also* Popular participation; War and popular participation

Democratic Party, U.S., 82, 93

Dictatorship of the proletariat, 101–3, 194–96, 202–3, 206–7, 247–48, 323–28

Distribution, 10, 36–39

Division of labor, socialism and, 34–36, 306–7, 308. *See also* International division of labor

Domestic economy, 10, 36–37

East-West conflict, 9, 80, 81, 86

Eastern Europe, 171

Economic policy: central planning and, 20–21; ideology and, 228–30, 232–48. *See also* Central planning; Economic policy in Nicaragua; Economics and politics in transition

Economic policy in Nicaragua: and absence of "social pedagogy," 158–60; and fragmentation of the state, 151–53; and lack of operating strategy, 153–55, 161–63; and limits of class struggle, 156–58; and nature of state, 155–56, 163–65; paradigm emphasizing economic recovery, 179; political costs of, 160–63

Economics and politics of transition, 17–27, 143–65, 215–17, 253–58

Economism, 175, 217–18, 314

El Salvador, 89

Elections, 22, 83, 270, 276, 279

Employment, politics and, 257–58

Engels. *See* Marxist theory

Ethiopia, 107, 109, 132–33
Exports, Export sector: accumulation
of surplus and, 43; and articulation
of different forms of production,
30, 32; central planning and, 45;
changes in, 52*n;* Cuban economy
and, 60–61, 64–65; and economics
of transition, 17–18, 55, 58, 73,
173–75; and industrialization,
34–35, 49; and land takeovers,
183–84; and politics, 253–54; pre-
and post-revolutionary, 35; and
state-private sector relations,
185–86; workers in, 36, 254–55
External finance, 12, 13, 54–77. *See
also* Foreign exchange sources

Financing. *See* External financing
Ford administration, 87, 88
Foreign credits, 47–48
Foreign debt, 63
Foreign exchange sources, 59–74. *See
also* External finance
Foreign investment, 32, 50, 61,
62–63, 65, 69, 174, 183
Foreign policy. *See* Imperialism; U.S.
foreign policy
Foreign trade, 28, 29, 40

Gender interests, 283–86, 290,
299–300
Gender issues, 23–24
Gender-related issues, 25, 227–28.
See also Women's emancipation
Ghana, 256–57
Global capitalism, 12–16, 25, 55
Grenada, 26, 266–67
Guatemala, 26, 80
Guevara, Che, 16, 52*n*–53*n,* 268,
273, 306–7, 308

Ideology in transition model, 211–32;
appropriate Marxism and, 223–24;
and politics, 231–48; of popular
sectors in Nicaragua, 159–60, 178;
as subjective factor, 309. *See also*
Marxist theory
Imperialism: and transition to

socialism, 9–10, 22, 24–27,
231–32, 243–46; and relation
between economics and politics,
147, 161–63. *See also* U.S. foreign
policy; U.S. imperialism; War and
popular participation
Imports, 29, 56
Indigenous peoples, 324–25
Industrialization, 49–50, 53*n,* 138,
186–89, 221
Inflation, 45–46, 53*n,* 152, 255–56
International division of labor in
transition model, 28, 32, 34–36, 50
International Monetary Fund (IMF),
61, 63, 67, 68, 72
Iranian revolution, 85–86

Japan, and global system, 11–12

Kissinger, Henry, 81–83, 86, 87

Labor: in export sector, 35;
productivity, 37–38, 48; supply,
and emancipation of women,
295–96; in transition model,
19–20, 36–39; in underdeveloped
capitalism, 36–37
Land distribution, 125–29, 183–84.
See also Agrarian reform
Law of value, 20, 40–41, 44, 45
Legal reform, 290–91, 296–97
Lenin, 16; on agrarian question,
101–6; on bureaucracy, 207–10; on
cultural revolution, 220; on
dictatorship of proletariat, 202–3,
206–7; on ideology, 214; on
principles of socialism, 197; and
transition debate, 31, 303–4. *See
also* Marxist theory
Literacy campaigns, 16, 33, 256
Loans. *See* Foreign exchange sources
Luxemburg, Rosa, 220, 265–66
Luxury consumption goods
production, 29–30, 38, 43, 56–57

Marx, Karl: on agrarian socialist
transformation, 98–100, 137;
concept of "productive labor," 52*n;*

on revolutionary morale, 315; and transition to socialism, 9, 16, 27*n*. *See also* Marxist theory

Marxist theory: and analysis of U.S. intervention abroad, 84; and "centralism" vs. "populism," 224–25; definitions of, 215–19; on democracy, 21, 224–25, 264–66; as ideology, 219–22; and dictatorship of the proletariat, 194–96, 203; importance of, 210–11; interpretations of, 215–19; and Lenin's concept of the state, 201–10; Stalinist, 220–22; and subjective factor in popular participation, 305–10; and transition to socialism in third world, 10, 16, 29–30, 56–59, 192–211, 222–30, 303–4; variants of, 213–15; and withering away of the state, 198–201, 203–8. *See also* Ideology and transition to socialism

Mass organizations in transition to socialism, 114–15, 127, 156, 257, 272–79, 297, 322–23

Masses, vanguard and, 22–23, 246–48

Material incentives, 37–38, 52*n*–53*n*

Mexican revolution, 80, 89

Military aggression. *See* Imperialism; U.S. foreign policy; U.S. imperialism and revolutionary societies; War and popular participation

Miskito Indians, 260, 278, 324–25

Mixed economy, 18–20, 145–46, 254. *See also* Mixed economy in Nicaragua

Mixed economy in Nicaragua, 171–89; and inherited social structures, 172–76; overpoliticization of, 175–77; paradigms shaping economic policies, 177–82; role of small and medium-sized producers, 176–77; state-private sector relations, 183–89

Money income, 255–57

Moral incentives, 37–38, 52*n*–53*n*

Mozambique, 47–48, 70; agrarian

reform in, 106, 116–17, 130–31; external financing of, 69–72; "ideological work" in, 212–13; lack of model for transition, 17

Multilateral loans, 61

National unity in Nicaragua, 23, 144, 149, 160–65

Nationalization of land, 106–9, 98–100. *See also* Agrarian reform; State sector

Natural resources, 35, 71

Neighborhood organizations, 274

Nicaragua: agrarian reform in, 106, 108, 109, 111–13, 126–29, 136; articulation of forms of production in, 19; and Carter administration, 83; central planning in, 20–21; compared with other revolutions, 286–87; creation of political party in, 312–13; democracy in, 278–79, 292–93; economy of, *see* Mixed economy of Nicaragua; foreign currency sources, 72–74; lack of model for, 17; neighborhood organizations in, 274; organization of new state in, 252–53; political decisions on wages in, 257; political pluralism in, 271; principal social force in, 310–19; private sector in, 253; relationship between economics and politics in, *see* Economics and politics in transition; relationship between third force and vanguard in, 317–18; revolutionary alliances in, 303–28; role of military forces in, 276, 316–17; third social force and, 311–19; U.S. imperialism and, 26, 80, 88–90; women in, *see* Women's emancipation; youth as third force in, 313–15

Nixon Doctrine, 85–86

North Korea, 80, 267. *See also* Korea

North Vietnam, 80, 108. *See also* Vietnam

Paris Commune, 196–98, 202, 204, 278

Peasantry: role in revolution, 226–27; role in transition to socialism, 123–24, 125, 129, 137, 172, 229, 310–19, 325–26. *See also* Collectivization of peasantry

Petty bourgeoisie, 33, 47, 242–43

Planning. *See* Centralized planning

Political pluralism, 159, 178, 261, 270, 271–72, 276, 279, 292–93

Politics of transition, 21–24, 249–62; assumption of power and organization of new state, 251–53; and defense, 252; and democracy, 258–62; and inherited political structures, 249–50; and lack of foreign exchange, 59; self-reliance and, 55. *See also* Economics and politics of transition; Ideology in transition model

Popular classes, 159–60, 218–19, 239–41

Popular militias, 275–76, 277

Popular mobilization, 33, 47, 48, 51

Popular participation, 22, 305–10. *See also* War and popular participation

Popular power, in Cuba, 269–70

Poverty, 15, 298

Prices, 34, 35–36, 39–43, 44, 58, 59, 152–53

Primitive socialist accumulation, 43, 47–48

Private bank loans, 61, 68, 74

Private sector in Nicaragua, 179–81, 293, 328–29; agrarian reform and, 99–100, 106, 108. *See also* State, in Nicaragua

Production during transition to socialism: articulation of different forms of, 18–20, 30–34, 40, 45, 47; emphasis on, 178–79; global nature of, 50; Marxist views of, 235–36, 306–7; social control over, 20–21; socially necessary labor time for, 37

Proletarianization, 237–38

Proletariat: absence of, 22, 23; and class in power after revolution, 237–41, 310; relationship with state and party, 244–46. *See also*

Dictatorship of the proletariat; Worker-peasant alliance

Raw materials, 36, 56

Reagan administration, 73, 81, 83, 84–96

Regional development banks, 61

Religious community, and U.S. foreign policy, 94, 95–96

Religious freedom, 259–60

Revolutionary alliances in Nicaragua, 323–28

Revolutionary party, democracy and, 271–72, 277–78. *See also* Vanguard

Revolution, 9; causes of, 15; democracy and, 266–67; role of peasantry in, 226–27; third force and, 311–19

Rural proletariat, in Nicaragua, 113, 126–27, 172–73, 183–84

Russian revolution, 80, 100, 102–6, 214–15, 219–22

Sanctuary movement, 94–95

Self-reliant development, 54–59

Social classes, in Nicaragua, 148–49, 173–74, 237–41

Social relationships, 307–9

Social wages, 256–57

Socialism, 10; in Chile, 68–69; and democracy, *see* Democracy; fundamental questions on, 10; in Mozambique, 70–72; and Nicaragua, 72; state ownership and, 19–20; in Tanzania, 65–67. *See also* Actually existing socialism

Somacista legacy, Nicaraguan economy and, 113, 151, 154, 172–77, 183

Soviet Union: and Angola, 87; and capitalist world, 12; Cuban economy and, 63–65; and financing of transitional economies, 74; and Marxism, 219–22, 225–27; organization of agriculture in, 103–6, 138–39; and shift of revolutionary struggles to third world, 9; and Stalinism, 105–6, 220, 228–29; and "war commun-

ism," 51–52. *See also* Actually existing socialism; Russian revolution
Speculators, 150, 153
State: Marxist theory on, 197–98; proletarian and nonproletarian, 237–38. *See also* Dictatorship of the proletariat; State, in Nicaragua; State sector; Withering away of the state
State farms, 109–19, 131, 134–35, 138–39
State, in Nicaragua, 163–65; central role of, 155–56; economic policy and, 151–53, 177–82; independence of unions from, 273; relations with private sector, 183–89; society relations in transition, 10, 259–60; and war and popular participation, 319–23
State sector, 19–20, 32–33, 40–41, 44, 64, 106
Subjective factor, 305–10, 315
Suppliers' credits, 61–62
Surplus in transition model, 31–32, 39–43, 45, 47–49, 51, 286–89, 297–99
Syria, 107, 108, 109

Tanzania, 65–67, 122–24, 137
Technology: labor productivity and, 48; transfers, 12, 13, 18, 28
Third social force, 23–24, 311–19
Trade, 12, 13, 31, 35–36, 50–51, 73

Underdevelopment: in capitalist countries, 36–37; and transition, 9–10, 21–22
Unemployment, 15, 257–58
Unions, 272–74
U.S. foreign policy, 26, 60, 61, 68, 70–71, 76, 82, 93–94. *See also* U.S. imperialism
U.S. imperialism and revolutionary societies, 79–96; and Angola, 82–83, 86–88; and Carter administration, 83–84; and Democratic Party, 82; and domestic opposition, 90–93; emergent alternatives, 93–94; historical background, 80–81; and

Iranian revolution, 85–86; and Nicaragua, 88–90; and political polarization, 94–96; and realignment of U.S. foreign policy, 81–84; and U.S. interests, 84–85

Vanguard, 21, 22–23, 25, 218–19, 242–47, 310–19, 323–28
Vietnam, 81, 92, 119–22, 136–37, 171
Villagization, 122–24, 130–31

Wage goods, 37, 49
War and popular participation, 24–27, 50–52; army and, 316; bureaucracy and, 319–23; and revolutionary alliances, 303–28; and role of state, 319–23; and role of vanguard, 310–19; and subjective factor, 309–10. *See also* Popular participation
Western European loans, 69, 71, 73, 74
Withering away of the state, 198–201, 203–8
Women's emancipation, 294–96, 300; and agricultural cooperatives, 128, 135–36; and autonomous women's movement, 23–24, 274–75; and conceptualizing women's interests, 282–86; legal reform and, 296–97; in Nicaragua, 280–300; and private sector, 293; and revolutionary alliances, 326–27; and U.S. imperialism, 92, 291–92
Worker participation, 24, 43–46, 115–16
Worker-peasant alliance, 98–103, 137–39, 221, 241–42
Worker self-management, 275
Working class. *See* Proletariat
World Bank loans, 61, 66–67, 72–73
World economy. *See* Global capitalism

Yemen, 107, 109, 133
Youth, as third force, 313–15
Yugoslavia, 52*n*

Zimbabwe, 83, 107, 108